GOSPELS
ONE

GOSPELS

ONE

The Four Gospels Interwoven into One Narrative

RAY BUMGARDNER

ARPress
ILLUMINATING IDEAS
EMPOWERING VOICES

ARPress
45 Dan Road Suite 36
Canton MA 02021

Hotline: 1(800) 220-7660
Fax: 1(855) 752-6001

Ordering Information:
Quantity sales. Special discounts are available on quantity purchases by corporations, associations, and others. For details, contact the publisher at the address above.

Printed in the United States of America.

ISBN-13:   Softcover   979-8-89389-584-1
           eBook   979-8-89389-585-8

Library of Congress Control Number: 2024920930

1

John

Luke

Mark

Matthew

CONTENTS

Author's Note 1

Prologue: Between the Testaments...................................... 3

The Writers Of The Gospels 11

Index By Scripture..21

Gospels One...27

Appendix..413

AUTHOR'S NOTE

This work began as a series of lessons for a Bible study class. At that time, no thought was given to the possibility that a book would be the final result of the study. In researching material for the individual lessons, therefore, no records were made of the sources of the material being gathered. After completing the study, there was such a large amount of material that had been used for the study that the writer decided at the last moment to consolidate it into a book. Regretfully, because the decision to make a book of the project did not arise at the beginning of the study, there is no bibliography attached. However, there are many instances within the manuscript in which the authority for the information used is cited. I deeply regret that credit for all the information received from outside sources cannot be given to the proper person or authority.

I trust that the failure of the author to provide a list of source materials will not detract from the acceptance or the enjoyment of the information given, especially since the reader will not be able to use the same sources of information to check the truth or reliability of the information contained herein.

PROLOGUE:
BETWEEN THE TESTAMENTS

There is a period of approximately four hundred years of Jewish history which is not recorded in the Bible except in the Catholic versions. Many world events which occurred during that period of time had a great impact on the Jewish people and the nation of Israel. Knowledge of those events would lead to a greater understanding of the New Testament. Also, knowledge of the political climate of the time in which Jesus lived on the earth would further enhance our understanding of some things recorded in the Gospels.

The information which has been assembled here is from various sources, including the views of many biblical scholars. Because there is, in many instances, no consensus of opinion among those scholars, it is doubtful that their opinions could be considered authoritative even though many of those opinions do have merit.

Roughly four hundred years before the birth of Jesus, the Old Testament record of the Jewish nation ended. However, much can be gleaned from the Apocrypha and from the Jewish historian Flavius Josephus. The political events which established the atmosphere prevalent during the earthly lifetime of Jesus occurred during the latter part of that four-hundred year period.

The Old Testament record of the Jewish people ended, and the period between the testaments began with the Israelites being held captive by and under the domination of the Persian Empire. The rule of the Persians had begun with the conquest of Babylon by Cyrus the Great in 539 BC. At that time, the Jewish nation was being held captive by the Babylonians and the Jews were a part of the spoils of war taken by the victorious Persians. Unlike the Babylonians, though, the Persians encouraged the growth and preservation of national religions and cultures among the nations which they held captive. They even aided the Jews in the rebuilding and upkeep of their temple in Jerusalem.

In 480 BC, the Persians, under Xerxes, attempted conquests in Europe but were defeated and driven back into Asia. One of the countries the Persians had conquered, in the course of their invasion of Europe, was Macedonia.

A man named Philip (Philip II) was able to ascend to power in Macedonia in 359 BC. Philip spent the next twenty years strengthening and consolidating his power and was able to extend his rule over all of Greece. Seeking revenge against Persia for its foray into Macedonia more than a century earlier, in 337 BC, Philip began planning a war to conquer and punish them. In 336 BC, though, before Philip could put his plans into effect, he was assassinated. Philip's empire passed into the hands of his son Alexander, later to be known as Alexander the Great. Alexander was twenty years old when he succeeded his father as ruler.

In 334 BC, acting on the plans his father had formulated, Alexander led his army across the Hellespont and began his conquests in Asia. Perhaps because of the importunities of a deputation of priests and leading citizens who called on him and because he had encountered no resistance by the Jews, Alexander bypassed Jerusalem. From there, he launched his offensive against Egypt. Final conquest of the Persian Empire came to fruition in 331 BC.

It is reported that one of the ambitions of Alexander was to have a completely Hellenized world empire. To that end and immediately after his conquests, he began to spread Greek culture and language into all the conquered territories. But before this dream could be realized, Alexander died. He was thirty-two years old at the time of his death.

Unlike his father, Alexander had no heirs to whom his empire could be passed down, and there was no single person strong enough to wrest control of it from the other aspirants. The empire which Alexander had so fiercely dedicated himself to building was in the end divided between several of his generals.

Ptolemy Soter was given control of Egypt and Palestine. Soter established a line of Greek kings who ruled their empire from Alexandria, a city conceived and built by Alexander. Soter carried many Jews captive from Palestine to Egypt. His successor, Ptolemy Philadelphus, however, freed all the Jewish captives and allowed all of those who wished to do so to return to their homeland. Many of them chose to remain in Alexandria.

Seleucus, founder of the dynasty of the Seleucids, superseded Alexander in the East and established his capital at Antioch in Syria. In Asia Minor, in Macedonia, and in Greece, rival kings fought for power but none of them was able to gain any great or long-lasting advantage over the others. In addition, the Seleucids and the Ptolemys struggled constantly for control of Palestine. During most of the third century BC, the Ptolemys were able to prevail, but near the beginning of the second century BC, the Seleucids gained the upper hand. Under the rule of both kingdoms, the Jews were subjected to Hellenizing influences. Greek culture was attractive to many of the Jews and had a great impact on the religion of some Jews as well.

Alexander's dream of having the whole world speak Greek was very nearly realized as Greek became the universal language between differing linguistic groups much as French was the universal language a century or so ago and as English is now. Greek was the language of trade, education, and writing even for people who preserved and used their own oral language. In the second century BC, so many Jews, mostly those outside of Palestine, neither spoke nor read Hebrew that it became necessary to translate the Jewish scriptures, the Old Testament, into Greek. This task was accomplished in Alexandria, one of the major centers of Jewish population outside of Palestine. The version of the Old Testament which resulted from this translation was called the Septuagint from the fact that seventy people were involved in the translation. It was the version best known by the early Christians and has been the primary source of subsequent translations.

Many Jews admired and began to emulate the Greeks. This caused a division among them. One party, called the Hellenists, favored the

Greek culture, while the other, the Hasidim, remained conservative and clung to the old ways. The Hasidim believed that the Greek religion, with its many gods and goddesses, was incompatible with Judaism and the one God. The great differences in the religious beliefs of the two groups led to internal strife so great that the Seleucid king was forced to intervene.

Antiochus IV, also known as Epiphanes, ascended the Seleucid throne in 175 BC upon the death of his father, Antiochus the Great, and ruled until 163 BC. Epiphanes became a bitter enemy of the majority of the Jews, and with the help of some of the leading Jewish families which had become Hellenists, he transformed Jerusalem into a Greek city. There was, of course, resistance by some of the adherents of Judaism, and because of that resistance, Antiochus tried to root out and destroy Judaism completely. To that end, he forbade the Jews to sacrifice, to practice circumcision, or to read the Law. When the Jews continued to resist, Antiochus had a statue of the Greek god Zeus placed in the temple, and he sacrificed pigs on the altar. For all pious Jews, that act contaminated the temple to such an extent that it was unfit for use in any form or in any act of worship.

That current situation was intolerable to all pious Jews, the Hasidim, and in 167 BC, some of them, led by a priest named Mattathias, revolted. Mattathias was aided by his five sons, Judas Maccabaeus, Jonathan, Simon, John, and Eleazar.

In 166 BC, Mattathias died, and his son Judas assumed leadership of the rebelling Jews. Judas proved to be a very capable military leader and tactician. The Maccabees, called that after Judas Maccabaeus, won battle after battle, some of them against tremendous odds. In 165 BC, the rebelling forces reconquered Jerusalem. They immediately purified and rededicated the temple according to the pattern advocated in the scriptures.

After accomplishing the task of freeing Judea, Judas became the first of a line of priest-kings to govern there. Judas served as priest-king from 166 BC until his death in 160 BC. After the death of Judas, his brother Jonathan succeeded him and governed until 142 BC. Upon the death of Jonathan, another brother, Simon, succeeded to the throne and ruled until 134 BC. The Hasmoneans, the line of priest-kings, continued to rule Judea as long as it remained an independent nation.

After suffering through more than four centuries of foreign domination, Judea was able to remain an independent nation for only a little more than a hundred years. It was able to keep from being swallowed up by any one of its larger neighbors only by the judicious use of treaties and agreements, including some with Rome. That fragile independent state lasted until 63 BC, when Judea was conquered by Roman forces under Pompey. From 63 BC until the fall of the Roman Empire several centuries later, Judea was governed directly or indirectly by the Romans.

During the early years of the Roman Empire, it was in constant turmoil due to internal strife. Ambitious men sought to take command of the empire with first one then another gaining control. In 27 BC, Octavius, also known as Augustus, became emperor and put an end to the internal strife and dissension. Octavius was emperor at the time of the birth of Jesus. He died in AD 14 and was succeeded by Tiberius. Tiberius was emperor of Rome during the entire ministry of Jesus. He died in AD 37.

After the conquest of Judea by Rome, it was governed by men appointed by the Romans. One of those governors was Antipater. Antipater was from Idumea, formerly known as Edom, the traditional home of the descendants of Esau. Upon the death of Antipater, his son Herod succeeded him. Herod's first wife, Mariamne I, was a descendent of the rebellious priest Mattathias through his son Simon, the third of the three brothers to govern the independent state of Judea as priest kings. In 41 BC the government of Rome made Judea a Roman province, and Herod, later to be known as Herod the Great, was made tetrarch of it. The term "tetrarch" is believed to have been most commonly used to designate a ruler over one fourth of a province, but the exact meaning is not now known of a certainty.

In 37 BC, Herod was appointed king of Judea by the Roman senate. He was not, however, a monarch but remained responsible to Rome. During the reign of Herod the Great Judea was once again, but for the last time, ruled by a king.

Herod was, like his father, from Idumea, a region south of Judea. Herod wanted to be known as a Jew, and he wanted the Jews in Judea to like and admire him. In spite of this, he was very unpopular with the Jewish people, and it was probably to mitigate that unpopularity that he built the magnificent temple in Jerusalem which was in use by the Jews during the time Jesus was on earth. Herod was also a great admirer of the Greek culture, and his admiration was shown in the architecture of the temple and in the other buildings which he ordered to be built.

Herod was ruling Judea as its king at the time of the birth of Jesus. It was he who, after the Magi told him of the birth of the king of the Jews, was responsible for ordering the slaughter of the infants and thereby forcing Joseph to take Mary and Jesus to Egypt. Herod died in 4 BC.

In accordance with his wishes, Herod's kingdom was divided into three parts, one for each of three of his sons. Archelaus became ethnarch (ruler of the people) of Judea, Samaria, and Idumea; Antipas was made tetrarch (ruler of one fourth of a province) of Galilee and Perea, an area east of the Jordan River; and Philip became ruler of Iturea, Gaulanitis, and Trachonitis, an area north of Galilee.

Archelaus reigned in Judea for only about ten years, until AD 6. He was deposed by the Romans and exiled to Vienne (or Gaul, as that part of France was then called). There is a town in France today which is named Vienne, but whether or not it is the same town, we don't know. After Archelaus was deposed, Judea was made a Roman province again and the rule over it was given to men who held the office of procurator. The word "procurator" had much the same meaning as the term "agent" means to us today. The position was one of patronage and was usually given to members of well known or wealthy families and usually in return for favors previously done for the empire. When Joseph learned that Herod the Great was dead, he returned with Mary and Jesus from Egypt. He settled in Galilee rather than in Judea, because Archelaus was ethnarch of Judea (Matt. 2:22-23). The scriptures do not tell why Joseph feared Archelaus, only that he did. The scriptures also say that Joseph settled in Nazareth in order to fulfill the prophecy that Jesus would be known as a Nazarene.

At that time, the rule of the Romans was comparatively benign. The Jews were free to come and go as they wished and, under the Sanhedrin and the high priest, they had a degree of self-government. The carrying out of an execution, however, was forbidden and could be imposed on criminals for any crimes whatever only with the consent and cooperation of the Romans.

Pontius Pilate was appointed procurator of Judea about AD 26 and served in that capacity for about ten years. He was recalled to Rome in AD 36 and charged with oppression. He was convicted and banished to Vienne, where he died about ten years later.

Herod Antipas, tetrarch of Galilee and Perea, was the person responsible for the death of John the Baptist. He was a full brother of Archelaus through his father's third wife, Malthake. Philip the tetrarch was a half brother of these two. Philip's mother was Cleopatra, not the notorious Egyptian queen, but the fourth wife of Herod the Great. Herod Philip whose wife Herodias married Antipas was a different Philip, another half brother whose mother was Mariamne II, Herod the Great's second wife.

After the first examination of Jesus by Pilate, as an act of courtesy on the part of Pilate, Jesus was sent to Herod Antipas for further examination and questioning although Antipas had no authority in Judea. Jesus was sent back to Pilate after Antipas had finished questioning and mocking Him.

Herod Agrippa (or King Agrippa) about whom we read in the chapters 25 and 26 of Acts was the great grandson of Herod the Great through Herod's first wife Mariamne I. Berenice, also mentioned in chapters 25 and 26 of Acts, was Agrippa's sister. Another sister, Drusilla, married Felix who was procurator of Judea from AD 52 to AD 60. When Drusilla married Felix, she was already married to Aziz, king of Emesa.

THE WRITERS OF THE GOSPELS

The names of the four people who are credited with writing the four books of the Bible known as the Gospels are very well known to almost everyone with even a rudimentary knowledge of the Bible, but not a great deal is known about some of the men themselves.

The four accounts of the Gospel are popularly attributed to the following people:

> Matthew-one of the apostles;

> Mark-who may or may not have seen Jesus and who was a companion of Paul and Barnabas in their missionary work and a cousin of Barnabas; Luke-at times a companion of Paul and who probably never saw Jesus; and John-another one of the apostles.

> Scholars in general believe the following about these men:

Matthew (meaning "gift of God" in Hebrew)

Tradition has it that the Gospel of Matthew was written by the apostle Matthew. The truth, however, cannot be determined with any degree of certainty. It is apparent, though, that the book was written by a Jew in an effort to present Jesus to the Jews as the Messiah.

Most (or many) biblical scholars believe that the Gospel of Matthew was, in fact, a very careful compilation from at least three separate sources. They believe that Matthew may have been the author of one of those sources or that he could have been the compiler of the book.

Very little is known about Matthew other than what appears in the accounts of his being called by Jesus and in the lists in which all the apostles are named. He is known to have been a publican (or tax gatherer). As a publican, he was looked upon by Jews, in general, with malice and scorn.

At that time and in that place, tax collecting was done very much differently from how it is done in this country today. Taxes here are a certain percentage added to purchases or a certain rate on the value of real or personal property or a certain rate on income and so on. All of this is in accordance with rules of law passed by elected representatives. Tax collecting in the days of Jesus under the Romans was quite different. Basically, each tax collector was required by the government to collect a certain amount in taxes from his particular territory. A collector was not limited to collecting a certain percentage of a man's income or a certain rate on the value of his property but could assess whatever he thought the individual could pay. He had the authority to levy whatever amount of tax on each person he desired and to collect by whatever means was necessary. This could have been as fair or as unfair as the collector wanted to make it. Publicans often became wealthy, because they were allowed to keep any excess money they collected; hence, the intense hatred of the Jews for publicans. In the scriptures, references to publicans often have them paired with sinners.

Except for records in three of the accounts of the Gospel telling of Jesus having called Matthew to follow Him, only one other event in the life of Matthew is recorded. That was the party Matthew gave for Jesus and for which Jesus was severely criticized by the Jews for socializing with publicans and sinners.

Traditions and legends attribute various activities to Matthew, as well as various methods and locations concerning his martyrdom. None of those stories or legends has been or can be substantiated.

The Gospel of Matthew is considered by some biblical scholars to be the narrative written by Mark with slight alterations and with other material inserted in appropriate places. A review of chapters 3 and 4, for instance, will reveal that they are almost identical to the narrative by Mark. In Matthew, there is then inserted chapters 5 through 7 comprising what is called "the Sermon on the Mount" after which Mark's narrative is continued in chapter 8 and part of chapter 9.

Even if what the scholars believe about the book and its writer is true (and there can be no certainty about that as there is no way of knowing whether it's true or not), what this book alone contains about Jesus and His life and His sayings is essential to a fuller knowledge of Jesus and the enrichment which that knowledge brings.

Mark (meaning "large hammer" in Latin)

Mark's Jewish name was John. He adopted the Roman surname of Marcus or Mark. Mark was a cousin of Barnabas and a companion of Paul and, by tradition, later a companion of Peter. It was to the home of Mark's mother, Mary that Peter went when he was delivered from prison by the angel and where the servant girl Rhoda left him standing at the gate while she ran back inside and announced that he was waiting at the gate.

The information contained in Mark's account of the Gospel is believed by many biblical scholars to have been from the mind of Peter and is supposed to have been written after the deaths of both Paul and Peter, both in martyrdom, in Rome. This could present a problem in chronology. If Mark wrote after the deaths of Peter and Paul, and if, as some sources believe, Matthew was martyred also, when did Matthew have the opportunity to copy Mark's manuscript?

Mark accompanied Barnabas and Paul when these two men began their first missionary journey from Antioch in Syria in about AD 46. For some reason which was not recorded, he left the missionaries and returned to Jerusalem before the completion of the journey. Paul considered Mark to have deserted them, and in about AD 49, when Paul and Barnabas were planning their second missionary journey, Paul's belief caused a disagreement between him and Barnabas causing them to split up, and Barnabas took Mark and sailed for Cyprus, while Paul chose Silas to accompany him.

Nothing more is written about Mark for about ten years when Paul referred to him in some of his letters as a fellow worker, as a comfort to Paul in prison, and as a useful assistant. There is also mention of Mark concerning his possible visit to the church in Colossae but nothing about whether or not the visit took place. The final reference we have to Mark is by Peter in his first letter from Rome in which he referred to Mark as "my son Mark."

In chronological order, the Gospel according to Mark is believed by some to have been the first one written. It is believed to have been used extensively in the writing of the Gospels of Matthew and Luke and to have been the basis for both those writings.

Of the six hundred sixty verses comprising the Gospel of Mark, six hundred of them are found substantially the same in the Gospel of Matthew and three hundred fifty of them are found in Luke's writing. Minor changes were made by both Matthew and Luke in some of Mark's writing for the sake of clarity, brevity, reverence, and accuracy. The scholars may be right-but, perhaps, they dismiss too easily the ability and influence of the Holy Spirit.

The Gospel of Mark begins with the account of the ministry of John the Baptist and then follows immediately with the beginning of the ministry of Jesus Himself. This beginning was probably due to the fact that the source from which Mark received his knowledge of Jesus did not include knowledge of the birth and early life of Jesus. Certainly, if it is true that Mark's source of information was Peter, probably the only way he could have had additional information about Jesus would have been either that Peter had learned about the early life of Jesus or by revelation of the Holy Spirit either to Peter or to Mark.

Of the accounts of the Gospel attributed to Matthew, Mark, and Luke, this is considered by the scholars to be by far the most important, because they consider the other two to have been built from and on this one.

Luke (probably a diminutive of the Latin name Lucas)

Luke's name is recorded only three times in the scriptures, but he is acknowledged to be the writer of the account of the Gospel which bears his name and of the book Acts of the Apostles. The name appears in Colossians 4:14, where reference is made to him as "the beloved physician," in 2 Timothy 4:11 in which Paul stated that only Luke was with him, and in Philemon 24, where the writer stated that Luke (among others) sends greetings.

Luke stated in the introduction to his account of the Gospel that many others had written accounts of the Gospel or as he put it, "those things which are most surely believed among us." He stated, further, that what he wrote was delivered to him by those who were eyewitnesses from the beginning and were ministers of the word.

Scholars offer much speculation about Luke-that he was by birth a gentile, possibly an early convert to Christianity, probably a Syrian and from Antioch, and possibly at one time a slave educated as a physician. Internal evidence in his Gospel and other scriptures confirms that he was indeed a physician.

Luke, from the evidence found in Acts, accompanied Paul on his second missionary journey across the Aegean Sea from Troas in Asia Minor to Philippi in Greece. Six years later, when Paul was on his third missionary journey, Luke returned with Paul from Philippi to Jerusalem. He also accompanied Paul on his final missionary journey from Caesarea to Rome, where he remained with Paul throughout Paul's imprisonment. Luke himself does not appear to have been a prisoner but seems to have been free to minister to Paul.

Many conflicting traditions and legends have grown up surrounding Luke as was the case with so many other New Testament people. Relics purporting to be the bones of Luke were removed from Thebes in Boeatia to Constantinople by order of Constantine II. These relics were later preserved in the Church of the Apostles.

Other traditions depict Luke as living to the age of eighty four and dying a natural death, still others of his being martyred, and of being an artist as well as a physician (pictures of Mary, the mother of Jesus, were supposed to have been painted by him in the Syrian Church in Jerusalem, at Santa Maggiore in Rome, and in several other places). Furthering the tradition that he was an artist, a painting by the artist Rogier van der Weyden (1399-1464) depicts Luke painting a portrait of Mary as she was nursing the infant Jesus.

John (meaning "God has been gracious" in Hebrew)

There should be no doubts as to the identity of the writer of the book of John, but remarkably among scholars, there appears to be less certainty about the identity of the writer of this account of the Gospel than of any of the others. This may be due to the fact that there are more men named "John" in the New Testament than those with any other name.

Some scholars believe there are nine men with the name "John" included in the New Testament, and list them as: John the Baptist; John (or Jonah), the father of Peter; John, listed with Annas, Caiaphas, Alexander and "all who were of high priestly descent"; John Mark, the evangelist; John, the beloved disciple; John, son of Zebedee; John the Evangelist; John, the Elder; and John the Divine.

Of these men, as possible candidates for the authorship of the book of John, immediately there can be eliminated the first four men listed—John the Baptist, Peter's father, the relative of Annas, and John Mark. Of the others and scholars have differing views on this, all of them may have been the same person. The scholars mostly agree that the Gospel of John and the First Epistle of John were written by the same man. In the minds of many of these scholars, there is some doubt concerning the others on the list, with a complete lack of harmony among them, each having doubts for reasons different from the reasons of the others.

John the son of Zebedee and brother of James was in all probability a fisherman as was his father. Tradition has it that John's mother, Salome, was the sister of Mary the mother of Jesus; although, there is no biblical evidence to support such a belief. However, an inference that this could have been true could be drawn from three passages: Matthew 27:56, Mark 15:40, and John 19:25. In these passages, the women who were present at the crucifixion of Jesus were listed. If Mary and Salome were indeed sisters, then John would have been a cousin to Jesus and would have known Him all his life. That would then account for the fact that the mother of James and John was emboldened to ask of her nephew (which Jesus would have been) that her sons be given special consideration, which request is recorded in Matthew 20:20-21.

Again according to scholars, the probability is great that the son of Zebedee, the beloved disciple, and the evangelist are all the same person. There is some doubt in their minds that this man is the same as the one who referred to himself as "the Elder" in the Second and Third Epistles of John. But they do concede the possibility that they were the same man. They base their opinion on the differences in the styles of writing in the various documents.

John, a relative of Annas the high priest, was certainly a different man from any of the others. This man is mentioned only in Acts 4:6. In addition, the man called simply "another disciple" in John 18:15 is in all probability the apostle John. This man was known to the high priest and was admitted with no questions to the place where Jesus was being examined. Apparently, his presence in that place at that time went unchallenged leading to speculation that perhaps Peter's presence would also have gone unchallenged if he had not denied being acquainted with Jesus.

Although scholars don't consider it a certainty that the apostle John was the same person as the one who was called "the Divine" and was the writer of the book of Revelation, they do acknowledge the probability that they were the same person. Certainly considering the time the Revelation was written, John could have been the writer as the Revelation is dated about the year AD 96. Internal evidence in Revelation and the evidence furnished by ancient Christian writers strongly support the belief that the apostle John was the writer of this book.

The apostle John seems to have been a business man with much more of the world's goods than some of the other disciples. In Mark 1:20, it is stated that Zebedee along with James and John had servants to help in their fishing business. John 19:27 strongly suggests that John owned a home. Perhaps it was because of the affluence of Zebedee and his family that John was known to the high priest.

It would be a great satisfaction, an allaying of curiosity, to know without doubt the identities of all the men called John and a certainty of the authorship of the books of the New Testament about which there is a question. We can be thankful, though, for the message contained in those books and what that message means to Christians in all ages and all over the world.

Readers of this work should be reminded again of what was written earlier concerning the beliefs of the biblical scholars whose opinions and comments were given, that is, that the opinions vary, sometimes widely, from scholar to scholar and that none of them should be accepted unconditionally. Those opinions are what each scholar believes from having studied the New Testament and contemporary history colored by his own prejudices and preconceived ideas, and even in those instances in which scholars most agree on any one topic, is there any guarantee that their combined opinion is the correct one.

To illustrate, it was stated earlier concerning the Gospel of Matthew that scholars in general believe that Matthew's account of the Gospel was a compilation from at least three different sources and that Mark's account was used extensively by Matthew in compiling his book. Another source stated emphatically that such an opinion is absurd and asks, "Why should Matthew have to copy from one who had *not* been an eyewitness of things that he himself had seen with his own eyes and heard with his own ears over and over and over?" In reply, and without advocating either position, a logical explanation would be that Mark's account of the Gospel was incomplete, and since Matthew was an eyewitness of the things about which he wrote, he expanded Mark's account for the sake of accuracy and to provide additional information which Mark did not include in his account.

Also previously reported were the opinions of some scholars who believe that Luke, too, drew heavily on Mark's Gospel in writing his own. However, Luke himself made the statement that what he wrote was delivered to him by those who were eyewitnesses from the beginning and were ministers of the word. If this statement of Luke is to be believed and taken literally it would seem to preclude any possibility that he used the writings of Mark in any way in the writing of his own account of the Gospel as Mark could not have been an "eyewitness from the beginning."

Of the original twelve apostles, we have no exact knowledge of what eventually happened to most of them, Judas Iscariot and James the son of Zebedee being the exceptions as accounts of the death of both of them are included in the *New Testament*. Also, in the book of Acts there are reports of incidents involving Philip and Peter and mention is made of some of the other apostles. Many traditions, surely including some myths, have arisen about the later lives of many of the apostles. Writings purporting to have been by some of them have been found but none have been positively verified as having been written by the ones to whom they were attributed. Relics which are claimed to be of some of the apostles are scattered among many of the older churches, and stories of their travels and travails are well known in those areas. Traditions include where those apostles preached and the manner, mostly in martyrdom, of their deaths.

A writer by the name of William Steuart McBirnie has written a book about the traditions which have grown up around the lives, especially the later lives, of the twelve apostles and certain other men of the Bible including, of course, all four men named as authors of the four accounts of the Gospel. The book is entitled *The Search for the Twelve Apostles* and was published by Tyndale House Publishers, Inc. Mr. McBirnie has apparently done a great deal of research into his subject and has produced a very scholarly work. However, much of the material in the book is of such a nature that the truth surrounding the traditions reported cannot be verified, especially that the relics so carefully preserved in many of the churches named as their repository are in fact the bones of the persons of whom they purport to be. Of course, Mr. McBirnie does not guarantee the accuracy of the traditions reported, only the fact of the existence of those traditions.

It would be interesting to know whether those traditions are fact or fiction, but they are of no special religious value as the tenets of Christianity are clearly set forward in the *New Testament* as it exists today.

Index By Scripture

	Matthew			Mark			Luke			John	
Ch.	Verse	Sec.	Ch.	Verse	Sec.	Ch.	Verse	Sec.	Ch.	Verse	Sec.
1	1-17	10	1	1	1	1	1-4	2	1	1-5	1
	18-25	8		2-8	18		5-25	3		6-8	17
2	1-12	12		9-11	19		26-38	4		9-14	1
	13-15	13		12-13	21		39-56	5		15	17
	16-18	14		14-15	31		57-66	6		16-18	1
	19-23	15		16-20	34		67-80	7		19-34	22
3	1-12	18		21-34	36	2	1-7	8		35-51	23
	13-17	19		35-39	37		8-20	9	2	1-12	24
4	1-11	21		40-45	38		21-39a	11		13-25	25
	12	29	2	1-12	39		39b	15	3	1-21	26
	13-16	33		13-17	40		40-52	16		22-36	27
	17	31		18-22	41	3	1-18	18	4	1-3	29
	18-22	34		23-28	46		19-20	28		4-42	30
	23-25	37	3	1-6	47		21-22	19		43	31
5	1-2	50A		7-12	48		23-38	20		44	33
	3-12	50B		13-19	49		1-3	21		45	31
	13-16	SOC		20-30	57		14-15	31		46-54	32
	17-48	50D		31-35	59		16-30	33	5	1-15	44
6	1-18	SOC		1-20	60		31-41	36		16-47	45
	19-34	50F		21-23	SOC		42-44	37	6	1	73
7	1-6	50G		24-25	50G		1-11	35		2-14	74
	7-11	50H		26-29	61		12-16	38		15-21	75
	12	501		30-34	63		17-26	39		22-71	77

Ch	Ref	Pg	Ch	Ref	Pg	Ch	Ref	Pg	Ch	Ref	Pg
	13-23	50J		35-41	66		27-32	40	7	1	78
	24-29	50K	5	1-21	67		33-39	41		2-10	94
8	1	51		22-43	42	6	1-5	46		11-30	95
	2-4	38	6	1-6a	68		6-11	47		31-53	96
	5-13	51		6b-13	69		12-16	49	8	1	96
	14-17	36		14-16	71		17-20a	50A		2-11	97
	18	66		17-20	28		20b-26	50B		12-59	98
	19-22	93		21-29	70		27-30	50D	9	1-41	99
8	23-27	66	6	30-31	72	6	31	501	10	1-21	100
	28-34	67		32	73		32-36	50D		22-42	110
9	1	67		33-44	74		37-42	50G	11	1-46	111
	2-9	39		45-52	75		43-45	50J		47-54	112
	9-13	40		53-56	76		46-49	50K		55-57	159
	14-17	41	7	1-23	78	7	1-10	51	12	1-11	138
	19-26	42		24-30	79		11-17	52		12-19	139
	27-34	43		31-37	80		18-35	53		20-50	142
	35-38	69	8	1-10	81		36-50	55	13	1-2	163
10	1	69		11-13	82	8	1-3	56		3-20	162
	2-4	49		14-21	83		14-15	60		21-30	163
	5-16	69		22-26	84		16-18	SOC		31-35	165
	17-23	153		27-30	85		19-21	59		36-38	167
	24-42	69		31-38	86		22-25	66	14	1-31	169
11	1	69	9	1	86		26-40	67	15	1-27	169
	2-19	53		2-13	87		41-56	42	16	1-33	169
11	20-30	54	9	14-29	88	9	1-6	69	17	1-26	170
12	1-8	46		30-32	89		7-9	71	18	1	171
	9-14	47		35-50	91		10	72		2-11	173
	15-21	48	10	1-12	128		11-17	74		12-14	174
	22-37	57		13-16	129		18-21	85		15-18	176
	38-45	58		17-27	130		22-27	86		19-23	174
	46-50	59		28-31	131		28-36	87		24	175
13	1-23	60		32-34	133		37-43A	88		25-27	176
	24-30	62		35-45	134		43b-45	89		28-38	178
	31-35	63		46-52	135		46-50	91		39-40	180
	36-43	64	11	1-11	139		51-56	113	19	1-3	181
	44-53	65		12-14	140		57-62	93		4-16	180

Ch.	Verse	Sec.	Ch.	Verse	Sec.	Ch.	Verse	Sec.	Ch.	Verse	Sec.
	54-58	68		15-18	141	10	1-24	54		17-24	182
14	1-2	71		19-26	140		25-37	101		25-30	184
	3-5	28		27-33	143		38-42	102		31-42	185
	6-12	70	12	1-12	145	1	103	20		1-18	187
	13a	73		13-17	147		2-4	SOE		19-25	190
	13b-21	74		18-27	148		5-8	103		26-29	191
	22-23	75		28-34	149		9-13	SOH		30-31	194
	34-36	76		35-37	150		14-23	57	21	1-24	192
15	1-20	78		38-40	151		24-32	58		25	194
	21-28	79		41-44	153		33	SOC			
	29-31	80	13	1-31	154		34-36	SOF			
	32-39	81		32-37	155		37-54	104			
16	1-4	82	14	1-2	159	12	1A	82		Act	
	5-12	83		3-9	138		1b	83	Ch.	Verse	Sec.
	13-20	85		10-11	160		2-9	69	1	2-3	194
	21-28	86		12-16	161		10	57		4-11	195
17	1-13	87		17-21	163		11-12	154			
17	14-21	88	14	22-25	166		13-21	105			
	22-23	89		26	171		22-34	SOF			
	24-27	90		27-31	167		35-48	106			
18	1-11	91		32-42	172		49-56	107			
	12-13	120		43-52	173		57-59	SOD			
	14	91		53	175	13	1-9	108			
	15-35	92		54	176		10-17	109			
19	1-12	128		55-65	175		18-21	63			
	13-15	129		66-72	176		22-23	116			
	16-26	130	15	1-5	178		34 35	152			
	27-30	131		6-15	180	14	1-14	117			
20	1-16	132		16-20	181		15-24	118			
	17-19	133		21-32	182		25-35	119			
	20-28	134		33-41	184	15	1-10	120			
	29-34	135		42-47	185		11-32	121			
21	1-11	139	16	1	185	16	1-13	122			
	12-17	141		2-11	187		14-17	123			
	18-22	140		12-13	189		18	50D			
	23-27	143		14	191		19-31	124			

	28-32	144	15-18	193	17	1-2	91
	33-46	145	19-20	195		3-4	92
22	1-14	146				5-10	125
	15-22	147				11-19	114
	23-33	148				20-21	115
	34-40	149				22	155
	41-46	150				23-25	154
23	1-36	151				26-36	155
	37-39	152				37	154
24	1-35	154			18	1-8	126
	36-51	155				9-14	127
25	1-13	156				15-17	129
	14-30	157				18-27	130
	31-46	158				28-30	131
26	1-5	159				31-34	133
	6-13	138				35-43	135
	14-16	160			19	1-10	136
	17-19	161				11-27	137
	20-25	163				28-44	139
	26-29	166				15-48	141
	30	171			20	1-8	143
	31-35	167				9-19	145
	36-46	172				20-26	147
	47-56	173				27-40	148
	57	175				41-44	150
	58	176				45-47	151
26	59-68	175			21	1-4	153
	69-75	176				5-33	154
27	1-2	178				34-38	155
	3-10	177			22	1-2	159
	11-14	178				3-6	160
	15-26	180				7-13	161
	27-31	181				14-20	166
	32-44	182				21-23	163
	45-56	184				24-30	164
	57-61	185				31-34	167

	62-66	186				
28	1-10	187				
	11-15	188				
	16-20	193				

	35-38	168
	39	171
	40-46	172
	47-53	173
	54a	175
	54b-62	176
	63-71	175
23	1-7	178
	8-12	179
	13-25	180
	26-38	182
	39-43	183
	44-49	184
	50-56	185
24	1-12	187
	13-35	189
	36-43	190
	44-49	194
	50-53	195

GOSPELS ONE

1 Introductions from Mark and John

(Mark 1:1; John 1:1-5, 14, 9-13, 16-18)

(1) This is the beginning of the gospel of Jesus Christ, the Son of God.

(2) In the beginning was the Word, and the Word was with God, and the Word was God. (3) The Word was in the beginning with God. (4) All things were made through Him, and without Him nothing was made that has been made. (5) In Him was life, and the life was the light of men. (6) The light shone in the darkness, and the darkness did not overcome it. (7) The Word became flesh and dwelled among us and we beheld His glory, glory as of the only begotten of the Father, full of grace and truth.

(8) The Word was the true light which enlightens everyone coming into the world. (9) He was in the world and the world was made through Him, but the world did not know Him. (10) He came to His own people and those who were His own did not receive Him. (11) But He gave to all who did receive Him, those who believe in His name, the right to become children of God. (12) Those who received Him were born not of blood, nor of the will of the flesh, nor of the will of man, but of God. (13) Of His fullness we have all received grace upon grace. (14) The Law was given through Moses but grace and truth came through Jesus Christ. (15) No man has seen God at any time but the only begotten of God, who is in the bosom of the Father, has told of Him.

27

Notes: The word "gospel" means "good news" or "good tidings." Originally, the phrase was "good spell" but through much usage was shortened to its present form. The use of the word now is limited almost exclusively to the Word of God or, in some instances, to testify to the absolute truth of a statement such as "the gospel truth."

The descriptive phrase "the Son of God" is used to proclaim unequivocally the divinity of Jesus.

Mark's introduction to his account of the Gospel consists of only the one sentence and is followed immediately by an account of the ministry of John the Baptist. John's introduction, however, is quite different from other statements in the New Testament. There is a striking similarity between the beginning of John's account of the Gospel and the opening words of the Old Testament.

John declared that Jesus existed with God in the "beginning," that Jesus existed with God before the world was created. John stated that Jesus was the Word of God incarnate, that before His incarnation, He existed and that when the world was made, it was made by the will of God through Jesus. In His prayer recorded in John 17:5, Jesus said, "And now, Father, glorify Me together with Yourself, with the glory which I had with You before the world was." In John 3:13, Jesus said, "And no one has ascended into heaven, but He who descended from heaven, even the Son of Man." Paul wrote in Ephesians 4:9-10, "Now this expression, 'He ascended,' what does it mean except that He also had descended into the lower parts of the earth? He who descended is Himself also He who ascended far above all the heavens, that He might fill all things."

John called Jesus the light of men, a light shining in darkness. As cold is the natural state and is relieved by heat, so darkness is the natural state and is relieved by light. In John 8:12, John wrote, "Then Jesus spoke to them again, saying, 'I am the light of the world. He who follows Me shall not walk in darkness, but have the light of life.'" And in John 9:5, Jesus said, "As long as I am in the world, I am the light of the world." And in John 12:46, "I have come as a light into the world, that whoever believes in Me should not abide in darkness."

2 Luke's Preface (Luke 1:1-4)

(1) Inasmuch as many have undertaken to draw up an account of the things which have been fulfilled among us, (2) just as those who from the beginning were eyewitnesses and ministers of the gospel have delivered them to us, (3) it seemed fitting to me as well, having investigated everything carefully from the beginning, to write it out for you in order, most excellent Theophilus, (4) that you might know the truth concerning the things you have been taught.

Notes: Luke prefaced his account of the Gospel with the reason for writing it. It was written specifically for a person, whom Luke addressed as "Theophilus," which in Greek means "lover of God." It is possible that Theophilus was not an individual but was a class or group of people who were "lovers of God."

The name "Theophilus," however, was the actual name of at least one person of whom we know. Flavius Josephus, the Jewish historian, in his *Antiquities of the Jews* (book XVII, chapter V, paragraph 3), wrote that Vitelius "deprived Jonathon of the high priesthood, and gave it to his brother Theophilus." Also, in book XIX, chapter VI, paragraph 2, Josephus wrote, "And when Agrippa had entirely finished all the duties of the Divine worship, he removed Theophilus, the son of Ananus, from the high priesthood, and bestowed that honour of his on Simon, the son of Boethus, whose name was also Canthera, whose daughter king Herod married, as I have related above." It is not known whether this man (or if there were two different men with the name "Theophilus," one of those men) was the person addressed by Luke or if there was yet another person with that name.

A further indication that Theophilus was a person is that Luke addressed him as "most excellent." That form of address would have been used in speaking to or of an individual rather than a group of people. Only in three other places in the New Testament is that form of address found and in all three places it is used by the speaker in addressing a high public official in Acts 23:26 in a letter from the commander of Paul's guard, which read, "Claudius Lysias, to the most excellent governor Felix, greetings," in Acts 24:3 by an attorney named Tertulius who said, ". . . we acknowledge this in every way and everywhere, most excellent Felix, with all thankfulness ...," and in Acts 26:25, "But Paul said, 'I am not out of my mind, most excellent Festus, but I utter words of sober truth.'"

To have been addressed as "most excellent" indicated that the person being addressed was an official of some sort. Commentators suggest that Theophilus could have been a Roman or a Greek official who had been converted to Christianity and desired to know more about the gospel of Christ. There is no record of a high priest named Theophilus being converted, but if he had been, he would have been addressed in that manner.

Perhaps because of the wording of Luke's preface, it could be deduced that the accounts of the Gospel which had been written prior to that time were incomplete or inaccurate. It could be further deduced that Luke may have collected fragmentary accounts which had been written by others and had, after extensive and intensive investigation, made a compilation of his own and incorporated those fragmentary accounts into a complete and accurate narrative.

Luke stated, too, that his purpose in writing his account of the Gospel was to further reinforce the beliefs of Theophilus, who had already been instructed, probably verbally, with a full account of the Gospel.

There is no indication that Theophilus had asked that the account be written so that he would have it on hand as a ready reference or whether the work was entirely a voluntary effort by Luke. Either way, it was made public so that it is a part of the canon of the New Testament.

3 Annunciation of John the Baptist (Luke 1: 5-25).

(1) In the days of Herod king of Judea there was a priest named Zacharias of the course of Abijah. Zacharias had a wife of the daughters of Aaron whose name was Elizabeth. (2) They were both righteous before God, walking blamelessly in all the commandments and ordinances of the Lord. (3) But they had no child because Elizabeth was barren and they were both advanced in years.

(4) Zacharias was performing his priestly service before God in the appointed order of his course. (5) According to the custom of the priestly

office the lot fell on him to enter the temple of the Lord and burn incense. (6) And the whole multitude of the people were praying outside at the hour of incense burning, (7) when there appeared to Zacharias an angel of the Lord standing on the right side of the altar of incense. (8) Zacharias was troubled when he saw the angel and fear gripped him.

(9) But the angel said to Zacharias, "Do not be afraid, Zacharias. Your supplication has been heard and your wife Elizabeth will bear you a son and you will name him John. (10) You will have joy and gladness and many will rejoice at his birth, (11) for he will be great in the sight of the Lord. He will drink no wine nor strong drink; and he will be filled with the Holy Spirit even while he is still in his mother's womb. (12) He will turn many of the sons of Israel to the Lord their God,

(13) and he will go as a forerunner before the Messiah in the spirit and power of Elijah 'To turn the hearts of the fathers back to the children' and the disobedient to the wisdom of the righteous and to make ready a people prepared for the Lord."

(14) Zacharias said to the angel, "How shall I know this is true? I am an old man and my wife is advanced in years, too."

(15) The angel said to Zacharias, "I am Gabriel who stands in the presence of God, and I was sent to speak to you and to bring you this good news. (16) You shall be silent and not able to speak until the day these things take place because you did not believe my words, which shall be fulfilled in their proper time."

(17) The people were waiting for Zacharias and wondering at his delay in the temple. (18) When he came out he was not able to speak to them and they realized that he had seen a vision in the temple. He kept making signs to them but remained mute. (19) And when the time of his priestly service was ended he went back home.

(20) After these days Elizabeth his wife became pregnant; and she kept herself in seclusion for five months, saying, (21) "This is the way the Lord has dealt with me in the days when he looked with favor upon me to take away my disgrace among the people."

Notes: Zacharias was a priest of the course or order of Abijah. During the reign of David the priests were so numerous that they could not all serve at the altar. To alleviate this, David divided the priests into twenty-four courses, each course to serve for one week at a time. The course of Abijah was the eighth in order.

Confirming or emphasizing what Gabriel told Zacharias Jesus said in Matthew 11:11, "Truly, I say to you that among those born of women there has not arisen anyone greater than John the Baptist; yet he who is least in the kingdom of heaven is greater than he." And referring to John in Matthew 3:3, Jesus said, "For this is the one referred to by Isaiah the prophet, saying, 'The voice of one crying in the wilderness, "Make ready the way of the Lord. Make His paths straight.""'

Jesus didn't explain what He meant when he said that the least person in the kingdom of heaven was greater than John, but as an assumption it could have been because John died before the establishment of the kingdom. Although saved under the Law, he would not be a Christian in the New Testament sense. Albert Barnes, in his commentary, wrote, "It [that is, being the least in the kingdom of heaven] here probably means, in preaching the kingdom of God, or the gospel. It could hardly be affirmed of the obscurest and most ignorant Christian that he had clearer views than John or Isaiah; but the apostles of the Saviour, of the first preachers who were with Him and heard His instructions, it might be said that they had more correct apprehension than any of the ancient prophets, or than John."

The daily tasks of the priests were assigned by lot, or, we might say, they gambled for the different tasks. On that day, the lot had fallen on Zacharias to burn incense in the temple, that is, in that part of the temple which was the Holy Place. According to Exodus 30:7-8, incense was to be burned there twice daily, in the morning and at twilight. The recipe for the composition of the incense is found in Exodus 30:34-38. The incense made from that recipe was holy to God and could not be used or burned for any other purpose on pain of being cut off from the rest of God's people. And only the incense made by the formula could be burned in the temple. Perhaps the "strange fire" for which Nadab and Abihu, the sons of Aaron, were condemned in Leviticus 10:1 was the burning of incense made from a formula other than that one which had been authorized by God.

Zacharias was told by Gabriel that John would drink neither wine nor strong drink. In that day, wine was drunk by almost everyone, all classes of people. It was a very light wine, probably no stronger than new cider. What was meant by the term "strong drink" is not known but possibly it was wine which had been made stronger than ordinary wine by the addition of sugar to fermented figs, dates, or palm juice. Distilled alcoholic drinks were unknown at that time. The distillation process for making liquors was not discovered until about the ninth or tenth centuries AD in Arabia. Ironically, distilled spirits were immediately banned by the Arabians. Probably "strong drink" referred merely to old wine, wine that was so old that it had had time to ferment and become strong enough in alcoholic content to make a person drunk.

The name "Gabriel" is a combination of two Hebrew words which together mean "man of God." Gabriel was the angel sent by God with a message to Daniel. He was the angel who was sent some time later to tell Mary that she had been chosen by God to be the mother of the Savior. Gabriel's name appears in the scriptures only those three times.

Elizabeth, like Zacharias, was of the tribe of Levi. We are not told of which tribe Mary was born, but both genealogies, the one in Matthew and the other in Luke, show that Mary's husband Joseph was of the tribe of Judah. The assumption would ordinarily be that Mary, being kin to Elizabeth, was also of the tribe of Levi. However, upon her marriage to a member of another tribe, a woman would become a member of the tribe of her husband. That is, perhaps, what had happened to someone in Elizabeth's lineage, taking her out of the tribe of Judah and into the tribe of Levi.

4 The Birth of Jesus Foretold (Luke 1:26-38)

(1) Now after six months the angel Gabriel was sent to Nazareth, a city in Galilee, (2) to a virgin who was engaged to a man named Joseph, a descendent of David. The virgin's name was Mary.

(3) The angel went in and said to Mary, "Hail to you who are highly favored. The Lord is with you."

(4) Mary was greatly troubled by this saying and was wondering as to what kind of salutation this might be.

(5) The angel said to her, "Do not be afraid, Mary, for you have found favor with God. (6) You will conceive in your womb and bear

a son and you shall name Him Jesus. (7) He will be great and will be called the Son of the Most High. The Lord God will give Him the throne of His father David. (8) He will reign over the house of Jacob forever and His kingdom will have no end."

(9) Mary asked the angel, "How can this be since I am a virgin?"

(10) The angel said to her, "The Holy Spirit will come upon you and the power of the Most High will overshadow you, and for that reason the holy offspring shall be called the Son of God. (11) Your relative Elizabeth has also conceived a son in her old age and she who was called barren is now six months pregnant. (12) For no word from God will be without power."

(13) Mary said, "Behold the bondslave of the Lord! Let it be done to me according to your word." And the angel departed from her.

Notes: Mary's home was in Nazareth but no definite information is given as to whether or not Nazareth was Joseph's home as well. Considering the means of travel available to the ordinary person in those days and since they eventually returned to Nazareth to live we should probably assume that Nazareth was Joseph's home also.

Judging from information given later in the scriptures Joseph intended or wished to make their home in Judea but changed his mind after learning that Archelaus had succeeded his father Herod the Great as ruler there. No reason is given as to why Joseph refused to be in subjection to Archelaus.

5 Mary Visits Elizabeth {Luke 1:39-56)

(1) After that Mary arose and hurried to a city in the hill country of Judea (2) where she entered the house of Zacharias and greeted Elizabeth. (3) When Elizabeth heard Mary's greeting the baby leaped in her womb and Elizabeth was filled with the Holy Spirit.

(4) Elizabeth cried out with a loud voice and said, "Blessed are you among women and blessed is the fruit of your womb!

(5) What reason is there for the mother of my Lord to come to me? (6) I ask this because when the sound of your greeting reached my ears

the baby leaped in my womb. (7) Blessed is she who believed for there will be a fulfillment of what has been spoken to her by the Lord."

(8) Mary said, "My soul does exalt the Lord (9) and my spirit has rejoiced in God my Savior. (10) He has looked at the humble state of His bondslave, and from this time on all generations will call me blessed. (11) The Mighty One has done great things for me. Holy is His name! (12) 'And His mercy is from generation to generation on those who fear Him.' (13) He has done mighty things with His arm. He has scattered those who were proud in the thoughts of their heart.

(14) He has put down rulers from their thrones and has exalted those who were humble. (15) 'He has filled the hungry with good things'; and sent away the rich with empty hands. (16) He has given help to Israel His servant to remember His mercy,

(17) as He spoke to our fathers, to Abraham and his descendents forever."

(18) And Mary stayed with Elizabeth about three months and then returned to her own home.

Notes: The word "arose" in verse one means the same as "setting out" and means starting out as on a journey.

What is meant here by "hill country" is the hill country of Judea, the area in and around Jerusalem. The name of the town where Zacharias lived with Elizabeth is not known. Some scholars speculate that it was Jerusalem, others that it was Hebron, and still others that it was some Levitical city and Zacharias lived there when he was not performing his priestly duties.

The distance from Nazareth to Jerusalem was about seventy miles on a direct line but, of course, farther by road. That distance could have been greater or lesser, depending upon which side of Jerusalem the home of Zacharias and Elizabeth was located. The method of transportation Mary used is not known. If she walked, it would have taken her from three to four days to make the journey, because the average distance a person could walk in a day would have been perhaps twenty but not more than thirty miles. By riding a donkey the time would have been shorter because a donkey would have traveled faster and farther in a day.

Apparently, Mary didn't know about the pregnancy of Elizabeth until the angel Gabriel told her. Mary then hurried to visit Elizabeth to share Elizabeth's joy and, perhaps, to share her own good news with Elizabeth.

We don't know how much time had passed between the visit of Gabriel to Mary and her arrival at the home of Elizabeth, but during that period of time the Holy Spirit had been visited upon Mary and she was pregnant with Jesus.

The only way Elizabeth could have known Mary's condition before Mary had a chance to tell her (assuming that all the facts of the matter have been recorded in the scriptures) was by revelation of the Holy Spirit, both to Elizabeth and to the baby she carried. A fact which should always be kept in mind is that not all information concerning things not pertinent to our salvation has been revealed in the scriptures. In John 20:30-31, John wrote, "Many other signs therefore Jesus also performed in the presence of the disciples, which are not written in this book; but these have been written that you may believe that Jesus is the Christ, the Son of God; and that believing you may have life in His name." I think we must also assume that in addition to the signs Jesus performed and which were not written down, many other details of lesser importance were omitted.

The word "Lord" in that day, in addition to being used to refer to God or to the promised Messiah was sometimes used to address or denote a superior, a master, a teacher or some ruler such as a governor. It is clear, though, that from the manner in which Elizabeth used the word in verse 5 above that she was referring to divinity. The word was commonly used by the Jews to refer to the expected Messiah but whether or not they used it to confirm their belief in the divinity of the Messiah is not now clear.

Mary was blessed in two ways by being chosen to be the mother of the Messiah and because she believed the message of Gabriel. By being blessed, though, she did not become an object of worship as is believed by some. To worship a person or to pray to a person, either dead or alive, even one who has been blessed by God is idolatry.

6 The Birth of John the Baptist (Luke 1:57-66)

(1) The time had come for Elizabeth to give birth and she bore a son. (2) Her neighbors and her relatives heard that the Lord had lavished His great favor upon her and they rejoiced with her. (3) Now on the eighth day they came to circumcise the child and they were going to call him Zacharias after his father, (4) but Elizabeth said, "No, not so! He shall be called John."

(5) But they said to her, "There is none of your relatives who is called by that name."

(6) So they made signs to Zacharias asking what he wanted the child to be called. (7) Zacharias asked for a tablet and wrote, "His name is John." And they were all astonished.

(8) Immediately Zacharias' mouth was opened and his tongue loosed and he began to speak praising God. (9) Fear came upon all those living around them and all these things were being talked about in all the hill country of Judea. (10) All who heard what had happened kept it in mind asking, "What then will this child turn out to be?" For the hand of the Lord was certainly with him.

Notes: The eighth day after birth was the day on which a male child was required to be circumcised under the Law. Genesis 17:12 reads, in part, "Then Abraham circumcised his son Isaac when he was eight days old, as God had commanded Him." Paul wrote in Philippians 3:5 that he had been circumcised on the eighth day.

Traditionally, a child was named at the time of his circumcision and it was the custom to name the first son after the father or another close relative. Gabriel had told Zacharias that his son was to be named John, and Zacharias had told Elizabeth, of course, probably in writing (the same way he had communicated with the other people there) because he was unable to speak.

A writing tablet was usually a smooth piece of wood covered with wax into which the message was scribed by use of a stylus. Writing on waxed boards was temporary and could not be preserved for any great length of time. More permanent writing would have been on parchment or papyrus.

The fear which the people felt was probably reverential awe. What had occurred (Zacharias regaining his power of speech after a nine-month loss) would certainly have been enough to cause such fear. Verse 6 above seems to indicate either that Zacharias was deaf as well as dumb or that the people thought he was since they made signs to him rather than speaking to him. At any rate, the sudden return of the power of speech to Zacharias after its absence for such a long time would have convinced the people that God was responsible both for the loss of speech and the regaining of it.

7 Zacharias's Song and Prophecy (Luke 1:67-80)

(1) Zacharias was filled with the Holy Spirit and prophesied, saying, (2) "Blessed is the Lord God of Israel for He has visited us and accomplished redemption for His people. (3) He has raised up a horn of salvation for us in the house of David His servant. (4) He promised through the mouths of His holy prophets from old (5) salvation 'from our enemies,' and 'from the hand of all who hate us,' (6) to show mercy toward our fathers, and to remember His holy covenant. (7) He swore an oath to Abraham our father (8) to grant that we, being delivered from the hand of our enemies, might serve Him without fear (9) in holiness and righteousness before Him all our days. (10) And you, child, will be called the prophet of the Most High, for you will go on 'before the Lord to prepare His ways' (11) to give to His people the knowledge of salvation by the forgiveness of their sins. (12) Because of the tender mercy of our God, with which the sunrise from on high shall visit us

(13) 'to shine upon those who sit in darkness and the shadow of death,' to guide our feet into the way of peace."

(14) The child continued to grow and to become strong in spirit. He lived in the desert until the day of his public appearance to Israel.

Notes: To "be filled with the Holy Spirit" means to turn over your life to God, to be guided by His will through the Holy Spirit, and to be sanctified to do His will as revealed by the Holy Spirit. To "prophesy" means, among other things as in this scripture, to praise God as when Zacharias said in verse 2 above, "Blessed is the Lord God of Israel."

The Greek word translated "visited" in verse 2 above is "episkeptomai." It means "to inspect, to select, to go to see, relieve" and was usually translated as "look out" or "visit."

"Redeemed" means, of course, ransomed. People are subject to God's Law, and since everyone breaks that law, they must pay the price of redemption to escape the penalty. Jesus paid the price of redemption for all people who want to be redeemed, a future event for Old Testament believers and a past event for New Testament believers. At that time redemption was still in the future for all of God's people.

A desert is not always a treeless place of burning sands, but today looking at what was then Judea, a person might think that the whole country was nothing but desert. Even though it may look drab now, it does look much better than it did in 1945 before the Jews conquered it and formed the present nation of Israel.

In the days when John lived there, the land south of the Dead Sea was desert. To the east of that desert was an area of brush and scrub trees with a strip of forest running in a north south direction through its center. To the east of that area of brush and scrub trees was another stretch of desert. At the southern end of the Dead Sea, there was a fairly large oasis.

8 The Birth of Jesus (Matt. 1:18-25; Luke 2:1-7)

(1) The birth of Jesus was this way. His mother Mary had been betrothed to Joseph but before they came together she was found to be with child by the Holy Spirit. (2) Joseph her husband, being a righteous man and not wanting to disgrace her, wanted to divorce Mary secretly. (3) But when he was considering this an angel of the Lord appeared to him in a dream and said, "Joseph, son of David, do not be afraid to take Mary as your wife because that which is conceived in her is of the Holy Spirit. (4) She shall bear a Son and you shall call His name Jesus. It is He who will save His people from their sins."

(5) All this took place so that what was spoken by the Lord through the prophet might be fulfilled, saying, (6) "Behold, a virgin shall be with child and shall bear a Son and they shall call His name Immanusel (which translated means 'God with us')."

(7) So Joseph arose from his sleep and did what the angel of the Lord commanded him. He took Mary as his wife (8) and kept her a virgin until she gave birth to a son.

(9) Now in those days a decree went out from Caesar Augustus that a census be taken of all the Roman Empire. (10) This was the first census taken while Quirinius was governor of Syria. (11) All the people were proceeding to register for the census, everyone going to his own city. (12) Because he was of the house and family of David, Joseph went up from the city of Nazareth in Galilee to Bethlehem in Judea, the city of David,

(13) to register with Mary who was espoused to him and was with child.

(14) While they were in Bethlehem the time was completed for Mary to give birth, (15) and Mary gave birth to her firstborn son and wrapped Him in swaddling cloths and laid Him in a manger because there was no room for them in the inn. (16) And they called the child's name Jesus.

Notes: Because Mary was pregnant before she and Joseph were married, according to the Law, Joseph could have publicly denounced Mary but he didn't want to do that, so he had decided to break the betrothal privately. The Law of Moses was very clear regarding the situation in which Joseph found himself. Any man who found that his wife was not a virgin, what was to be done to the man if he charged falsely that his wife was not a virgin, and what was to be done to the woman if the man's charge was true are dealt with in Deuteronomy 22:13-21. Verses 20 and 21 reads, "But if this charge is true, that the girl was not found a virgin, then they shall bring out the girl to the doorway of her father's house, and the men of her city shall stone her to death because she committed an act of folly in Israel, by playing the harlot in her father's house; thus you shall purge the evil from among you." The truth of the charges, if they had been made, would have been evident if Joseph had made them publicly.

Isaiah 7:13-14 reads, "Then he said, 'Listen now, 0 house of David! Is it too slight a thing for you to try the patience of men, that you will try the patience of my God as well? Therefore the Lord Himself will give you a sign: Behold, a virgin will be with child and bear a Son, and she will call His name Immanuel.'"

Caesar Augustus was also known as Octavius and reigned as emperor over the Roman Empire from 27 BC until his death in AD 14. Of course, the whole world to him was the Roman Empire.

History records that Quirinius probably served two terms as governor of Syria of which Palestine was then a part. The first term was from 6 BC to 4 BC and the second from AD 6 to AD 9. There was a census in both of his terms as governor. Luke states that the census taken at the time of the birth of Jesus was that one taken during Quirinius's first term as governor. The second census was probably the one to which it is referred in Acts 5:37.

In verse 15 above, it is stated that "there was no room for them in the inn." "Inn" here is preceded by a definite article, "the," which would indicate that there was only one inn in Bethlehem. There would probably have been no need for more than one inn in a town as small as Bethlehem was at that time.

When Joseph and Mary arrived in Bethlehem, they found that the inn was already filled to capacity. They must have traveled slowly because it was so close to the time for Mary to deliver her child. They may have left Nazareth in what they assumed would be plenty of time to get a room at the inn, or perhaps they failed to anticipate the number of people who would be in Bethlehem. At any rate, the only space they could find which would give them some shelter was in a stable. Although not stated in the scriptures, the stable was probably a part of the inn. The size of the inn is not known, but it was probably a small one as Bethlehem was not on a major caravan route.

Inns at the time Jesus was born were quite different from the inns with which we are familiar. The word "inn" conveys to us a picture of a large house with a number of bedrooms and a large dining room. In the early days of this country, inns were plentiful. In Colonial Williamsburg, inns have been restored or rebuilt, and we can now see first hand what they were like. Through the years, inns have mostly been replaced by hotels which were built larger and larger as the need and architectural knowledge increased. In the past fifty years or so, the most common form of lodging for travelers has come to be motels, a name coined by combining syllables of the original term by which they were called, "motor hotel."

First-century inns (also known as caravansaries or caravanserais because they were used mostly as stopping places for caravans) were usually built on trade routes and would sometimes be at the site of an oasis rather than in a town. The ground floors and the open space around the buildings were used to shelter the beasts of burden and the wares and baggage of the travelers. The upper floors were for the use of the travelers. Surrounding all this, there would sometimes have been a high wall of local stone or sun-dried brick to protect against thieves and robbers. When all the rooms were filled or a traveler could not afford the price of a room, he would usually sleep in the courtyard. In bad weather, these less-fortunate travelers would seek shelter in the arcades among the animals.

It was the custom of the Jews to wash a child in water immediately after it was born. After that the baby was rubbed with salt and wrapped in swaddling cloths. Swaddling cloths were bands or blankets which closely confined the limbs of the infants. Ezekiel 16:4 reads, "As for your birth, on the day you were born your navel cord was not cut, nor were you washed with water for cleansing; you were not rubbed with salt or even wrapped in cloths."

The birth place of the Messiah was prophesied in Micah 5:2 as follows: "But as for you, Bethlehem Ephrathah, too little among the clans of Judah, from you One will go forth for Me to be ruler of Israel. His goings forth are from long ago, from the days of eternity."

9 The Visit of the Shepherds {Luke 2:8-20)

(1) In the vicinity of Bethlehem there were some shepherds who were staying out in the fields at nights to keep watch over their flock, (2) and an angel of the Lord suddenly appeared standing before them and the glory of the Lord shone around them, and the shepherds were very frightened.

(3) The angel said to the shepherds, "Do not be afraid. I bring you good news of a great joy which will be for all the people. (4) Today in the city of David there has been born for you a Savior who is Christ the

Lord. (5) This will be a sign for you-you will find a baby wrapped in swaddling cloths and lying in a manger."

(6) Suddenly there appeared with the angel a multitude of the heavenly host praising God and saying, (7) "Glory to God in the highest and on earth peace among men of good will."

(8) When the angels had gone away from the shepherds into heaven the shepherds said to one another, "Let us hurry to Bethlehem and see this thing that has happened which the Lord has made known to us."

(9) Then the shepherds went in haste and found Mary and Joseph and the baby, and the baby was lying in a manger. (10) When they had seen this they made known the statement which had been told them about this Child. (11) Those who heard it wondered at the things which were told to them by the shepherds. (12) And Mary treasured all these things pondering them in her heart. (13) The shepherds returned to their flock glorifying and praising God for all that they had heard and seen, just as had been told to them.

Notes: The fact that the shepherds remained outdoors at night indicates that the time of the year was probably somewhere between April and October, because between those dates, the weather would have been warm enough for the shepherds to have stayed outside all night. In the latter part of December, the weather would have been too cold for them to have been outside, so we can rest assured that the date on which the Christian world celebrates the birth of Jesus, December 25, is not the date on which He was actually born to Mary.

Instead of" ... keeping watch over their flock by night...," the correct phrasing would more properly have been something like "... keeping the night watches over their flock. .. " or, as Albert Barnes suggests, ". . . tending their flock by turns through the night watches... " The time between, what to us would be, 6:00 p.m. and 6 a.m., for them, would have been divided into four watches of three hours each rather than as we tell time by hours in that time period. Time designations during the night would have been according to the number of the watch. As the first hour of the day would have been the time between 6:00 and 7:00 a.m., the first watch would have been the time between 6:00 p.m. and 9:00 p.m.

The shepherds were simple men, neither sophisticated nor well-cultured as were the scribes and Pharisees. They believed what the angel told them-that Jesus was the promised Messiah. It is doubtful that the scribes and Pharisees would not have been skeptical, and certainly they would not have believed without diligently checking the Messianic prophecies and the genealogy of Joseph. Later, after Jesus had begun His ministry, most of them never did come to believe. They were not even convinced by the miracles Jesus performed in their own presence. That was probably because they didn't want to believe.

10 The Genealogy of Joseph (Matt. 1:1-17)

(1) This is the genealogy of Jesus Christ, the son of David, the son of Abraham.

(2) To Abraham was born Isaac; and to Isaac Jacob; and to Jacob Judah and his brothers; (3) and to Judah were born Perez and Zerah by Tamar; and to Perez was born Hezron; and to Hezron Ram; (4) and to Ram was born Amminadab; and to Amminadab Nahshon; and Nahshon Salmon; (5) and to Salmon was born Boaz by Rahab; and to Boaz was born Obed by Ruth; and to Obed Jesse; (6) and to Jesse was born David the king.

To David was born Solomon by her who had been the wife of Uriah; (7) and to Solomon was born Rehoboam; and to Rehoboam Abijah; and Abijah Asa; (8) and to Asa Jehoshaphat; and to Jehoshaphat Joram; and Joram Uzziah; (9) and to Uzziah Jotham; and to Jotham Ahaz; and to Ahaz Hezekiah; (10) and to Hezekiah Manasseh; and to Manasseh Amon; and to Amon Josiah; (11) and to Josiah Jeconiah and his brothers, at the time of the deportation to Babylon.

(12) After the deportation to Babylon to Jeconiah was born Shealtiel; and to Shealtiel Zerubbabel; (13) and to Zerubbabel Abiud; and to Abiud Eliakim; and to Eliakim Azor; (14) and to Azor Zadok; and to Zadok, Achim; and to Achim Eliud; (15) and to Eliud Eleazar; and to Eleazar Matthan; and to Matthan Jacob; (16) and to Jacob was born Joseph the husband of Mary by whom was born Jesus, who is the Christ.

(17) The number of generations from Abraham to David were fourteen; and from David to the deportation to Babylon were fourteen

generations; and from the deportation to Babylon until the time of Christ were fourteen generations.

Notes: Because of the Messianic prophecies, the Jews kept very careful records of the genealogies of their people. Only in this way could there be an accurate account of the people in the different tribes especially those in the Messianic line. From the Old Testament prophecies, they knew that the Messiah would be from the tribe of Judah (Gen. 49:9-10), a descendant of Jesse (Isa. 11:10), and that He would be born in Bethlehem (Mic. 5:2). Only through their records of genealogies would the Jews know if the Messiah, when He came, fit all the criteria of family antecedents as prophesied in the scriptures. In this way, they could know exactly which person would fit all the conditions as described by the prophets. The genealogy as given by Matthew was to prove to the Jews that Jesus fit those prophecies.

The word "son" as used by the Jews could mean any number of things. It could mean an actual son, a grandson, a descendent, an adopted son, a disciple, or a person who was so loved or regarded that he was considered as close as a son. In this case, the word is used to mean that Jesus was a descendent of David. In the same way, it is used to show that Jesus was a descendent of Abraham, to whom the promise was made that all nations would be blessed through the seed of (or a descendent of) Abraham. Because the promise was to Abraham, it was important that the lineage of the Messiah be traced to him too. Of course, the lineage of all Jews would go back to Abraham, because he was the ancestor of all Jews and it was to him that God's promise was made.

It may be noted, too, that Rahab, the harlot of Jericho, was a progenitor of the Messiah as was Ruth, a Moabite woman. Perhaps, those two women being ancestors of the Messiah was God's way of telling us that His salvation was open to all nations and to all kinds and classes of people.

If the Old Testament record is checked concerning the lineage given here as being that prior to Abraham, it will be found that not all the people between Adam and Abraham are listed. That does not necessarily mean that the record of Matthew is incorrect. It could be that Matthew included only enough of the record to prove that the genealogy of Jesus met the requirements of the Messiah as prophesied. Further, the record following David also has omissions which were probably made for the same reason.

More on that subject later.

11 Jesus Presented at the Temple (Luke 2:21-39a)

(1) When the child Jesus was eight days old, the age for circumcision, He was named Jesus, the name given by the angel before He was conceived in the womb.

(2) When the days for their purification according to the Law of Moses were completed Joseph and Mary brought Jesus up to Jerusalem to present Him to the Lord (3) (as it is written in the Law of the Lord, "Every first-born male that opens the womb shall be called holy to the Lord"), (4) and to offer a sacrifice according to what was said in the Law of the Lord, "A pair of turtledoves or two young pigeons."

(5) Now there was a man in Jerusalem whose name was Simon and this man was righteous and devout looking for the consolation of Israel, and the Holy Spirit was upon him. (6) It had been revealed to him by the Holy Spirit that he would not see death before he had seen the Lord's Christ. (7) So he came in the Spirit into the temple. When the parents of Jesus brought in the child Jesus to carry out for Him the custom of the Law

(8) Simon took Jesus into his arms and blessed God and said,

(9) "Now, Lord, You do let Your bond-servant depart in peace according to Your word, (10) for my eyes have seen Your salvation, (11) which You have prepared in the presence of all the people, (12) 'A light of revelation to the Gentiles' and the glory of Your people Israel."

(13) Joseph and Mary were amazed at the things which were being said about Jesus. (14) And Simon blessed them and said to Mary His mother, "This child is appointed for the fall and rise of many in Israel and for a sign to be opposed---{15} and a sword will pierce even your own soul-to the end that thoughts from many hearts may be revealed."

(16) There was also a prophetess, Anna the daughter of Phanuel, of the tribe of Asher. She was advanced in years and had lived with a

husband seven years after her marriage (17) and then as a widow to the age of eighty-four. She never left the temple, serving night and day with fastings and prayers.

(18) At that very moment she came up and began giving thanks to God, and continued to speak of Jesus to all those who were looking for the redemption of Jerusalem.

(19) And they performed everything according to the Law of the Lord.

Notes: According to the Law of Moses as recorded in Leviticus 12:3, eight days after His birth, Jesus was circumcised. It was at that time that the child was named Jesus in accordance with the instructions given to Mary in section 4 above (Luke 1:31). This probably took place in Bethlehem, but we have no information concerning the length of time Joseph and Mary remained in Bethlehem after the birth of Jesus because of the census, or, for that matter, for any other reason. After Luke 2:1-5, no further mention is made in the scriptures of the census which Augustus had ordered to be made and was the reason for the presence of Joseph and Mary in Bethlehem.

From the text, it would appear that no great amount of time had passed between the circumcision of Jesus and the trip of Joseph and Mary with Jesus to the temple in Jerusalem. Actually, there had been thirty-two days between those two events. There is no information given in the Scriptures as to the route Joseph took in traveling between Bethlehem and Jerusalem, that is, whether he and his family went back to Nazareth and then to Jerusalem or went directly from Bethlehem to Jerusalem.

Under the Law of Moses as recorded in Leviticus 12:2-5, a woman was unclean after having given birth. If the child was a male, the length of time the woman was unclean was forty days, but if the child was a female, the woman was unclean for eighty days. It was after the passage of the forty days that was required for the purification of Mary that Joseph took her and Jesus to Jerusalem to present Jesus to the Lord according to the Law (Exod. 13:2) and to offer the sacrifice required by the Law as stated in the text.

The Law as given in Leviticus 12:6-8 reads as follows: "And when the days of her purifying are fulfilled, for a son, or for a daughter, she shall bring a lamb a year-old for a burnt offering and a young pigeon, or a turtledove, for a sin offering, unto the door of the tent of meeting, unto the priest; and he shall offer it before Jehovah, and make atonement for her; and she shall be cleansed from the fountain of her blood. This is the law for her that beareth, whether a male or a female. And if her means suffice not for a lamb, then she shall take two turtledoves, or two young pigeons; the one for a burnt-offering, and the other for a sin-offering; and the priest shall make atonement for her, and she shall be clean."

Evidently, Joseph and Mary were from among the poorer class of people in Israel. The scriptures do not say that for Mary only turtledoves or pigeons were sacrificed, but the failure to mention a lamb in the quotation from the Law indicates that the sacrifice was of turtledoves or pigeons only.

Albert Barnes, in his commentary, speculated that by sacrificing turtledoves or pigeons, Mary was showing her poverty, and that Jesus, Himself coming to earth in a state of poverty, showed that He did not dishonor the poor.

12 The Visit of the Wise Men (Matt. 2:1-12)

(1) After Jesus was born in Bethlehem of Judea, in the days of Herod the king, Magi from the East arrived in Jerusalem and asked, (2) "Where is He who has been born King of the Jews? We saw His star in the East and have come to worship Him."

(3) When Herod the king heard this he was troubled, he and all Jerusalem with him. (4) Gathering together all the chief priests and scribes of the people Herod began to inquire of them where the Christ was to be born.

(5) They said to him, "In Bethlehem of Judea, for so it has been written by the prophet, (6) 'And you, Bethlehem, land of Judah, are by no means least among the leaders of Judah; for out of you shall come forth a Ruler, who will shepherd My people Israel.'"

(7) Then Herod secretly called the Magi and ascertained from them the time the star appeared. (8) He sent them on to Bethlehem and said

to them, "Go and make careful search for the Child and when you have found Him report to me that I may come and worship Him." (9) Having heard the king the Magi went their way and the star which they had seen in the East went on before them until it came and stood over where the Child was. (10) When they saw the star they rejoiced exceedingly with great joy, (11) and they went into the house and saw the Child and Mary His mother, and they fell down and worshiped Him. Opening their treasures they presented to Jesus gifts of gold and frankincense and myrrh. (12) But having been warned by God in a dream not to return to Herod they departed for their own country by another way.

Notes: There was a very good reason for always stating that Bethlehem was in Judea-there was a town named Bethlehem in Galilee also. That other Bethlehem, the one in Galilee, was in the territory which had been assigned to the tribe of Zebulon as recorded in Joshua 19:15. Of course, the only reason we are familiar with the town of Bethlehem in Judea is that in prophecy the event had been foretold, that Jesus was to be born there, and that the prophecy had been fulfilled.

Herod was called a king, but his authority was only that of a governor or regent. He received his office by appointment from Rome and his occupancy of that office was dependent on the good will of the emperor in Rome. At the time of the birth of Jesus Herod had reigned about thirty-four years. He was responsible for having built the magnificent temple which was being used during the ministry of Jesus. The Romans destroyed that temple in AD 70 and only the base of the west wall still remains. This Herod is known to historians as Herod the Great because of his military prowess and his talent for governing and defending the realm.

The word "Magi" is translated "wise men" in the King James Version of the Bible. Magi is the plural form of magus and a Magus is defined in Webster's dictionary as "a member of a hereditary priestly class among the ancient Medes and Persians." Smith's Bible Dictionary says of them: "Originally they were a class of priests among the Persians and Medes, who formed the king's privy council, and cultivated astrology, medicine and occult natural science. They probably learned of Jehovah when they came into contact with the Israelites when both nations were being held captive by Nebuchadnezzar. Among all the nations of the world the religion of the Persians had the greatest similarity to that of the Jews in that both believed in one god and had no idols."

Ellicott writes, "The Magi express the feeling which the Roman historians Tacitus and Seutonius tell us sixty or seventy years later had been for a long time very widely diffused. Everywhere throughout the East men were looking for the advent of a great king who was to rise from among the Jews. It had fermented in the minds of men, heathen as well as Jews, and would have led them to welcome Jesus as the Christ had he come in accordance with their expectations."

In verse 6 above, in answer to Herod's question concerning where the Christ was to be born, the chief priests and scribes quoted him the passage quoted here, which is from Micah 5:2.

Myrrh is obtained from the bark of a plant, *Balsamodendron myrrha*. It first appears in the form of a gum but hardens into small yellowish drops. Myrrh was one of the ingredients used in making the "oil of holy ointment," the recipe of which is given in Exodus 30:23-25. It was also used in the purification of women (Esther 23:12), as a perfume (Ps. 45:8) and for embalming (John 19:39).

Frankincense is an incense obtained from a vegetable resin and was used primarily for sacrificial fumigation. The "frank" part of the word means that the incense burns freely for a long time and with a steady flame giving off its odor as it burns. According to Exodus 30:34, frankincense was one of the ingredients in the incense which was to be burned upon the altar and the incense made from this formula was not to be used as a perfume by anyone-it was to be "holy to you for the Lord."

An interesting observation is that the Magi went into the "house" where they found Mary and Jesus. This indicates that, contrary to all the manger scenes we see in December, Joseph and Mary and Jesus were no longer staying in the stable when the Magi made their visit. Assuming that Jesus had been taken to the temple in Jerusalem (which was only about six miles from Bethlehem) before the visit of the Magi, their visit would have been no sooner than forty days after the birth of Jesus and at least that length of time after the shepherds had come to worship the Messiah. Thus the shepherds and the Magi would not have visited Jesus and His family in Bethlehem at the same time. As shown by our knowledge of later events, the visit of the Magi could have been almost two years after the birth of Jesus but was probably not more than about one year later.

The only account of the visit of the Magi is in Matthew and nowhere does he state, infer nor imply that their number was three. Since "magi" is plural, their number could have been anywhere from two upwards. By tradition, in later years, their number was arbitrarily determined to have been three. Also by tradition, they have come to be thought of as eastern kings named Gaspar, Melchior, and Belthazar and have been honored in "sainthood" by the Catholic Church as patron saints of travelers.

13 The Flight into Egypt (Matt. 2:13-15)

(1) When the Magi had departed an angel of the Lord appeared to Joseph in a dream and said, "Arise and take the Child and His mother and flee to Egypt. Remain there until I tell you; for Herod is going to search for the Child to destroy Him."

(2) So Joseph arose and took the Child and His mother by night and departed for Egypt (3) and stayed there until the death of Herod so that what was spoken by the Lord through the prophet might be fulfilled, "Out of Egypt did I call My Son."

Notes: If we need it, this should be proof enough for us that God can and does look after His own. God warned the Magi not to go back through Jerusalem and report their findings to Herod, but He also warned Joseph that Herod was intent on destroying the newly born "king" and that he should take Mary and Jesus to Egypt for safety.

Although also under Roman rule, Egypt was a separate province from Judea and Herod had no power there. Upon the death of Alexander, his empire had been divided between the Seleucids and the Ptolomys; the Ptolomys reigning in Egypt and the Seleucids in Asia Minor. Judea had passed back and forth between those two empires several times until the Romans had stabilized their empire and at the time of the birth of Jesus, Judea was not a part of the Egyptian province.

The death of Herod is believed by most scholars to have occurred in the year 4 BC or possibly 3 BC. The flight of Joseph, Mary and Jesus to Egypt and return was in fulfillment of the prophecy in Hosea 11:1, "Out of Egypt I called My Son."

It is interesting to note that the flight to Egypt was one of the only two times that Jesus was ever outside the boundaries of Palestine. It is also interesting that it was to Egypt that the family of Israel (Jacob) fled and in Egypt that the Israelites grew into a nation, and that it was from out of Egypt that the children of Israel proceeded in order to establish their home in Palestine.

14 Massacre of the Babies by Herod (Matt. 2:16-18)

(1) When Herod saw that he had been tricked by the Magi he became very enraged. He sent and slew all the male children who were in Bethlehem and in all its environs and who were two years old and younger according to the time which he had ascertained from the magi. (2) Then that which was spoken through Jeremiah the prophet was fulfilled, (3) "A voice was heard in Ramah, weeping and mourning, Rachel weeping for her children, and she refused to be comforted because they were no more."

Notes: The Magi had not intended to trick Herod nor to mock him (as the King James Version reads) but having been warned in a dream not to return through Jerusalem, they understood the dream to have been a warning, and they did as they had been instructed to do.

Probably Herod had originally intended only to have Jesus put to death, but having been thwarted by not having received the required information from the Magi and angered because of that, in order to be sure of killing this new "king" whom he assumed would be a rival for his own kingdom, he now had to have all the male children of the right age killed. What Herod evidently failed to understand was that the new "king" was no more able to become the political ruler over Judea than he himself had been. It was the Roman emperor who had the power to choose a ruler, and he could and would choose anyone who suited him whether or not Herod approved.

The prophecy concerning the murder of the children is found in Jeremiah 31:13 which reads, "A voice is heard in Ramah, lamentation and bitter weeping. Rachel is weeping for her children; she refuses to be comforted for her children, because they are no more."

The only person named Rachel about whom anything is written in the Bible is the second (and favorite) wife of Jacob. Judah, the fourth son of Jacob, was the ancestor of Jesus (supposedly) and his descendants, the tribe of Judah, were the Israelite settlers of Judea. Rachel, however, was not the mother of Judah and, therefore, not the ancestor of the majority of the inhabitants of Judea. No explanation is given for the reason Rachel instead of Leah was named in that passage. It was Leah, the first wife of Jacob, who was the mother of Judah and, presumably, the ancestor of most of the children who were murdered because of Herod's order. There were, however, probably people of all the tribes of Israel living in Judea at that time, and perhaps, in that case, some of the slaughtered babies were descendants of Rachel.

Ramah was a town in Judea located about five miles north of Jerusalem and was often mentioned in the Old Testament, most frequently in the book of I Samuel. Ramah was the town in which Samuel was born, had lived, and was buried. It is believed that by the time the New Testament was written, the name of the town had been changed to Arimathea. If that is true, Ramah, now Arimathea, was the home of the man named Joseph who claimed the body of Jesus after His crucifixion. Ramah was once a large fortified city, but only a few poor huts remain today to show that it ever existed. A Mohammedan mosque which was once a Catholic church sits near the site of the grave of Samuel and now lies in near ruin.

15 Return to Nazareth (Matt. 2:19-23; Luke 2:39b)

(1) When Herod was dead an angel of the Lord appeared in a dream to Joseph in Egypt and said, (2) "Arise and take the Child and His mother and go into the land of Israel for those who sought the Child's life are dead."

(3) Then Joseph arose and took the Child and His mother and came into the land of Israel. (4) But when he heard that Archelaus was

reigning over Judea in place of his father Herod he was afraid to go there. Being warned by God in a dream Joseph departed for the regions of Galilee (5) and went and resided in a city called Nazareth so that what was spoken through the prophets might be fulfilled, "He shall be called a Nazarene."

Notes: When Joseph was told by an angel in a dream that it was safe to return to Israel, apparently, he had intended to make a home for himself and his family in Judea, but upon learning that Archelaus would be ruling in Judea, he changed his mind about living there. Archelaus was one of the three sons of Herod the Great, who inherited the kingdom and was allowed by the Romans to rule in accordance with his father's wishes. He became the ruler over that part of the kingdom which included Judea. He is reputed to have been a cruel man with a tyrannical disposition and a temperament much like that of his father. The scriptures don't give a reason why Joseph feared Archelaus, but Joseph probably knew of the character and reputation of Archelaus, and knowing what his father was like, it isn't very difficult to imagine how Joseph must have felt. Archelaus was deposed by the Romans in AD 6 for his cruelty and injustice. He was exiled to Vienne in what is now France. Through another dream, God told Joseph to go to Nazareth in Galilee to live. Nazareth had been the home of Mary before her marriage to Joseph, but it isn't known whether or not it had also been the home of Joseph.

In this passage of the scripture, it is stated that Joseph's decision to live in Nazareth was a fulfillment of that which was spoken through the prophets, "He shall be called a Nazarene." Such a prophecy is not found recorded in the Old Testament. In fact, the word "Nazarene" is not listed in *Strong's Exhaustive Concordance of the Bible* as appearing at all in the Old Testament. Albert Barnes, in his commentary, addressed this subject in detail and part of his explanation is as follows: "When Matthew says that the prophecies were 'fulfilled,' his meaning is, that the predictions of the prophets that he would be of a low and despised condition, and would be rejected, were fully accomplished in his being an inhabitant of Nazareth, and despised as such." This is borne out in John 1:46, which reads, "And Nathaniel said to him, 'Can any good thing come out of Nazareth?'" and in John 7:41 and 52, which read, "Still others were saying, 'Surely the Christ is not going to come from Galilee, is he?' ... They answered and said to him, 'You are not also from Galilee, are you? Search and see that no prophet arises out of Galilee.'"

16 The Child Jesus Visits Jerusalem (Luke 2:40-52)

(1) Jesus continued to grow and become strong, becoming full of wisdom and the grace of God was upon Him.

(2) Now every year the parents of Jesus went to Jerusalem at the Feast of the Passover. (3) And when Jesus was twelve years old they went up to the Feast according to their custom. (4) As they were returning home after spending the full number of days, the boy Jesus stayed behind in Jerusalem. His parents were unaware of it (5) but supposed Him to be in the caravan and went a day's journey. Then they began looking for Him among their relatives and acquaintances. (6) When they did not find Him they returned to Jerusalem looking for Him. (7) After searching for three days they found Him in the temple sitting in the midst of the teachers both listening to them and asking them questions. (8) And all who heard Him were amazed at His understanding and His answers.

(9) When His parents saw Jesus they were astonished and His mother said to Him, "Son, why have You treated us this way? Your father and I have been anxiously looking for You."

(10) Jesus said to them, "Why is it that you were looking for Me? Did you not know that I had to be about the things of My Father?" (11) But Joseph and Mary did not understand the statement which Jesus had made to them.

(12) Jesus went down with His parents and came to Nazareth and He continued in subjection to them and His mother treasured all His words in her heart.

(13) Jesus kept increasing in wisdom and stature and in favor with God and men.

Notes: As with all children, the body of Jesus grew with the years and became strong. But the wisdom of Jesus may have far exceeded that of other children. It doesn't seem reasonable that Jesus would have to learn everything as other children did. He had existed with God before the world was made, and surely, He didn't suddenly lose all the knowledge He had when He was born on the earth, but the scripture says that Jesus increased in wisdom as well as in stature. If such was actually the case, and I have no doubt that it was, God did take away from Jesus some of the knowledge which He had had since before the world was made.

Perhaps, the grace of God that was upon Him, rather than being unmerited favor such as is shown to sinners when they obey, was simply God's favor and the love of a father for a son. It would seem, too, that whatever knowledge Jesus did possess, and even at the tender age of twelve, it must have been considerable, He could not let it be known to the people around Him lest they be convinced that He was some sort of demon as He was accused of being later during His ministry.

Deuteronomy 16:16 says, "Three times in a year all your males shall appear before the Lord your God in the place which He chooses, at the Feast of Unleavened Bread and at the Feast of Weeks and at the Feast of Booths, and they shall not appear before the Lord empty-handed." Jewish males were not considered to have reached their manhood until they were twelve years old. It is probable that this was the first time Jesus had been required to go to Jerusalem for the feast although He had probably gone previously with His parents, because Joseph and Mary had been accustomed to go to Jerusalem for the feasts every year.

The "full number of days" for the Feast of the Passover was eight. The Passover was celebrated on the first day, and the Feast of Unleavened Bread during the other seven.

Albert Barnes wrote, "It may seem very remarkable that parents should not have been more attentive to their only son... " It is possible, or even probable, that Jesus was not an only son by the time He was twelve years old. We know that He had at least four brothers and two sisters and most of them may have (or could have) been born by the time Jesus was twelve. If Mary had had a child every two years, which is a reasonable length of time between children, she would have had six children, including Jesus, by the time Jesus was twelve years old. If that's the case, it's not quite so remarkable that the absence of Jesus from the company was not noticed until after the first day's journey. There could be any number of reasons for their negligence, but speculation would be useless because one could never be sure of what was the truth.

It seems remarkable, too, that Joseph and Mary did not understand what Jesus said to them. After all that had happened, the announcement by the angel Gabriel, the virgin birth, the adoration of the shepherds and the Magi, the dreams in which God had warned them, it would seem to be unreasonable that they still didn't understand that Jesus, their Son, was the Messiah, or at least someone who was very, very special. Whether or not Joseph ever came to believe is not known. And even of Mary, we have no scriptural evidence that she became a Christian.

Sometimes, it's in the seemingly little things that we find the greatest confirmation of the truth of the scriptures. It says here that Jesus "went down" to Nazareth from Jerusalem. Jerusalem is located in high mountainous country and the elevation of Nazareth is much less. As we look at a map today, it would look as though Nazareth was above Jerusalem simply because the orientation of the map would make it seem so. But Luke was referring to elevation when he wrote that they went down to Nazareth just as one would say that he went down from Denver to Kansas City or from Asheville to Charlotte or from Lake Tahoe to Los Angeles.

17 The Mission of John the Baptist (John 1:6-8, 15)

(1) There came a man sent from God whose name was John.

(2) He came as a witness that he might bear witness of the light so that all might believe through him. (3) He was not the light but came that he might bear witness of the light.

(4) John bore witness of Him who was the light and cried out saying, "This is He of whom I said, 'He who comes after me has a higher rank than I for He existed before me.'"

Notes: Reading that passage, those few words, it may seem to some to be rather inconsequential. However, John had already been preaching repentance to the Jews in Judea and in Galilee (and not in Samaria) and was well known throughout the land. Many people had the mistaken belief that John was the Messiah. For this reason, John was emphatic in his denial that he, John, was the Messiah but only a prophet with a mission to tell the Jews of the imminent coming of the true Messiah.

Jesus is presented in many passages as the light of the world. He said of Himself in John 8:12, "I am the light of the world. Anyone who follows Me will never walk in darkness because he will have the light of life." The fact that John the apostle wrote that Jesus was the light probably comes from having been told by Jesus Himself that He was the light of the world. John the apostle believed that Jesus was the light (or the One who was to enlighten the world so that the whole world would have the opportunity to believe on Jesus and be saved), so he called Jesus the light.

The purpose or mission of John the Baptist was to announce to the Jews the imminent coming of the Messiah. For Jesus to have made that claim of Himself without John having done so beforehand would have made him a target for scoffers, but John's standing with the people would have made his prediction of the coming of the Messiah an event to have been anticipated. After having made the announcement that the Messiah was coming and then to have introduced Jesus as that Messiah would have given Jesus much greater stature and believability with the people.

John was performing the duty for which he had been born. It was he who fulfilled the prophecy of Isaiah 40:3, "The voice of one who cries in the wilderness, 'Prepare ye the way of the Lord, make straight in the desert a highway for our God.'"

18 John Preaches and Baptizes Penitents

(Matt. 3:1-12; Mark 1:2-8; Luke 3:1-18)

(1) In the fifteenth year of the reign of Tiberius Caesar when Pontius Pilate was governor of Judea, when Herod was tetrarch of Galilee, when his brother Philip was tetrarch of the region of Iturea and Trachonitis and when Lysanias was tetrarch of Abilene, (2) in the high priesthood of Annas and Caiaphas, in the wilderness the Word of God came to John the son of Zacharias. (3) Then he went into the wilderness of Judea in the region of the Jordan River and began preaching a baptism of

repentance for the forgiveness of sins saying, "Repent, for the kingdom of heaven is at hand." (4) For John was the one referred to by Isaiah the prophet saying, "The voice of one crying in the wilderness, make ready the way of the Lord, make His paths straight. (5) Every ravine shall be filled up and every mountain and hill shall be brought low and the crooked shall become straight and the rough roads smooth, (6) and all flesh shall see the salvation of God."

(7) Now John wore a garment of camel's hair and a leather belt about his waist. His food was locusts and wild honey.

(8) All the country of Judea and all of the district around the Jordan and all the people of Jerusalem were going out to John and they were being baptized by him in the Jordan River, confessing their sins. (9) But when John saw many of the Pharisees and Sadducees coming for baptism he said to them, "You brood of vipers, who warned you to flee from the wrath to come? (10) First bring forth fruit in keeping with repentance

(11) and do not suppose that you can say to yourselves, 'We have Abraham for our father'; for I say to you that God is able from these stones to raise up children to Abraham. (12) The axe is already laid at the root of the trees. Every tree therefore that does not bear good fruit is cut down and thrown into the fire."

(13) And the multitude were questioning him saying, "Then what shall we do?"

(14) And he would say to them, "Let the man who has two tunics share with him who has none and let him who has food do likewise."

(15) Some tax gatherers also came to be baptized and they said to John, "Teacher, what shall we do?"

(16) John said to them, "Collect no more than what you have been ordered to."

(17) Some soldiers also were questioning him saying, "And what about us, what shall we do?"

He said to them, "Do not take money from anyone by force nor accuse anyone falsely and be content with your wages."

(18) Now while the people were in a state of expectation and all were wondering in their hearts about John as to whether he might be the Christ (19) John said to them all, "As for me, I baptize you with

water but One is coming who is mightier than I and I am not fit to untie the thong of His sandals. He will baptize you with the Holy Spirit and fire. (20) His winnowing fork is in His hand to thoroughly clear His threshing floor and to gather the wheat into His barn, but He will bum up the chaff with unquenchable fire."

(21) So with many other exhortations also he preached the gospel to the people.

Notes: According to historians Tiberius Caesar succeeded Augustus as Emperor of Rome in AD 14. Pontius Pilate was appointed to govern Judea in AD 26. Herod Antipas, tetrarch of Galilee, and his brother Philip, tetrarch of Iturea and Trachonitis, had succeeded their father, Herod the Great, in those areas. Herod had died in either 3 or 4 BC. Depending upon what time of the year in AD 14 and how far into the fifteenth year of the reign of Tiberius the ministry of John began, the year could have been anywhere between AD 27 and AD29.

"Lysanias" and "Abilene" are both mentioned only here and nowhere else in the Bible. Abilene is an area north of Iturea. Annas, one of the high priests mentioned here, appears three times in the Gospels and once in Acts, and Caiaphas is mentioned eight times in the Gospels and once in Acts, too.

The wilderness of Judea was that land along the Jordan River and the edge of the Dead Sea. It is rocky, mountainous, rough, thinly forested country, and was sparsely populated. During the time of Joshua, there were six cities located in the wilderness as listed in Joshua 15:61-62.

The "garment of camel's hair" was not the fine cloth from which expensive coats are made today. It was probably a coarse, cheap cloth made from the long shaggy hair of camels.

Monks and poorer classes of people still wear garments made from that hair. A leather girdle or wide belt completed John's wardrobe.

The land of Canaan has been described in the Bible as a land flowing with milk and honey, as in Exodus 3:8 and 17. The "wild honey" may have been from bees which built their hives in fissures and clefts of rocks and trees. They are said to have been plentiful at that time as they are still. Also in that area, there is another type of wild honey which is called wood honey. That kind of honey is produced by small insects and deposited on tree leaves from which it flows in large quantities. It is an inferior product, and it is said that it is still produced in some parts of the Near East.

There are several species of locust trees-black locust, honey locust, and carob. The fruit of these trees are long flat pods which contain a gelatinous substance which has a sweetish taste. It is edible but not particularly tasty. That is *not* the kind of locusts on which John subsisted. The locusts that John ate were the insects by that name, the same insects that were one of the plagues in Egypt. Locusts are similar to grasshoppers but can fly great distances. They have been known to fly into an area in such great numbers that they blot out the sky. They can blanket an area and decimate the crops in that area in a very short time. In Utah, in the mid-nineteenth century, that occurred, and the area was saved only by a great influx of seagulls which flew in and ate the locusts. There is a monument in Salt Lake City to those seagulls.

The common locust is brown and grows to about three inches in length. There are a great many references to locusts in the Old Testament. They gather in great numbers and sometimes are so thick that they obscure the sun (Exod. 10:15, Judg. 6:5, Jer. 46:23), their appetite is voracious (Exod. 10:12 and 15, Joel 4:1 and 7), in flight they make a great noise (Joel 2:5, Revelation 9:9), their progress is irresistible (Joel 2:8-9), they enter dwellings and even eat the woodwork of houses (Exod. 10:6, Joel 2:9-10), they do not fly at night (Nah. 3:17) and the sea destroys a great number of them (Exod. 10:19, Joel 2:20).

M. Olivier in his book *Voyage dans l'Empire Ottoman*, which roughly translated means "A Journey Through the Ottoman Empire," makes this statement about locusts: "With the burning south winds of Syria there come from the interior of Arabia and from the most southern parts of Persia clouds of locusts, whose ravages to these countries are as grievous and nearly as sudden as those of the heaviest hail in Europe. We witnessed them twice. It is difficult to express the effect produced on us by the sight of the whole atmosphere filled on all sides and to a great height by an innumerable quantity of these insects, whose flight was slow and uniform, and whose noise resembled that of rain; the sky was darkened, and the light of the sun considerably weakened. In a moment the terraces of the houses, the streets, and all the fields were covered by these insects, and in two days they had nearly devoured all the leaves of the plants. Happily they lived but a short time, and seemed to have migrated only to reproduce themselves and die; in fact, nearly all we saw the next day had paired, and the day following, the fields were covered with their dead bodies."

Locusts have been used for food from earliest times. Herodotus speaks of a Libyan nation whose people dried their locusts in the sun and ate them with milk. The more common method, however, was to pull off the legs and wings and roast them in an iron dish. Then they were thrown into a bag and eaten like parched corn, each person taking a handful when he chose *(Biblical Treasury)*. They are also prepared for food in a variety of other ways. Sometimes they are ground and pounded and mixed with flour and water and made into cakes. Sometimes they are salted and eaten; sometimes smoked, boiled, or roasted; or perhaps stewed or fried in butter.

That and wild honey was the fare of John the Baptist.

19 Jesus Baptized by John in the Jordan River

(Matt. 3:13-17; Mark 1:9-11; Luke 3:21-22)

(1) When all the people were being baptized by John, Jesus arrived from Nazareth in Galilee coming to John at the Jordan River to be baptized by him. (2) But John tried to dissuade Jesus saying, "I have need to be baptized by You and instead You come to me."

(3) Answering, Jesus said to John, "Permit it at this time for in this way it is fitting for us to fulfill all righteousness."

Then John baptized Jesus.

(4) After being baptized Jesus came up immediately from the water and while He was praying He saw the heavens open up and the Spirit of God in bodily form like a dove descending upon Him and a voice came out of heaven and said, "You are My beloved Son. In You I am well pleased."

Notes: John probably chose to baptize in the Jordan River because that was one of the very few places in Judea with water deep enough and plentiful enough to be used for that purpose. If John had chosen to baptize in Galilee, he would have had the Sea of Galilee at his disposal. The Sea of Galilee is a freshwater lake. At that location, of course, there would have been many fewer people because of the distance to Judea and Jerusalem.

Today, many people make pilgrimages to that area to be baptized in the Jordan River supposedly at the same place Jesus was baptized and to emulate His baptism there. They suppose that by doing so their baptism (even though it may be a second baptism) is more meaningful than a baptism at some other place may have been.

20 The Real Genealogy of Jesus through Mary

(Luke 3:23-38)

(1) When He began His ministry Jesus Himself was about thirty years of age, supposedly being the son of Joseph, the son-in-law of Eli (2) the son of Matthat, the son of Levi, the son of Melchi, the son of Jannai, the son of Joseph, (3) the son of Mattathias, the son of Amos, the son of Nahum, the son of Hesli, the son of Naggai, (4) the son of Maath, the son of Mattathias, the son of Semein, the son of Josech, the son of Joda, (5) the son of Joanan, the son of Rhesa, the son of Zerubbabel, the son of Shealtiel, the son of Neri, (6) the son of Melchi, the son of Addi, the son of Cosam, the son of Elmadam, the son of Er, (7) the son of Joshua, the son of Eliezer, the son of Jorim, the son of Matthat, the son of Levi, (8) the son of Simeon, the son of Judah, the son of Joseph, the son of Jonam, the son of Eliakim, (9) the son of Melea, the son of Menna, the son of Mattatha, the son of Nathan, the son of David, (10) the son of Jesse, the son of Obed, the son of Boaz, the son of Salmon, the son of Nahshon, (11) the son of Amminadab, the son of Admin, the son of Ram, the son of Hezron, the son of Perez, the son of Judah, (12) the son of Jacob, the son of Isaac, the son of Abraham, the son of Terah, the son of Nahor, (13) the son of Serug, the son of Reu, the son of Peleg, the son of Heber, the son of Shelah, (14) the son of Caiman, the son of Arphaxad, the son of Shem, the son of Noah, the son of Lamech, (15) the son of Methuselah, the son of Enoch, the

son of Jared, the son of Mahalaleel, the son of Cainan, (16) the son of Enosh, the son of Seth, the son of Adam, the son of God.

Notes: This is the only place where the Bible says anything about the age of Jesus when He began His ministry. Reconciling that statement with calculations of dates by historians, we can check its accuracy. Tiberius succeeded Augustus in AD 14, and John's ministry began in the fifteenth year of the reign of Tiberius (John 3:1). Jesus was born two years before the death of Herod the Great, who died in 3 BC or 4 BC, meaning that Jesus was probably born sometime between 3 BC and 6 BC. Depending upon what part of the year it was in AD 14 that Tiberius began to reign and what part of the fifteenth year of his reign John's ministry began would mean that John began his ministry sometime between AD 27 and AD 29. According to all those dates and all the "ifs, ands, and buts," that means that Jesus could have been between thirty and thirty-five years when He began His ministry. Assuming a date of around 3 BC for His birth, Jesus could very well have been thirty years old. At that, Luke did not give an exact age of Jesus, saying He was "about thirty," whether a guess on his part or a guess by another person who was his source for the information he had about Jesus or a revelation by the Holy Spirit, we have no way of knowing. Regardless, the age of Jesus when He began His ministry is of no particular importance. What is important is that the Bible and world history do not contradict each other.

According to Numbers 4:3 and 47, the priests of the tribe of Levi were to serve in the tent of meeting from the age of thirty to the age of fifty. This has no special significance for Jesus as He was not of the tribe of Levi. However, there must have been some good reason the priests were not to begin to serve until after their thirtieth birthday. In speculating about this, it may be that their service was deferred until they reached the age of thirty, because by that age, they would have had time to have gained experience, knowledge and wisdom, and the respect of the people.

In Psalms 110:4 and in several places in the book of Hebrews, Jesus is said to have been a priest after the order of Melchizedek. Too, in several places in Hebrews, Jesus is said to be the High Priest of Christians. As a priest in that sense, it might have seemed fitting that Jesus begin His ministry at the same age priests were to begin their service and that it not begin until that time for the same reason, whatever that reason.

Jesus was supposedly the son of Joseph, that is, he was believed to be the son of Joseph by all who knew the family. The circumstances surrounding the conception and birth of Jesus would not have been believed until the time He came to be acknowledged as the Messiah, the Son of God, and then only because the prophets had foretold those things.

The genealogies as given here and in section 10 (Matt. 1) differ greatly. No explanation of the differences is given in the scriptures other than that of Matthew's genealogy ending with ". . . and to Jacob was born Joseph the husband of Mary by whom was born Jesus, who is the Christ," and that Luke's begins with "Jesus... supposedly being the son of Joseph, the son-in-law of Eli, the son of Matthat... "etc.That would seem to be explanation enough, but-there are several schools of thought among biblical scholars as to the reasons for (and an explanation of) the differences between the two genealogies. The most common explanation, the most widely accepted, is what certainly seems to be the correct one, and that is that the genealogy in Matthew is that of Joseph and that the one in Luke is that of Mary. In view of the wording in each of the genealogies that would certainly seem to be the correct explanation.

21 Jesus Tempted By Satan

(Matt. 4:1-11; Mark 1:12-13; Luke 4:1-13)

(1) Jesus, full of the Holy Spirit, returned from the Jordan and was led about by the Spirit in the wilderness (2) for forty days to be tempted by the devil. Jesus ate nothing during the forty days and when they had ended He was hungry. (3) Then Satan the tempter came to Jesus and said, "If You are the Son of God command that these stones become bread."

(4) Jesus answered him, "It is written, 'Man shall not live on bread alone, but on every word that proceeds out of the mouth of God.'"

(5) Then the devil took Jesus into Jerusalem the holy city and had Him stand on the pinnacle of the temple (6) and said to Him, "If You are the Son of God throw Yourself down for it is written, 'He will give His angels charge concerning You to guard You,' (7) and, 'On their hands they will bear You up lest You strike Your foot against a stone.'"

(8) Jesus answered him, "Again it is written, 'You shall not put the Lord your God to the test.'"

(9) Then the devil took Jesus to a very high mountain and showed Him all the kingdoms of the world and their glory in a moment of time. (10) The devil said, "I will give You all this domain and its glory for it has been handed over to me and I give it to whomever I wish. (11) Therefore if You will bow down and worship me it shall all be Yours."

(12) Then Jesus said to him, "Begone, Satan! For it is written, 'You shall worship the Lord your God and serve Him only.'"

(13) When the devil had finished every temptation he departed until an opportune time and then the angels came and ministered to Jesus.

Notes: It should be obvious that the reason Jesus was led by the Holy Spirit into the wilderness (regarding "wilderness," see notes on section 18) and there fasted for forty days and forty nights was so that His body would be weakened by the lack of nourishment, and because of His weakness, He would be less able to resist the temptations Satan was about to offer. When the body is weakened by the lack of food and drink, the other faculties of a person, mental and spiritual, are weakened as well. Physically, mentally, and spiritually, Jesus was, after the forty days, at the lowest point of resistance in His life, both past and future, except, of course, when he was being tried and crucified.

Jesus, being full of the Holy Spirit, was led by the Spirit, or under the influence of the Spirit, into the wilderness for the express purpose of being tempted by the devil. The reason Jesus was to be tempted was to show that, even in His weakened physical condition, He would be able to resist the temptations. Those temptations were the most compelling ones that Satan could devise, and if Jesus was able to resist even those, it would show His followers that with the help of the Holy Spirit they could do so too.

When Satan said, "If You are the Son of God... " he wasn't indicating that he was having any doubts that he was talking to the Son of God. He was saying what he did say to make the temptation even stronger by seeming to doubt the truth. It is very difficult for some people to resist when someone says to them, "If such and so... " That's like a dare to them and makes them want to prove themselves. Satan, of course, knew that and tried to use it to his advantage when he was tempting Jesus.

The first quotation from the scriptures which Jesus cited is from Deuteronomy 8:3, and it reads, "And He humbled you and let you be hungry, and fed you with manna which you did not know, nor did your fathers know, that He might make you understand that man does not live by bread alone, but man lives by everything that proceeds out of the mouth of the Lord."

The second quotation is similar to Deuteronomy 6:13, "You shall fear [or reverence] only the Lord your God, and you shall worship [or serve] Him, and swear by His name."

And the third is from Deuteronomy 6:16, "You shall not put the Lord your God to the test, as you tested Him at Massah."

It might be well to observe here that temptations, real temptations, must meet certain conditions. The tempter, in this case Satan, must be able (or at least believed to be able) to deliver what he holds out to the person being tempted. The person being tempted must believe that the tempter will, if his conditions are met, deliver it. If the person being tempted does not believe that the tempter can deliver and will deliver, there is no temptation. Furthermore, the person being tempted must be able to succumb to the temptation. If he is unable to succumb for whatever reason, there is no temptation.

Regarding the temptations of Jesus, Satan had the power to deliver what he said he would deliver and Jesus, being one with God, knew that Satan was able to deliver, else there would have been no temptation. It was as a man whose body had been weakened by forty days of fasting who was being tempted. Jesus was confronted with very real temptations which He, in the form of man, could have accepted because if God (or the Holy Spirit) had been helping Jesus to resist the temptations they would not have been true temptations.

Remember, too, what Jesus said in John 8:44, "You are of your father the devil, and you want to do the desires of your father. He was a murderer from the beginning, and does not stand in the truth, because there is no truth in him. Whenever he speaks a lie, he speaks from his own nature; for he is a liar, and the father of lies."

22 The Testimony of John the Baptist (John 1:19-34)

(1) This is the witness of John to whom the Jews sent priests and Levites from Jerusalem to ask him, "Who are you?"

(2) John, whom many of the people thought to be the Christ, denied it and confessed, "I am not the Christ."

(3) They asked him, "What then? Are you Elijah?" John said, "I am not."

"Are you the Prophet?" John answered, "No."

(4) Then they said to him, "Tell us who you are so that we may give an answer to those who sent us. What do you say about yourself?"

(5) John said, "I am 'a voice of one crying in the wilderness, "Make straight the way of the Lord,"' as Isaiah the prophet said."

(6) Now they had been sent by the Pharisees, (7) and they asked him, "If you are not the Christ nor Elijah nor the Prophet then why are you baptizing?"

(8) John answered, "I baptize in water but among you stands One whom you do not know. (9) It is He who comes after me, the thong of whose sandal I am not worthy to untie."

(10) These things took place in Bethany beyond the Jordan where John was baptizing.

(11) The next day John saw Jesus coming to him and said,

"Behold the Lamb of God who takes away the sin of the world!

(12) This is He of whom I said, 'After me comes a Man who has a higher rank than I for He existed before me.' (13) I did not recognize Him, but in order that he might be manifested to Israel I came baptizing in water."

(14) John bore witness saying, "I have beheld the Spirit descending as a dove out of heaven and He remained upon Him. (15) I did not recognize Him but He who sent me to baptize in water said to me, 'He

upon whom you see the Spirit descending and remaining upon Him, this is the one who baptizes in the Holy Spirit.' (16) I have seen and have borne witness that this is the Son of God."

Notes: John had become well known and his fame had spread among the people of Judea and Galilee. People from all over those areas were coming to him to be baptized for repentance. His message was one that touched the people and caused them to think about their sins and their salvation in a way that was foreign to their religious leaders. The preaching of John could probably be compared favorably to that of the gospel preachers who held those great revival meetings of a hundred or more years ago.

The people to whom John was preaching seemed reluctant to accept him as only the simple man that his clothing indicated him to be. They wondered if perhaps John was one of the great prophets who had been resurrected to bring them the message he was preaching. John's fame and the speculations of the people reached the ears of the religious leaders and they sent some of their number to John to find out more about him.

The Jewish ruling body, called simply "the council" in some versions of the Bible and the "Sanhedrin" in others, is not mentioned in the Old Testament. The origin of this assembly is unknown. Some scholars trace it back to the seventy elders who were appointed to aid Moses in his work. Numbers 11:16- 17 says, "The Lord said to Moses: 'Bring Me seventy of Israel's elders who are known to you as leaders and officials among the people. Have them come to the Tent of Meeting, that they may stand there with you. I will come down and speak with you there, and I will take of the Spirit that is on you and put the Spirit on them. They will help you carry the burden of the people so that you will not have to carry it alone.'" Others believe that that assembly did not exist after the Israelites reached Palestine.

From what little information there is in the New Testament, the Sanhedrin seems to have been made up of the chief priests, or the heads of the twenty-four courses into which the priests were divided; elders who were men of age and experience; scribes and lawyers, that is, people who supposedly had intimate knowledge of the Law of Moses. The number of members is thought to have been seventy-one.

Albert Barnes wrote that the fact that John denied being the Christ is proof that he was not an imposter. There were expectations of the imminent coming of the Messiah and John, with the reputation he had already established among the people, could easily have taken advantage of those expectations and proclaimed himself to have been the Christ. The people were ready and willing to accept him as such and to follow him.

John also said he was not Elijah or "That Prophet." The identity of "That Prophet" is unknown. The Jews might have thought that not only Elijah would return before the appearance on earth of the Messiah but that Jeremiah would return also. Some people speculate that Jeremiah was "That Prophet." Others think it might have been the person to whom Moses referred in Deuteronomy 18:15 when he said, "The Lord your God will raise up to you a prophet like me from among your brothers. To him you shall listen." God confirmed in verse 18 of the same scripture that such a prophet would be sent.

In those days when Jesus was on earth, there were three major religious sects and several minor ones. The major sects were Pharisees, Sadducees, and Essenes. The people who were questioning John were of the sect of the Pharisees. The Pharisees were the most numerous, the wealthiest, and the strictest in their religious observances. The beliefs of the Pharisees were in many respects the same as Christians with two main exceptions-they believed that God owed them special favor and consideration and that they were justified before God by keeping the Law of Moses as interpreted by themselves. They were self-righteous and proud, believing themselves to be superior to the common people whom they held in low esteem.

John called Jesus "the Lamb of God." In prophesying about the Messiah, Isaiah wrote in 53:7, "He was oppressed and He was afflicted, yet He did not open His mouth, like a lamb that is led to slaughter, and like a sheep that is silent before its shearers, so He did not open His mouth." In the book of Revelation, "Lamb" is used numerous times as a metaphor for Jesus.

John also told the people that it was Jesus, the Lamb of God, who would take away the sins of the world. Peter wrote in 1:24 of his First Epistle, "... He Himself bore our sins in His body on the cross, that we might die to sin and live in righteousness; for by His wounds you were healed." Revelation 1:5 says,"... Jesus Christ, the faithful witness, the first-born of the dead, and the ruler of the kings of the earth. To Him who loves us, and released us from our sins by His blood." In saying that Jesus would take away the sins of the world he was, in effect, telling those Pharisees that the Jews who had once been the preferred people of God would not be the only ones to whom the kingdom of God would be available. No, the whole world would have the same opportunity as the Jews to become children of God.

According to what John said, he was not personally acquainted with Jesus in spite of the fact that they were related. John lived in the hill country of Judea, and Jesus grew up in Nazareth. The Holy Spirit, which had sent John on his errand to baptize the penitent, revealed to John the identity of Jesus, and how he would be able to recognize Jesus.

23 Jesus Makes His First Disciples (John 1:35-51)

(1) The next day John was standing with two of his disciples

(2) and he looked at Jesus as He walked nearby and said, "Behold the Lamb of God!"

(3) The two disciples heard him speak and they followed Jesus. (4) Jesus turned and saw them following Him and said to them, "What do you seek?"

They said to Him, "Rabbi (which translated means "teacher"), where are You staying?"

(5) Jesus said to them, "Come and you will see."

They came, therefore, and saw where Jesus was staying and they stayed with Him that day for it was then about the tenth hour.

(6) One of the two who heard John speak and followed Jesus was Andrew, Simon Peter's brother. (7) He first found his own brother Simon and said to him, "We have found the Messiah (which translated means 'Christ')." (8) Andrew then took Simon to Jesus.

Jesus looked at Simon and said, "You are Simon the Son of John. You shall be called Cephas (which is translated 'Peter')."

(9) The next day Jesus determined to go forth into Galilee and He found Philip. Jesus said to Philip, "Follow Me."

(10) Philip was from Bethsaida, the city of Andrew and Peter. (11) Philip found Nathanael and said to him, "We have found Him of whom Moses in the Law and also the Prophets wrote, Jesus of Nazareth, the son of Joseph."

(12) Nathanael asked Philip, "Can any good thing come out of Nazareth?"

Philip said to him, "Come and see."

(13) Jesus saw Nathanael coming to Him and said to him, "Behold an Israelite indeed in whom is no guile!"

(14) Nathanael said to Jesus, "How do You know me?"

Jesus answered, "Before Philip called you, when you were under the fig tree, I saw you."

(15) Nathanael answered Him, "Rabbi, You are the Son of God. You are the King of Israel."

(16) Jesus asked Nathanael, "Do you believe because I said to you that I saw you under the fig tree? You shall see greater things than these."

(17) Jesus continued, "Truly, truly, I say to you, you shall see the heavens opened and the angels of God ascending and descending on the Son of Man."

Notes: The day after John testified that Jesus was the Son of God, upon hearing John say that Jesus was the Lamb of God, two of John's disciples left John and followed Jesus. They set an example for all people who would be Christians. Christians do not follow after men nor do they obey the commandments of men, but instead follow only Jesus and obey His commandments.

Apparently, those two disciples of John were very religious men, intent on searching out the person best suited to lead them in their religion. When John told them that Jesus was the Lamb of God, they knew or believed that Jesus was who John said He was. There was no further need for them to follow John after he had pointed out the Messiah. Now they would follow the Messiah.

One of those two disciples was Andrew. The name of the other one was not given, but scholars believe it to have been John, the son of Zebedee. John, the apostle, in writing his account of the Gospel, never referred to himself by name-he most often referred to himself as "the disciple whom Jesus loved." The fact that no further information is given about the second disciple seems to confirm that the second disciple might have been John.

The purpose or mission of John the Baptist was to point out that Jesus was the fulfillment of the Old Testament prophecies. In stating his purpose in preaching and baptizing, John had quoted from Isaiah 40:3, "The voice of one crying in the wilderness, 'Prepare the way of the Lord, make straight in the desert a highway for our God.'" The fact that he denied being the Messiah is proof that John was sincere. He was in a perfect position to claim he was the Messiah or that he was Elijah or Moses or one of the other prophets reincarnated. Whatever he claimed for himself would have been believed. And what he claimed about Jesus was believed by some of his listeners including two of his own disciples. That should be the only purpose of all preachers-to point the way to Jesus and to refuse to make disciples for themselves.

It's interesting to note that in several verses there are given translations of certain words-rabbi, Messiah, Cephas. This is an indication that John's Gospel was not written exclusively for the Jews, because those words would not need to have been translated for Jews, but they would have needed to be translated for anyone who was not familiar with the language of the Jews.

Albert Barnes noted in his commentary that the two men asked Jesus where He was staying probably because they wanted to be with Jesus and to be instructed by Him. It would have been simpler to go with Jesus to the place where He was staying to talk with Him there than to try to talk with Him where they were. That would have limited their time with Jesus, and they wanted to be with Him longer than would have been possible, standing there by the wayside. From this time until Jesus was crucified, there were few times when the disciples of Jesus were not with Him or near Him.

Further along in the scriptures, there is evidence that some women who believed in Jesus also followed Him and ministered to Him. When the women began to do that is unclear as the scriptures do not give us that information.

At that time, it appears that the city of Nazareth and the Nazarenes did not enjoy a good reputation. To be called a Nazarene or even a Galilean was an expression of contempt for people in that country. Nathanael was expressing the popular view of Nazareth and the Nazarenes.

To be without guile was to be honest. Jesus saw Nathanael as an honest man, a person who did not say one thing to your face and something else behind your back. Jesus not only knew what Nathanael had done, but what he thought and his secret thoughts were without guile.

24 The First Miracle of Jesus at the Wedding in Cana

(John 2:1-12)

(1) On the third day there was a wedding in Cana of Galilee and the mother of Jesus was there. (2) Jesus and His disciples were also invited to the wedding.

(3) When the wine was gone the mother of Jesus said to Him, "They have no wine."

(4) Jesus said to His mother, "Woman, what have I to do with that? My hour has not yet come."

(5) Mary said to the servants, "Whatever He says to you, do it."

(6) Now there were six stone waterpots set there for the Jewish custom of purification containing twenty or thirty gallons of water each.

(7) Jesus said to the servants, "Fill the waterpots with water." The servants filled the waterpots up to the brim.

(8) Then Jesus said to them, "Draw some out now and take it to the headwaiter." They did so.

(9) When the headwaiter tasted the water which had now become wine he did not know where it came from (but the servants who had drawn the water knew). The headwaiter then called the bridegroom (10)

and said to him, "Every man serves the good wine first, and when men have drunk freely, then he serves the wine that is poorer. You have kept the good wine until now."

(11) Jesus did this beginning of His signs in Cana of Galilee. He manifested His glory and His disciples believed in Him.

(12) After this Jesus, His mother, His brothers and His disciples went down to Capemaum and stayed there a few days.

Notes: This was the first in chronological order of the recorded miracles of Jesus. Jesus may have performed other miracles prior to this one, but this is the first of them to have been performed publicly and to have been recorded. A confirmation that this was true was the actions of Mary. She was positive that Jesus could remedy the situation and reduce the embarrassment of there being a shortage of wine for the celebrants at the wedding, and it was for that reason that she told the servants to do whatever Jesus told them to do.

Can't you picture Mary at that time? Like most mothers, she had complete faith in what her Son could and would do. And like most mothers, she quietly and firmly insisted that Jesus do what He had been in the habit of doing for the past thirty years-obeying her. Even though Jesus protested that His hour had not yet come, she just smiled her mother's proud smile and told the servants to do as Jesus asked.

What Mary did and the fact that the servants obeyed her instructions when she told them to do whatever Jesus told them to do was an indication that Mary was known to them, perhaps as a close friend or relative of the host or hostess or of the bride or groom.

Cana was a small town about five miles northeast of Nazareth on the road toward the Sea of Galilee and about twelve miles from the seashore. According to John 21:2, Cana of Galilee was the home of Nathanael. According to Albert Barnes, it was called Cana of Galilee in order to differentiate it from another Cana in the land of the tribe of Ephraim; however, there is no mention either in the Old Testament or the New Testament of another town named Cana. There was a river named Kanah on the border of Ephraim but no town. In Joshua 19:28, there is a town named Kanah in the territory of Asher. Whether or not that is the Cana to which Barnes referred is not known.

At that time, the only disciples Jesus is known to have had were Peter, Andrew, Philip, Nathanael, and the unnamed disciple, who is thought to have been John. And if John was there, then James, his brother, might have been there too. After the wedding, Jesus went to Capernaum with his disciples, His brothers, and His mother. Capernaum was about twenty miles from Cana on the northern coast of the Sea of Galilee.

The information in verse 12 above raises a question to which there is no answer in the scriptures: What of Joseph and the sisters of Jesus? When Jesus returned to his own country and preached, the people there raised the questions recorded in Matthew 13:55-56: "Is not this the carpenter's son? Is not His mother called Mary, and His brethren, James, and Joses, and Simon, and Judas? And His sisters, are they not all with us?" This passage, together with Mark 6:3, leaves no doubt that Jesus had sisters. But what about Joseph? The wording in the passage in Matthew seems to indicate that Joseph was still alive and was known to the speaker, but the wording in Mark 6:3 is a little different. It says there, "Is not this the carpenter, the son of Mary, the brother of James, and Joses, and Judas, and Simon, and are not His sisters here with us?" This says that Jesus was the carpenter, perhaps indicating that Joseph was dead or, at best, no longer a carpenter. Regardless, there is no definite answer in the scriptures.

25 Jesus Cleanses the Temple at the First Passover of his Ministry (John 2:13-25)

(1) The Passover of the Jews was at hand and Jesus went up to Jerusalem. (2) He found in the temple those who were selling oxen and sheep and doves, and the moneychangers were also there. (3) He made a scourge of cords and drove them all out of the temple with their sheep and oxen, and He poured out the coins of the moneychangers and overturned their tables. (4) To those who were selling the doves He said, "Take these things away. Stop making My Father's house a house of merchandise."

(5) The disciples of Jesus remembered that it was written, "Zeal for Thy house will consume me."

(6) The Jews therefore came around and asked Jesus, "What sign of authority do You have to show us for these things that You do?"

(7) Jesus said to them, "Destroy this temple and in three days I will raise it up."

(8) The Jews said, "It took forty-six years to build this temple and You say You will raise it up in three days?"

(9) But Jesus was speaking of the temple of His body. (10) When He was raised from the dead His disciples remembered that He had said this and they believed the Scriptures and the word which Jesus had spoken.

(11) Now when Jesus was in Jerusalem at the Passover during the feast many believed in His name because they were seeing the signs which He was doing. (12) But Jesus did not put His trust in men for He knew all men (13) and He did not need anyone to bear witness concerning man for He Himself knew what was in man.

Notes: There's a saying, "There is nothing new under the sun." We know from our own experience that tradesmen will go anywhere they are allowed to go if they believe they can sell their wares there. Back in the days of Jesus, this was true, even of the temple, the house of God. This could not have been done without the cooperation or connivance of the high priest.

It will be noted that Jesus did not hurt nor destroy anything. He drove out the sheep and oxen and overturned the tables of the moneychangers, but He did not turn loose the doves. He told the sellers of the doves to "take these things away."

The quotation about which it was written that the disciples remembered later, "Zeal for Thy house will consume me," is from Psalms 69:9.

It was the custom of the parents of Jesus to go to Jerusalem every year for the feast of the Passover. Luke 2:41 reports, "Now His parents went to Jerusalem every year at the feast of the Passover." Jesus, as a mature male Jew, was required to continue to do that.

26 Jesus and Nicodemus Discuss the New Birth

(John 3:1-21)

(1) Now there was a man of the Pharisees named Nicodemus who was a ruler of the Jews. (2) He came to Jesus by night and said to Him, "Rabbi, we know that You have come from God as a teacher for no one can do these signs that You do unless God is with him."

(3) Jesus said to him, "Truly, truly, I say to you, unless one is born again he cannot see the kingdom of God."

(4) Nicodemus said, "How can a man be born when he is old? Can he enter a second time into his mother's womb and be born?"

(5) Jesus answered, "Truly, truly, I say to you, unless one is born of water and the Spirit he cannot enter into the kingdom of God. (6) That which is born of the flesh is flesh and that which is born of the Spirit is spirit. (7) Do not marvel that I said to you, 'You must be born again.' (8) The wind blows where it wishes and you hear the sound of it but do not know where it comes from and where it is going. This is so of everyone who is born of the Spirit."

(9) Nicodemus asked Jesus, "How can these things be?"

(10) Jesus said, "Are you the teacher of Israel and do not understand these things? (11) Truly, truly, I say to you, we speak that which we know and bear witness of that which we have seen but you do not receive our witness. (12) If I told you earthly things and you do not believe how shall you believe if I tell you heavenly things? (13) No one has ascended into heaven except He who descended from heaven, the Son of Man. (14) As Moses lifted up the serpent in the wilderness even so must the Son of Man be lifted up (15) so that whoever believes in Him may have eternal life.

(16) "For God so loved the world that He gave His only begotten Son so that whoever believes in Him should not perish but have eternal life. (17) For God did not send the Son into the world to judge the world but so that the world should be saved through Him. (18) He who believes in Him is not judged. He who does not believe has been judged already because he has not believed in the name of the only begotten Son of God. (19) This is the judgment that the light is come into the world and men loved the darkness rather than the light because their

deeds were evil. (20) Everyone who does evil hates the light and does not come to the light lest his deeds should be exposed. (21) But he who practices the truth comes to the light that his deeds may be manifested as having been wrought in God."

Notes: This is our introduction to the man named Nicodemus.

He is written about in two other places in the scriptures, John 7:50 and John 19:39, being identified both times as the man who went to Jesus by night.

It's amazing to what lengths some people will go to willfully misunderstand the Bible, that is, to assign to certain passages meanings that will tend to enhance or prove their own particular pet beliefs. The statement of Jesus that we must be born again illustrates that point.

There are people who believe that there are two kinds of Christians, those who are born again and those who are not born again. They call the ones who have been born again "fundamentalists." We often hear of people who are called "born-again Christians" as though they are of a different religion or denomination than other Christians. Jesus made it very plain that there is only one kind of Christian-a born again Christian. If a person is born again, he is a Christian, and if he has not been born again, he is not a Christian. To say "born again" and "Christian" together is redundant as, biblically, those two terms mean the same thing.

There's another area in which people become purposely obtuse and that is in regard to baptism. Jesus said, "... Unless one be born of water and of the Spirit, he cannot enter into the kingdom of God." There are those people who will argue that the water of which Jesus spoke is not the water of baptism, but the water involved in a physical birth. If a person believes you become a Christian by your own choice through obedience, it should be obvious to them that if such a belief is true, that is, that Jesus was speaking of the water involved in a physical birth, that God would be condemning some people to hell at the time they are born, that the choice was His and not theirs, and that His choices are arbitrary, a belief that is completely foreign to the teachings of the New Testament. It is not the way of God to conceal the way to the kingdom of heaven or to hide that way in obscure or confusing language. And nothing is kept back for fear of offending anyone, regardless of their wealth, social position, rank, or for any other reason.

Nicodemus, being not only a Jew but a ruler of the Jews, would have been familiar with the Jewish rite of baptizing Gentile converts into Judaism. Apparently, the idea of that rite being applied to Jews was an absurdity to Nicodemus as Jews were believed to be physically born into the kingdom of God and did not ever have to be baptized into it. We don't know, of course, the reason for Nicodemus' question about entering again into a mother's womb, whether he was honestly puzzled by Jesus's reference to being born again or if he was only being facetious because of the perceived absurdity of the statement.

27 Jesus and John Both Baptizing and John's Second (Last) Testimony (John 3:22-36)

(1) After these things Jesus and His disciples came into the land of Judea and there Jesus was spending time with the disciples and baptizing. (2) John also was baptizing in Aenon near Salim because there was much water there and people were coming and were being baptized. (3) John had not yet been thrown in prison.

(4) Then there arose a discussion on the part of John's disciples with a Jew about purification. (5) They came to John and said to him, "Rabbi, He who was with you beyond the Jordan, the One to whom you have borne witness, is baptizing and all are coming to Him."

(6) John said, "A man can receive nothing unless it has been given to him from heaven. (7) You yourselves bear me witness that I said, 'I am not the Christ,' but, 'I have been sent before Him.' (8) He who has the bride is the bridegroom; but the friend of the bridegroom who stands and hears him rejoices greatly because of the bridegroom's voice. And so this joy of mine has been made full. (9) He must increase but I must decrease.

(10) "He who comes from above is above all but he who is of the earth is from the earth and speaks of the earth. He who came from heaven is above all. (11) He bears witness of what He has seen and heard but no man receives His witness. (12) He who has received His witness has set his seal to this, that God is true. (13) For He whom God has sent

speaks the words of God because He gives the Spirit without measure. (14) The Father loves the Son and has given all things into His hand.

(15) He who believes in the Son has eternal life but he who does not obey the Son shall not see life but the wrath of God abides on him."

Notes: There must have been some lapse of time between the time Jesus had the discussion with Nicodemus, and this is the next recorded incident. Jesus had gone to Jerusalem, which was in Judea, to observe the Passover, and Nicodemus went to Him while He was in Jerusalem. In verse 1 above, it says that Jesus "came into the land of Judea" which indicates, but does not prove, that Jesus had left Judea and had now returned. Perhaps, as He often did, Jesus had gone off somewhere to meditate and pray and to be with His disciples. But as it had quickly become a normal thing, wherever Jesus was, there the people came to Him, and He taught them and baptized them. According to John 4:2, Jesus Himself did not baptize, His disciples were actually performing that physical act for Him.

At that same time, John was baptizing people at a place called Aenon which was near another place called Salim because there was much water there. This is the only passage in the Bible in which either of those places was mentioned. According to the maps, Salim was in Samaria approximately twenty-one miles due south of the southern tip of the Sea of Galilee and about two miles west of the River Jordan. Aenon is said to have been the name of springs or waters which were in abundance in that place.

This is to be the last time we are told that John was doing any baptizing. This is also the last time John testified of Jesus.

The disciples of John had a disagreement with a certain Jew or some Jews. Some versions of the Bible say there was one Jew, and other versions state that there was more than one. The discussion or dispute was about purification. What the exact cause of the dispute was, was not recorded. We can speculate, however, that since the baptism of John was for repentance that the disagreement centered on the relative merits of baptism by John and baptism by Jesus. Possibly the disciples of John, being loyal to him, thought his baptism to be of greater efficacy for purification than that of Jesus.

28 John the Baptist Imprisoned

(Matt. 14:3-5; Mark 6:17-20; Luke 3:19-20)

(1) Herod the Tetrarch himself had sent and had John arrested and bound because John had reproved him for marrying Herodias, his brother Philip's wife, and about all the other wicked things Herod had done. (2) John had been saying, "It is not lawful for you to have your brother's wife."

(3) Herodias had a grudge against John and wanted to put him to death and could not do so (4) because Herod was afraid of the multitude who regarded John as a prophet. And too, Herod was afraid of John, knowing that he was a righteous and holy man, and kept him safe. When Herod heard John he was very perplexed, but he used to enjoy listening to him.

Notes: The relationship in the *menage a trois* against which John preached, the preaching of which eventually resulted in his death, was, to say the least, an unholy mess. Herod the Great had six sons by either four or five different wives: Philip II, Archelaus, Aristobulus, Antipas, Philip I, and Antipater. Herodias was the daughter of Aristobulus. She married her uncle, Herod Philip I. Later she left that uncle and married her half uncle, Herod Antipas. Antipas was tetrarch of Samaria and Idumea. John had been preaching that Antipas had no right to marry Herodias because she was still married to her first husband, Philip I, who was the half brother of Antipas.

29 Jesus Leaves Judea to Return to Galilee

(Matt. 4:12; John 4:1-3)

(1) Now when Jesus heard that John had been taken into custody and also that the Pharisees had heard that Jesus was making and baptizing more disciples than John (2) (although Jesus Himself was not baptizing but His disciples were) (3) He left Judea intending to return to Galilee.

30 Jesus at Sychar in Samaria (the Woman at the Well)

(John 4:4-42)

(1) To get from Judea to Galilee Jesus had to pass through Samaria. (2) He came to a city of Samaria called Sychar which was near the parcel of ground that Jacob gave to his son Joseph, (3) and Jacob's well was there, too. Jesus, being wearied from His journey, was sitting by the well. It was about the sixth hour (4) and there came a woman of Samaria to draw water.

Jesus said to her, "Give Me a drink." (5) His disciples had gone away into the city to buy food.

(6) The Samaritan woman said to Jesus, "How is it that You, being a Jew, ask me for a drink since I am a Samaritan woman?" (For Jews have no dealings with Samaritans.)

(7) Jesus said to the woman, "If you knew the gift of God and who it is who says to you, 'Give Me a drink,' you would have asked Him and He would have given you living water."

(8) The woman said to Jesus, "Sir, You have nothing to draw with and the well is deep. From where do You get that living water? (9) Are You greater than our father Jacob who gave us the well and drank of it himself together with his sons and his cattle?"

(10) Jesus said to her, "Everyone who drinks of this water shall thirst again (11) but whoever drinks of the water that I shall give him shall never thirst. The water that I shall give him shall become in him a well of water springing up to eternal life."

(12) The woman said to Jesus, "Sir, give me this water so I will not be thirsty nor come all the way here to draw."

(13) Jesus said, "Go, call your husband and come here."

(14) The woman answered, "I have no husband."

Jesus said to her, "You have well said, 'I have no husband';

(15) The woman said, "Sir, I perceive that You are a prophet. (17) Our fathers worshiped in this mountain and you people say that in Jerusalem is the place where men ought to worship."

(18) Jesus said to her, "Woman, believe Me, an hour is coming when neither in this mountain nor in Jerusalem shall you worship the Father. (19) You worship that which you do not know. We worship that which

we know for salvation is from the Jews. (20) But an hour is coming, and now is, when the true worshipers shall worship the Father in spirit and truth. Of such people the Father seeks to be His worshipers. (21) God is spirit and those who worship Him must worship in spirit and truth."

(16) for you have had five husbands and the one whom you now have is not your husband. This you have said truly."

(22) The woman said to Jesus, "I know that Messiah is coming (He who is called Christ). When that One comes He will declare all things to us."

(23) Jesus said to her, "I who speak to you am He."

(24) At this point the disciples of Jesus came and they marveled that He had been speaking with a woman yet no one said, "What do you seek?" or, "Why do You speak to her?"

(25) So the woman left her waterpot and went into the city and said to the men, (26) "Come and see a man who told me all the things that I have done. Can this be the Christ?" (27) Then they all went out of the city and were coming to Jesus.

(28) In the meanwhile the disciples were requesting Jesus to eat, saying, "Rabbi, eat."

(29) But Jesus said to them, "I have food to eat that you do not know about."

(30) The disciples then were asking each other, "Has anyone brought Him anything to eat?"

(31) Jesus said to them, "My food is to do the will of Him who sent me and to accomplish His work. (32) Do you not say, 'There are yet four months and then comes the harvest'? Look, I tell you, lift up your eyes and look on the fields and see that they are white for harvest. (33) Already he who reaps is receiving wages and is gathering fruit for life eternal so that he who sows and he who reaps may rejoice together. (34) For in this case the saying is true, 'One sows and another reaps.' (35) I sent you to reap that for which you have not labored. Others have labored and you have entered into their labor."

(36) From that city many of the Samaritans believed in Jesus because of the word of the woman who testified, "He told me all the things that I have done."

(37) So when the Samaritans came to Jesus they were asking Him to stay with them, so He stayed there two days.

(38) Many more believed because of the word of Jesus. (39) They were also saying to the woman, "It is no longer because of what you said that we believe for we have heard for ourselves and know that this One is indeed the Savior of the world."

Notes: From Judea to Galilee, the shortest route was through the province of Samaria, and that's the route Jesus took. There was a road which ran almost due north from Jerusalem through Sychar and on down to the southern tip of the Sea of Galilee. Sychar was about thirty miles from Jerusalem and about forty miles from the Sea of Galilee. Jews usually refused to pass through Samaria, choosing instead to cross the Jordan River and travel to the east of it until they reached Galilee.

The scripture says that to get from Judea to Galilee Jesus had to pass through Samaria, but no reason is given as to why He had to go that way. We can speculate that it was for the very purpose of causing to happen what did happen, that is, the encounter with the Samaritan woman and the Samaritans.

The town of Sychar was near Mount Gerizim, which was the holy mountain of the Samaritans, about five miles southeast of the City of Samaria and about fifteen miles west of the Jordan River.

The purchase of a parcel of land by Jacob is recorded in Genesis 33:19. Scholars speculate that it was this parcel or another one nearby that Jacob gave to Joseph as recorded in Genesis 48:21-22. Whether or not the parcel Jacob is said to have bought in Genesis 33 was the same parcel of land he gave to Joseph as recorded in Genesis 48 we don't know, but in Joshua 24:32 it states that it was in the parcel Jacob bought in Genesis 33 that the bones of Joseph were buried.

There is no record in the Old Testament of this well which the Samartian woman said was Jacob's well. It may have been just a myth or a tradition which had been handed down through the generations or it could as easily have been a well which Jacob did dig, the event not having been recorded in the scriptures. There is still a well, which is dry now, in that vicinity which the people point out as being Jacob's well.

This seems to have been the only place about which it was recorded that the people asked Jesus to stay longer. Many Jews followed Jesus around from place to place and stayed to listen to Him when he chose to speak to them, but this is the only place where He is asked to stay longer. It is to the credit of the Samaritans that they were willing, even anxious, to find out more about the kingdom of God. One must wonder if later on the Samaritans lost their faith as did so many of the Jews who were followers of Jesus at one time. However, it must be remembered that when Philip preached in Samaria, the Samaritans were receptive of his message, perhaps remembering Jesus and what He had said to them when He was there in this present occasion.

Only here and in 1 John 4:14 is the expression "the Savior of the World" found. Jesus told the woman that He was the Messiah. Whether or not she repeated that statement to the other Samaritans and whether or not Jesus Himself repeated it later, the Samaritans believed that He was the Messiah and that the Messiah was the Savior of the world.

31 Jesus Arrives in Galilee and Begins to Preach

(Matt. 4:17; Mark 1:14-15; Luke 4:14-15; John 4:43, 45)

(1) And after the two days Jesus went forth from Sychar and returned to Galilee in the power of the Spirit, (2) and John had already been taken into custody.

(3) So when Jesus came to Galilee, the Galileans received Him, having seen all the things He did in Jerusalem at the feast; for they themselves also went to the feast. (4) And from that time Jesus began preaching and teaching in their synagogues, (5) and saying, "The time is fulfilled; repent and believe in the gospel for the kingdom of God and heaven is at hand." (6) And Jesus was praised by all and news about Him spread through all the surrounding district.

Notes: The "two days" in verse 1 above are the two extra days Jesus stayed in Sychar, Samaria.

The phrase in verse 1 above about Jesus being in the power of the Spirit means that Jesus was being led by the Holy Spirit, the Spirit always being with Him except during His crucifixion.

The Galileans received and accepted Jesus because of what they had seen Him do and had heard of Him doing when He was in Jerusalem rather that because of anything He had said. Many (if not all) of them had been to the Feast of the Passover as was probably their custom. In earlier scriptures, it was said that Joseph and Mary, together with many other people from Galilee, customarily traveled to Jerusalem for the Feast of the Passover.

32 Jesus Heals the Son of a Nobleman at Cana

(John 4:46-54)

(1) Jesus went again to Cana of Galilee where He had made the water into wine. And there, too, was a certain royal official whose son was sick at Capernaum. (2) When the nobleman heard that Jesus had come out of Judea into Galilee he went to Jesus and asked Jesus to come down and heal his son who was at the point of death.

(3) Jesus said to the official, "Unless you people see signs and wonders you will not believe."

(4) The royal official answered, "Sir, come down before my child dies."

(5) Jesus said to him, "Go your way. Your son lives."

The man believed the word that Jesus spoke to him and he started off to return home. (6) As he was going down, his slaves met him and told him that his son was living. (7) He inquired of them the hour at which his son began to get better.

They said to him, "Yesterday at the seventh hour the fever left him."

(8) So the father knew that it was at that hour in which Jesus said to him, "Your son lives"; and he himself believed together with his whole household.

(9) This is again a second sign that Jesus performed when He had come out of Judea into Galilee.

Notes: There are often small signs, sometimes missed or overlooked, which attest to the truth of what is written in the scriptures. One of them is in this passage. It says that the nobleman asked Jesus to come down from Cana to Capernaum and heal his son. Capernaum was on the northern coast of the Sea of Galilee, and Cana was in more mountainous country to the west and a little bit south of Capernaum. The words, ". . . come down...," were accurate, then, because Jesus would have had to go from the high altitude at Cana to a lower altitude at Capernaum.

Although some time had passed since Jesus performed His first miracle, turning the water into wine, concerning this miracle, the healing of the nobleman's son, it is interesting to note that it was performed in the same place as the first one. This was not the second miracle of Jesus but it is the second of which we have knowledge of the details. The reason the Galileans received Jesus so gladly and the reason the nobleman knew to go to Jesus about the sickness of his son was because of the signs (or miracles) Jesus did while He was in Jerusalem during the Feast of the Passover and, possibly, the miracle of turning the water into wine may have become known throughout the area of Cana.

33 Jesus Is Rejected at Nazareth and Dwells at Capernaum

(Matt. 4:13-16; Luke 4:16-30; John 4:44)

(1) Jesus came to Nazareth where He had been brought up and, as was His custom, He entered the synagogue on the Sabbath and stood up to read. (2) The book of the prophet Isaiah was handed to Him. He opened the book and found the place where it was written, (3) "The Spirit of the Lord is upon Me because He anointed Me to preach the gospel to the poor. He has sent Me to proclaim release to the captives and recovery of sight to the blind, to set free those who are downtrodden, (4) to proclaim the favorable year of the Lord."

(5) Jesus closed the book, gave it back to the attendant and sat down. The eyes of all in the synagogue were fixed upon Him, (6) and He said to them, "Today this scripture has been fulfilled in your hearing."

(7) All the people were speaking well of Jesus and wondering at the gracious words which fell from His lips. They were saying, "Is this not the son of Joseph?"

(8) Jesus said to them, "No doubt you will quote this proverb to Me, 'Physician, heal yourself! Whatever we heard was done at Capernaum, do here in your home town as well.'

(9) "Truly I say to you, no prophet is welcome in his home town. (10) But I say to you in truth, there were many widows in Israel in the days of Elijah, when the sky was shut up for three years and six months, when a great famine came over all the land. (11) Yet Elijah was sent to none of them except to Zarephath in the land of Sidon to a woman who was a widow.

(12) There were many lepers in Israel in the time of Elisha the prophet, and none of them was cleansed except Naaman the Syrian."

(13) All those in the synagogue were filled with rage as they heard these things (14) and they rose up and cast Jesus out of the city. They led Him to the brow of the hill on which their city had been built in order to throw Him down the cliff. (15) But passing through their midst Jesus went His way. (16) Jesus Himself testified that a prophet has no honor in his own country.

(17) Leaving Nazareth, Jesus came and settled in Capernaum, which is by the sea in the region of Zebulon and Naphtali. (18) This was to fulfill what was spoken through Isaiah the prophet, saying, (19) "The land of Zebulon and the land of Naphtali, by the way of the sea beyond Jordan, Galilee of the Gentiles: (20) The people who were sitting in darkness saw a great light and to those who were sitting in the land and shadow of death upon them a light dawned."

Notes: The scripture Jesus read is from Isaiah 61:1. The story of Elijah and the widow of Zarephath is recorded in 1 Kings 17, and the story of Elisha and Naaman the leper is told in 2 Kings 5.

We don't know whether it was the custom of Jesus to enter into a synagogue wherever He happened to be on the Sabbath day and read from the scriptures or if it had been His custom to read the scriptures in the synagogue at Nazareth every Sabbath day as He was growing up and before He began His ministry. It would seem, though, that if He had often read the scriptures in the synagogue at Nazareth, He would have been well-known that there would have been no question of His identity.

The word "gracious" as used in this scripture to describe the words which Jesus spoke is not the same word which was used in the scriptures to mean the grace of God. This word is from the Greek word meaning graciousness of manner or gratifying. The dictionary defines it, in part, as marked by kindness, courtesy, tact, delicacy, charm, or good taste.

When the people asked, "Isn't this the son of Joseph?" it indicated two things. First, that Jesus was a person with whom they were personally familiar, at least, to some extent. He lived among them for about twenty-eight to thirty years and, because they did know who He was, they couldn't accept Him as someone special. That seems to be a common human failing, and it's probably the origin of the saying, "Familiarity breeds contempt!"

Second, judging from the way the question was worded, that Joseph the husband of Mary, was still alive, known to the people and possibly still living in Nazareth. At a later date, Jesus went back to Nazareth and the tone of the comments about Jesus at that time indicated that Joseph was still alive and worked at carpentry in Nazareth.

The Bible gives very little information about the character and activities of Joseph after the return of him and his family from Egypt. From what is written, he seems to have been a God-fearing man, considerate and concerned about the welfare and safety of Mary and Jesus. He was never defiant either toward God or the authorities. He did not live in Judea because of his fear of Archelaus. These things we can gather from earlier passages, but of his later life we know nothing. We can surmise (and that's all it is, a supposition) from the passages cited that he was still alive when Jesus was preaching, or at least when Jesus began preaching, but any actual knowledge of him after that time is nil.

The scriptures do not specifically state that it was a miracle which allowed Jesus to escape the angry mob by walking through the midst of them, but it seems to have been. A person isn't usually allowed to just walk away from an angry mob which is intent on throwing him over a cliff.

After leaving Nazareth, Jesus went to live in Capernaum which was in fulfillment of the prophecy in Isaiah 9:1-2. Capernaum was located on the northern coast of the Sea of Galilee in the land which had been allotted to the descendants (tribe) of Naphtali.

34 Jesus Calls the Four Fishermen

(Matt. 4:18-22; Mark 1:16-20)

(1) As Jesus was walking along by the Sea of Galilee He saw the two brothers, Simon who was called Peter and Andrew, casting a net into the sea, for they were fishermen.

(2) Jesus said to them, "Follow Me and I will make you become fishers of men." (3) They immediately left their nets and followed Him.

(4) Going on from there a little farther Jesus saw two other brothers, James and John, the sons of Zebedee. They were in the boat with Zebedee their father mending their nets. Jesus called them (5) and they left their father Zebedee in the boat with the hired servants and followed Him.

Notes: One might think this was a duplication of an earlier passage in which it was stated that Peter, Andrew, Philip, and Nathaniel (and possibly John) became disciples of Jesus. We know, too, from earlier passages, that there were some disciples of Jesus with Him at various times, but we don't know who they were, possibly only those four or five but also possibly other people whose names we are never to know. Too, Jesus had told only Philip to follow Him. Because some of the disciples of Jesus were invited to the wedding in Cana, a person might get the idea that some of the events in the life of Jesus as reported are out of order, but the "water to wine" miracle at Cana was said in the scriptures to have been the beginning of the signs of Jesus.

This is the first place in the scriptures where the apostle James is mentioned and, if the unknown disciple in that earlier passage was not John, the first time John is mentioned. Two more disciples have now been added in the persons of James and John. At this point, six of the twelve men who are to become apostles have been chosen.

Scholars believe that the fact that Zebedee had hired servants working for him means that his financial status was higher than that of most of the people in Israel. Not only did he have two sons working with him, he had a plurality of hired men working for him. Also the fact that there were at least five men in the boats mending nets indicates that the boat was rather large.

The area in and around the Sea of Galilee is often shown in the scriptures to have been one of the main areas of the work of Jesus. It was called by at least three other names: the Sea of Tiberias, the Sea of Chennereth, and the Lake of Gennesaret. Its surface was about six hundred feet lower than the level of the Mediterranean Sea. There were many cities along its banks, including Capemaum, Bethsaida, Magdala, Tiberias, and other cities only a very short distance away. That area is said to have been the most beautiful part of Palestine. Josephus called it a perfect paradise. Its water is still sweet and clear, and it's still full of fish. At its lowest point, it's about a hundred sixty-five feet deep. There are many storms there, probably due to the movement of the air currents in the nearby hills.

The time which many people use to speculate about unknowable things is usually time wasted, but sometimes we can learn from such speculation. For instance, the personality of Jesus must have been so magnetic that the sheer force of it persuaded men to follow Him. Why else would people be willing to give up the life they knew to follow a stranger to an unknown destiny? It couldn't have been His looks because Isaiah wrote in 53:2, "... He hath no form nor comeliness; and when we shall see Him, there is no beauty that we should desire Him." The NIV words it like this, "He had no beauty or majesty to attract us to Him, nothing in His appearance that we should desire Him."

35 The Miraculous Draught of Fishes (Luke 5:1-11)

(1) Now as Jesus was standing by the lake of Gennesaret the multitudes were pressing around Him and listening to the Word of God. (2) Jesus saw two boats lying at the edge of the lake but the fishermen had gotten out of them and were washing their nets. (3) Jesus got into the boat which was Simon's and asked Simon to put out a little

way from the land. Jesus sat down and began teaching the multitude from the boat.

(4) When Jesus had finished speaking He said to Simon, "Put out into the deep water and let down your nets for a catch."

(5) Simon answered, "Master, we worked hard all night and caught nothing, but at Your bidding I will let down the nets."

(6) When they had done this they enclosed a great quantity of fish and their nets began to break. (7) They signaled to their partners in the other boat for them to come and help. Those who were in the other boat came and they filled both of the boats with fish so that they began to sink.

(8) But when Simon Peter saw that, he fell down at the feet of Jesus and said, "Depart from me, for I am a sinful man, O Lord!" (9) Amazement had seized him and all his companions because of the catch of fish which they had taken, (10) as it did also to James and John, the sons of Zebedee, who were partners with Simon.

Jesus said to Simon, "Do not fear. From now on you will be catching men."

(11) When they had brought their boats to land they left everything and followed Jesus.

Notes: It is possible that this is the same incident as that which was recorded in the previous section but written in much greater detail. Neither Peter nor Andrew nor James wrote an account of the Gospel, and John did not record this miraculous draft of fishes. John did, however, record a similar incident in chapter 21 of his Gospel account, which happened after the resurrection of Jesus.

Gennesaret is mentioned by both Matthew and Mark, but Luke is the only one of the Gospel writers to call it a lake. There was a plain named Gennesaret bordering the lake to the northwest, and it was this land and not the lake to which Matthew and Mark were alluding. Scholars say that in the Old Testament writings, it was called the sea of Chinnereth. There was a city on the shores of the lake called Chinnereth as reported in Joshua 19:35, and the "sea of Chinnereth" is mentioned in Numbers 34:11. The lake was most often called the "Sea of Galilee" in the New Testament. John 6:1 says, "After these things, Jesus went over the sea of Galilee, which is the sea of Tiberias." There was a city on the shore of the lake named Tiberias to which John referred in verse 23 of that same chapter. That city had been built by Herod Antipas and named in honor of the Roman emperor. In the KJV, whether the reference is to Galilee, Gennesaret, Tiberias, or Chinnereth, the word "sea" preceding it is not capitalized leaving one to wonder if the reference was to "the sea (or lake) which is located at or near that place" or the "sea (or lake) named that."

Concerning the fishing boats, the Jewish historian Flavius Josephus wrote that there were about two hundred thirty of them on the lake and that each of them had a crew of four or five men.

When Peter told Jesus that he had been fishing all night, it makes one wonder what kind of fishing they did at night. In Thomson's book *The Land and the Book*, he writes, "Peter here speaks of toiling all night; and there are certain kinds of fishing always carried on at night. It is a beautiful sight. With blazing torch the boat glides over the flashing sea, and the men stand gazing keenly into it until their prey is sighted, when, quick as lightning, they fling their net or fly their spear; and often you see the tired fishermen come sullenly into the harbour in the morning having toiled all night in vain."

36 Jesus Teaches and Heals in Capernaum

(Matt. 8:14-17; Mark 1:21-34; Luke 4:31-41)

(1) Jesus and His disciples went into Capernaum, a city of Galilee, and on the Sabbath Jesus entered the synagogue and began to teach. (2) Those in the synagogue were amazed at His teaching for He was teaching them as one having authority and not as the scribes.

(3) There was a man in the synagogue who was possessed by the spirit of an unclean demon and he cried out with a loud voice, (4) "Ha! What do we have to do with You, Jesus of Nazareth? Have You come to destroy us? I know who You are-the Holy One of God!"

(5) Jesus rebuked the demon, "Be quiet and come out of him!"

(6) Throwing the man down in the midst of those in the synagogue, the demon cried out with a loud voice and came out of the man without doing him any harm.

(7) The people were all amazed so that they began discussing this happening among themselves. They were saying, "What is this? A new teaching with authority? For with authority and power He commands even the unclean spirits and they obey Him!"

(8) Immediately the news about Jesus went out into every locality in all the surrounding district of Galilee.

(9) After they had come out of the synagogue, Jesus went with Simon and Andrew into their home together with James and John. (10) Now Simon's mother-in-law was lying sick and suffering from a high fever and they spoke to Jesus and made request of Him on her behalf. (11) Jesus came and stood over her and taking her by the hand Jesus rebuked the fever and it left her and immediately she arose and began to serve them.

(12) When evening was come, even during and after the setting of the sun, the people brought to Jesus all who were ill and those who were demon-possessed. (13) The whole city had gathered at the door, (14) and Jesus laid His hands on every one of them and healed those who were ill with various diseases. (15) Demons were coming out of many also, crying out and saying, "You are the Son of God!" Rebuking the demons Jesus would not allow them to speak because they knew Him to be the Christ. (16) He did this in order that what was spoken through Isaiah the prophet might be fulfilled, "He Himself took our infirmities and carried away our diseases."

Notes: It was the custom of the presiding priest or elder in a synagogue to read from the scriptures and then to invite anyone who wished to do so to speak to the people. This custom was written about in Acts 13:14-15 which says, "But when they departed from Perga, they went to Antioch in Pisidia, and went into the synagogue on the Sabbath day, and sat down. And after the reading of the law and the prophets, the rulers of the synagogue sent unto them, saying, 'Ye men and brethren, if ye have any word of exhortation for the people, say on.'" In His ministry, Jesus often availed Himself of that privilege.

The scribes were considered to have been the most authoritative of the Pharisees, that is, they were supposed to know more about the scriptures than anyone else. The teaching of Jesus in the synagogue at Capernaum was recognized by the people He was teaching to have been different from that of the scribes. Jesus didn't teach the way the scribes taught. Evidently, he taught things the scribes didn't know. The scribes taught what they had learned from the scriptures, that is, the Old Testament. They also taught from the *Talmud* or the Oral Law. This book was used as a companion to the five books of Moses which contained the written law. The *Talmud* was by tradition the Oral Law which had been passed by word of mouth from Moses to Joshua and then on to others until it was eventually written down. The scribes could teach only what they had learned-they were without authority. But what Jesus taught was recognized as truth although not a part of the written Law of Moses or the Oral Law. A king or emperor has authority because there is no one higher in authority. A judge has authority in a courtroom because that's his reason for being there. A father exercises authority, because his children do not have the knowledge nor the ability nor the experience to take care of themselves.

Jesus also exercised His authority even over the unclean spirit which He cast out of the man, further amazing the people who saw it happen and impressing them even more with His authority. The proof was that even the unclean spirits were forced to obey the word of Jesus. And not only that, but the spirit was unable to speak and tell the people the true identity of Jesus, because Jesus didn't yet want the people to know that He was the Messiah.

According to this scripture, Peter lived in Capemaum with his brother Andrew and, it is assumed, his wife, because Peter's wife's mother apparently lived there too. We have no information about Peter's wife, whether she lived with him, was dead, or they were divorced. It would be unusual, to say the least, for the mother of a divorced woman to live with the woman's ex-husband, so the matter of a divorce must surely be disregarded. However, it would not have been at all unusual for the mother of either one of a married couple to have lived with the couple or for her to live with her offspring's spouse if the offspring was dead.

This passage is proof, too, that the Catholic Church is in error concerning its belief that Peter, a married man, was never married and was the first pope. Catholics believe that the popes are the spiritual descendants of Peter, but Catholic priests, bishops, cardinals, and popes are forbidden to marry. In 1 Timothy 3:2, Paul wrote that a bishop must be the husband of one wife. And in chapter 4, same book, it says, "Now the Spirit speaketh expressly, that in the latter times some shall depart from the faith, giving heed to seducing spirits, and doctrines of devils; . . . forbidding to marry... "And Hebrews 13:4 says, "Marriage is honourable to all..."

The quoted passage is from Isaiah 53:4. According to scholars the verse in Hebrews reads, "Surely He hath borne our griefs, and carried our sorrows," and they say that from the Greek in the New Testament, it should have been translated exactly the same. The word translated "griefs" in Isaiah and the word translated "infirmities" here both mean diseases, maladies, sicknesses, infirmities, and refer to physical problems. Jesus bore those infirmities away from all the hundreds, perhaps thousands, of people he healed of their physical problems. The "sorrows" in Isaiah and "sicknesses" in Matthew refer to grief and mental anguish, and as the Messiah, Jesus offered a way to take those away too. For all who obey His commandments, Jesus took away their sin and assured them of a place in heaven. It more properly belongs in a study of Isaiah, so we won't delve deeply into it here, but this verse in Isaiah is telling why Jesus should not be despised as it was stated He would be in the previous verse. Compare Psalms 103:3 which says, "Who forgiveth all thine iniquities; who healeth all thy diseases..."

37 Preaching and Healing in Galilee

(Matt. 4:23-25; Mark 1:35-39; Luke 4:42-44)

(1) In the early morning, while it was still dark, Jesus arose and went out to a lonely place and was praying there.

(2) Simon and his companions hunted for Jesus (3) and when they found Him they said to Him, "Everyone is looking for You." And the people would have tried to keep Jesus from going away from them.

(4) Jesus said to them, "Let us go somewhere else to the towns nearby for I must preach the kingdom of God to the other cities also. It was for that purpose that I was sent out."

(5) Jesus went about in all Galilee, teaching in the synagogues and proclaiming the gospel of the kingdom and healing every kind of disease and every kind of sickness among the people.

(6) The news about Jesus went out into all Syria and there was brought to Him all who were ill, taken with various diseases and pains, demoniacs, epileptics and paralytics and He healed them.

(7) And great multitudes followed Him from Galilee and Decapolis and Jerusalem and Judea and from beyond the Jordan.

Notes: It must be terrible to never have any privacy. Many public figures including some of the better known entertainers of theater, television, and motion pictures sometimes complain that they can never go places like lesser-known people can go because they're mobbed by people wanting autographs, pictures, and such. Perhaps, that was the way it was with Jesus. His fame had already spread throughout the region, even to places He had never been and would never go. People from those places came to Him to hear Him or to be healed by Him. It was even necessary for Him to try to slip away so that He could have some time alone to pray.

At that time, there were many Jewish synagogues scattered throughout the Jewish world. There was said to have been about four hundred eighty of them in Jerusalem alone. Synagogues were apparently a recent addition to the religious life of Jews. The word "synagogue" appears only once in the Old Testament in Psalms 74:8 and then only in the KJV and ASV. It is translated variously in other versions as "shrines," "meeting places," "the meeting place of God," and "every place where God was worshiped in the land." According to Strong's concordance, the word that was translated "synagogue" in Psalms meant a number of things, including: an appointment or a fixed time or season, a feast, etc. Synagogues were mentioned by Josephus many times in his history of the times before Christ, but no dates were given. Jesus, and later the apostles, often went into the synagogues on the Sabbath day and used those occasions to teach the gospel to the Jews.

Teaching and preaching and healing were the three things which Jesus did most in His ministry, and healing was probably the one most sought after by His audiences. But if healing brought the people, healing gave Jesus the opportunity to teach and preach to them.

We are familiar with many of the diseases that Jesus healed, but one with which we are not familiar nowadays is the casting out of demons. Only in the world of entertainment do we hear of demons speaking through a man, or perhaps, it is believed or practiced within some religious sects. Whether or not people still become demon-possessed or if that phenomena has passed away, in the days of Jesus's visit to earth it was a reality. Jesus spoke to the demons, and they spoke to Him. Jesus had power over them, and they knew Him.

Decapolis was a region located mostly east of the Jordan River. The word *decapolis* is Greek and simply means "ten cities." One of the cities was west of the Jordan River and the other nine were to the east of it.

38 A Leper Is Healed

(Matt. 8:2-4; Mark 1:40-45; Luke 5:12-16)

(1) It happened that while Jesus was in one of the cities a man who was full of leprosy was there also. When the leper saw Jesus he fell to his knees and bowed his face to the ground and implored Jesus, saying, "Lord, if You are willing, You can make me clean."

(2) Moved by compassion, Jesus stretched out His hand and touched the leper and said to him, "I am willing. Be cleansed." And immediately the leprosy left the man and he was clean.

(3) Jesus ordered the man to tell no one, "But go and show yourself to the priest and make an offering for your cleansing just as Moses commanded for a testimony to them."

(4) But the man went out and began to proclaim it freely and spread the news about and great multitudes gathered to hear Jesus and to be healed of their sicknesses. (5) Because of the multitudes Jesus could no longer publicly enter a city but stayed out in unpopulated areas, and people were coming to Him from everywhere.

(6) But Jesus Himself would often slip away to the wilderness alone and pray.

Notes: For centuries, leprosy was one of the most horrible and dreaded diseases a person could have. The disease has now been almost eliminated. For years, there was a leper colony on one of the Hawaiian Islands, but it has now been closed, because there's no longer a need for it.

Leprosy was highly contagious. It was also very painful. It takes a long time to develop, sometimes as long as five years, and it can take up to fifty years to become fatal. Two thousand years ago, it was always fatal. In those days, no one except Jesus would have deliberately touched a leper. The fact that He did is a proof that He was able to heal leprosy.

In those days, not all skin diseases were leprosy, but leprosy was feared when any rash or skin infection appeared. In Leviticus chapters 13 and 14, it tells what must be done when a skin rash appeared on anyone. The leper whom Jesus healed here was living under the Law of Moses, and according to the Law, he was required to be examined by a priest who would make a determination as to whether or not he still had leprosy. If the priest determined and proclaimed that the person was now clean, there was a certain sacrifice that the former leper was required to make.

It was not surprising that the leper was so deliriously happy that he had been cleansed of his leprosy that he forgot what Jesus had told him to do. And it's understandable that a person who had been cured of a painful and fatal disease could forget. It might also be expected that a person would have a greater dread of the years of pain to which he could look forward than of the eventual death the disease would bring. But obedience to the commandments of God and of Christ is essential to salvation. We don't know anything more about this leper, whether the man's disobedience was forgiven him or if he had to pay for it.

39 Jesus Heals a Paralytic

(Matt. 9:2-8; Mark 2:1-12; Luke 5:17-26)

(1) When Jesus had come back to Capemaum several days later it was spread around that He was at home. (2) So many people were gathered together that there was no longer any room, even near the door, and Jesus was speaking the word to them. (3) There were also

Pharisees and teachers of the Law there who had come from every village of Galilee and Judea and from Jerusalem, and the power of the Lord was present for Jesus to perform healing.

(4) And there were some men who were carrying a bed on which lay a man who was paralyzed, and they were trying to bring him in to set him down in front of Jesus. (5) Being unable to get to Jesus on account of the crowd, they removed the roof above Jesus, and when they had dug an opening, they let down the pallet on which the paralytic was lying.

(6) Jesus, seeing the faith of those who brought the paralytic, said to the paralytic, "My son, your sins are forgiven you."

(7) The scribes and Pharisees began to reason among themselves, saying, "This man is speaking blasphemies. Who but God alone can forgive sins?"

(8) Jesus, perceiving in His spirit that they were reasoning that way within themselves, immediately asked them, "Why are you reasoning about these things in your hearts? (9) Which is easier, to say to the paralytic 'Your sins are forgiven,' or to say, 'Arise, take up your pallet and walk'? (10) But in order that you may know that the Son of Man has authority on earth to forgive sins," He turned and said to the paralytic, (11) "I say to you, rise, take up your pallet and go home."

(12) The paralytic rose and immediately took up the pallet and went out in the sight of all so that they were all amazed and were glorifying God, saying, "We have never seen anything like this."

Notes: From this text, it appears that Jesus had a home in Capernaum where He dwelt when He was there. There is no information as to whether the house in which He lived was owned or rented by Him or if He was an invited guest in the home of someone else. But judging from what He said in Matthew 8:20, "The foxes have holes, and the birds of the air have nests, but the Son of Man hath not where to lay His head," it is most likely that He was the invited guest of one of His disciples, possibly even one of the men who were to become apostles.

Some versions of the Bible say that the man who was brought to Jesus through the roof of the house was sick of the palsy, while others say he was a paralytic. According to the Greek dictionary, the meaning of the word in Greek could have either, or both, of those meanings, but "paralytic" seems to be, judging by the context, the intended meaning.

With our knowledge of modern-home architecture, it's difficult to imagine how the men who were carrying the paralytic could make a hole in the roof through which they could lower the man. But houses at that time and in that place were built much differently from ours. Those houses were built around a central courtyard with the roof being nearly flat and with a dirt floor. Most of them had only one floor or story. And there was usually only one opening in the outer wall, a door into a porch, or possibly with a latticed window directly above the door. From the porch or from the open space in the center of the house, the courtyard, there would have been a stairway which led to the roof. There would have been a balustrade or railing around the outside edge of the roof and another around the edge of the courtyard. The roof would not extend over the courtyard but would overlook it. On the ground floor, there would be a door from each of the rooms onto the courtyard. And there would be a covered gallery around the courtyard so that in rainy weather a person could go from one room to another without getting wet.

The roofs of houses were used for many purposes. Rahab hid the Israelite spies on such a roof (Josh. 2:6). Samuel talked with Saul on the roof (1 Sam. 9:25). David walked around on the roof in the evening and saw Bathsheba who was bathing on her roof (2 Sam. 11:2). And Peter went up on the roof to pray (Acts 10:9).

40 The Call of Matthew and His Feast

(Matt. 9:9-13; Mark 2:13-17; Luke 5:27-32)

(1) Jesus went out again by the seashore and all the multitude were coming to Him and He was teaching them. (2) As Jesus was passing on from there He saw Matthew (or Levi), the son of Alphaeus, a tax-gatherer, sitting in the tax office. Jesus said to Matthew, "Follow Me!" And Matthew left everything and rose up and followed Jesus.

(3) Matthew gave a big reception for Jesus in his house and there was a great crowd of tax-gatherers and others there who were reclining at table with them.

(4) When the scribes of the Pharisees saw that Jesus was eating with the sinners and tax-gatherers they asked His disciples, "Why is He eating and drinking with tax-gatherers and sinners?"

(5) But when Jesus heard this He said to them, "It is not those who are healthy who need a physician but those who are ill. (6) Go and learn what this means, 'I desire compassion and not sacrifice,' for I did not come to call the righteous but to call sinners."

Notes: Matthew, the seventh of the twelve who were to become apostles, was chosen. Matthew, in his account of the Gospel, wrote that the man's name was Matthew but both Mark and Luke called him Levi. Mark wrote that Levi was the son of Alphaeus. Another one of the twelve who was called later was James; he was called James the Less or James the Younger and was also said to have been the son of Alphaeus. Whether or not this Alphaeus was the same man we have no way of knowing, because there is nothing in the scriptures stating that Matthew and James were brothers. We know that such a relationship existed between Peter and Andrew and James and John, the sons of Zebedee, and that these relationships were noted in the Scriptures. Because the name Alphaeus is from the same Aramaic word as the name Clopas (or Cleophas), some scholars believe that these two were indeed brothers. The women who are named as being present at the crucifixion of Jesus include in some accounts "the mother of James" and in other accounts "the wife of Clopas." This leads to further speculation among scholars that "the mother of James" *and* the "wife of Clopas" (or Alphaeus) were the same person and that this is proof that the two men, Matthew and James the Less, were sons of the same man and, if not full brothers, they could have been half-brothers if the mother of James was not also the mother of Matthew.

This subject was addressed in the *Introduction,* but a publican or, as he is called in some versions, a tax gatherer, was one of the most despised of all men by the Jews, one of their own working with and for the Romans. The Pharisees classed all tax collectors with sinners, the people who made no pretense at being religious. Most publicans were rich because they could collect as much money from each person as that person could pay, fair or not. He could keep for himself all the money he collected in excess of the amount he was obligated to turn over to the Romans. Whether or not Matthew was rich it doesn't say, but it does say that he had a house and that he gave a big party to honor Jesus and to which a great crowd of publicans and others were invited.

Apparently, Matthew's house was not constructed on the same plan as the average house. The fact that he could probably afford a much larger and nicer house may have been the reason. At any rate, the Pharisees and their scribes could see that Jesus and His disciples were there, and they knew that the other guests were "publicans and sinners." Or perhaps, these Pharisees were bold enough to enter the house, because they evidently were in a position to see who was there and to ask the disciples of Jesus why Jesus was eating with publicans and sinners.

The quotation of Jesus, "I desire mercy and not sacrifice," is from Hosea 6:6.

41 The Discourse of Jesus on Fasting

(Matt. 9:14-17; Mark 2:18-22; Luke 5:33-39)

(1) John's disciples and the Pharisees were fasting and they came and said to Jesus, "The disciples of John often fast and offer prayers. The disciples of the Pharisees also do the same, but Your disciples eat and drink. Why is this?"

(2) Jesus said to them, "Can you make the attendants of the bridegroom fast while the bridegroom is with them? (3) The days will come when the bridegroom is taken away from them and they will fast in those days."

(4) Jesus also told them a parable: "No one sews a patch of unshrunk cloth on an old garment. Otherwise the patch pulls away from it, the new from the old, and a worse tear results; and the piece from the new will not match the old. (5) No one puts new wine into old wineskins. Otherwise the new wine will burst the skins and the wine will be spilled out and the skins will be ruined. (6) But new wine must be put into fresh wineskins. (7) And no one, after drinking old wine wishes for new for he says, 'The old is good enough.'"

Notes: To fast means to abstain from food or drink either from necessity or as a religious observance. Fasting is first mentioned in the Bible in Judges 30:26 which reads, "Then all the children of Israel, and all the people, went up, and came to the house of God, and wept, and sat there before the Lord, and fasted that day until even, and offered burnt offerings and peace offerings before the Lord." You may remember that while his first child by Bathsheba was sick, David fasted and wept, hoping that God would be gracious and let the child live.

In the Old Testament, fasting seems to have been one of the means by which people implored God to help them. It was most often an expression of grief or sorrow. Even without any religious significance, people sometimes fast simply because they have no desire for food when they are confronted by catastrophe or sorrow. They don't consciously decide not to eat, but they don't eat simply because they have no appetite for food. Fasting, then, becomes to some extent an expression of grief. That fact is the foundation for fasting as a religious rite. When the soul is oppressed, the body doesn't desire food. When we want to get closer to God, to pray or to meditate, abstention from food seems to make us able to accomplish our purpose with greater ease.

In the time of Christ, the Jews fasted often. There were several annual periods of fasting including one to commemorate their sorrow for the capture of Jerusalem by Nebuchadnezzer, one to show their sorrow for the burning of the temple, and one of sorrow for the murder of Gedaliah whom the king of Babylon had made governor over the cities of Judah. The Pharisees fasted twice a week simply as a rite which they had made into a tradition. In addition, the Jews fasted ceremoniously at various other times and whenever they felt some need to do so.

The disciples of John may have been fasting because, as you may recall, John had been imprisoned by Herod Antipas. John probably would have had no regard for the traditions of the Jews if they had only a ritualistic meaning, so his disciples were probably fasting in the manner of David and not according to the traditions of the Pharisees.

In reply to the question as to why His disciples didn't fast, Jesus used a point of reference that all of them understood. They knew that it was proper and fitting that at a wedding as long as the bridegroom was present or as long as the wedding festivities were in progress, none of the attendants would fast or mourn. A wedding was a time of joy and celebration. The disciples of John surely understood that Jesus was comparing Himself to the bridegroom and His disciples to the attendants and that as long as He was with them, there was no occasion for fasting or mourning. Those things would come later.

Another illustration Jesus made was to the folly of patching an old garment with a new piece of cloth. When I was a child, all my clothing was bought one or two sizes too large. That was done for two reasons: first, so that I wouldn't outgrow it before it wore out and, second, to allow for shrinkage when it was washed. Almost all fabrics shrunk the first couple of times they were washed. Later manufacturers began preshrinking the fabric before it was made into garments. When that was done, the garments were labeled "sanforized," the name of the process used to preshrink them. Nowadays, it would probably be difficult to find clothing that had not been preshrunk.

It was the fact that new cloth would shrink upon washing, and the old cloth, to which Jesus was referring, would not shrink. The shrinking of the new cloth would cause a greater tear in the garment than the tear which was being repaired.

Many of the containers for liquids which were in use in Jesus's day were made from the skins of animals, especially if the product for which the container was to be used was to be transported. The skin bottles were used mostly for water or wine. The entire skins of sheep or goats, and sometimes oxen, were prepared in a special way and used as containers for liquids. Since the main methods of transportation were on foot or on an animal, some of the skins could be quite large, depending on the strength of the animal which was to carry the product. Even though earthenware containers were available, skin bottles could be transported much more easily. Two ox skins, for example, could be connected together and slung onto a camel, one skin on each side of the animal. This was much easier than making racks or harnesses to which earthen vessels could be strapped.

Over time, the skin bottles would become tender. New wine would continue to ferment to some degree after being put into a wineskin. Old skins would have no elasticity still in them and would tear open because of the increase in pressure caused by fermentation. New skins would have a great deal of elasticity and would stretch with the increase in pressure.

What Jesus meant by these last two illustrations was that the doctrines He brought were different from the doctrines which the Jews had been observing for centuries. Trying to live by both the old doctrines and traditions and the new ones that Jesus brought would confuse people, because the two sets of doctrines, the old Law and the gospel of Jesus, were incompatible.

42 A Woman Healed and Jairus's Daughter Raised

(Matt. 9:18-26; Mark 5:22-43; Luke 8:41-56)

(1) While Jesus was saying these things there came to Him an official of the synagogue named Jairus. And Jairus fell down at the feet of Jesus and began entreating Him, "My only daughter who is twelve years of age is at the point of death she may even be dead already. Please come and lay Your hands on her that she may get well and live."

(2) So Jesus went off with Jairus, and Jesus' disciples and a great multitude were following and the multitude was pressing in on Him. (3) A woman who had had a hemorrhage for twelve years (4) and had endured much at the hands of many physicians and had spent all that she had and was not helped at all, but rather had grown worse, (5) after hearing about Jesus came up in the crowd behind Him and touched His cloak. (6) She thought, "If I just touch His garments I shall get well."

(7) Immediately the flow of her blood was dried up and she felt in her body that she was healed of her affliction.

(8) Jesus asked, "Who is the one who touched Me?"

While they were all denying it Peter said, "Master, the multitude are crowding and pressing in upon You."

(9) But Jesus said, "Someone did touch Me, for I was aware that power had gone out of Me."

(10) When the woman saw that she had not escaped notice she came trembling and fell down before Jesus and declared in the presence of all

the people the reason why she had touched Jesus and how she had been immediately healed.

(11) Jesus said to the woman, "Daughter, your faith has made you well. Go in peace."

(12) While Jesus was still speaking someone came from the house of the synagogue official and said, "Your daughter has died. Do not trouble the Teacher any more."

(13) But when Jesus heard this He said to Jairus, "Do not be afraid any longer. Only believe and she shall be made well."

(14) When Jesus came to the official's house He saw the flute-players and a commotion and heard a noisy disorder and people weeping and wailing. (15) Jesus said to them, "Why make a commotion and weep? Depart, for she has not died but is asleep."

(16) The people began laughing at Jesus, knowing that the girl had died. But putting them all out Jesus allowed no one to enter with Him except Peter, John and James and the girl's father and mother. Jesus entered the room where the child lay,

(17) and taking her by the hand Jesus said to her, "Talitha kum!" (which translated means, "Little girl, I say to you, arise!"

(18) The child's spirit returned and she rose up immediately and began to walk. And Jesus gave orders that something be given to her to eat. (19) Her parents were amazed and Jesus instructed them to tell no one what had happened.

(20) But the news of what Jesus had done went out into all the land.

Notes: Like so many of the people with whom Jesus came into contact during His ministry, Jairus is mentioned only in one passage. He was said to be a ruler of the synagogue, probably one of the elders who looked after the synagogue. In Matthew's account, Jairus said that his daughter was dead, but in the accounts of both Mark and Luke, he is reported to have said that she was dying or on the point of death. Sometimes people say that something has happened when in actuality it is only on the point of happening or its happening is inevitable. That's probably the meaning Matthew assigned to what Jairus said.

Matthew wrote that the woman touched the hem of Jesus's garment, Mark wrote that she touched the garment of Jesus, and Luke wrote that she touched the border of the garment. The garment in question was the outer garment of Jesus, a cloak or mantle. This garment was comprised of a large square of cloth that was worn thrown over the shoulders. The hem was actually a fringe or tassel of loose threads. The Jews were told to wear such a hem or fringe to distinguish them from people of other nations. Numbers 15:38-39 reads, "Speak to the sons of Israel, and tell them that they shall make for themselves tassels on the comers of their garments throughout their generations, and that they shall put on the tassel of each comer a cord of blue. And it shall be a tassel for you to look at and remember all the commandments of the Lord, so as to do them and not follow after your own heart and your own eyes, after which you played the harlot."

In the near East, of which Israel was and is a part, since before the time of Christ, it has been the custom to make quite a show of grief at the death of someone. Friends and relatives of the deceased, especially the women, wail mournfully and ceaselessly. This usually went on for up to about eight days, and this was done especially at the funeral. The mourners sometimes hire professional mourners and minstrels and musicians as an aid in the mourning process. The mourners sometimes cut themselves, pull out their own hair, throw dust or ashes into the air or lie in dust or ashes, and tear their clothing as a visible sign of their anguish and grief.

The Jews, however, were forbidden to cut themselves or to pull out their own hair. They showed their grief by howling, by music, by the concealment of their chins, by tearing their outer garments, by refusing to wash or anoint themselves, by refusing to talk to others, by throwing ashes or dust into the air, and by lying in ashes or dust. In 2 Samuel 12, there is the account of how David handled grief.

After Jesus had restored life to the daughter of Jairus, He told her parents to give her something to eat. She had been restored to life by extraordinary means, but now she must be sustained by ordinary means. She had to eat but for her to do that nothing out of the ordinary was necessary.

It makes one wonder why Jesus told the girl's parents not to tell anyone what He had done. The people who were outside the house knew the girl was dead. Shortly, they would know that she was alive again. It's possible that when Jesus told the crowd outside the house that the girl was not dead but sleeping that He was setting the stage for a doubt to be raised in the minds of the people who had laughed at Him. The five people who were with Jesus were enough witnesses to establish the truth of the miracle. We know that later, even people who had witnessed Jesus performing miracles refused to believe that He was the Christ. If they refused to believe after seeing Jesus perform miracles, what *would* make them believe?

We read in many places in the scriptures that Jesus told the beneficiaries of some of His miracles not to tell anyone about what He had done. The incident in the following section is another example of that.

43 Two Blind Men and a Dumb Demoniac Healed

(Matt. 9:27-34)

(1) As Jesus passed on from there two blind men followed Him crying out, "Have mercy on us, Son of David."

(2) After Jesus had come into the house the blind men came up to Jesus and He said to them, "Do you believe that I am able to do this?" They said to Jesus, "Yes, Lord."

(3) Then Jesus touched their eyes and said, "Be it done to you according to your faith."

(4) The eyes of the blind men were opened, and Jesus sternly warned them, "See that you let no man know about this!" (5) But they went out and spread the news about Jesus in all that land.

(6) As the men who had been blind were going out, a dumb man, demon possessed, was brought to Jesus. (7) After the demon was cast out the dumb man spoke, and the multitude marveled, saying, "Nothing like this was ever seen in Israel."

(8) But the Pharisees were saying, "He casts out demons by the ruler of demons."

Notes: To the Jews, "the Son of David" meant the Messiah, and by calling Jesus the Son of David, the blind men were saying that they believed Jesus was the Messiah. The fact that these men regained their sight after Jesus said to them, "Be it done to you according to your faith," is further proof that they believed Jesus to be the Messiah, otherwise they would not have received their sight.

The scripture doesn't say so, but evidently the person or persons who were leading the blind men followed Jesus right into the house where He was staying. It was probably the same people who had told the blind men of the power of Jesus to heal, and even to restore the dead to life, because the blind men could not have seen the Power of Jesus for themselves.

Just as it is required of people who become Christians today, Jesus asked the blind men for a verbal confession of their faith in Him, a belief that He could do what they asked Him to do. This is not to show God we believe, nor to confirm to ourselves our belief in Jesus, but to show the world that we love God enough to become His servants.

The people about whom we read who were possessed of demons were incapacitated in different ways. The Gerasene demoniac named Legion was very strong physically because of the demons which were in possession of his body. He couldn't be kept bound, even with chains, because he was able to break any of the bonds that were put on him. This man was made dumb by the demon with which the man was possessed.

Isn't it usually true that people who don't want to believe in God and in Jesus can always find some reason not to believe! The Pharisees didn't want to believe that Jesus was the Messiah, so they accused Him of being a demon Himself and of deriving His power from the ruler of demons. They accused Him of the same thing in other places in the scriptures, too, such as in Matthew 12:24 and Mark 3:22. They couldn't deny that Jesus had performed miracles because they had seen Him do some of them, but they could and did try to discredit Him by saying that His power was from Satan instead of from God.

44 Jesus Heals an Impotent Man on the Sabbath

(John 5:1-15)

(1) After these things there was a feast of the Jews and Jesus went up to Jerusalem.

(2) Now there is in Jerusalem by the sheep gate a pool which is called in Hebrew Bethesda. It had five porticoes. (3) In these lay a multitude of those who were sick, blind, lame and withered waiting for the moving of the waters, (4) for they believed that an angel of the Lord went down at certain seasons into the pool and stirred up the water. After the stirring up of the water, whoever then stepped into the pool first was made well from whatever disease with which he was afflicted.

(5) A certain man was there who had been thirty-eight years in his sickness. (6) When Jesus saw him lying there and knew that he had already been a long time in that condition He said to the man, "Do you wish to get well?"

(7) The sick man answered Jesus, "Sir, I have no man to put me into the pool when the water is stirred up and while I am coming another steps down before me."

(8) Jesus said to the man, "Arise, take up your pallet and walk." (9) Immediately the man became well and took up his pallet and began to walk.

Now it was the Sabbath on that day. (10) Therefore the Jews were saying to him who was cured, "It is the Sabbath and it is not permissible for you to carry your pallet."

(11) But the man answered them, "He who made me well was the one who said to me, 'Take up your pallet and walk.'"

(12) They asked him, "Who is the man who said to you, 'Take up your pallet and walk'?"

(13) But he who was healed did not know who it was for Jesus had slipped away while there was a crowd in that place.

(14) Afterward Jesus found the sick man whom He had healed in the temple and said to him, "Look, you have become well. Do not sin any more so that nothing worse may befall you."

(15) The man went away and told the Jews that it was Jesus who had made him well.

Notes: The scriptures do not tell us which feast this was. There were a total of three times each year when the men were required to go to Jerusalem to a feast. Deuteronomy 16:16 reads, "Three times in a year all your males shall appear before the Lord your God in the place which

He chooses, at the Feast of Unleavened Bread and at the Feast of Weeks and at the Feast of Booths, and they shall not appear before the Lord empty-handed." The *KN* translates the word "tabernacles" instead of "booths." But the scripture doesn't say which feast this was, that it was one of the three feasts to which all the males were required to attend. It could have been some other feast and that Jesus went to Jerusalem at that time merely because He wanted to be there.

The sheep gate is supposed to have been just north of the temple mount and the pool called Bethesda just north of the sheep gate. The meaning of "Bethesda" was "house of kindness." That was certainly an appropriate name for the pool considering the reputation it had for healing.

The latter part of verse 3 and all of verse 4 above, which explain the reputation of the pool for healing, are believed by some scholars to have been inserted into the text at a later date by some copier of the scriptures as an explanatory note telling why the people waited there by the pool. The insertion may have been made in order to explain the statement of the lame man when he said that there was no one to help him when the water was stirred. That passage does not appear in the text of some versions of the Bible.

Because those verses were omitted in earlier texts of the scriptures, it's unclear as to whether the truth of the belief in the curative powers of the pool was real or imagined. Believing, as we do, in the power of God, we can accept the phenomenon of the healing power of the water, but under the circumstances we are not obliged to do so since the scripture doesn't tell us whether that belief was a myth or the truth.

It might seem strange that Jesus asked the man if he wanted to be healed. A person would think that there would be no question as to whether or not he wanted to walk again. One writer suggested that because of his condition, the man may have had such a large income from begging that he may not have wanted to be healed.

The Law concerning observance of the Sabbath is found in Exodus 20:8-11 and Deuteronomy 5:12-15. In Exodus, the passage says, "Remember the sabbath day, to keep it holy. Six days you shall labor and do all your work, but the seventh day is a sabbath of the Lord your God; in it you shall not do any work, you or your son or your daughter, your male or your female servant or your cattle or your sojourner who stays with you. For in six days the Lord made the heavens and the earth, the sea and all that is in them, and rested on the seventh day; therefore the Lord blessed the sabbath day and made it holy."

The Law of Moses didn't say that small things such as picking up a mat were work. It was the traditions which had grown up and been foisted on the people by the Pharisees and others of their ilk who had tried to make it a sin to pick up a pallet or to walk more than a certain distance on the Sabbath. Jesus at another time said that it was not a sin to help an ox out of a ditch on the Sabbath. Jesus said in Matthew 23:2-4, "The scribes and the Pharisees have seated themselves in the chair of Moses; therefore all that they tell you, do and observe, but do not do according to their deeds; for they say things, and do not do them. And they tie up heavy loads, and lay them on men's shoulders; but they themselves are unwilling to move them with so much as a finger."

Moreover, the day may not have been a seventh-day Sabbath as Sabbaths are generally accepted to be. In Leviticus 23:3, it says, "Six days shall work be done; but the seventh day is the sabbath of rest, an holy convocation ...." The NIV renders "holy convocation" as "sacred assembly." We don't know which Jewish feast was meant in verse 1 above, but writers generally agree that it was probably the Passover. If it was the Passover, Leviticus 23 says that following the Passover there was to be seven days of the Feast of Unleavened Bread. The first and seventh days of the feast were to be "holy convocations" or "sacred assemblies." That would mean that there were two Sabbaths only six days apart and there was the possibility that another Sabbath, the weekly seventh-day Sabbath, would be between those two Sabbaths. Further, Leviticus 23:24 says, "In the seventh month, on the first day of the month, shall ye have a sabbath, a memorial of blowing of trumpets... " The first day of the seventh month would fall on different days of the week in different years and that Sabbath would then not be on the seventh day of the week in all years. Also, we know that the term "Sabbath" was not limited in use to mean only the seventh-day of rest Sabbath, because according to the Law as recorded in Leviticus 25, there was to be a Sabbath for the land, a year of rest for the land after having been farmed for six years.

What the lame man who was healed did should be an example to everyone. When Jesus saw the man later, he was in the temple. What the man was actually doing in the temple we don't know, but knowing the purpose of the temple in the religious life of the Jews, we can certainly make an assumption.

45 Jesus Defends Himself for Healing on the Sabbath

(John 5:16-47)

(1) Because Jesus was doing these things on the Sabbath the Jews were persecuting Him. (2) But Jesus answered them, "My Father is working until now and I Myself am working."

(3) For this reason the Jews were seeking all the more to kill Jesus because He not only was breaking the Sabbath but also was calling God His own Father, making Himself equal with God. (4) Jesus, therefore, said to them, "Truly, truly, I say to you, the Son can do nothing of Himself unless it is something He sees the Father doing. Whatever the Father does, these things the Son also does in like manner. (5) For the Father loves the Son and shows Him all things that He Himself is doing. And greater works than these will he show Him that you may marvel. (6) For just as the Father raises the dead and gives them life even so the Son also gives life to whom He wishes.

(7) For not even the Father judges any one but He has given all judgment to the Son (8) in order that all may honor the Son even as they honor the Father. He who does not honor the Son does not honor the Father who sent Him.

(9) "Truly, truly, I say to you, he who hears My word and believes Him who sent Me has eternal life and does not come into judgment, but has passed out of death into life.

(10) "Truly, truly, I say to you, an hour is coming and now is, when the dead shall hear the voice of the Son of God, and those who hear shall live. (11) For just as the Father has life in Himself even so He gave to the Son also to have life in Himself, (12) and He gave the Son authority to execute judgment because He is the Son of Man.

(13) "Do not marvel at this for an hour is coming in which all who are in the tombs shall hear His voice (14) and shall come forth, those who did the good deeds to a resurrection of life, those who committed evil deeds to a resurrection of judgment.

(15) "I can do nothing on My own initiative. As I hear I judge, and My judgment is just because I do not seek My own will but the will of Him who sent Me.

(16) "If I alone bear witness of Myself My testimony is not true. (17) There is another who bears witness of Me and I know that the testimony which He bears of Me is true.

(18) "You have sent to John and he has borne witness to the truth. (19) But the witness which I receive is not from man. I say these things so that you may be saved. (20) He was the lamp that was burning and was shining and you were willing to rejoice for a while in his light. (21) But the witness which I have is greater than that of John; for the works which the Father has given Me to accomplish, the very works that I do, bear witness of Me, that the Father has sent Me. (22) And the Father who sent Me, He has borne witness of Me. You have neither heard His voice at any time nor seen His form. (23) And you do not have His word abiding in you for you do not believe Him whom He sent.

(24) "You search the Scriptures because you think that in them you have eternal life, but it is these that bear witness of Me, (25) and you are unwilling to come to Me that you may have life.

(25) "I do not receive glory from men, (27) but I know you, that you do not have the love of God in yourselves.

(28) "I have come in My Father's name and you do not receive Me. If another shall come in his own name you will receive him.

(29) "How can you believe when you receive glory from one another and you do not seek the glory that is from the one and only God?

(30) "Do not think that I will accuse you before the Father. The one who accuses you is Moses in whom you have set your hope. (31) For if you believed Moses you would believe Me, for Moses wrote of Me. (32) But if you do not believe his writing how will you believe My words?"

Notes: We don't know what form the persecution of Jesus by the Jews took, but at this time, it doesn't seem to have been physical. It was probably all verbal, consisting of the Jews trying to ruin the reputation of Jesus, to destroy His popularity, and to portray Him to the people as a breaker of God's Law. Instead of trying to make a mature determination as to whether or not Jesus really was the Messiah, they ignored everything they had seen that proved He was the Messiah and assumed that He was not. People haven't changed a great deal since the days of Jesus-they still believe only what they want to believe.

In addition to persecuting Jesus, the Jews began looking for an opportunity to kill Him. Under Roman law, no one had the power to pass or carry out a death sentence except the Romans themselves. If we assume that the Jews were sincere in their belief that Jesus was not the Messiah but a lawbreaker, we could almost commend them for doing what they were commanded to do in Exodus 31:15 and Exodus 35:2, "For six days work may be done but on the seventh day there is a sabbath of complete rest, holy to the Lord, whoever does any work on the sabbath day shall surely be put to death." Even if the Jews were sincere, though, it is rather far fetched for them to classify the healing of a sick man as work under the Law. Would a man who had been gored by an ox or one who broke his leg on the Sabbath be compelled to lie where he fell until the Sabbath day was over? Certainly not! Were the Israelites forbidden to repel an invader on the Sabbath? The Pharisees would have condemned Jesus for doing for a man what any one of them would have done for his own sick cattle. They would not have considered that to have been work and deemed to be worthy of death.

We can see in the conduct of the Jews what envy can do to corrupt men. Envy makes people do things they wouldn't do otherwise. Envy of one's neighbors is so rife that there's a popular phrase with which we're all familiar-"keeping up with the Joneses." If the Jews had the power to heal sick people, they would have used it at every opportunity, even on the Sabbath and probably would have insinuated or intimated that it was because of their piety that they had that power. Further, if Jesus had been one of them, a close associate, they would probably never have uttered a word of criticism against Him.

In the beginning, God did His work in six days and rested from the work of creation on the seventh day. But God had not ceased to work. He didn't sit back on the Sabbath and refuse to answer prayers. He never ceased to make the sun shine on the Sabbath. He never ceased to make it rain on the Sabbath. All the laws of nature which God had set in motion continued to function on the Sabbath just as they did on the other six days of the week. Because God was His Father and He was one with God, Jesus didn't stop doing the work God had sent Him to do and which was allowed under the Law because the day was a Sabbath.

In His statement, "My Father is working until now and I Myself am working," Jesus said in effect that He was equal with God and that the same exemption from the Law concerning work which applied to God also applied to Him. Jesus knew His answer would offend the Jews, but by that answer, He taught us another valuable lesson-we are not to withhold the truth because we might become endangered because of it or because it might offend someone. The fault was not in the truth that Jesus spoke but in the sinners who would not accept it as the truth.

Jesus as a man could do nothing by His own power, but as a part of God, He could do anything. By being able to do anything showed that Jesus had the approval and cooperation of God. Jesus said in John 10:30, "I and My Father are one." And in John 17:31, "... that they may all be one; even as You, Father, are in Me, and I in You, that they also may be in Us; that the world may believe that You did send Me." Jesus said, too, that whatever God the Father did, the Son did also, thus confirming that He was one with God in power and in the exemption from all laws-Jewish, Roman, and natural.

The Jews didn't doubt the power of God to raise the dead. He had done so on at least two other occasions of which they knew-the son of the widow of Sarepta through Elijah (1 Kings 17:22) and the Shunamite's son through Elisha (2 Kings 4:32-35). Jesus also had that power as we have already seen in the case of Jairus's daughter and on at least two other occasions still to come. Whether or not any of these Jews had been at the resurrection of Jairus's daughter, certainly the story was well known in the area and surely some of them would have heard about it. Jesus's power was not confined to physical life but included spiritual life as well. In John 11:25-26, Jesus said, "I am the resurrection and the life; he who believes in Me shall live even if he dies, and everyone who lives and believes in Me shall never die." And in Ephesians 2:1 Paul wrote, "And you hath He quickened [made alive], who were dead in trespass and sins."

Jesus said that whoever listened to what He said and believed in God had eternal life and had passed out of death into life. The meaning of this is that everyone who comes to believe in Jesus as the Son of God and obeys His commandments has been transformed from a lost condition into a saved condition. Listening to the words of Jesus is not just hearing with the ears, it is doing what He tells us to do. But according to the apostle John there is even more required. He wrote in 1 John 3:14, "We know that we have passed out of death into life, because we love the brethren." Also in 1 John 4:8 he wrote, "The one who does not love does not know God, for God is love." If God is love then so is Jesus. It was for love of us that Jesus came into the world and suffered death and the grave so that we might live.

46 Jesus Defends His Disciples for Plucking Ears of Grain on the Sabbath

(Matt. 12:1-8; Mark 2:23-28; Luke 6:1-5)

(1) At that time, which was the Sabbath, Jesus went through the grainfields and His disciples, being hungry, began to pick the heads of grain and to eat.

(2) When the Pharisees saw this they said to Jesus, "Look, your disciples do what it is not lawful to do on the Sabbath."

(3) Then Jesus said to them, "Have you not read what David did when he and his companions became hungry, (4) how he entered the house of God in the time of Abiathar the high priest. They ate the consecrated bread which was not lawful for him nor those with him to eat, but for the priests alone? (5) Or have you not read in the Law that on the Sabbath the priests in the temple break the Sabbath and are innocent?

(6) "But I say to you that something greater than the temple is here. (7) But if you had known what this means, 'I desire compassion and not a sacrifice,' you would not have condemned the innocent.

(8) "The Sabbath was made for man and not man for the Sabbath. (9) Consequently the Son of Man is Lord even of the Sabbath."

Notes: Before the disciples of Jesus could eat the heads of grain which they picked, they had to rub it between the palms of their hands to separate the chaff from the grain. The chaff could not be eaten, but it was lighter in weight than the grain so that by gently blowing on the mixture of grain and chaff, the chaff could be blown away leaving only the grain.

Even though the field of grain belonged to someone else, the disciples weren't stealing it. Deuteronomy 23:25 says, "When you enter your neighbor's standing grain, then you may pluck the heads with your hand, but you shall not wield a sickle in your neighbor's standing grain." A sickle is a long sharp curved blade attached to a long handle made especially for harvesting grain crops.

It appears that wherever Jesus went and whatever He did, there were Pharisees there to keep track of Him. They were there again at this time, watching when the disciples picked the heads of grain to eat. They accused Jesus's disciples of breaking the Law as recorded in Exodus 34:21, "You shall work six days, but on the seventh day you shall rest; even during plowing time and harvest you shall rest." Technically, it may be supposed if one wanted to press the issue, what the disciples did could have been called harvesting.

Jesus reminded the Pharisees that David and his men ate the hallowed or consecrated shewbread or, as the NASV records it, the bread of Presence. That incident is recorded in 1 Samuel 21:6. The bread involved was bread that had been replaced on the altar by fresh bread. Only the priests and their families were allowed by Law to eat that bread (Lev. 24:5-9). Jesus reminded the Pharisees, too, that the priests profane the Sabbath, but because their duties are required under the Law, they are not sinning. Probably the act, or one of the acts, to which Jesus was referring was a part of the Law as recorded in Numbers 28:9-10, "Then on the Sabbath day two male lambs one year-old without defect, and two-tenths of an ephah of fine flour mixed with oil as a grain offering, and its libation: This is the burnt offering of every Sabbath in addition to the continual burnt offering and its libation." Also in Exodus 35:3, it says, "You shall not kindle a fire in any of your dwellings on the Sabbath day." A fire was required for the burnt offerings, although that would not be in a dwelling. The priests were required by Law to do something that the Law forbade others to do.

47 Jesus Heals a Withered Hand on the Sabbath

(Matt. 12:9-14; Mark 3:1-6; Luke 6:6-11)

(1) Jesus departed from there and, it being the Sabbath, He entered their synagogue to teach. There was a man in the synagogue whose right hand was withered. (2) The scribes and the Pharisees were watching Jesus closely to see if He healed on the Sabbath hoping that they might find reason to accuse Him.

(3) But Jesus knew what the scribes and Pharisees were thinking and He said to the man with the withered hand, "Arise and come forward!" The man arose and came forward.

(4) Jesus said to the scribes and Pharisees, "What man shall there be among you who shall have one sheep and if it falls into a pit on the Sabbath will not take hold of it and lift it out?

(5) Of how much more value is a man than a sheep! So then, I ask you, is it lawful on the Sabbath to do good or to do evil, to save a life or to destroy it?"

(6) After looking around at them with anger, grieved at their hardness of heart, Jesus said to the man, "Stretch out your hand!" The man stretched out his hand and it was restored to normal, like the other.

(7) But the Pharisees were filled with rage and went out and immediately began taking counsel with the Herodians against Jesus, as to how they might destroy Him.

Notes: Matthew's account of the Gospel reads their synagogue but both Mark and Luke wrote the synagogue. Matthew was perhaps referring to the synagogue which the Pharisees in the preceding section attended, but this probably would have no other significance.

We don't often read about Jesus becoming angry and even more seldom do we think of Him being angry. We know, too, that it is not a sin to become angry. Jesus had anger on occasion, and we know that He had no sin. It's what we do because of anger that may be sinful. What was it that made Jesus angry on this occasion? The scriptures say it was because of the hardness of the hearts of the scribes and Pharisees. They thought that blindly following their traditions or their interpretation of the Law was more important than a person badly in need of help.

The Herodians were the partisans of Herod Antipas. If you remember, Herod Antipas was the one who had John the Baptist imprisoned, because John was telling everyone that the marriage of Antipas to Herodias was adulterous because Herodias was still married to Philip, the brother of Antipas. The scribes and Pharisees plotted with the Herodians to have Jesus killed. We don't know for sure why the Herodians were involved, but we can assume that it was because of the religious relationship of John and Jesus, not their family kinship.

This incident happened about two years or more before the crucifixion of Jesus and already the Scribes and Pharisees were conspiring against Jesus. It took them all that time to find a way to have Him killed. The hatred of the Pharisees for Jesus was not because He did not keep the Law of Moses, or that He profaned the Sabbath, but that He knew the hypocrisy in their hearts. Jesus knew what they were really like. He knew their thoughts and the motives behind their actions, and they knew that He knew. But worst of all, Jesus accused them of their hypocrisy for all the world to hear.

48 Jesus Working Miracles at the Sea of Galilee

(Matt. 12:15-21; Mark 3:7-12)

(1) Jesus, aware of the plotting against Him, withdrew to the sea with His disciples and a great multitude from Galilee followed. From Judea, (2) Jerusalem, Idumea, beyond the Jordan, and from the vicinity of Tyre and Sidon a great multitude heard of all that Jesus was doing and came to Him.

(3) Jesus told His disciples that a boat should stand ready for Him because of the multitude, so that they might not crowd Him, (4) for

He had healed many with the result that all those who had afflictions pressed about Him in order to touch Him.

(5) Whenever the unclean spirits beheld Jesus they would fall down before Him and cry out, "You are the Son of God!"

(6) Jesus healed all those who came to Him (7) and warned them not to make Him known (8) in order that what was spoken through Isaiah the Prophet might be fulfilled.

(9) "Behold, My Servant whom I have chosen, My beloved in whom My soul is well-pleased! I will put My Spirit upon Him and He shall proclaim justice to the Gentiles.

(10) "He will not quarrel nor cry out, nor will any one hear His voice in the streets.

(11) "A battered reed He will not break off and a smoldering wick He will not put out until He leads justice to victory.

(12) "And in His name the Gentiles will hope."

Notes: There is no evidence that Jesus was ever in Tyre or Sidon or even in any part of Syria, although that part of Syria once comprised part of the promised land of the Israelites. There is no evidence that He was ever in Idumea either, yet His fame had spread to all those outlying areas and people from those places were coming to Him to be healed of whatever ailments they had. Also, it must be noted that most of the people from Tyre and Sidon and Idumea would have been Gentiles, although some of them may have been Jews living in those regions.

The prophecy quoted is from Isaiah 41:1-4 and, of course, referred to the coming of the Messiah.

A reed is a very fragile plant and is easily broken. It is used here as a simile for the poor and downtrodden people. The sense in which it is used is that the Messiah will not add to the burdens of the weak and fragile people as most conquerors do.

A smoldering wick refers to the wick of a lamp which continues to smolder after the lamp has run out of oil. The flame of such a wick is also a very fragile thing and also refers to the weak and downtrodden people of the world. The Messiah would not quench that flame but would nurture it.

The last part of the quotation from Isaiah was to confirm the fact that salvation through the Messiah was for the whole world, both Jews and Gentiles, and everyone who would obey His commandments.

49 The Twelve Apostles Selected

(Matt. 10:2-4; Mark 3:13-19; Luke 6:12-16)

(1) It was at this time that Jesus went off to the mountain to pray and He spent the whole night in prayer to God. (2) When day came He summoned those disciples whom He Himself wanted and they came to Him. (3) He appointed twelve of them, whom He also named as apostles, that they might be with Him and that He might send them out to preach (4) and to have authority to cast out the demons. (5) Now the names of the twelve apostles are: the first, Simon, whom Jesus also called Peter; Andrew his brother; (6) James, the son of Zebedee; John the brother of James (to them He gave the name "Boanerges," which means "Sons of Thunder"); (7) Philip; Bartholomew; Thomas; Matthew the tax-gatherer; James the son of Alphaeus; Thaddeus (also known as Judas), the son of James; (8) Simon the Cananaean (also called the Zealot); and Judas Iscariot, the one who later betrayed Jesus.

Notes: The mountain to which Jesus went to pray is not identified, but it is probably the same hill or mountain on which He sat to deliver His Sermon on the Mount, as that sermon followed closely in time after the events related here.

Wouldn't it be interesting and inspiring to know exactly what Jesus and His Father said to each other on this and similar occasions? The conversations between Jesus and His Father probably would not have been anything like the same type of communication that a mortal would have in like circumstances. When mortals pray, it's what would be called a unilateral, or one-sided, conversation. We speak to God and hope He hears us. We hope that our hearts are right and our lives are such that He will hear us. We can't testify that He does hear our every prayer. We can only believe that He does. Thinking back, it seems that at some of the times when I was most anxious for God to hear me and to answer my prayer positively that the very thing about which I was praying was what was keeping God from hearing me. That is, I'm so busy thinking about my problem that I'm not giving proper attention to my prayer.

The prayer of Jesus when He prayed all night to God was probably like a conversation between a father and son. The scriptures don't say what that conversation was about, but the implication is that it was concerning the twelve men who would shortly be chosen to be apostles. Perhaps they were discussing the different qualities that different ones of the disciples possessed and their fitness to be an apostle. Perhaps more than the twelve were considered and then their number was narrowed down to those who were eventually chosen.

The twelve men who were chosen to be apostles are sometimes referred to as the twelve disciples and sometimes as the twelve apostles. These twelve were both disciples and apostles. Many, many people were disciples of Jesus but only the twelve, at that time, were apostles. In the Greek language disciples are pupils or learners while apostles means those sent out, in this instance, the men sent out to preach and teach and having the power to heal and perform other miracles.

The twelve apostles were: Peter and Andrew; James and John, the sons of Zebedee; Philip; Bartholomew, meaning son of Tolomai, and named Nathaniel; Thomas, also called Didymus; James, the son of Alphaeus; Judas or Thaddaeus, the son of James; Simon, also called the Cananaean; Simon Zelotes, or Simon the Zealot; and Judas Iscariot. Iscariot was not the surname of Judas but indicated that he was from the town of Kerioth. In the same way, Magdalene was not Mary's surname but only indicated that she was from the town of Magdala.

50 The Sermon on the Mount

A. Preparation and Beginning (Matt. 5:1-2; Luke 6:17-20a)

(1) Jesus descended with the apostles and stood on a level place. There was a great multitude of His disciples and a great throng of people from all Judea and Jerusalem and the coastal region of Tyre and Sidon (2) who had come to hear Him and to be healed of their diseases. Those who were troubled with unclean spirits were also being cured.

(3) All the multitude were trying to touch Jesus for power was coming from Him and healing them all.

(4) Jesus withdrew from the midst of the multitude up on the side of the mountain and after He sat down His disciples came to Him. (5) Turning His gaze on His disciples Jesus opened His mouth and began to teach them.

Notes: This scripture states that there were three classes of people with Jesus-apostles, disciples and people from Judea, Jerusalem and the coastal region of Tyre and Sidon. It further states that when Jesus withdrew from the crowd of people and went up on the side of the mountain that His *disciples* came to Him. It's unclear from the language of the passage whether only the disciples (which would include the apostles) came to Jesus or if the whole multitude of people including the "great throng of people" also followed Him to the side of the mountain and heard the sermon. It seems, though, from the language of the passage that only the disciples heard the sermon.

When "the Sermon on the Mount" is mentioned most people think only of the account beginning in chapter 5 of Matthew, but there are two accounts, the one in Matthew and another in Luke's Gospel. Matthew's account is much longer than Luke's, there being one hundred seven verses in Matthew's account compared to only thirty verses in Luke's account. The language of Matthew is much more beautiful than that in Luke. It is from Luke's account that some scholars deduce that Luke may have been a slave at one time, citing as their reason the passage in Luke 6:24-26 and noting that there is a feeling of bitterness in Luke's writing that isn't present in Matthew's. Those verses are not included in Matthew's Gospel. Luke's account has little of the beauty of language that is in Matthew's and is much harsher in its phrasing.

B. *The Beatitudes* (Matt. 5:3-12; Luke 6:20b-26)

(6) "Blessed are the poor in spirit for theirs is the kingdom of heaven.

(7) "Blessed are those who weep and mourn for they shall laugh and be comforted.

(8) "Blessed are the humble for they shall inherit the earth.

(9) "Blessed are those who hunger and thirst for righteousness for they shall be satisfied.

(10) "Blessed are the merciful for they shall receive mercy.

(11) "Blessed are the pure in heart for they shall see God.

(12) "Blessed are the peacemakers for they shall be called sons of God.

(13) "Blessed are those who have been persecuted because of their righteousness for theirs is the kingdom of heaven.

(14) "Blessed are you when men hate you and revile you and persecute you and ostracize you and heap insults and say all kinds of evil against you and spurn your name as evil on account of Me. (15) Rejoice and be glad in that day and leap for joy for your reward in heaven is great, for so their fathers persecuted the prophets who were before you.

(16) "But woe to you when all men speak well of you for in the same way their fathers used to treat the false prophets. (17) And woe to you who are rich for you are receiving your comfort in full. (18) Woe to you who are well-fed now for you shall be hungry. Woe to you who laugh now for you shall mourn and weep.

Notes: The word "bless'd" or "bless-ed" is translated from the Greek word *makarios* (mak-ar'-ee-os). It means fortunate, well off, or happy. This is not the same Greek word which was used in Matthew 14:19 concerning the blessing of the five loaves or in Matthew 26:26 in which Jesus blessed the bread at the time of the last supper. That word is "eulogeo" (you-log-eh'-o), which means to thank or invoke a benediction upon, to praise.

Sometimes statements are made which sound good when spoken but are not in accordance with what the scripture actually says. In a Bible class some years ago, the teacher, a former elder in another congregation, made the statement that a person couldn't be saved unless he was everything which was covered by *all* the beatitudes. But two of the beatitudes are ones over which a person has no control and another in which a person must have an opportunity before he can fulfill its requirements. The two over which a person has no control are those about being persecuted because of their righteousness and about being hated and reviled. The other one is about being a peacemaker. A person may desire to be a peacemaker but never have the opportunity to do so.

The last three verses above are those from Luke and which do not appear in the Gospel of Matthew.

C. *Instruction and Duties* (Matt. 5:13-16; Mark 4:21-23; Luke 8:16-18, 11:33)

(19) "You are the salt of the earth, but if the salt has become tasteless how will it be made salty again? It is good for nothing anymore except to be thrown out and trampled underfoot by men.

(20) "You are the light of the world. A city set on a hill cannot be hidden. (21) Men do not light a lamp and put it in a secret place or under the peck measure but put it on the lampstand and it gives light to all who are in the house. (22) Nothing is hidden that shall not become evident nor anything secret that shall not be known and come to light. Let your light shine before men in such a way that they may see your good works and glorify your Father who is in heaven. If anyone has ears to hear let him hear."

Notes: Salt was used as a condiment and as a preservative. Without the taste, it is useless for either purpose. This is a parable of sorts in which Jesus is comparing the people who believe and obey His commandments, Christians, and their activities to the purpose for which salt is used. It is through people that a taste is created for a greater knowledge of the gospel, and it is through people that the purity of the gospel is preserved. Regardless of the fact that a far greater number of people who claim to be Christians do not consider the Bible to be authoritative, the Bible still remains the only guide to the will of God.

D. *Relations to Old Testament and Tradition* (Matt. 5:17-48; Luke 6:27-30, 32-36, 12:57-59, 16:18)

(23) "Do not think that I came to abolish the Law or the Prophets. I did not come to abolish but to fulfill. (24) Truly I say to you, until heaven and earth pass away not the smallest letter or stroke shall pass away from the Law until all is accomplished. (25) Whoever then breaks one of the least of these commandments, and so teaches others, shall be

called least in the kingdom of heaven; but whoever keeps and teaches them shall be called great in the kingdom of heaven. (26) I say to you, unless your righteousness surpasses that of the scribes and Pharisees you shall not enter the kingdom of heaven.

(27) "You have heard that the ancients were told, 'You shall not commit murder' and 'Whoever commits murder shall be liable to the court.' (28) But I say to you that everyone who is angry with his brother shall be guilty before the court and whoever shall say to his brother, 'Raca (good-for-nothing),' shall be guilty before the supreme court and whoever shall say, 'You fool,' shall be in danger of the hell of fire. (29) If therefore you are presenting your offering at the altar and there remember that your brother has something against you (30) leave your offering there before the altar and go your way. First be reconciled to your brother and then come and present your offering. (31) And why do you not even on your own initiative judge what is right?

(32) "Make friends quickly with your opponent at law in an effort to settle with him while you are with him on the way in order that your opponent may not deliver you to the judge and the judge deliver you to the officer and you be thrown into prison. (33) Truly I say to you, you shall not come out of there until you have paid the last farthing.

(34) "You have heard that it was said, 'You shall not commit adultery'; (35) but I say to you that everyone who looks on a woman to lust for her has committed adultery with her already in his heart. (36) If your right eye makes you stumble tear it out and throw it from you for it is better for you that one of the parts of your body perish than for your whole body to go into hell. (37) If your right hand makes you stumble cut it off and throw it from you for it is better for you that one of the parts of your body perish than for your whole body to go into hell.

(38) "It was said, 'Whoever divorces his wife shall give her a certificate of dismissal' (39) but I say to you that everyone who divorces his wife, except for the cause of unchastity, and marries another commits adultery. He also makes her whom he divorced commit adultery if she marries again. And whoever marries a divorced woman commits adultery.

(40) "Again, you have heard that the ancients were told, 'You shall not make false vows but shall fulfill your vows to the Lord.' (41) But

I say to you, make no oath at all, either by heaven for it is the throne of God, (42) or by the earth for it is the footstool of His feet, or by Jerusalem for it is the city of the great King. (43) Nor shall you make an oath by your head for you cannot make one hair white or black. (44) But let your statement be, 'Yes, yes' or 'No, no,' for anything beyond these is of evil.

(45) "You have heard that it was said, 'An eye for an eye and a tooth for a tooth,' (46) but I say to you, do not resist him who is evil. If someone strikes you on your right cheek turn and offer him the other also. (47) If any one wants to sue you and take your shirt let him have your coat also. (48) If any one shall force you to go one mile with him go with him two. (49) Give to whoever asks of you and do not turn away from him who wants to borrow from you but rather if anyone borrows what is yours do not demand it back.

(50) "You have heard that it was said, 'You shall love your neighbor and hate your enemy.' (51) But I say to you who hear, love your enemies, do good to those who hate you, (52) bless those who curse you, pray for those who persecute you (53) in order that you may be sons of your Father who is in heaven for He causes His sun to rise on the evil and the good and sends rain on the righteous and the unrighteous. (54) If you love those who love you what credit is that to you? Even the sinners and tax-gatherers love those who love them. (55) And if you greet your brothers only what do you do more than others do? Do not even the Gentiles do the same? (56) If you do good only to those who do good to you what credit is that to you? Even sinners do the same thing. (57) If you lend to those from whom you expect to receive what credit is that to you? Even sinners lend to sinners in order to receive back the same amount.

(58) "But love your enemies and do good. Lend expecting nothing in return and your reward will be great (59) and you will be sons of the Most High, for He Himself is kind to the ungrateful and evil. (60) Be merciful just as your Father is merciful. (61) Therefore you are to be perfect as your heavenly Father is perfect."

Notes: The sect of the Pharisees divided the Old Testament Laws into two categories-those of great importance and those of lesser importance.

In order to keep some of their traditions, which they considered to be as binding on them as the Law, they would break the lesser laws and teach that it was all right to do so. Jesus taught that such thinking was not right and that the people who taught such things, the scribes and Pharisees, would not enter the kingdom of heaven. He also taught that people who weren't more righteous than the scribes and Pharisees would not enter the kingdom of heaven either.

In the views of biblical scholars and differing religious organizations, there are great differences of opinions as to the meaning of what Jesus said about divorce and remarriage.

Most denominations accept divorce for any reason and remarriage after an unscriptural divorce as a matter of little importance. The Catholic Church differs from most Protestant denominations in that their rules for divorce and remarriage are much stricter. They are sometimes able to get around their rules, however, by granting annulments when their rules will not allow divorces. Generally speaking, members of some fundamentalist churches are much more conservative in their treatment of the issue of divorce and remarriage than most denominational churches. There are times, though, when the elders or men of the congregation are too timid to enforce their beliefs on the members of their flocks and allow unscriptural marriages to exist without any form of discipline being enforced.

The Romans had a rule that permitted any of their soldiers to compel any person they chose to carry their baggage for one mile, but they could not under the law compel anyone to carry it further than that. In the Roman Empire, a mile was measured as one thousand six hundred twenty (1,620) yards as compared to one thousand seven hundred sixty (1,760) yards for a statute mile as measured in this country. The Roman mile as walked off by the soldiers was not measured in yards, however, but was supposed to be equal to one thousand (1,000) paces, a considerably shorter distance.

The teaching of Jesus concerning revenge is very difficult for some people to accept and to abide by. Well-known historical feuds such as that between the Hatfields and McCoys and the range war between cattlemen and sheepmen on the western frontier probably started that way. There was a slight, and the person slighted was determined to get even, leading to a full-scale war between the factions.

The original rendering of "hell fire" as used regarding the calling of someone a fool was "gehenna of fire," gehenna meaning "valley of Hinnom." That valley was just south of the city of Jerusalem. It was said to have originally been a very pleasant little valley until in a time of idolatry, it was where an idol of the false god Moloch was worshiped and to whom children were sacrificed. After the return of the Jews from captivity, the place was held in such low esteem that it became a garbage dump. Every kind of waste including dead carcasses was dumped there, and of a necessity, fires were kept burning continuously. It was an extremely loathsome sight to everyone in and around Jerusalem and the meaning of what Jesus said would have been clear to all of them. Anyone consigned to that place would have been extremely miserable. This did not refer to the final resting place of those who die without God.

The opponent or adversary about which Jesus spoke did not refer to God as some people would have us believe nor is it possible to negotiate salvation with God after death as those same people advocate.

Concerning the eye and right hand that offend, I hardly think Jesus expected or intended that to be taken literally. Rather, He meant that if what we cherish most will keep us out of heaven, then we must get rid of that cherished item, whatever it is. Some of the turmoil a well-known church is experiencing in regard to the ungodly sexual appetites of some of their leaders is a prime example.

E. About Almsgiving, Prayer, and Fasting (Matt. 6:1-18; Luke 11:2-4)

(62) "Beware of practicing your righteousness in order to be seen by men otherwise you have no reward with your Father who is in heaven. (63) Therefore when you give alms do not do as the hypocrites do sounding a trumpet before you in the synagogue and in the streets so that you will be honored by men. Truly I say to you, they have their reward in full. (64) But when you give alms do not let your left hand know what your right hand is doing (65) so that your alms may be in secret, and your Father who sees in secret will repay you.

(66) "When you pray you are not to be as the hypocrites, for they love to stand and pray in the synagogues and on the street corners in

order to be seen by men. Truly I say to you, they have their reward in full. (67) But when you pray go into your inner room, and when you have shut the door, pray to your Father who is in secret and your Father who sees in secret will repay you. (68) When you are praying do not use meaningless repetitions as the Gentiles do for they suppose that they will be heard for their many words. (69) Therefore do not be like them, for your Father knows what you need before you ask Him. (70) When you pray, pray then in this way: Our Father who is in heaven, hallowed is Your name. (71) Your kingdom come. Your will be done on earth as it is in heaven. (72) Give us this day and every day our daily bread. (73) Forgive us our sins and our debts as we also forgive our debtors. (74) Do not lead us into temptation, but deliver us from evil, for Thine is the kingdom and the power and the glory forever. Amen. (75) For if you forgive men for their transgressions your heavenly Father will also forgive you. (76) But if you do not forgive men then your Father will not forgive your transgressions.

(77) "Whenever you fast do not put on a gloomy face as the hypocrites do, for they neglect their appearance in order to be seen fasting by men. Truly I say to you, they have their reward in full. (78) But you, when you fast anoint your head and wash your face (79) so that you may not be seen fasting by men but only by your Father who is in secret and your Father who sees in secret will repay you."

Notes: There are people, sad to say, who use their church membership as a business advantage. In one congregation of which I knew, the members were urged to patronize a certain automobile dealer because he was a member of that church.

Although his name was on the membership roll, he was seldom if ever seen at any service. Jesus said, in essence, that whatever advantage he received in this life because of his name being on the church roll, he would receive no reward in heaven for it having been there.

The prayer that Jesus gave as an example of how people should pray to God is most often called "the Lord's Prayer." It's true that Jesus spoke those words to His disciples, but as far as the scriptures record, Jesus never prayed that prayer. In that sense, it was not the Lord's Prayer, but was to be used as a model for the prayers of the disciples.

For that reason it's sometimes, and more accurately, called "the model prayer" rather than "the Lord's Prayer." Further, it is not a model for the prayers of Christians, but only for the disciples *before* the coming of the kingdom of heaven which occurred when Peter preached that first gospel sermon on the day of Pentecost. Prayers of Christians are to be in the name of Jesus.

In the New Testament record, fasting is mentioned a number of times and several times Paul stated that he had fasted. People were said to have contemplated a problem by prayer and fasting, but nowhere in the scriptures are Christians instructed to fast or is there any commandment to the effect that fasting is required of any Christian. The Jews often fasted ritualistically, but that ritual was not carried over into Christianity. Prayer is very comforting and sometimes beneficial, but nowhere is anyone commanded to fast.

F. Contrasting Security of Heavenly Treasures with Earthly Anxieties (Matt. 6:19-34; Luke 11:34-36, 12:22-34)

(80) "Do not lay up for yourselves treasures upon earth where moth and rust destroy and where thieves break in and steal. (81) But lay up for yourselves treasures in heaven where neither moth nor rust destroys and where thieves do not break in or steal. (82) Sell your possessions and give to charity. Make yourselves purses which do not wear out, an unfailing treasure in heaven, for where your treasure is there your heart will be also.

(83) "The lamp of the body is the eye so if your eye is clear your whole body will be full of light. But if your eye is bad your whole body will be full of darkness. Then watch out that the light that is in you may not be darkness. (84) If your whole body is full of light with no dark part in it, it shall be wholly illumined as when the lamp illumines you with its rays.

(85) "No one can serve two masters for either he will hate one and love the other or he will hold to one and despise the other. You cannot serve God and riches. (86) For this reason I say to you, do not be anxious for your life as to what you shall eat or what you shall drink, nor for your body as to what you shall wear, for life is more than food and the body than clothing. (87) Consider the birds of the air, how they do not sow

nor reap nor gather into barns and storehouses, and yet your heavenly Father feeds them. Are you not worth more than they? (88) Which of you by being anxious can add a single cubit to his life's span? (89) Then if you cannot do even such a little thing, why are you anxious about other matters? (90) Why are you anxious about clothing? Consider the lilies and how they grow. They neither toil nor spin but I tell you that even Solomon in all his glory did not clothe himself like one of these. (91) If God so arrays the grass of the field which is alive today and tomorrow is thrown into the furnace, will He not do much more for you, 0 you of little faith? (92) Do not be anxious then about what you are to eat or what you will drink and with what you will clothe yourselves. (93) All these things the Gentiles eagerly seek after but your heavenly Father knows that you need all these things. (94) Seek first His kingdom and His righteousness and all these things shall be added to you.

(95) Do not be anxious about tomorrow for tomorrow will care for itself. Each day has enough trouble of its own. (96) Do not be afraid, little flock, for your Father has chosen gladly to give you the kingdom."

Notes: In the days when Jesus walked the earth life, of course, was much simpler than it is now. Modern men and women must think more and plan more in order to feed and dress and house themselves and their families. Jesus wasn't saying that we shouldn't do that. He was saying that we should not put undue emphasis on that part of our lives. A person cannot neglect his spiritual life in order to accumulate the material things of the world. He must have faith that God will help him get the things that are needed. Nor can a person spend all his time amassing wealth, buying fancy clothes and expensive homes and powerful automobiles, going nightclubbing, marrying and divorcing and remarrying, and then say to the world, "Oh, by the way, in case you can't tell it by my actions, I'm a Christian." It just doesn't work that way.

G. *Concerning Judging Others* (Matt. 7:1-6; Mark 4:24-25; Luke 6:37-42)
(97) "Do not pass judgment and you will not be judged; do not condemn and you shall not be condemned; pardon and you will be pardoned. (98) Give and it will be given to you-good measure, pressed down, shaken together, running over, they will pour into your lap. (99)

Take care what you listen to for in the way you judge you will be judged, and by your standard of measure it shall be measured to you, (100) and more will be given to you. More will be given to him who has and even what he has will be taken away from him who has not.

(101) "A blind man cannot guide a blind man or they will both fall into a pit. (102) A pupil is not above his teacher but everyone, after he has been fully trained, will be like his teacher.

(103) "Why do you look at the speck in your brother's eye but do not notice the log that is in your own eye? (104) Or how can you say to your brother, 'Brother, let me take out the speck that is in your eye,' when you yourself do not see the log that is in your own eye? You hypocrite, first take the log out of your own eye and then you will see clearly to take out the speck that is in your brother's eye.

(105) "Do not give what is holy to dogs, and do not throw your pearls before swine lest they trample them under their feet and turn and tear you to pieces.

Notes: Judging others is one of the habits that many of us have that we should break. I don't mean that if we see a brother committing a sin, we shouldn't remind him that what he's doing is a sin. Some of those people to whom we point out their sins will accuse us of judging them, though, and claim that by judging them we are also sinning. But pointing out a person's sin isn't judging-that's what the scriptures command us to do as in Galatians 6:1. We are to point out the sins of others so that they can be restored to full fellowship with other Christians.

H. Concerning Prayer (Matt. 7:7-11; Luke 11:9-13)

(106) "And I say to you, ask and it shall be given to you; seek and you shall find; knock and it shall be opened to you.

(107) Every one who asks receives, and he who seeks finds, and to him who knocks it shall be opened.

(108) "What man is there among you who when his son shall ask him for a loaf will give him a stone? (109) Or suppose one of you fathers is asked by his son for a fish the father will not give him a snake instead. Or if he is asked for an egg, he will not give his son a scorpion. (110) Then if you, being evil, know how to give good gifts to your children

shall not your Father who is in heaven give the Holy Spirit and much more of what is good to those who ask Him?

Notes: The old biblical writers tell of a white scorpion that, when rolled up, would resemble an egg. The scorpion to which Jesus referred here is about two to three inches long, of the animal grouping called Arachnids, of which spiders are also members. This scorpion, like all scorpions, has a stinger in its tail. A scorpion is similar in appearance to a lobster, but, of course, is much smaller. The white scorpion of Judea has a sting, it is said, about as severe as that of a wasp. Some scorpions, such as those in the western part of the United States, have a sting which hurts much more and is much more dangerous.

I. The Golden Rule (Matt. 7:12; Luke 6:31)

(111) "Treat others and do for them the same way that you would have them treat you and do for you for this is the Law and the Prophets."

Notes: This is probably, with the possible exception of John 3:16, the best known passage in the entire Bible. People who know nothing else about the Bible are familiar with this statement and know that it comes from the Bible. Usually the way it is expressed is, "Do unto others as you would have them do unto you." But that particular language is not used in any of the more accurate versions of the Bible. In the KJV, Luke 6:31 reads, "And as ye would that men should do to you, do ye also to them likewise," and Matthew 7:12 reads, "Therefore all things whatsoever ye would that men should do to you, do ye even so to them; for this is the law and the prophets."

J. Broad and Narrow Ways and False Prophets (Matt. 7:13-23; Luke 6:43-45)

(112) "Enter by the narrow gate for the gate is wide and the way is broad that leads to destruction and there are many who enter by it. (113) The gate is small and the way is narrow that leads to life and there are few who find it.

(114) "Beware of the false prophets who come to you in sheep's clothing but inwardly are ravenous wolves. (115) You will know them

by their fruits for each tree is known by its own fruit. (116) Men do not gather figs from thorn bushes nor do they pick grapes from a briar bush. (117) Also, every good tree bears good fruit, but the corrupt tree bears bad fruit. (118) A good tree cannot produce bad fruit nor can a corrupt tree produce good fruit. (119) Every tree that does not bear good fruit is cut down and thrown into the fire, (120) so then, you will know them by their fruits. (121) The good man out of the good treasure of his heart brings forth what is good, and the evil man out of an evil heart brings forth what is evil, for the mouth speaks from that which fills the heart.

(122) "Not every one who says to Me, 'Lord, Lord,' will enter the kingdom of heaven but only those who do the will of My Father who is in heaven. (123) Many will say to Me in that day, 'Lord, Lord, did we not prophesy in Your name and in Your name cast out demons and in Your name perform many miracles?' (124) And then I will declare to them, 'I never knew you. Depart from Me, you who practice lawlessness.'"

Notes: There are about five hundred or so different churches whose members call themselves Christians. All these churches exist because men try to make their church what they want it to be, instead of trying to get into the one church which God established and to be what God wants them to be.

People want to believe that God doesn't mean what He said. They want to think that whatever they choose to believe has God's approval. What Jesus said in this passage should be enough to convince them otherwise.

K. The Two Builders and the Conclusion (Matt. 7:24-29; Luke 6:46-49)

(125) "Why do you call Me. 'Lord, Lord,' and do not what I say? (126) Everyone who hears these words of Mine and acts upon them may be compared to a wise man who, when building his house, dug deep and laid a foundation upon the rock. (127) When the rain descended and the floods came and the winds blew and burst against that house it did not fall for it had been founded upon the rock. (128) But everyone who hears these words of Mine and does not act upon them will be like a foolish man who built his house upon sand without any foundation.

(129) When the rain descended and the floods came and the winds blew and burst against that house it fell, and great was the ruin of that house." (130) The result was that when Jesus had finished these words the multitudes were amazed at His teaching, (131) for He was teaching them as one having authority and not as their scribes.

Notes: In this passage, Jesus is speaking expressly to those people who think that all they have to do to be saved is to believe that God and His Son exist. It shows clearly that they are wrong in believing that and that belief alone is not enough, that a person has to act on those beliefs in order to be saved.

51 Jesus Heals the Centurion's Servant

(Matt. 8:1, 5-13; Luke 7:1-10)

(1) When Jesus had completed all his discourse in the hearing of the people He came down from the mountain and went to Capernaum, and great multitudes followed Him. (2) When Jesus had entered Capernaum there came word to Jesus of a certain centurion who had a slave who was very dear to him and this slave was sick and at the point of death. (3) The centurion had heard of Jesus and sent Jewish elders with a message to Jesus asking Him to save the life of the slave, asking, "Sir, my servant is lying paralyzed at home, suffering great pain."

(4) The Jewish elders earnestly entreated Jesus, saying, "He is worthy for You to grant this to him for he loves our nation, and it was he who built us our synagogue."

(5) Jesus said to them, "I will come and heal him."

(6) Now Jesus started on His way with them, and when He was already not far from the house the centurion sent friends to say to Him, "Lord, do not trouble Yourself further for I am not fit for You to come under my roof. (7) For this reason I did not even consider myself worthy to come to You, but just say the word and my servant will be healed. (8) For indeed, I am a man under authority with soldiers under me. I say to this one, 'Go!' and he goes, and to another, 'Come!' and he comes, and to my slave, 'Do this!' and he does it."

139

(9) Now when Jesus heard this He marveled and turned and said to the multitude that was following Him, "Truly I say to you, I have not found such great faith with anyone in Israel.

(10) I say to you that many shall come from east and west and recline at table with Abraham, and Isaac, and Jacob in the kingdom of heaven (11) but the sons of the kingdom shall be cast out into outer darkness and in that place there shall be weeping and gnashing of teeth."

(12) Jesus said to the friends of the centurion, "Go your way. It has been done for him as he has believed."

(13) When the friends of the centurion returned to the house they found that the slave was in good health having been healed that same hour.

Notes: There is an account of this incident in both Matthew's Gospel and Luke's Gospel. There are some differences in the two accounts, causing some scholars to believe that there are two different incidents involving two different centurions. Luke states that the centurion sent the Jewish elders to Jesus to request that He heal the centurion's servant, but Matthew says that the centurion approached Jesus himself and asked for Him to heal the slave. It is difficult to believe that there could have been two different Roman centurions both of whom had a beloved servant (or slave) who was sick unto death and that both centurions used exactly the same words in requesting that the servant be healed and that Jesus used exactly the same words in His reply. The differences in the two accounts could have been caused because the two men who reported it saw the incident from two different perspectives. Or it could have been that the centurion did personally speak to Jesus and the Jewish elders confirmed to Jesus that he, the centurion, was worthy of having his request fulfilled. Further, Matthew may have been present and saw exactly what happened, whereas it is highly unlikely that Luke was there, but that he received his information from some other source.

What the centurion said indicated that he considered himself to be very much inferior to Jesus. When he said that he too was a man with authority, he was not comparing himself to Jesus in that respect, but rather, he was drawing a parallel. He was saying in effect that although he had authority over some men, he was under the authority of others, whereas Jesus had no earthly superior and His authority extended over even disease, demons and death.

As Job is often cited as an exemplar of patience, Jesus presented this Roman centurion to the Jews as an exemplar of faith. Contrary to the way Jews in general felt toward Romans, these Jews (in or near Capernaum) had great respect for this Roman because he loved the Jewish nation and had built their synagogue for them. If the Jews had not had such great respect for this centurion they probably would have resented what Jesus said about him and about the Jews. Or perhaps they did resent it but that fact wasn't recorded. Jesus said that people would come from the east and the west, Gentiles, to be with the patriarchs Abraham, Isaac and Jacob, and that some of the Jews would not be heirs to the kingdom of heaven. Some (or perhaps all) of the Jews believed that because they were Jews and descendants of Abraham, Isaac, and Jacob, their place in the kingdom of heaven was assured.

The expression "recline at table" was a literal reference to the manner of eating a meal at that time. The table on which the food was placed was low to the floor and the diners lay down beside it, propped up on pillows or their elbows, to eat.

Most of the world with which the Jews were familiar was under the military control of the Roman Empire. Most of the Roman officers with which the Jews came into contact were centurions, each a commander over one hundred soldiers. Most of the centurions about which we read in the Bible seem to have been friendly, or at least not hostile, to the Jews. This is the first chronologically about which we can read. Another was the one who, upon watching Jesus die on the cross, said of Him, "Surely this was the Son of God!" And of course, there was Cornelius. We don't know about the centurion who watched Jesus die, but this one and Cornelius both did much good for the Jews. A fourth centurion about which we read in the Bible was the one who was escorting Paul to Rome. He thought very highly of Paul and prevented the soldiers in his command from killing Paul and the other prisoners to make sure that none of them escaped.

52 Jesus Raises the Widow's Son at Nain (Luke 7:11- 17)

(1) Soon afterwards Jesus and His disciples went to a city called Nain and they were accompanied by a large multitude. (2) Now as Jesus approached the gate of the city, a dead man, the only son of his mother who was a widow, was being carried out, and a sizeable crowd from the city was with her. (3) When the Lord saw the widow He felt compassion for her and said to her, "Do not weep." (4) Then Jesus went up and touched the coffin and the bearers came to a halt. Jesus said, "Young man, I say to you, arise!" (5) And the dead man sat up and began to speak, and Jesus gave him back to his mother. (6) Fear gripped all the people and they began glorifying God, saying, "A great prophet has arisen among us!" and, "God has visited His people!" (7) This report concerning Jesus went out all over Judea and in all the surrounding district.

Notes: The city of Nain is southwest of the sea of Galilee about twenty-two or twenty-three miles from Capernaum and about two miles from Mount Tabor. This is the only place in the Bible in which the town of Nain is mentioned. It still exists but is much smaller than it was at one time. It is inhabited, or was before the state of Israel was established, by Jews, Christians, and Muslims.

The word "fear" used here is translated from the Greek word *phobos* and means to be put into great fear or great terror. It is certainly understandable that such an action as raising up a dead person would cause fear in the people and also that the news of that event would spread quickly to the far corners of the area.

53 John the Baptist Inquires of Jesus

(Matt. 11:2-19; Luke 7:18-35)

(1) Now the disciples of John reported to him all the things that Jesus was doing. (2) John was in prison when he heard of these works of Christ and, summoning two of his disciples, he sent them to Jesus

(3) telling them to ask Him, "Are You the One who is coming or shall we look for someone else?"

(4) When these men had come to Jesus they said, "John the Baptist has sent us to You, saying, 'Are You the One who is coming or shall we look for someone else?'" (5) At that very time Jesus cured many people of diseases and afflictions and evil spirits, and He granted sight to many who were blind.

(6) Jesus said to John's disciples, "Go and report to John the things which you hear and see: (7) the blind receive sight and the lame walk, the lepers are cleansed and the deaf hear, and the dead are raised up, and the poor have the gospel preached to them. (8) Blessed is he who keeps from stumbling over Me."

(9) When the messengers of John had left, Jesus began to speak to the multitude about John, "What did you go out into the wilderness to look at, a reed shaken by the wind? (10) But what did you go out to see, a man dressed in soft clothing? Look, those who dress in soft clothing and live in luxury are found in royal palaces. (11) But what did you go out to see, a prophet? Yes, I tell you, and one who is more than a prophet.

(12) This is the one about whom it was written, 'I sent My messenger before Your face, who will prepare Your way before You.' (13) Truly I say to you, among those born of women there has not arisen anyone greater than John the Baptist, yet he who is least in the kingdom of God is greater than he. (14) From the days of John the Baptist until now the kingdom of heaven suffers violence and violent men take it by force. (15) For all the prophets and the Law prophesied until John. (16) If you care to accept it, he himself is Elijah who was to come. (17) He who has ears to hear, let him hear."

(18) When all the people and the tax-gatherers heard this they acknowledged God's justice, having been baptized with the baptism of John. (19) But the Pharisees and the lawyers rejected God's purpose for themselves, not having been baptized by John.

(20) Jesus continued, "To what then shall I compare the men of this generation and what are they like? (21) They are like children who sit in the market place and call to one another, and they say, 'We played the flute for you and you did not dance, we sang a dirge and you did not weep.' (22) For John the Baptist has come eating no bread and

drinking no wine and you say, 'He has a demon!' (23) The Son of Man has come eating and drinking and you say, 'Look, a gluttonous man and a drunkard, a friend of tax-gatherers and sinners!' Yet wisdom is vindicated by all her deeds."

Notes: A person might wonder why John sent men to Jesus to find out if He was truly the person whose coming John had been sent to announce to the world. Was he doubting Jesus? Surely he had heard, like everyone else in Galilee and Judea, about all the things that Jesus had done and was doing. But John was in prison, and in those days, prisoners didn't enjoy the country estate atmosphere that prisoners have in this country today. Surely he could be excused for feeling low and wanting to be assured that his mission in life had been accomplished. It's possible that most Christians have some moments of doubt or wonder. Certainly, the apostles had their doubts while the body of Jesus lay in a tomb, and they weren't convinced until they saw for themselves that Jesus had really been raised from the dead.

The answer that Jesus sent to John was to remind John of the prophecies of Isaiah. Isaiah 35:5-6 says, "The eyes of the blind will be opened, and the ears of the deaf will be unstopped. Then the lame will leap like a deer, and the tongue of the dumb will shout for joy." And Isaiah 61:1, "The Spirit of the Lord God is upon me, because the Lord has anointed me to bring good news to the afflicted; He has sent me to bind up the brokenhearted, to proclaim liberty to captives, and freedom to prisoners..."

The Pharisees and the lawyers, in rejecting God's purpose for them, were not only rejecting John as a proclaimer of the good news about the coming of the Messiah, but they were rejecting the counsel of God that was given through John.

54 The Seventy Sent Out and Return, Jesus Upbraids Favored Cities, and Prayer and Invitation

(Matt. 11:20-30; Luke 10:1-24)

(1) Now after this the Lord appointed seventy others and sent them two and two ahead of Him to every city and place where He Himself was going to come.

(2) Jesus said to the seventy, "The harvest is plentiful but the laborers are few; therefore beseech the Lord of the harvest to send out laborers into His harvest.

(3) "Go your way. Look, I send you out as lambs in the midst of wolves. (4) Carry no purse, no bag, no shoes, and greet no one on the way.

(5) "Before you enter any house say, 'Peace be to this house.' (6) And if a man of peace lives there your peace will rest upon him; but if not, it will return to you. (7) Stay in that house eating and drinking what they give you for the laborer is worthy of his wages. Do not keep moving from house to house.

(8) "Whatever city you enter, if they receive you, eat what is set before you, (9) and heal those in that city who are sick and say to them, 'The kingdom of God has come near to you.'

(10) "But whatever city you enter and they do not receive you, go out into the streets and say, (11) 'Even the dust of your city which clings to our feet we wipe off in protest against you. Yet be sure of this that the kingdom of God has come near.'

(12) I say to you, it will be more tolerable in that day for Sodom than for that city."

(13) Then Jesus began to reproach the cities in which most of His miracles were done because they did not repent. (14) "Woe to you, Chorazin! Woe to you, Bethsaida! For if the miracles had been performed in Tyre and Sidon which occurred in you they would have repented long ago sitting in sackcloth and ashes. (15) Nevertheless, I say to you, it will be more tolerable for Tyre and Sidon in the day of judgment than for you. (16) And you, Capernaum, will not be exalted to heaven. You shall descend to Hades, for if the miracles which were

done in you had been done in Sodom it would have remained to this day. (17) Nevertheless, I say to you that it shall be more tolerable for the land of Sodom in the day of Judgment than for you.

(18) "The one who listens to you listens to Me, and the one who rejects you rejects Me, and he who rejects Me rejects the One who sent Me."

(19) The seventy returned with joy saying, "Lord, even the demons are subject to us in Your name."

(20) Jesus said to them, "I was watching Satan fall from heaven like lightning. (21) Listen, I have given you authority to tread upon serpents and scorpions, and over all the power of the enemy, and nothing shall injure you. (22) Nevertheless, do not rejoice in this, that the spirits are subject to you, but rejoice that your names are recorded in heaven."

(23) At that time Jesus rejoiced greatly in the Holy Spirit and prayed, "I praise You, 0 Father, Lord of heaven and earth, that You did hide these things from the wise and intelligent and did reveal them to babes. (24) Yes, Father, for thus it was well pleasing in Your sight. (25) All things have been handed over to Me by My Father, and no one knows who the Son is except the Father nor does anyone know who the Father is except the Son and anyone to whom the Son wills to reveal Him.

(26) "Come to Me, all you who are weary and heavy-laden, and I will give you rest. (27) Take My yoke upon you and learn from Me, for I am gentle and humble in heart and you shall find rest for your souls. (28) My yoke is easy and My load is light."

(29) Turning to the disciples Jesus said privately, "Blessed are the eyes which see the things you see, (30) for I say to you that many prophets and kings wished to see the things which you see and did not see them, and to hear the things which you hear and did not hear them."

Notes: In regard to the number of men Jesus sent out, some manuscripts report that there were seventy and others that there were seventy-two. Whether or not the number of men sent out has any significance, or whether that number matters at all, is unclear. Seventy (or seventy-two) was perhaps only the number of men qualified to do the work that they were sent out to do.

The site of the city of Chorazin is now unknown. Ancient references place it on the shore of the Sea of Galilee about two miles from Capernaum. Too, the site of Bethsaida is no longer known for sure. Bethsaida was the home of Philip, Peter, and Andrew and, since Peter and Andrew were fishermen (we don't know about Philip), was probably also on the shore of the sea of Galilee. Philip the tetrarch enlarged the city of Bethsaida and changed its name to Julia in honor of Caesar's daughter.

Scholars point out the probable site of Capernaum but the city itself no longer exists. Jesus said that those three cities, Chorazin, Bethsaida, and Capernaum, are places in which great works had been performed. He did not say that the works performed there had been performed by Him, but they probably had been performed by Him although there is no record anywhere in the Bible of Jesus having performed any miracles in Chorazin. In fact, these two passages are the only places in the entire Bible where that city is mentioned.

Tyre and Sidon were very prosperous cities. They were port cities on the Mediterranean Sea in what was then Phoenicia. Both cities still exist. Tyre is still known by its ancient name and Sidon is now called Seide or Saide.

Jesus made His home in Capernaum during at least a part of the time during His earthly ministry, and He did perform many miracles there. The term "exalted unto heaven" didn't mean that the inhabitants of Capernaum were destined to go to heaven but was a figurative term meaning that they were or had been uplifted. And the term "descend to Hades" didn't mean that they were destined for hell, but it was meant to show how low they would fall. The city was later destroyed and made completely desolate.

Because of the great wickedness of the people of Ninevah God sent Jonah there to preach to them. Jonah performed no miracles yet the people of Ninevah repented. Jesus preached and performed miracles in Capernaum, but the people there rejected Him and His message.

Jesus said at another time that we must become as little children in order to accept His word. In 1 Corinthians 1:18, Paul wrote about "the foolishness of preaching." Both of these references point out that the people who think of themselves as wise and learned have difficulty in accepting the simple truths of the gospel. Jesus didn't mean it literally when He said that God had purposely hidden the truth from the people who were wise and discerning, but that such people would not accept the message because of its simplicity. The people who were humble and not highly educated were able to see the truth because the simplicity of the truth was easily understood if one didn't let pride and haughtiness interfere.

The word "yoke" is used in various places in the Bible to mean various things, such as bondage or slavery, afflictions, punishment for sins, burdensome Old Testament ceremonies, etc. The bondage of the yoke of Jesus is called easy and the burden to be pulled (as oxen pulling a load) is light. This was being compared to the burden the people had been carrying; they were burdened by the yoke of the Roman Empire and by the rites and rituals required of them by the Law and by the traditions of the Jews.

The reference to Satan falling from heaven was symbolic of the victory of the seventy over the unclean spirits. The fact that the seventy could have been bitten by serpents or stung by scorpions without suffering any ill effects may have been symbolic of the victory over the forces of Satan, or it could have been only literal. You may remember that Paul was bitten by a poisonous serpent on his journey to Rome and that he suffered no ill effects.

Further information concerning the fall of Satan from heaven can be found in Isaiah 14:12f, Revelation 9:1, and Revelation 12:8-9. When he tempted Eve in the form of a serpent Satan had already fallen from heaven. Jesus said that He saw Satan fall. That is further confirmation that Jesus existed before the world was made.

55 A Penitent Woman Anoints the Feet of Jesus

(Luke 7:36-50)

(1) Now one of the Pharisees requested Jesus to dine with him, and so Jesus entered the Pharisee's house and reclined at table. (2) There was a woman in the city who was a sinner, and when she learned that Jesus was reclining at table in the Pharisee's house she came to Him and

brought an alabaster vial of perfume. (3) She stood behind Jesus at His feet weeping and began to wet His feet with her tears. She kept wiping Jesus' feet with the hair of her head and kissing them and anointing them with the perfume.

(4) When the Pharisee who had invited Jesus saw this he said to himself, "If this Man were a prophet He would know who and what sort of person this woman *is* who *is* touching Him, that she is a sinner."

(5) Jesus, knowing the Pharisee's thoughts, said to him, "Simon, I have something to say to you."

Simon replied, "Say it, Teacher."

(6) "A certain money lender had two debtors. One owed him five hundred denarii and the other fifty. (7) When they were unable to repay, he graciously forgave them both. Which of them then will love him more?"

(8) Simon answered and said, "I suppose the one whom he forgave more."

Jesus said to him, "You have judged correctly."

(9) And turning toward the woman Jesus said to Simon, "Do you see this woman? When I entered your house you gave Me no water for My feet but she wet My feet with her tears and wiped them with her hair. (10) You gave Me no kiss; but since the time she came in she has not ceased to kiss My feet. (11) You did not anoint My head with oil but she anointed even My feet with perfume. (12) For this reason I say to you, her sins which are many have been forgiven for she loved much, but he who is forgiven little loves little."

(13) Then Jesus said to the woman, "Your sins have been forgiven."

(14) Those who were reclining at table with Jesus began to say to themselves, "Who is this Man who even forgives sins?"

(15) Jesus said to the woman, "Your faith has saved you. Go in peace."

Notes: There is no information given in the Bible about the host at the dinner other than that his name was Simon. Some scholars speculate that the reason Jesus was invited to dine with Simon was because he, Simon, was trying to find some evidence against Jesus that the Jews could use to prosecute Him, but the language of the text doesn't support that opinion.

The town in which Simon lived and in which this incident happened is unknown, but, of course, there is no significance in its location.

The woman who came to Jesus was known by Simon and his guests and was known to have been a sinner. Whether she was a criminal, a prostitute, a thief, an adulteress or what, we don't know. We can deduce, though, that she was not a pauper because she possessed a vial of very expensive perfume. There is no evidence to support the belief of some scholars that this woman was Mary Magdalene.

Alabaster was made from carbonate of lime, found on the floors of limestone caves. At that time alabaster was considered to be the best material for making vases or vials to hold and preserve their ointments. Vessels made from alabaster were translucent in appearance. Alabaster is formed of the same material as marble but formed differently.

Sandals were the common footwear of that day and place and when people walked in the dirt and dust of the roads their feet, naturally, got dirty. It was the custom for a host to provide facilities for washing the feet of his guests. People of means usually had a servant who was assigned to perform that menial task.

56 Further Journeying of Jesus through Galilee

(Luke 8:1-3)

(1) Soon afterwards Jesus was going about from one city and village to another proclaiming and preaching the kingdom of God. With Him were the twelve (2) and also some women who had been healed of evil spirits and sicknesses: Mary who was called Magdalene from whom seven demons had gone out; (3) and Joanna the wife of Chuza, Herod's steward; and many others who were contributing to their support out of their private means.

Notes: Mary Magdalene is a familiar figure to Bible scholars, but Joanna is not mentioned anywhere else in the scriptures by name or is Chuza, Herod's steward, mentioned by name anywhere else.

The number of demons said to have gone out of Mary Magdalene was seven and in Jewish apocalyptic literature quite often that number is used as an indefinite amount, meaning many, rather than the definite number of seven. Which sense that number is used in this particular passage is not known, but since the writings of Luke are not apocalyptic, we can assume that the number was a definite seven. It may be pointed out here that Mary Magdalene was probably the most faithful of all the followers of Jesus. She watched the crucifixion and the burial of Jesus, she was one of those women who was said to be preparing the spices for the body of Jesus, and she was the first person to whom Jesus spoke after His resurrection. Some biblical scholars claim that before she was healed by Jesus she was a prostitute, but there is no scriptural evidence whatsoever to support such a belief. That she was a very troubled person before she met Jesus due to the demons which possessed her there can be no doubt, but beyond that fact anything else about her character and personal life is merely speculation and/or fabrication.

57 Jesus Heals a Blind Demoniac and Answers the Blasphemous Accusations of the Jews

(Matt. 12:22-37; Mark 3:20-30; Luke 11:14-23, 12:10)

(1) Jesus went into a house and the multitudes gathered again to such an extent that Jesus and those with Him could not even eat a meal. (2) When Jesus' own kinsmen heard of this they went out to take custody of Him, for they were saying, "He has lost His senses."

(3) Then there was brought to Jesus a man possessed of a demon who was also blind and dumb, and when Jesus had cast out the demon and healed him, the man spoke and could see.

(4) All the multitudes were amazed and began to say, "Can this man be the Son of David?"

(5) But when the Pharisees and the scribes who had come down from Jerusalem heard of it they said, "He is possessed by demons!" and "He casts out demons by the power of Beelzebul the ruler of the demons!" (6) And others, to test Jesus, were demanding of Him a sign from heaven.

(7) Knowing their thoughts Jesus called them to Him and began speaking to them in parables, "How can Satan cast out Satan? (8) Any kingdom divided against itself is laid waste, and any city or house divided against itself cannot stand. (9) If Satan casts out Satan he is divided against himself. How then shall his kingdom stand? (10) If I by Beelzebul cast out demons, by whom do your sons cast them out? Consequently they shall be your judges. (11) But if I cast out demons by the Spirit of God then the kingdom of God has come upon you.

(12) "When a strong man who is fully armed guards his own house his possessions are undisturbed (13) but when someone who is stronger attacks and overpowers him, that man takes away all the armor on which he had relied and carries off his possessions. (14) He who is not with Me is against Me and he who does not gather with Me scatters.

(15) "Truly I say to you, any sin and blasphemy shall be forgiven men except blasphemy against the Spirit shall not be forgiven. (16) Anyone who shall speak a word of blasphemy against the Son of Man it shall be forgiven him; but if anyone shall speak words of blasphemy against the Holy Spirit it shall not be forgiven him, neither in this age nor the age to come," (17) (because they were saying, "He has an unclean spirit.")

(18) "Either make the tree good and its fruit good or make the tree rotten and the fruit rotten, for the tree is known by its fruit. (19) You brood of vipers, how can you, being evil, speak what is good? For the mouth speaks out of that which fills the heart. (20) The good man out of his good treasure brings forth what is good and the evil man out of his evil treasure brings forth what is evil. (21) I say to you that every careless word that men shall speak they shall render account of it in the day of judgment. (22) For by your words you shall be justified and by your words condemned."

Notes: This section tells us what the relatives of Jesus thought of Him at this time in His ministry-they thought He was deranged! They had heard what Jesus was doing-preaching, healing the sick and infirm, casting out demons, and such like-and, thinking that He was delirious or deranged, they tried to restrain Him. We don't know the location of the house in which this happened, but since some of the relatives of Jesus were close enough to try to restrain Him, it was probably in Nazareth or some other town located close by. We don't have any information as to the relationship of Jesus to these people.

The only relatives of Jesus about whom we know are: His own family, Joseph, Mary, and the brothers and sisters of Jesus; Elizabeth and her son, John the Baptist; and the wife of Zebedee, the mother of James and John.

58 The Scribes and Pharisees Seek a Sign

(Matt. 12:38-45; Luke 11:24-32)

(1) Then some of the scribes and Pharisees answered Jesus saying, "Teacher, we want to see a sign from You."

(2) The crowds were increasing as Jesus began to speak saying, "This evil and adulterous generation seeks a sign and yet no sign shall be given to it but the sign of Jonah the prophet. (3) Just as Jonah was three days and three nights in the belly of the sea monster so shall the Son of Man be three days and three nights in the heart of the earth. (4) The men of Ninevah shall stand up with this generation at the judgment and shall condemn it because they repented at the preaching of Jonah and something greater than Jonah is here.

(5) "The Queen of the South shall rise up with the men of this generation at the judgment and condemn them because she came from the end of the earth to hear the wisdom of Solomon and something greater than Solomon is here.

(6) "Now when the unclean spirit goes out of a man it passes through waterless places seeking rest and does not find it. (7) Then it says, 'I will return to the house from which I came,' and when it comes it finds that house unoccupied, swept, and put in order. (8) Then it goes in and takes along with it seven other spirits more wicked than itself and they go in and live there, and the last state of that man is worse than the first. That is the way it will also be with this evil generation."

(9) While Jesus said these things one of the women in the crowd raised her voice and said to Him, "Blessed is the womb that bore You and the breasts at which You nursed."

(10) But Jesus said, "On the contrary, blessed are those who hear the Word of God and observe it."

Notes: It may seem ridiculous to us that the people who had just seen Jesus cast out a demon from a man who was dumb and blind and then had restored the man's voice and sight were asking that He show them a sign, presumably a sign to prove that He was the Messiah. They wanted further proof that Jesus came from or was sent by God.

It's possible, though, even though the scriptures don't say so, that the people who were asking for a sign were new arrivals and had not witnessed the latest miracle of Jesus. In that case what they were saying was that they, too, wanted to see a sign from Him as proof that what they had just been told by the people who had witnessed this miracle was true. Perhaps they were thinking back to Moses and the signs which accompanied those things Moses had done-thunder, lightning, or manna-or some equally dramatic sign such as a comet shooting across the sky or darkness at noon.

Keep in mind the words Jesus spoke here about being in the heart of the earth three days and three nights. That prophecy of His will be discussed later in the proper context.

Like the parables of Jesus, His reference to the men of Nineveh condemning the present generation, this was figurative language. The preaching of Jonah was not accompanied by any miraculous signs, yet the people of Nineveh repented. Contrasting the men of Nineveh to the (then) present generation, that generation did not believe Jesus even though His words were accompanied by signs and miracles. People who didn't know God believed and repented but the people who were supposed to be God's own chosen people didn't believe nor repent.

Nineveh was a very ancient city. It was founded only a few generations after the flood by Asshur. It was the capital of the Assyrian Empire and was situated on the banks of the Tigris River to the northeast of Babylon. It was said that its population at the time of Jonah was about six hundred thousand. The promised destruction of Nineveh, in forty days if its inhabitants did not repent, was delayed for two hundred years after the inhabitants repented at the preaching of Jonah. It was conquered by the Babylonians about 600 BC. A hundred forty years earlier, the destruction of Nineveh had been foretold. "But with an overwhelming flood he will make an utter end of the place thereof" (Nah. 1:9). And "The gates of the river shall be opened, and the palace shall be dissolved" (Nah. 2:6). During the Babylonian siege, a great flood of the Tigris River washed away part of the walls of the city. The Babylonians entered the city through that breach and thus were able to conquer and destroy the city.

The Queen of the South was the Queen of Sheba. She had traveled a great distance because she had heard of the wisdom of Solomon and wanted to ask him questions. She was convinced of the greatness of Solomon by the wisdom of the answers to her questions and without seeing any signs or miracles, but that generation of the Jews would not believe Jesus even after seeing signs and miracles. For that reason, the Queen of Sheba would be a witness against the Jews at the judgment.

Sheba was a town or small country, probably located in Arabia and probably founded by and named for one of the four men by that name about which we can read in the Old Testament, the most likely being the great grandson of Ham, the son of Noah.

This passage tells of another person who was possessed by seven unclean spirits. In this passage, as in the other one, the number seven probably refers to an indefinite number rather than to the literal number seven.

The lesson to be learned from the story of the unclean spirit returning to its former home with seven others is this: when sins have been forgiven and worldly thoughts have been taken out of the lives of people who have been converted to Christ, those evil things must be replaced by good things or the evil things will return to occupy that vacant space. There is a saying that nature abhors a vacuum. If the inner person is left empty, after salvation has been reached, sin will find a way to return. But if those evil things are replaced by good things, there will be no space for sin to lodge when it tries to return. Further, it seems to be a truism that if a person gains salvation and later loses it, that person will sink lower than he was in the beginning.

59 The Mother and Brothers of Jesus Seek Him

(Matt. 12:46-50; Mark 3:31-35; Luke 8:19-21)

(1) While Jesus was still speaking to the multitudes His mother and His brothers arrived and while they were standing outside unable to get to Him because of the crowd they sent word to Him and called Him. (2) Someone in the multitude that was sitting around Jesus said to Him, "Your mother and Your brothers are standing outside seeking to speak to You."

(3) But Jesus answered the one who was telling Him and said, "Who is My mother and who are My brothers?"

(4) And looking about on those who were sitting around Him and stretching out His hand toward His disciples Jesus said, "Behold My mother and My brothers! (5) For whoever shall do the will of My Father who is in heaven he is My brother and sister and mother."

Notes: There is at least one religious body which teaches and holds to the doctrine that Jesus had no physical blood brothers or sisters, teaching instead that in the scriptures, people said to be His brothers and sisters were, in fact, cousins, claiming that it was in this manner that Jesus sometimes spoke of cousins. The Greek word used in the text here, though, is *"adelphos"* (a-del-fos'), the same word used in Matthew 13:55 which reads, "Is this not the carpenter's son? Is not His mother called Mary, and His brothers, James and Joseph and Simon and Judas?" It is also the word used to describe the relationship of Peter and Andrew and of James and John.

Jesus, in speaking of His mother and brothers, was not showing disrespect for them or any lack of love and affection. He was using this incident to call His hearers' attention to what was to follow. He was pointing out to them that the closest and tenderest relationship which can exist on earth is the kinship of one Christian to another. He indicated that His relationship to His disciples was even closer than His blood relationship to His mother and His brothers.

60 The Parable of the Sower

(Matt. 13:1-23; Mark 4:1-20; Luke 8:4-15)

(1) Another day Jesus went out of the house and was sitting by the sea, (2) and great multitudes gathered about Him so that He got into a boat and sat down, and the whole multitude was standing on the beach. (3) Jesus taught them many things in parables and said to them in His teaching, "Listen to this! A sower went out to sow. (4) As he sowed the seed some of them fell beside the road and the birds came and ate them. (5) Other seed fell upon the rocky places where they did not have much soil and immediately they sprang up because they had no depth of soil, (6) but when the sun had risen they were scorched, and because they had no root they withered away. (7) Other seed fell among the thorns and the thorns came up and choked them out. (8) Still others fell on the good soil and yielded a crop, some a hundred-fold, some sixty, and some thirty." (9) As He said these things He would call out, "He who has ears to hear, let him hear."

(10) As soon as Jesus was alone, His followers along with the twelve asked Him, "Why do You speak to them in parables?"

(11) Jesus answered, "To you it has been granted to know the mysteries of the kingdom of heaven, but to them it has not been granted so they get everything in parables. (12) Whoever has, to him shall more be given and he shall have an abundance; but whoever does not have, even what he does have shall be taken away from him. (13) Therefore I speak to them in parables because while seeing they do not see and while hearing they do not hear, nor do they understand. (14) In their case the prophecy of Isaiah is being fulfilled, which says, 'You will keep on hearing, but will not understand; and you will keep on seeing, but will not perceive; (15) for the heart of this people has become dull, and with their ears they scarcely hear, and they have closed their eyes lest they should see with their eyes, and hear with their ears, and understand with their heart and turn again, and I should heal them.' (16) But blessed are your eyes because they see, and your ears because they hear. (17) For truly I say to you that many prophets and righteous

men desired to see what you see and did not see it and to hear what you hear and did not hear it."

(18) Then Jesus asked them, "Do you not understand this parable? How will you understand all the parables? (19) Hear then the parable of the sower.

"The seed is the word of God. The sower sows the word.

(20) The word that is sown beside the road is the ones who hear the word and immediately Satan comes and takes away the word which has been sown in them so that they may not believe and be saved. (21) The ones on whom seed was sown on the rocky places are those who hear the word and immediately receive it with joy, (22) yet they have no firm root in themselves but are only temporary. Then when affliction or persecution arises because of the word immediately they fall away. (23) Others are the ones on whom seed was sown among the thorns. These are the ones who have heard the word, (24) but the worries of the world, the deceitfulness of riches, and the desires for other things enter in and choke the word and it becomes unfruitful. (25) The ones on whom seed was sown on the good ground are the ones who have heard the word in an honest and good heart and understand and accept it, who indeed bear fruit, some a hundredfold, some sixty, and some thirty."

Notes: The word "parable" is translated from the Greek word *parabole*, which means a fictitious narrative of common life which conveys a moral.

The parables of Jesus, and this one in particular, the parable of the sower, have been preached and taught to the point that most churchgoing people are very familiar with them. As stated at the beginning of this work, the purpose of this study is not to sermonize but to teach about obscure things and unfamiliar references so that the readers will have a better background for understanding those things.

The prophecy which Jesus quoted is recorded in Isaiah 6:9-10.

Until now, Jesus had taught the people openly, saying in plain language whatever He had to say and making enemies in the process. This had caused a lot of controversy among the people who were not ready to believe what Jesus taught or that He was the Son of God. On one occasion, some of the unbelievers had already tried to throw Him over a cliff in order to kill Him.

Consequently, Jesus was changing His manner of speaking to the multitudes, among whom were His most implacable enemies, the scribes and Pharisees, and instead of speaking plainly, He was now teaching the people in parables. By teaching in parables, Jesus could teach the same lessons He had been teaching without incurring the same risks and, more importantly, without constant controversy and interruptions. He could explain to those who were close to Him in private, as He did in this instance, the meanings and applications that were unclear to them. And the people who did believe in Jesus and who wanted to learn from Him could apply the principles He taught in the parables and in that way learn the lessons Jesus wanted them to learn. At the same time, the enemies of Jesus who followed Him around only to try to find some sin or blasphemy of which to accuse Him, would ignore the lessons He taught and fail to apply them to themselves.

The pious people of understanding who wanted to increase their knowledge of Jesus, the Father and righteousness, by diligence could do so. But people who were motivated by other things-unbelief, arrogance, a desire for wealth or acclamation, to achieve or protect a position in society or the church-would not only not grow spiritually, but their desires would cause their knowledge of the Law and the prophets to be forgotten or adulterated by their traditions and lack of interest.

61 Parable of the Seed Growing of Itself (Mark 4:26-29)

(1) Jesus continued, "The kingdom of God is like a man who casts seed upon the ground (2) and goes to bed at night and gets up by day. The seed sprouts up and grows-how, he himself does not know. (3) The earth produces crops by itself; first the blade, then the head, then the mature grain in the head.

(4) And when the crop permits, he immediately puts in the sickle, because the harvest has come."

62 Parable of the Tares (Matt. 13:24-30)

(1) Jesus presented another parable to them, saying, "The kingdom of heaven may be compared to a man who sowed good seed in his field. (2) But while he was sleeping his enemy came secretly and sowed tares among the wheat and went away. (3) When the wheat sprang up and bore grain the tares became evident also. (4) Then the slaves of the landowner came and said to him, 'Sir, did you not sow good seed in your field? How then does it have tares?' (5) The landowner said to them, 'An enemy has done this!' And the slaves said to him, 'Do you want us to go and gather up the tares?' (6) But the landowner said, 'No, because while you are gathering up the tares you may root up the wheat with them. (7) Allow both to grow together until the harvest, and in the time of the harvest I will say to the reapers, "First gather up the tares and bind them in bundles to burn them up, then gather the wheat into my barn."'"

Notes: Tares are a weed called "darnel" or "false grain," a member of the vetch family. The dictionary defines vetch as "any of a genus (Vicia) of herbaceous twining leguminous plants including some grown for fodder and green manure." And "fodder" is defined as "something fed to domestic animals; esp. coarse food for cattle, horses, or sheep." The main source of fodder in this country is the leaves of corn plants which are stripped from the stalk, tied into "hands" and allowed to dry before being gathered up and stored.

63 Parables of (A) Mustard Seed and (B) Leaven

(Matt. 13:31-35; Mark 4:30-34; Luke 13:18-21)

(1) Jesus said, "To what shall we compare the kingdom of God or by what parable shall we present it? (2) It is like a mustard seed which, though smaller than all the seeds, when planted in the ground it grows up and becomes a tree larger than all the garden plants (3) and forms large branches so that the birds of the air come and nest in it."

(4) Jesus spoke to them again in another parable, "To what shall we compare the kingdom of God? (5) It is like leaven which a woman took and hid in three pecks of meal until the meal was all leavened."

(6) All of the things which Jesus spoke to the multitude were spoken only in parables (7) so that what was spoken through the prophet might be fulfilled, as it was written, "I will open My mouth in parables; I will utter things hidden since the foundation of the world." (8) But Jesus was explaining everything privately to His own disciples.

Notes: The prophecy cited here by Jesus is from Psalms 78:2.

64 The Parable of the Tares Explained (Matt. 13:36-43)

(1) Jesus left the multitudes and went into the house. Then His disciples came to Him and said, "Explain to us the parable of the tares of the field."

(2) Jesus said, "The one who sows the good seed is the Son of Man (3) and the field is the world. As for the good seed, these are the sons of the kingdom and the tares are the sons of the evil one. (4) The enemy who sowed the tares is the devil. This harvest is the end of the age and the reapers are angels. (5) Therefore just as the tares are gathered up and burned with fire so shall it be at the end of the age. (6) The Son of Man will send forth His angels and they will gather out of His kingdom all stumbling blocks and those who commit lawlessness (7) and will cast them into the furnace of fire where there shall be weeping and gnashing of teeth. (8) Then the righteous will shine forth as the sun in the kingdom of their Father. He who has ears let him hear."

65 Additional Parables:
(A) The Hidden Treasure; (B) The Pearl of Great Price;
(C) The Net; (D) The Householder (Matt. 13:44-53)

(1) "The kingdom of heaven is like a treasure hidden in the field which a man found and hid. From joy over it he goes and sells all that he has and buys that field.

(2) "Again, the kingdom of heaven is like a merchant seeking fine pearls. (3) Upon finding one pearl of great value he went and sold all that he had and bought it.

(4) "Again, the kingdom of heaven is like a dragnet cast into the sea and gathering fish of every kind. (5) When it was filled the fishermen drew it up on the beach. Then they sat down and gathered the good fish into containers but the bad they threw away. (6) So it will be at the end of the age. The angel shall come forth and take out the wicked from among the righteous (7) and will cast them into the furnace of fire. There shall be weeping and gnashing of teeth.

(8)"Have you understood all these things?" They answered Jesus, "Yes."

(9)Jesus said to them, "Therefore every scribe who has become a disciple of the kingdom of heaven is like a head of a household who brings forth out of his treasure things new and old."

(10) When Jesus had finished these parables He departed from there.

66 Jesus Stills a Storm (Matt. 8:18, 23-27; Mark 4:35-41; Luke 8:22-25)

(1) One day when evening had come Jesus saw that there was a crowd around Him and He said to His disciples, "Let us go over to the other side of the lake."

(2) Then Jesus and His disciples got into a boat and launched out. Leaving the multitude, the disciples took Jesus along with them in the boat just as He was, and there were other boats with Him. (3) As they were sailing along Jesus fell asleep and there arose a great storm, and a fierce gale of wind descended upon the lake. (4) Waves were breaking over the boat so much that the boat was filling up and they began to be swamped and to be in danger. (5) The disciples went to Jesus in the stern where He was asleep on the cushion and awoke Him.

(6) The disciples said, "Master, save us. Do you not care that we are about to perish?"

(7) Jesus said to them, "Why are you timid, you men of little faith?" (8) Then He arose and rebuked the wind and said to the sea, "Hush, be still." Then the wind died down and became perfectly calm. (9) The disciples were fearful and amazed and said to one another, "Who then is this who commands even the winds and the water and they obey Him?"

Notes: Because of the arrangement of the terrain around the Sea of Galilee that area is subject to sudden violent squalls. In his book, *The Land and the Book*, Dr. Thomson wrote the following: "Small as the lake is, and placid, in general, as a molten mirror, I have repeatedly seen it quiver, and leap, and boil like a cauldron, when driven by fierce winds from the eastern mountains."

Even after the disciples had seen all the things that Jesus had done before this-turning water into wine, healing the sick, lame, deaf, dumb, blind, lepers, and even restoring life to dead people-they were still amazed at the power of Jesus. They were still learning the extent of that power.

67 Gerasene Demoniacs Healed

(Matt. 8:28-34, 9:1; Mark 5:1-21; Luke 8:26-40)

(1) They sailed to the other side of the sea into the country of the Gerasenes which is opposite Galilee. (2) Then, when Jesus had come out of the boat onto the land, two men who were demon-possessed came out of the tombs among which they had been living and met Him. (3) One of them was so exceedingly violent that no one could pass by on that road. He had not put on clothing for a long time and no one was able to bind him any more, even with a chain. (4) He had often been bound with shackles and chains but the chains had been torn apart and the shackles broken in pieces by him, and no one was strong enough to subdue him. (5) Constantly, night and day, among the tombs and in the mountains he was crying out and gashing himself with stones.

(6) Seeing Jesus from a distance this man had run up and bowed down before Him, (7) and, crying out with a loud voice, he said, "What have I to do with You, Jesus, Son of the Most High God? Have You

come here to torment me before the time? I implore You before God, do not torment me!"

(8) Jesus commanded the spirit, "Come out of the man, you unclean spirit!" (9) Many times the spirit had seized the man and he had been bound and kept under guard. Yet he had burst his fetters and been driven by the demon into the desert.

(10) Jesus asked him, "What is your name?"

He answered, "Legion," for many demons had entered him.

(11) The demons entreated Jesus earnestly not to command that they depart the country nor be sent into the abyss. (12) Now there was at a distance from them a herd of many swine feeding there on the mountain side. (13) The demons began to entreat Jesus, saying, "If You are going to cast us out, send us into the herd of swine."

(14) Jesus gave them permission, saying, "Begone!"

Coming out, the unclean spirits entered the swine and the herd rushed down the steep bank into the sea, about two thousand of them, and all of them were drowned in the sea.

(15) When the herdsmen who tended the swine saw what had happened, they ran away and reported it in the city and out in the country, including the incident of the demoniacs.

(16) Then the people went out to see what had happened. They came to Jesus and found the man from whom the demons had gone out sitting down at the feet of Jesus, clothed and in his right mind, the very man who had had the legion, and they became frightened. (17) Those who had seen it described to the others what had happened to the demon-possessed man, and about the swine. (18) Then all the people of the country of the Gerasenes and the surrounding district asked Jesus to depart from them for they were all gripped with great fear.

(19) As Jesus was getting into the boat to depart the man from whom the demons had gone was begging Jesus that he be allowed to accompany Him. (20) Jesus did not give the man permission but said to him, "Go home to your people and report to them what great things the Lord has done for you and how He had mercy on you."

(21) The man departed and began to proclaim in Decapolis what great things Jesus had done for him, and everyone marveled.

(22) When Jesus had again crossed over in the boat to His own city on the other side, a great multitude gathered about Him and welcomed Him for they had all been waiting for Him, and He stayed by the seashore.

Notes: The province of Gaulanitis bordered the northeastern shore of the Sea of Galilee, and directly across the sea to the east of the town of Magdala in the southwestern corner of Gaulanitis was the town of Gergesa or Gerasa, the spelling varying with the different versions of the Bible. Gerasa was supposed to have been governed by the inhabitants of the town of Gadara which was one of the ten cities of the province of Decapolis (the word *Decapolis* in the Greek language meaning "ten cities"). In the vicinity of Gerasa there is said to be the only place on the eastern shore of the Sea of Galilee where a steep hill goes all the way down to the water.

Matthew, whose account of this incident is much shorter than the others, wrote that there were two men who were demoniacs, but both Mark and Luke wrote of only one man. Since, of the three, only Matthew was an eyewitness, I am inclined to believe his account is the more accurate, although neither Mark nor Luke wrote that there was *only* one. They could have known about the second man but wrote only about the first since he may have been the only one who could not be bound nor controlled.

Also, both Mark and Luke say this was the country of the Gerasenes but Matthew wrote that it was the country of the Gadarenes. The incident did not happen in either city but only Gerasa is on the coast of the Sea of Galilee. Gadara was about twelve or fourteen miles south of Gerasa and about six miles from the coast. It is likely that Matthew said it was the country of the Gadarenes because it was the Gadarenes who administered the affairs of the town of Gerasa.

These men were living in the tombs-not among the tombs, but in the tombs. The tombs of that time were mostly caves or hollowed out rocks. Some of the caves were very extensive, being entered by steps carved into the floors. It was not unusual for very poor people who did not have homes of their own to live in the tombs among the dead. It would not have been unusual, either, to find demoniacs living in the tombs.

These demons, as had others about whom we have already read, knew Jesus for who He was, the Son of God. And they knew of His power over them. From what they said, it seems that they not only knew that they would have to face God's judgment but that they knew what that judgment would be. Their immediate concern was that God's judgment would be visited on them at that time rather than at the end of the ages.

A unit of a particular size in the Roman army was called a legion. The number of men in a legion varied through the ages, but at that time a legion numbered six thousand men, three thousand infantrymen, and three thousand cavalrymen. Since many demons had entered "Legion" the name, although probably an exaggeration, might have been appropriate.

The only purpose for which swine are used is for food. Since the Jews did not eat pork nor were they permitted by law to raise or to trade in swine, it follows that the inhabitants of the area, or at least the owner(s) of the swine, were not Jews. That land had once been a part of the Promised Land in which the Israelites had settled. It was part of the inheritance of the tribe of Manessah, but those settlers had long since been carried away into captivity and the land appropriated by others.

The man Legion did far more to spread the name and fame of Jesus by doing what Jesus told him to do than he could ever have done by following after and being with Jesus. That's what happened to the early Christians-they were scattered abroad by fear of persecution when they would have pref erred to remain in or around Jerusalem. And because they did disperse, the gospel was spread much faster than it would have been if they had remained together in Jerusalem.

68 Jesus Returns to Nazareth and Is Again Rejected

(Matt. 13:54-58; Mark 6:1-6a)

(1) Jesus went out from there and came to His home town and His disciples followed Him.

(2) When the Sabbath had come Jesus began to teach in the synagogue. The many listeners were astonished, saying, "Where did this man get these things, and what is this wisdom given to Him, and such miracles as these performed by His hands? (3) Is not this the carpenter's son and is not His mother called Mary? His brothers, James and Joseph and Simon and Judas, and His sisters, are they not all with us?" And they took offense at Him.

(4) Jesus said to them, "A prophet is not without honor except in his home town and among his own relatives and in his own household."

(5) Jesus could do no miracles there except that He laid His hands upon a few sick people and healed them, and He wondered at their unbelief.

Notes: It was the custom of Jesus to go to a synagogue each Sabbath day and teach the people there. Luke wrote in Luke 4:16, "... as was His custom He entered the synagogue on the Sabbath and stood up to read." His custom would have been for Jesus to have gone to *a* synagogue rather than to the synagogue in Nazareth. If it had been the custom of Jesus to read, or teach, in the synagogue in Nazareth the people would have become accustomed to him being there and would not have taken offense when He did so on this occasion.

The wording in Matthew's account seems to indicate that Joseph was still living at that time, and that Joseph and Mary and their other children still lived in Nazareth. Joseph and Mary had four sons who were called by name. And the people said, "And His sisters, are they not *all* with us?" indicating that there were at least two sisters and possibly, even probably, more than two because they said, ". . . are they not all with us?"

However, whereas in Matthew's account the people asked, "Is this not the carpenter's son... ?" Mark records that they asked, "Is this not the carpenter?" That does not mean that Joseph was not there or that he was dead, but only that Jesus had also worked as a carpenter and that the people of Nazareth knew Him as such.

The town of Nazareth was a small obscure village not mentioned even once in the Old Testament or the Jewish Talmud or in any of the writings of Josephus, the Jewish historian. Perhaps its obscurity was the reason Joseph chose it as their home when he and Mary with Jesus returned from Egypt.

Not once in the scriptures is it recorded that Jesus sought out any of His relatives, even His mother, or to visit any of them. At this time, however, He may have been in Nazareth for that very purpose. At that time, too, it is probable that none of the brothers or sisters of Jesus believed that He was the Messiah. John 7:5 says, "For not even His brothers were believing in Him." One would think that if Mary and Joseph believed that Jesus was the Messiah, or even if only Mary did, that their other children, the brothers and sisters of Jesus, would have believed in Him too.

69 Journeying in Galilee, the Twelve
Are Instructed and Sent Forth

(Matt. 9:35-10:1, 10:5-16; 10:24-11:1;
Mark 6:6b-13; Luke 9:1-6, 12:2-9)

(1) Jesus went about all the cities and the villages, teaching in their synagogues and proclaiming the gospel of the kingdom, and healing every kind of disease and every kind of sickness. (2) Seeing the multitudes He felt compassion for them because they were distressed and downcast like sheep without a shepherd.

(3) Then Jesus said to His disciples, "The harvest is plentiful but the workers are few. (4) Therefore beseech the Lord of the harvest to send out workers into His harvest."

(5) Then Jesus summoned His twelve disciples and began to send them out in pairs. He gave them power and authority over the demons and unclean spirits, and told them to proclaim the kingdom of God. (6) Before sending out the twelve Jesus gave them instructions, saying, "Do not go in the way of the Gentiles and do not enter any city of the Samaritans, (7) but rather go to the lost sheep of the house of Israel.

(8) "And as you go, preach, saying, 'The kingdom of heaven is at hand.'

(9) "Heal the sick, raise the dead, cleanse the lepers, cast out demons; freely you received, freely give.

(10) "Do not take gold or silver or copper in your purse or money belts, (11) or bread or a bag for your journey, or even two tunics, or sandals, or a staff; for the worker is worthy of his support.

(12) "Into whatever city or village you enter inquire who is worthy in that town; and whatever house you enter abide there until you leave. (13) As you enter the house give it your greeting. (14) If the house is worthy let your greeting of peace come upon it, but if it is not worthy let your peace return to you.

(15) "Wherever they do not receive you nor heed your words, as you go out of that house or that city, shake off the dust from your feet as a testimony against them. (16) Truly I say to you, it will be more tolerable for the land of Sodom and Gomorrah in the day of judgment than for that city.

(17) "Realize that I send you out as sheep in the midst of wolves, so be as shrewd as serpents and as innocent as doves.

(18) "A disciple is not above his teacher nor a slave above his master. (19) It is enough for the disciple that he become as his teacher and the slave as his master. If they have called the head of the house Beelzebul, how much more the members of his household! (20) Therefore do not fear them for there is nothing covered that will not be revealed and nothing hidden that will not be known. (21) What I tell you in the darkness speak in the light and what you hear whispered in your ear in the inner rooms proclaim upon the housetops.

(22) "And I say to you, My friends, do not fear those who kill the body but are unable to kill the soul and after that have no more that they can do. But I will warn you whom to fear: fear the one who after He has killed has authority to cast into hell. Yes, I tell you, fear Him who is able to destroy both soul and body in hell. (23) Are not five sparrows sold for two cents and two sparrows sold for a cent? Yet not one of them will fall to the ground and be forgotten before God, your Father. (24) The very hairs of your head are all numbered. (25) Therefore do not fear, for you are of more value than many sparrows.

(26) "I say to you, every one who shall confess me before men the Son of Man will also confess before My Father who is in heaven and the angels. (27) But whoever shall deny Me before men, I will also deny before My Father who is in heaven and the angels.

(28) "Do not think that I came to bring peace upon the earth; I did not come to bring peace but a sword. (29) I came to set a man against his father and a daughter against her mother, and a daughter-in-law against her mother-in-law. (30) A man's enemies will be the members of his own household.

(31) "He who loves father or mother more than he loves Me is not worthy of Me and he who loves son or daughter more than he loves Me is not worthy of Me. (32) He who does not take his cross and follow Me is not worthy of Me. (33) He who has found his life shall lose it and he who has lost his life for My sake will find it.

(34) "He who receives you receives Me and he who receives Me receives Him who sent Me. (35) He who receives a prophet in the name of a prophet shall receive a prophet's reward and he who receives a righteous man in the name of a righteous man shall receive a righteous man's reward. (36) Whoever in the name of a disciple gives to one of these little ones even a cup of cold water to drink, truly I say to you, he shall not lose his reward."

(37) When Jesus had finished giving instructions to His twelve disciples He departed to teach and preach in their cities.

(38) The twelve went into the villages and preached the gospel and that men should repent. (39) They cast out many demons and anointed with oil many sick people and healed them.

Notes: The common people of that time and place were said to be distressed and cast down. They were burdened not only by the Law but by the traditions which had been added through the ages and which were sometimes contrary to the Law but considered by their religious leaders to be just as binding as the Law. Coupled with that, they were also a conquered people, subject to the whims and dictates of their conquerors. Theirs was a pastoral society, and Jesus likened them to sheep without a shepherd, therefore, without guidance or protection. Too, Jesus knew that many of them hungered for the true Word of God and were ready to receive the word which He brought to them, like a wheat field with the grain ripe and ready for the reaper's scythe.

Jesus sent the twelve disciples out in pairs. They could have covered more ground and preached to more people if they had been sent out alone, but there were good reasons for them to go out in pairs. The Law required two witnesses to establish the truth so by going out in pairs each of them could confirm the truth of what the other preached.

This first commission given to the twelve disciples restricted them to preaching only to the Jews but the second commission which they were given, the Great Commission as it is called, was for them to preach to *all* people everywhere. Jesus was sent only *to* the Jews but not just *for* the Jews.

Jesus told the disciples to preach, "The kingdom of heaven is at hand." That was the same message that John the Baptist preached.

Jesus said that a worker was worthy of being supported. If there was nothing else in the scriptures on the subject, this would authorize support for preachers. In 1 Timothy 5:18 Paul wrote essentially the same thing. Also in 1 Corinthians 9:14 Paul wrote, "Even so hath the Lord ordained that they which preach the gospel should live by the gospel." Some preachers refuse to accept a "salary" preferring to call it "support" instead. But whether they call it support or salary they are entitled to be paid.

To the Jews, the dust of heathen places was impure and was to be shaken off their feet when they left those places. Since the twelve disciples were going only to the Jews in Jewish cities, to shake the dust off their feet when leaving a town or house where they were rejected was a sign that they considered those people to be no better than heathens. It was a renunciation of the places and people who rejected them.

The Jews considered a serpent to be a symbol of wisdom. Perhaps this was a carryover from their years in Egypt where the Egyptians also deemed a serpent to be a symbol of wisdom. The dove was a symbol of peace, gentleness, and inoffensiveness.

Records show that during the times when Christians were being persecuted so severely, quite often it was their relatives who turned them in to the authorities for their religious beliefs. Religious differences are sometimes a major cause of strife. There was war in Northern Ireland between Protestants and Catholics for years. In India, the different religious groups are at war with each other, and this was a major reason for Pakistan splitting off from India to become a separate nation. Muslims wage holy war against non-Muslims. And during the "dark ages," Catholics persecuted unbelievers and non Catholics unmercifully in the name of God. It's not uncommon for families to be divided because of religion. Jesus didn't say that the purpose of His coming was to set family members against each other, but that that would be the result of His coming. Micah 7:5-6 says, "Do not trust in a neighbor; do not have confidence in a friend. From her who lies in your bosom guard your lips. For son treats father contemptuously, daughter rises up against her mother, daughter-in-law against her mother-in-law; a man's enemies are the men of his own household." Quite often, too, a person will refuse to obey the commandments of God and will change his religious beliefs because his father or mother was a member of a particular denomination or religion because "if it's good enough for the parents (or whoever), it's good enough for them." When Jesus said that there would be enmity within families that may have been a part of what He meant.

In some of the Amish sects, members can be excommunicated for minor offenses. If, for instance, it was the father of a family who was excommunicated, the other family members could not speak to him nor even eat at the same table with him.

Jesus told the disciples to expect to be treated in the same way that He was treated. Jesus was accused of performing miracles in the name of Beelzebul. Beelzebub was the name of the god of the Ekronites (2 Kings 1:2) and means literally "the lord or god of flies." Beelzebub was supposed to protect the Ekronites from the hoards of flies which abounded in their country. The Jews adopted the name "Beelzebub" as a name for Satan to express their contempt for him. They changed the name from "Beelzebub" to "Beelzebul," the last "b" to an "l", and it's in that form that the word was used in this passage. By changing the last letter as they did, the meaning was changed to "the god of dung or filth," which expressed even greater aversion and contempt for Satan. Since Jesus was treated with contempt by some of the Jews, the disciples could expect to be treated with contempt, too.

It was a part of the sentence of those who were condemned to die on a cross that they must carry their own cross to the place of execution. It is evident from what Jesus said on several occasions that He knew well in advance of the fact that He would die on a cross. He knew, too, as did all those who lived under the rule of Rome, that death on a cross was a disgraceful way to die, and He was reminding the disciples that for them (or anyone) to be worthy of the name "Christian," they must be willing to suffer disgrace and death.

The "little ones" to whom Jesus referred were the twelve disciples. They were spoken of as "little ones" because they had no rank or wealth and that whoever treated them kindly was doing so for them personally, rather than for any favor that they could be expected to do in return.

70 Herod's Birthday Feast and the Death of John the Baptist

(Matt. 14:6-12; Mark 6:21-29)

(1) A strategic day came when Herod on his birthday gave a banquet for his lords and military commanders and the leading men of Galilee. (2) When the daughter of Herodias herself came in and danced she pleased Herod and his dinner guests so much that the king said to the girl, "Ask me for whatever you want and I will give it to you."

(3) Herod swore to her, "Whatever you ask of me I will give it to you, up to half of my kingdom."

(4) The girl went out and asked her mother, "What shall I ask for?" Herodias said, "The head of John the Baptist."

(5) Immediately the girl came in haste before the king and asked, "I want you to give me right away the head of John the Baptist on a platter."

(6) Although the king was very sorry, because of his oath and of his dinner guests he was unwilling to refuse her. (7) Immediately the king sent an executioner commanding him to bring back John's head. The executioner went and beheaded John in the prison (8) and brought his head on a platter and gave it to the girl, and the girl gave it to her mother.

(9) When John's disciples heard about this they came and took away his body and laid it in a tomb and they went and reported to Jesus.

Notes: Some time before this, Herod Antipas had sent John the Baptist to prison at the insistence of his wife Herodias because John had told Herod and the people that Herod had no right to marry Herodias. The Gospels state that Herodias was married to Philip, a half-brother of

Antipas, but Josephus the Jewish historian wrote that it was not the brother of Antipas but another Philip to whom Herodias was married, and that the reason John criticized Antipas for marrying Herodias was that she was his niece and Jewish law forbade marriage between such close relatives. Herodias was the daughter of Aristobulus, another half-brother of Antipas through their father Herod the Great. Josephus wrote that Herodias first married an uncle named Herod Boethus and by him had a daughter named Salome. But Josephus also mentioned a marriage of Herodias to a member of the Herod family whose name was Philip, making her marriage to Antipas her third.

The name of the daughter of Herodias is not given in the scriptures, but historical records indicate that it was, in fact, Salome. The character of Salome has been attacked because of her violation of the tradition of modesty and propriety by dancing in public, a dance noted for wantonness. It was probably because of the excitement caused by the dance that Antipas was moved to make, and to keep, an oath contrary to the law. Salome is said to have been sixteen years old at the time, and the blame for what she did is laid at the feet of her mother, whose character was certainly subject to much criticism.

Roman law prohibited the execution of anyone except with the approval of Roman authorities, and Antipas violated that law. The scriptures do not tell why the Roman authorities did not punish Antipas for this breach of their law.

At that time, it was the custom of men in high office, such as was Antipas, to give a great feast or banquet for their higher ranking underlings and military commanders, but it was not the custom of women of good character to exhibit themselves scantily clad in public nor to dance in such a lascivious way as Salome is reported to have done.

Josephus wrote that the execution of John took place in the fortress of Machaerus, and from about the fourth century, there has been a place in Samaria which is honored as being the tomb of John.

When the disciples of John had buried the body of John, they did what all Christians should do when they experience some great loss or disturbance-they turned to Jesus!

71 Herod Hears of the Works of Jesus

(Matt. 14:1-2; Mark 6:14-16; Luke 9:7-9)

(1) King Herod the tetrarch heard of all that was happening for the name of Jesus had become well known, and he was greatly perplexed because the people were saying, "John the Baptist has risen from the dead and that is why miraculous powers are at work in Jesus."
(2) But some others were saying, "He is Elijah."
Still others were saying, "He is a prophet like one of those of old."
(3) Herod said, "I myself had John beheaded so who is this man about whom I hear such things?" And He kept trying to see Jesus.

Notes: Herod Antipas heard about Jesus, but he also heard that some of the people believed that Jesus was John the Baptist reincarnated, or else that He was Elijah or one of the other prophets. In order to satisfy himself about the truth of that rumor, Antipas wanted to see Jesus himself because he knew that John was dead, having himself seen John's head on a platter. The meeting between Jesus and Antipas didn't take place until Jesus was arrested and just before His crucifixion.

72 The Apostles Return and Report

(Mark 6:30-31; Luke 9:10)

(1) When the apostles returned they gathered together with Jesus and reported to Him all that they had done and taught. (2) Taking them with Him, Jesus withdrew privately to a city called Bethsaida.
(3) Jesus said to the apostles, "Come away by yourselves to a lonely place and rest a while." (For there were many people coming and going and Jesus and the twelve did not even have time to eat.)

Notes: Some biblical scholars have raised a question about the location given. The scripture says that Jesus and the twelve apostles withdrew privately to a city called Bethsaida. The conclusion of the scholars is that this place was *in the vicinity* of Bethsaida and that they returned *to the city* of Bethsaida. Not that the matter is material either way, but it does show to what extent some people will go to question the accuracy of the scriptures.

73 Jesus Crosses the Sea of Galilee

(Matt. 14:13a; Mark 6:32; John 6:1)

(1) Afterwards Jesus and the apostles went away in a boat by themselves to a lonely place on the other side of the Sea of Galilee (or Tiberias).

74 Jesus Feeds the Five Thousand

(Matt. 14:13b-21; Mark 6:33-44; Luke 9:11-17; John 6:2-14)

(1) The people saw Jesus and the apostles going and many recognized them and told others, and they all ran there together from all the cities and got there ahead of Jesus. (2) Disembarking, Jesus saw a great multitude, and He felt compassion for them because they were like sheep without a shepherd. He began to teach them many things about the kingdom of heaven and to cure those who had need of healing.

(3) Jesus went up on the mountain and there He sat with His disciples. (4) Now the Passover, the feast of the Jews, was at hand.

(5) When it was quite late in the evening the twelve came to Jesus, saying, "This place is desolate and it is already quite late. (6) Send the multitude away so that they may go into the surrounding villages and countryside and find lodging and get something to eat."

(7) Jesus, lifting up His eyes and seeing that a great multitude was coming to Him, said to the twelve, "They do not need to go away. You give them something to eat."

(8) They said to Jesus, "Shall we go and buy bread for them to eat?"

(9) Jesus said to Philip, "Where are we to buy bread that these may eat?" He said this to test Philip for He Himself knew what He was intending to do.

(10) Philip answered Jesus, "Two hundred denarii worth of bread is not sufficient for every one of them to receive even a little.

(11) Jesus asked, "How many loaves do you have? Go look!"

(12) When they had looked, one of them, Andrew Simon Peter's brother said to Jesus, "There is a lad here who has five barley loaves and two fish, but what are these for so many people?"

(13) Jesus said, "Bring them here to Me."

(14) Then Jesus commanded all the people to recline by groups on the green grass (15) and they reclined in companies of hundreds and fifties.

(16) Jesus then took the five loaves and the two fish and, looking up toward heaven, He blessed the food and broke the loaves and He kept giving them to the disciples to set before the multitude; and He divided up the two fish among them all.

(17) All the people ate and all were satisfied.

(18) After the people were all filled, Jesus said to His disciples, "Gather up the leftover fragments that nothing may be lost." (19) So they gathered up the fragments and filled twelve baskets from what was left over from the five barley loaves by those who had eaten. (20) There were about five thousand men who ate, besides the women and children.

(21) When the people saw the sign which Jesus had performed they said, "This is of a truth a Prophet who is to come into the world."

Notes: Of the four accounts of this incident in the four Gospels, only Matthew gives the information that the number of people was five thousand *men* plus unnumbered women and children. Matthew, of course, was writing to the Jews, and among the Jews, women and children were not permitted to eat with the men in public. Matthew probably emphasized the fact that the men did not eat with the women and children to show that nothing contrary to the laws or customs of the Jews was done.

It was unusual for a crowd of so many people to be gathered together in such a remote area. In a large city such as Athens or Rome or Jerusalem such a large crowd would not have been unusual, but the entire population of the cities of Capernaum or Bethsaida would probably have been only between two and three thousand people.

We don't know anything about the baskets which were filled with the leftover goods other than that they were there. Why they were there or from where they came, we don't know. Scholars suggest that they were probably baskets which were commonly used by the Jews to carry their food with them when they traveled away from home. Any Jew traveling through the lands of the Samaritans or the Gentiles would have found no place to buy food, kosher food, that is, as the Law required them to eat. It's possible that the twelve apostles had the baskets with them and that it was those baskets which were filled with the leftover bread.

Instead of "two hundred denarii," the NIV renders this phrase "eight months of a man's wages." The denarii were Roman coins and the value of one denarius was about one day's wages for the average working man and was about enough to support a family of four for one day.

75 Jesus Walks on Water

(Matt. 14:22-33; Mark 6:45-52; John 6:15-21)

(1) Jesus, perceiving that the people were intending to come and take Him by force to make Him king, determined to withdraw again to the mountain alone. (2) Immediately He made His disciples get into the boat and go ahead of Him to Bethsaida on the other side, while He Himself was sending the multitude away. (3) After bidding the disciples farewell He went up to the mountain by Himself to pray and when evening came He was still there alone.

(4) Now the sea began to be stirred up because a strong wind was blowing, (5) but the boat was already many stadia away from the land and was being battered by the waves, for the wind was contrary. (6) At about the fourth watch of the night Jesus was walking upon the sea. He intended to pass by the disciples but, seeing how they strained at the oars because of the wind being against them, He came to them.

(7) When the disciples saw Jesus walking on the sea they were frightened, and said, "It is a ghost!" And they cried out for fear.

(8) But Jesus spoke to them, "Take courage, it is I; do not be afraid."

(9) Peter answered, "Lord, if it is You, command me to come to You on the water."

(10) Jesus said, "Come!"

Peter then got out of the boat and, walking on the water, came toward Jesus. (11) But seeing the wind he became afraid and, beginning to sink, he cried out, "Lord, save me!"

(12) Immediately Jesus stretched out His hand and took hold of Peter and said to him, "O you of little faith, why did you doubt?"

(13) When Jesus and Peter got into the boat the wind stopped. (14) Those who were in the boat were astonished and worshiped Jesus saying, "You are certainly God's Son!" (15) They had not gained any insight from the incident of the loaves for their hearts were hardened.

Notes: It was evening when the disciples began their trip across the lake toward Bethsaida. They had gone about twenty-five to thirty furlongs or stadia when the wind became so strong that large waves were tossing the boat around. A furlong or stadia was about two hundred to two hundred twenty yards. A stadia was the distance the Greeks had established as the length of a foot race. The distance the disciples had rowed figures out to about three to four miles or five to six kilometers. The width of the lake is about eight or nine miles at its widest point so the disciples were literally in the middle of it.

In those days, the nights were divided into watches rather than in hours as were the days. A watch was three hours in length. Night (or watches) began at about what we would designate as six o'clock in the evening and ended at six o'clock in the morning, so it was between three and six o'clock in the morning and had taken the disciples from six to eight hours to reach the half way point of their trip. They were rowing instead of sailing, probably because the wind was too strong to permit the use of sails or else the wind was contrary to the direction they were intending to go. One can imagine how tired and sleepy the disciples must have been, having had no sleep and having rowed for from six to eight hours without rest from the previous days labors.

In the earlier times, the Jews had divided the night into three watches of four hours each. A watch was the length of time a soldier was required to stand guard, so each night three guards would stand watches of four hours each. But at this time, the number and length of the watches had been changed to four watches of three hours each, probably because the Romans divided their nights into four watches of three hours each.

In the armed forces of the United States, the standard tour of guard duty is two hours on watch and four hours off. In a twelve-hour tour, a guard would stand watch twice, and in a twenty-four-hour tour, he would stand watch four times.

Even if the disciples had not been so tired and sleepy, they probably could not have recognized Jesus in the darkness. Artists who paint the scene tend to picture the form of Jesus as glowing in the darkness. That's the way He was described in Revelation, but at this time, Jesus looked like any other man. To see someone walking on the water in the middle of a lake in a high wind would certainly have been frightening to anyone.

76 Jesus Performs Miracles at Gennesaret

(Matt. 14:34-36; Mark 6:53-56)

(1) When Jesus and the disciples had crossed over they came to land at Gennesaret and moored to the shore. (2) When they had come out of the boat the people immediately recognized Jesus. (3) They ran about that whole country and began to carry the pallets with those who were sick to the place where they heard Jesus was.

(4) Whenever Jesus entered a village or city or a countryside the people laid the sick in the market places and entreated Him that they might just touch the fringe of His cloak, and as many as touched it were made well.

Notes: Josephus described Gennesaret as a plain on the western shore of the Sea of Galilee. It was in the province of Galilee and was about four miles long with an average width of about two and a half miles. It was bounded on the east by the Sea of Galilee and on the west by a semicircular line of hills. Capernaum was located in this area.

77 Jesus at Capernaum; Many Disciples Forsake Him

(John 6:22-71)

(1) The next day the multitude that stood on the other side of the sea saw that there was only one small boat there and that Jesus had not entered into the boat with His disciples, but that the disciples had gone away alone. (2) There came other small boats from Tiberias close to the place where they ate the bread after the Lord had given thanks. (3) When the multitude saw that neither Jesus nor His disciples were there they themselves got into the small boats and went to Capernaum seeking Jesus. (4) When they found Him on the other side of the sea they said to Him, "Rabbi, when did You get here?"

(5) Jesus answered, "Truly, truly, I say to you, you seek Me, not because you saw signs, but because you ate the loaves and were filled.

(6) "Do not work for the food which perishes but for the food which endures to eternal life, which the Son of Man shall give to you, for on Him the Father, even God, has set His seal."

(7) They asked Jesus, "What shall we do that we may work the works of God?"

(8) Jesus said to them, "This is the work of God-that you believe in Him whom He has sent."

(9) They said to Jesus, "What then do You do for a sign that we may see and believe You? What work do You perform?

(10) Our fathers ate the manna in the wilderness, as it is written. 'He gave them bread out of heaven to eat.'"

(11) Jesus said to them, "Truly, truly, I say to you, it is not Moses who has given you bread out of heaven but it is My Father who gives you the true bread out of heaven. (12) The bread of God is that which comes down out of heaven and gives life to the world."

(13) They said, "Lord, evermore give us this bread."

(14) Jesus answered, "I am the bread of life. He who comes to Me shall not hunger and he who believes in Me shall not thirst. (15) I said to you that you have seen Me and yet do not believe. (16) All that the Father gives Me shall come to Me and the one who comes to Me I will certainly not cast out. (17) I have come down from heaven, not to do

My own will, but the will of Him who sent Me. (18) This is the will of Him who sent Me, that of all that He has given Me I lose nothing, but raise it up on the last day. (19) It is the will of My Father that every one who beholds the Son and believes in Him may have eternal life and I Myself will raise him up on the last day."

(20) Then the Jews grumbled about Jesus because He had said, "I am the bread that came down out of heaven."

(21) They said, "Is not this Jesus, the Son of Joseph, whose father and mother we know? How does He now say, 'I have come down out of heaven'?"

(22) Then Jesus said to them, "Do not grumble among yourselves. (23) No one can come to Me unless the Father who sent Me draws him, and I will raise him up on the last day. (24) It is written in the prophets, 'And they shall all be taught of God.' Every one who has heard and learned from the Father comes to Me. (25) Not that any man has seen the Father except the One who is from God. He has seen the Father.

(26) "Truly, truly, I say to you, he who believes has eternal life. (27) I am the bread of life. (28) Your fathers ate the manna in the wilderness and they died. (29) This is the bread which comes down out of heaven so that one may eat of it and not die. (30) I am the living bread that came down out of heaven. If any one eats of this bread he shall live forever and the bread which I shall give for the life of the world is My flesh."

(31) The Jews began to argue with one another, asking, "How can this Man give us His flesh to eat?"

(32) Jesus said to them, "Truly, truly, I say to you, unless you eat the flesh of the Son of Man and drink His blood you have no life in yourselves. (33) He who eats My flesh and drinks My blood has eternal life and I will raise him up on the last day. (34) My flesh is true food and My blood is true drink.

(35) He who eats My flesh and drinks My blood abides in Me and I in him. (36) As the living Father sent Me, and I live because of the Father, so he who eats Me shall also live because of Me. (37) This is the bread which came down out of heaven, not as the fathers ate and died, but he who eats this bread shall live forever."

(38) These things Jesus said in the synagogue as He taught in Capernaum.

(39) Many of His disciples, when they heard this said, "This is a difficult statement. Who can listen to it?"

(40) But Jesus, conscious that His disciples grumbled at this, said to them, "Does this cause you to stumble? (41) Then what if you should behold the Son of Man ascending where He was before? (42) It is the Spirit who gives life. The flesh profits nothing. The words that I have spoken to you are spirit and are life. (43) But there are some of you who do not believe." For Jesus knew from the beginning who they were who did not believe and who it was that would betray Him.

(44) Jesus continued, "For this reason I have said to you that no one can come to Me unless it has been granted him from the Father."

(45) As a result of these sayings many of Jesus' disciples withdrew and did not walk with Him any more.

(46) Jesus said to the twelve, "Do you not want to go away also?"

(47) Simon Peter answered Him, "Lord, to whom shall we go? You have words of eternal life. (48) We have believed and have come to know that You are the Holy One of God."

(49) Jesus answered them, "Did I Myself not choose you, the twelve, and yet one of you is a devil?" (50) Now Jesus meant Judas the son of Simon Iscariot, for Judas, one of the twelve, was going to betray Jesus.

Notes: The city of Tiberias was situated about half way down the western coast of the Sea of Galilee. It was built by Herod Antipas to honor the Roman emperor Tiberias. There are very few places even in that dry country less suited for a city than the site chosen for the city of Tiberias. The weather is very hot there. It was built between a very high mountain and the sea and is about six hundred feet below sea level. The mountain shields the city from any breezes coming from the Mediterranean Sea, and the temperature there is known to have been as high as a hundred degrees at midnight.

It isn't known why the boatmen sailed from Tiberias to the shore of that part of the lake where Jesus had fed the five thousand men. The distance is only about eight miles. One writer speculated that the boatmen saw the crowds on the far shore and went to see if they could earn money by ferrying them to some other place.

The question that Jesus was asked, "What shall we do that we may work the works of God?" is a question that is still being asked today. And man in his ignorance of the Bible has come up with all sorts of answers-pilgrimages, fasts, penance, letting the hair grow long, cutting off all the hair, growing a beard, and any number of other things.

The people in this passage seem to have been comparing Jesus to Moses. The Messiah was supposed to be greater than Moses or any of the prophets. Moses (supposedly) had given their fathers manna-a complete food-every day for nearly forty years, and Jesus had fed more than five thousand people one meal. Such a comparison was unfavorable to Jesus, but the point they failed to see was that everyone received what he needed. The five thousand needed one meal, and the Israelites in the wilderness needed food every day for nearly forty years. And there was something else these Jews had forgotten: that the Israelites got very tired of eating manna every meal of every day for nearly forty years.

Jesus said that belief in Him was necessary for salvation, but belief encompasses more than just an acknowledgment that He exists. It's like saying you believe in air, but fail to breathe it. You can't believe in Jesus and fail to obey His commandments. Jesus was often asked to perform some sign to prove that He was who He said He was. Even after seeing Him perform many miracles-healing the sick, lame, blind, deaf and dumb, raising the dead, and many other things-they still asked for a sign. One writer wrote that this was like someone who had seen the sun, felt its heat, witnessed its light and its power to make things grow and all the other things the sun does, and then refuses to believe it exists unless they see some other sign.

The Jews grumbled or murmured against Jesus because He said He was the bread of life. But the Jews had been murmuring against something or someone ever since before they had come out of Egypt. They murmured against Moses, against Aaron, against God, against the manna, against Joshua, against Saul-in fact, when didn't they murmur against something?

Apparently, there were people in the crowd who had known or known of Jesus when He was growing up in Nazareth. Perhaps, they had lately come from there because in their murmuring they asked, "Is not this Jesus, the son of Joseph, whose father and mother we know?

How does He now say, 'I have come down out of heaven'?" This is a further indication that Joseph was still alive at that time. They said, "Whose father we know." If they had said, "Whose father we knew," it would perhaps have meant that Joseph was dead or else that he had gone to live somewhere else. As to what happened to Joseph, when he died or whatever else may have happened to him, the scriptures are silent and there is no further mention of him.

The scripture to which Jesus referred is from Isaiah 54:13 and reads, "And all thy children shall be taught of the Lord; and great shall be the peace of thy children." Remember what is written in Jeremiah 31:33-34, "'But this is the covenant which I will make with the house of Israel after those days,' declares the Lord. 'I will put My law within them, and on their hearts I will write it' and I will be their God, and they shall be My people. And they shall not teach again, each man his neighbor and each man his brother, saying, "Know the Lord," for they shall all know Me, from the least of them to the greatest of them,' declares the Lord, 'for I will forgive their iniquity, and their sin I will remember no more.'"

From a previous scripture we learned that Jesus had decided to teach people only in parables and never in plain language. What Jesus was saying here was a parable of sorts. This was in the same language that Jesus would later use when He instituted what we call "the Lord's Supper." We can understand to some extent the confusion of the Jews because the Law of Moses specifically prohibited the ingestion of blood because the blood was the life of the animal. But knowing this, we can wonder why they were taking the words of Jesus in a strictly literal sense when they should have been able to see that they were not meant to be taken literally.

Perhaps one of the reasons for the murmuring of the Jews and their forsaking of Jesus was that He was dashing their hopes of a Jewish kingdom set up on earth, a kingdom which would free them from the rule of the Romans and make them subjects of an earthly king, perhaps one like David.

The message of the Bible is a happy message, a message that gives hope to a sinful world, but there are some sad things written there, too. One of those sad things are these words, "From this time many of His disciples went back and walked with Him no more." It seems to be a truism that the first time a person does something that time is the hardest and after that it gets progressively easier-the second time a person leads singing is easier than the first time, the second theft is easier and the second murder and the second time a person misses services and so on. These people had other opportunities to return to Jesus, but it says they "walked with Him no more."

78 Jesus Talks about the Traditions of Men

(Matt. 15:1-20; Mark 7:1-23; John 7:1)

(1) Afterwards Jesus walked in Galilee, for He was unwilling to walk in Judea because the Jews were seeking to kill Him.

(2) The Pharisees and some of the scribes who had come from Jerusalem gathered together around Jesus. (3) They had seen that some of His disciples were eating their bread with impure, that is, unwashed hands. (4) (The Pharisees and all the Jews do not eat unless they carefully wash their hands, thus observing the traditions of the elders. (5) When they come from the market place they do not eat unless they cleanse themselves, and there are many other things which they have received in order to observe, such as the washing of cups and pitchers and copper pots.)

(6) The Pharisees and the scribes then asked Jesus, "Why do Your disciples not walk according to the tradition of the elders, but eat their bread with impure hands?"

(7) Jesus answered, "Why do you yourselves transgress the commandment of God for the sake of your tradition? (8) God said, 'Honor your father and mother,' and, 'Let him who speaks evil of father or mother be put to death.' (9) But you say, 'If a man says to his father or his mother, "anything of mine you might have been helped by is Corban" (that is to say, given to God),' (10) you no longer permit him to do anything for his father or his mother (11) thus invalidating the word of God by your tradition which you have handed down. And you do many other things such as that.

(12) "You hypocrites, rightly did Isaiah prophesy of you,

(13) 'This people honors Me with their lips, but their heart is far away from Me. (14) In vain do they worship Me, teaching as their doctrines the precepts of men.'"

(15) Summoning the multitude again Jesus said to them, "Listen to Me, all of you, and understand. (16) There is nothing outside the man which going into him can defile him, but the things which proceed out of the man are what defile the man."

(17) Then the disciples came and said to Jesus, "Do You know that the Pharisees were offended when they heard this statement?"

(18) Jesus said, "Every plant which My heavenly Father did not plant shall be rooted up. (19) Let them alone-they are blind guides of the blind, and if a blind man guides a blind man both will fall into a pit."

(20) After leaving the multitude Jesus entered the house and His disciples questioned Him. Peter said to Jesus, "Explain the parable to us."

(21) Jesus said to them, "Are you also without understanding? Do you not see that whatever goes into the man from outside cannot defile him (22) because it does not go into his heart but into his stomach and is eliminated?" (Thus Jesus declared all foods clean.)

(23) Jesus continued, "But the things that proceed out of the mouth come from the heart, and those things defile the man.

(24) Out of the heart come evil thoughts, murders, adulteries, fornications, thefts, false witness, slanders, (25) deeds of coveting and wickedness, deceit, sensuality, envy, pride, foolishness. (26) These are the things which defile the man, but to eat with unwashed hands does not defile the man."

Notes: The traditions of the elders (or ancients) required that all Jews wash their hands before eating anything, and, if they had been in a large crowd of people, they might be required to bathe their whole body. The Jews believed that God gave two sets of laws to Moses, one set written down and the other given orally. This Oral Law was the traditions so important to them. The traditions were supposed to have been handed down from Moses to Joshua and so down through the ages from generation to generation. In the time of Jesus, these traditions of the elders were still in oral form and were not written down until about AD 200. Instead of being handed down from Moses, it is more than likely that they originated after the return of the Jews from the Babylonian captivity. No evidence can be found today which would indicate their origination at an earlier time. "Corban" was a Greek word (from an older Hebrew form) meaning "dedicated" or "the treasury," which in turn meant that the money was already in the treasury and, therefore, untouchable for any reason.

The prophecy that Jesus quoted is from Isaiah 29:13, but the Hebrew text of the Old Testament and the Greek text of the New Testament are not translated in the same words in any of the versions of the Bible, although their meanings are obviously the same.

79 Healing the Syrophoenician Woman's Daughter

(Matt. 15:21-28; Mark 7:24-30)

(1) Jesus went away from there and withdrew into the district of Tyre and Sidon. When He had entered a house He wanted no one to know of it, yet He could not escape notice.

(2) Hearing of Him, a woman whose little daughter had an unclean spirit immediately came and fell at Jesus' feet. (3) Now the woman was a Gentile, of the Syrophoenician race, and she cried out, saying, "Have mercy on me, 0 Lord, Son of David. My daughter is cruelly demon-possessed."

(4) But Jesus did not answer her a word, and His disciples came to Him and kept saying to Him, "Send her away for she is shouting out after us."

(5) Jesus said, "I was sent only to the lost sheep of the house of Israel."

(6) But the woman came and bowed down before Jesus and said, "Lord, help me!"

(7) Jesus said to her, "Let the children be satisfied first, for it is not good to take the children's bread and throw it to the dogs."

(8) Then the woman said, "Yes, Lord, but even the dogs under the table feed on the children's crumbs which fall from the master's table."

(9) Jesus said, "O woman, your faith is great. Be it done for you as you wish. The demon has gone out of your daughter." And the woman's daughter was healed at once. (10) Going back to her home the woman found the child lying on the bed, the demon having departed.

Notes: The cities of Tyre and Sidon were located in Syria (or Phoenicia), a Roman province. Tyre was about thirty-five miles northwest of Capernaum on the coast of the Mediterranean Sea, and Sidon was about twenty-five miles further north on the coast. This is the only place in the scriptures in which it says that Jesus visited any foreign place other than Egypt as a child.

The fact that the woman called Jesus the Son of David shows that she had not only heard of His miraculous powers but that she was also familiar with the fact that the Jews expected the Messiah to ascend the literal throne of David and to rule over a free and independent Jewish homeland. The work of Jesus heretofore had been limited almost exclusively to the Jews, another exception being the Roman centurion whose servant Jesus healed. Any exceptions were made to people who believed in His divinity and in His power.

There are valuable lessons to be learned from this woman. First, we can learn that even in the face of God's silence, we should persist in our prayers. Sometimes, only because of our persistence, we are rewarded by having our prayers answered as we would like them to be answered. But we should always avoid the trap of vain repetition. That was one of the mistakes the Pharisees made. They thought that by repeating a request over and over, it would eventually be granted.

Second, we can learn that God is open to reasoning with us. God and Jesus are one, and the woman reasoned with Jesus because she had great faith in His powers, and because of that faith, her request was granted. Also you might remember that Abraham bargained with God concerning the destruction of Sodom and Gomorrah.

Third, the woman compared this miracle (so great to her) as only a crumb which had fallen from the table in its importance to Jesus and to His great powers. The Jews, and even the apostles, were continually being amazed by the power and variety of the miracles of Jesus, but this woman, a foreigner, never doubted the power of Jesus. She had faith great enough to believe that whatever Jesus wanted to do, He could do.

80 Jesus Returns to Decapolis and Heals Many

(Matt. 15:29-31; Mark 7:31-37)

(1) Departing from there Jesus went out from the region of Tyre and came through Sidon to the sea of Galilee in the region of Decapolis, (2) and having gone up to the mountains, He was sitting there. (3) And the multitudes came to Him bringing with them the lame, crippled, blind, dumb, and many others and they laid them down at Jesus' feet, and He healed them, (4) so that the multitude marveled as they saw the dumb speaking, the crippled restored, the lame walking and the blind seeing; and they glorified the God of Israel.

(5) One of those they brought to Jesus was deaf and spoke with difficulty, and they entreated Jesus to lay His hand upon the man. (6) Jesus took the man aside from the multitude alone and put His fingers into the man's ears and after spitting, touched the man's tongue, with the saliva; (7) and looking up to heaven with a deep sign, He said, "Ephphatha!" that is, "Be opened!"

(8) Then the man's ears were opened and the impediment of his tongue was removed and he began speaking plainly.

(9) Jesus gave them orders not to tell anyone, but the more He ordered them, the more widely they continued to proclaim it.

(10) The people were utterly astonished, saying, "He has done all things well; He makes even the deaf to hear and the dumb to speak."

Notes: Returning from Tyre and Sidon, Jesus crossed over the mountains and into Decapolis on the eastern side of the Jordan River. Jesus was probably sitting, because He was tired, having just completed a walking tour of about a hundred fifty miles or more.

Jesus had been in the region of Decapolis before, so He and His works were known to the people there. We may speculate that some of the same people who now came to Jesus for healing may have been in the crowd which asked Jesus to leave their neighborhood, because the herd of swine had been destroyed after Jesus had sent the demons into them.

One biblical writer suggested that the impediment in the speech of the deaf man was that he stammered. Another, citing Mark 7:35, deduced that the man was tongue-tied. It is probably safe to assume that the man had not been deaf from birth; otherwise, he probably would not have been able to speak at all. I say "probably" because deaf people nowadays are able to learn to speak well enough to be understood. Helen Keller is a notable example of this. There is also an actress who was deaf from birth but can now speak well enough to be understood. It's possible, then, that the man had been deaf from birth and had learned to speak and that that was the reason for the impediment in his speech.

"Decapolis" is a Greek word meaning "ten cities." Although it was now a Roman province, Decapolis had originally been organized by the Greeks. The Greek people were known for their thirst for knowledge-any kind of knowledge. Paul is recorded to have taken advantage of this thirst for knowledge to teach the gospel when he was in Athens. Acts 17:19-21 reads, "And they took him and brought him to the Areopagus, saying, 'May we know what this new doctrine is of which you speak? For you are bringing some strange things to our ears. Therefore we want to know what these things mean. For all the Athenians and the foreigners who were there spent their time in nothing else but either to tell or to hear some new thing." The Jews who lived in Decapolis had come under the influence of the Greeks, and the Greek culture and had been Hellenized to some extent, adopting many of the Greek customs.

81 Jesus Feeds Four Thousand

Matt. 15:32-39 and Mark 8:1-10)

(1) In those days, too, when there was a great multitude and they had nothing to eat, Jesus summoned His disciples to Himself and said to them, (2) "I feel compassion for the multitude because they have remained with Me now three days and have nothing to eat. (3) If I send them away fasting to their homes they will faint on the way, and some of them have come from a distance."

(4) Jesus' disciples answered Him, "Where will anyone be able to find enough to satisfy these men with bread here in the wilderness?"

(5) Jesus asked them, "How many loaves do you have?" They said, "Seven, and a few small fish."

(6) Then Jesus directed the multitude to sit down on the ground. (7) He took the seven loaves and the fish and, giving thanks, He broke them and started giving them to the disciples, and the disciples in turn gave them to the multitudes.

(8) All the multitude ate and were satisfied, and the disciples picked up seven full baskets of what was left over of the broken pieces. (9) Those who ate were four thousand men, besides women and children.

(10) Dismissing the multitudes, Jesus entered the boat with His disciples and they came to the region or district of Magadan, also known as Magdala or Dalmanutha.

Notes: This incident of feeding people miraculously is very similar to that which was recorded in Matthew 14:14-21 (section 74), that is, people had gathered to see and hear Jesus and to be healed of their ailments, but had not brought enough food to last them. The last time it had been a boy who had brought food. This time it appears that it was one or more of the disciples who had done so.

Jesus said the people had been with Him three days and now had nothing to eat. Because of the way the Jews counted time that could have meant anywhere between about twenty-six hours and seventy-two hours. As an extreme example, they could have counted any part of a day as a day so that an hour in one day, one whole day, and an hour in another day would have been counted as three days.

As was stated, when Jesus fed the five thousand men, here again when He fed the four thousand, that figure did not include women and children. The number of people who were actually fed in both cases could have been double the number given.

The fact that Matthew stated that Jesus and His disciples set sail for Magdala *(KJV* and NKJV) or Magadan (ASV, NASV, and NIV) and Mark stated that they went to Dalmanutha does not mean that the two writers contradicted each other. Magdala was the town from which Mary Magdalene came and was the same place called Magadan by some writers. It is probably the same town that was called Migdalel in Joshua 19:38 and that is now known as Mejdel. Nothing is known about a place, whether town or region, that Mark called Dalmanutha. It may also have been another name for Magdala or Magadan. A cave with the name "Talmanutha" has been found south of the plain of Gennesaret. Whether this is the location of Dalmanutha (or another name for it) or has no connection at all is an unanswered question.

82 Pharisees and Sadducees Seek a Sign

(Matt. 16:1-4; Mark 8:11-13; Luke 12:1a)

(1) There the Pharisees and Sadducees came out and began to argue with Jesus, asking Him to show them a *sign from heaven* to test Him.

(2) Sighing deeply in His spirit, Jesus said to them, "When it is evening you say, 'It will be fair weather for the sky is red,'

(3) and in the morning, 'There will be a storm today for the sky in red and threatening.' Do you know how to discern the appearance of the sky but cannot discern the signs of the times?

(4) Why does this evil and adulterous generation seek after a sign? Truly, no sign will be given this generation except the sign of Jonah."

(5) In the meantime so many people had gathered together that they trod upon one another, and leaving these people, Jesus again embarked and went away to the other side.

Notes: The Pharisees and Sadducees, so different in their philosophies or doctrines, had put aside their differences and joined together in an effort to find some means of causing trouble for Jesus. They wanted to test Him by asking that He show them a sign from heaven. What that sign could have been is a mystery since they didn't accept the healing of the sick, restoring sight to the blind, letting the deaf hear and the dumb speak, cleansing lepers, or making the lame to walk as signs from heaven. Moses had sent the manna, Samuel had caused it to thunder, and Isaiah had caused the sun to back ten steps on the stairway of Ahaz, or rather God had done those things through those men. What could Jesus possibly have done to convince them? Of course, the Pharisees and Sadducees were not really looking for a sign from heaven but were trying to find something to charge against Jesus, something of which they could accuse Him or cause Him to lose the respect of the people who were following Him.

It's a common saying nowadays, "Red sky at night; sailors' delight. Red sky at morning; sailors take warning." That means that if the sky is red at evening, the weather the next morning will be good, but that if the sky is red in the morning there will be bad weather. Most people, not even sailors, probably would not know that saying is from the Bible.

On other occasions the Jews had asked Jesus for a sign as proof that He was who He said He was. And as on those other occasions, Jesus did not give them such a sign. But He did tell them again that the only sign they would see was the sign of Jonah. Whether or not they understood what Jesus meant by that we don't know. We do know when He did give them the sign of Jonah, His return to life after three days and three nights in the tomb, most of them still did not believe in Him.

83 Jesus Warns of the Leaven of the Pharisees And Sadducees

(Matt. 16:5-12; Mark 8:14-21; Luke 12:1b)

(1) The disciples came to the other side and had forgotten to take bread. They did not have more than one loaf in the boat with them.

(2) Jesus said to His disciples first of all, "Watch out! Beware of the leaven of the Pharisees and Sadducees and of Herod, which is hypocrisy."

(3) The disciples began to discuss Jesus' words among themselves. They said, "He said that because we brought no bread."

(4) Jesus, aware of their thoughts, said to them, "O you of little faith, why do you discuss among yourselves because you have no bread? Do you not see or understand? Do you have a hardened heart? (5) Having eyes, do you not see? And having ears, do you not hear? Do you not remember (6) when I broke the five loaves for the five thousand? How many large baskets full of broken pieces did you pick up?"

They said to Jesus, "Twelve."

(7) "When I broke the seven for the four thousand, how many baskets full of broken pieces did you pick up?"

They answered Him, "Seven."

(8) "How is it that you do not understand that I did not speak to you concerning bread? But beware of the leaven of the Pharisees and Sadducees."

(9) Then the disciples understood that Jesus did not say to beware of the leaven of bread, but of the teaching of the Pharisees and Sadducees.

Notes: Jesus warned His disciples against the teachings of the Pharisees, the Sadducees, and the Herodians. The leaven (or teachings) of the Pharisees was tradition and formalism. The Sadducees didn't believe in life after death, and the Herodians were morally and politically corrupt.

The disciples later understood that Jesus was warning them that they must not let the doctrines of those three groups creep into their own lives. It might seem sometimes that Christians are guilty of doing just that. It's easy to understand and build doctrines on clear statements in the Bible, but sometimes people are mislead by an incorrect understanding of texts which are not so clear and form opinions based on those misunderstandings. Then those people try to bind their opinions on others as well.

Back in the eighteenth and nineteenth centuries there was a great movement which came to be known as the "restoration." Men of understanding tried to restore New Testament teachings in the churches. Those men studied and mostly held the same opinions about what the Bible taught. Since then, though, the New Testament church that they tried to restore has been fragmented and splintered by different groups within the church forming contrary opinions and trying to bind those opinions on the church as a whole. Issues such as how to provide for orphans and widows and old people, how to raise funds to support the church, instrumental music and so on have divided the church into a number of different institutions, each of them believing that they are correct in what they believe or that it makes no difference to their salvation just what they do believe.

Two different Greek words are translated into English as "baskets." The two meanings, though, are slightly different. The first meaning was a small basket and the other meant a larger basket or a food basket such as a picnic basket.

84 Jesus Heals a Blind Man at Bethsaida (Mark 8:22-26)

(1) Jesus and the disciples came to Bethsaida. There a blind man was brought to Jesus and those who brought him entreated Jesus to touch him. (2) Taking the blind man by the hand Jesus brought him out of the village. After spitting on his eyes and laying His hands upon the man, Jesus asked him, "Do you see anything?"

(3) The blind man looked up and said, "I see men, but I am seeing them like trees walking about."

(4) Then again Jesus laid His hands upon the man's eyes; and the man looked intently and was restored and began to see everything clearly.

(5) Then Jesus sent the man to his home, saying, "Do not even enter the village."

Notes: There were two towns named Bethsaida, or perhaps one town but with two separate parts. One town, a small one, was on the western side of the Jordan River. The other town or part, situated across the river on the eastern side of the Jordan, was much larger and prettier. The name of the town on the eastern side of the Jordan was properly Bethsaida Julias, being named for a daughter of the Roman emperor. The two towns were in two different provinces, the one to the west in Galilee and the one to the east in Gaulanitis.

It's evident that as soon as the people saw Jesus, they recognized Him because immediately they brought a blind man to have his sight restored.

Jesus put saliva (spit) on the man's eyes, whether for a therapeutic reason or just that Jesus chose to do so for no particular reason, we don't know. In restoring the sight of another man, Jesus had mixed dirt with spit and applied that to the man's eyes. In still other cases, Jesus just spoke and sight was restored.

This is the only occasion of which we know in which the miracle of Jesus was performed in two stages, and we don't know the reason for it having been done in that way.

According to indications, this man had not been blind from birth because he knew what trees looked like, and he knew the difference between the appearance of men and of trees.

85 The Great Confession

(Matt. 16:13-20; Mark 8:27-30; Luke 9:18-21)

(1) Now Jesus came into the district of Caesarea Philippi and, with His disciples, went out to the villages. (2) While He was praying He questioned the disciples, asking them, "Who do people say that I, the Son of Man, am?"

(3) They told Him, "Some say John the Baptist, and others say Elijah, and others say Jeremiah or that one of the prophets of old has risen again."

(4) Jesus asked the disciples, "But who do you say that I am?"

(5) Simon Peter answered and said, "You are the Christ, the Son of the living God!"

(6) Jesus said to Peter, "Blessed are you, Simon Barjonah, because flesh and blood did not reveal this to you. My Father who is in heaven revealed it. (7) I also say to you that you are Peter, and upon this rock I will build My church and the gates of Hades shall not overpower it.

(8) "I will give you the keys of the kingdom of heaven-and whatever you shall bind on earth shall have been bound in heaven and whatever you shall loose on earth shall have been loosed in heaven."

(9) Then Jesus warned the disciples that they should tell no one that He was the Christ.

Notes: The region to which Jesus went next was near the town of Caesarea Philippi, that is, the villages in the vicinity of Caesarea Philippi.

The original name of Caesarea Philippi was Paneas. Herod Philip had the town enlarged and beautified and he renamed it Caesarea to honor the emperor Tiberias Caesar. There was another town named Caesarea located on the coast of the Mediterranean Sea and to distinguish his city from the one on the Mediterranean, Philip added his own name to the name he had given the city thus making the full name of the town Caesarea Philippi. It is no longer called Caesarea Philippi but is now called Banias, a corruption of its original name. The town is at the foot of Mount Hermon and, except for Sidon, is probably the most northernmost point Jesus reached in any of His travels.

This passage is very familiar to most of us. It has been taught in classes and preached in sermons and has been used as proof of a doctrinal point. Some institutions take the passage as proof that Peter was the rock on which the church of Christ was built. A careful unbiased study will, however, show that it was the truth of the statement Peter made which was the rock upon which the church was built.

The phrase which Jesus so often used in referring to Himself, "the Son of Man," was meant to indicate His divinity. By asking His disciples who other people thought He was and then asking them who they thought He was may have been the method Jesus used to help the disciples think about that subject deeply enough to resolve their own thinking about the matter.

Matthew wrote in 14:2 that Herod Philip thought Jesus was John the Baptist reincarnated. When Jesus first began His ministry, people in general seemed to have accepted Him as the Messiah, but only as a man and not as the Son of God. And throughout the ministry of Jesus, people were ready to accept Him as a prophet, even though many of them didn't accord Him the honor and the acclaim which would have been due a prophet. In spite of all the evidence of the divinity of Jesus, His teachings and the miracles He performed, the Jews refused to accept Him as a spiritual Messiah-they wanted a physical, a political Messiah, at one time trying to take Him by force and make Him their earthly king.

Peter's answer to the question of Jesus as to who the disciples thought He was, wasn't given in a way to indicate that it was his opinion, but that what he said was a fact. As the "Anointed One," Jesus was the fulfillment of many Old Testament prophecies, but to fulfill some of those prophecies such as that He was of the lineage of David, Jesus had to be a man. Peter said that Jesus was the Son of the living God.

By using the term "living God," Peter and the prophets were calling attention to the fact that their God was alive and active in the lives of people in contrast to the blocks of stone or wood which some people worshiped as gods and which had never been alive.

The word "blessed" here means: extremely fortunate, happy, honored, and worthy of the approbation of God. "Simon Barjonah" means simply "Simon, son of Jonah."

By "flesh and blood," Jesus meant mortal man. No mortal person had made the revelation to Peter-it had been revealed to him by God, the Father of Jesus. In the past, Jesus had been called the Messiah by several people who had been witnesses or subjects of His miracles, but they had made the statement in such a way as to indicate wonder rather than a conviction of that fact. How else could this man perform such miracles! The knowledge Peter expressed had been given to him directly by God.

As stated earlier, this passage has become a part of the doctrine of several different religious groups but for differing reasons. There are several different interpretations of the statement by Jesus leading to different doctrinal beliefs. One interpretation is that by "rock" Jesus is referring to the truth of the statement Peter had just made. The words "Peter" and "rock" in this passage are two forms of the same Greek word for rock. "Rock" is the feminine form of the word and means a mass of rock or a very large rock. "Peter" is the masculine form and refers to a rock much smaller than that meant by "rock" but larger than the word which is translated "stone." This interpretation would mean, then, that Jesus had said in effect, "You are Peter. You have stated a fact and upon that fact, the fact which you have just stated, I am going to build My church."

Other religious groups take the position that Jesus was referring to Himself when He spoke of the rock upon which He would build His church. If this is true, Jesus would have been saying in effect, "You are Peter. You have said that I am the Christ, the Son of the living God. Upon Myself because I am the Son of God I will build My church."

Still others claim that Jesus was saying that Peter, the person, was the rock which would become the foundation of the church Jesus was going to build. That is the doctrinal belief of some, holding also that because Peter was the foundation of the church, he was also infallible in his teaching. There are several things which weaken the argument for that doctrine, which doctrine could otherwise seem to be a good one. In Acts 15, the advice of Peter was rejected and that of James was followed. Further, there is recorded an incident in which Peter was definitely in the wrong and for which cause Paul withstood him to his face. Those things seem to disprove the infallibility of Peter.

There are people, often referred to as "fundamentalists," the word sometimes used by other religious organizations in a deprecating manner, who are always striving to establish the truth of any and every passage in the Bible. These "fundamentalists" are convinced that the rock upon which Jesus would build His church was the truth of the statement Peter made. A building built on dirt or sand or swamp, anything less than firm rock, is not perfect and will not endure. If we are to believe that Peter was the foundation of the church, we are forced to believe that the foundation of the church is less than perfect because Peter, as we all know, was less than perfect.

Traditionally, ancient cities were most vulnerable to attack at their gates so the gates had to be more heavily fortified than the rest of the defensive walls. This was difficult because the gates were moveable and less easily fortified. Too, the gates of a city were the points from which attacks were launched against outside forces. The gates of Hades, heavily fortified, are the points from which Satan sallies forth to attack God's people.

Even though Peter was not the foundation upon which the church of Christ was built, he was given the keys of the kingdom of heaven. Subsequent scriptures reveal what that meant. Peter was given the honor of preaching the first gospel sermon to the Jews on that day of Pentecost, and Peter was given the honor of preaching the first gospel sermon to Gentiles when he delivered the gospel to Cornelius and his household. It is evident, then, that the "keys of the kingdom" are the words of the gospel message that leads to salvation. After the kingdom of heaven was opened to the Jews and then to the Gentiles, the "keys of the kingdom" were no longer needed. The "way" was now open to everyone. The other apostles and all who wished to do so would spread the message of the hope of heaven to others. Peter's only honor was in being the first to preach that message. The New Testament writers, including Peter, were only infallible when being led by the Holy Spirit. Evangelists, or any others, are infallible only when they are teaching the truth as revealed in the New Testament. Like all other people, when we express an opinion not backed up by the scriptures, we can be, and often are, wrong.

86 The Passion Foretold and Peter Rebuked

(Matt. 16:21-28; Mark 8:31-9:1; Luke 9:22-27)

(1) From that time Jesus began to teach and to show His disciples that He must go to Jerusalem, and suffer many things, and be rejected by the elders and chief priests and scribes, and be killed, and after three days rise again.

(2) Peter took Jesus aside and began to rebuke Him, saying, "God forbid it, Lord! This shall never happen to You."

(3) But turning around and seeing His disciples, Jesus rebuked Peter, and said, "Get behind Me, Satan! You are a stumbling block to Me, for you are not setting your mind on God's interests but on man's."

(4) Jesus summoned the multitude with His disciples and said to them, "If anyone wishes to come after Me let him deny himself and take up his cross daily and follow Me. (5) Whoever wishes to save his life shall lose it, and whoever loses his life for My sake and the gospel's, he is the one who will save it. (6) What will a man be profited if he gains the whole world and loses or forfeits his own soul? Or what will a man give in exchange for his soul?

(7) "Whoever is ashamed of Me and My words in this adulterous and sinful generation, of him will the Son of Man be ashamed when He comes in His glory, and the glory of the Father and the holy angels, and will recompense every man according to his deeds."

(8) Jesus continued to them, "Truly I say to you, there are some of those who are standing here who shall not taste of death until they see the kingdom of God after it has come with power."

Notes: At this time, Jesus began to tell His disciples in plain language what was going to happen to Him. When He told these things to His disciples, He did so openly and anyone else who was near could hear Him. Later, what Jesus said about His resurrection was used in testimony against Him to show that He had blasphemed.

The elders, the chief priests, and the scribes about whom Jesus said would reject Him were the classes of people who made up the Sanhedrin, the Jewish ruling council.

In calling Jesus aside and rebuking Him for what He had just said, Peter was showing that he did not yet fully understand the purpose behind Jesus corning down to earth. Peter had just acknowledged his belief that Jesus was the Son of God, but he had yet to understand what that meant to him and to the world.

The question arises now that if the twelve disciples had known the nature of the journey upon which they were beginning at the time they were called whether or not they would have been so willing to follow Jesus. Even after the resurrection of Jesus and just before His ascension, the disciples asked Jesus in Acts 1:6 if He was finally ready to restore the kingdom to Israel. It seems that even at that late date, they still had visions of the glory of an earthly kingdom for the Jews and the end of domination by foreigners.

Jesus knew at that time the manner of the death He was destined to suffer, that He would be crucified. And he used a cross as a symbol of the burden Christians might have to carry and the danger they might have to face. We read in the Bible about people who did cling to their faith in spite of the persecution, and secular history records that thousands of them chose a similar fate rather than renounce their faith. Jesus emphasized that the cross must be a constant reminder of their calling.

The words "life" and "soul" used in this passage are both translated from the same Greek word *psuche* (psoo-khay'). The references are to a temporal life which will end compared to a spiritual life which will never end.

To be ashamed of Jesus or His word is to deny Jesus. To believe in private but deny in public is to renounce faith in Jesus. Paul wrote in Romans 1:16, "For I am not ashamed of the gospel of Christ: for it is the power of God unto salvation to everyone that believes; to the Jew first, but also to the Greek." The Greek word used here, and in many other places where the power of God is meant, as opposed to other words translated "power," is from the Greek word *dunamis* (doo'-nam-is) and implies miraculous power. Certainly, there was miraculous power present at the time of the first gospel sermon-power to allow all those people to hear in their own language, power to convict people of their sins and make them want to be saved, power to make three thousand people respond to the message, and power to save all three thousand of them and give them eternal life.

In response to those people who believe that the kingdom of God is only in the future and only in heaven, the words of Jesus stating that some of the people who heard Him speak the words that day would still be alive when the kingdom was established should be proof enough that the kingdom of God is an earthly kingdom, that is, it's a spiritual kingdom on earth, a vehicle to transport the saved to heaven at the proper time.

Words to think on: Why did Jesus say, "Get behind Me, Satan!"? Was Jesus calling Peter by the name "Satan"? Or were those words meant to be only an exclamation?

87 The Transfiguration

(Matt. 17:1-13; Mark 9:2-13; Luke 9:28-36)

(1) Six or eight days later Jesus went up to a high mountain to pray and took with Him Peter and James and John his brother, and brought them up there by themselves.

(2) While Jesus was praying He was transfigured before them. The appearance of His face became different and shone like the sun, and His garments became white and glistening, so white as no fuller on earth can clean them. (3) There were two men talking with Jesus-Moses and Elijah-{4} who, appearing in glory, were speaking of His departure which He was about to accomplish at Jerusalem.

(5) Now Peter and his companions had been overcome with sleep but when they were fully awake they saw the glory of Jesus and the two

men standing with Him. (6) And as the two men were parting from Jesus Peter said to Jesus, "Lord, it is good for us to be here. Now let us make three tabernacles: one for You, and one for Moses, and one for Elijah"-not realizing what he was saying, for they were all terrified.

(7) While Peter was still speaking, a bright cloud formed and began to overshadow them, and they were afraid. (8) And a voice came from out of the cloud saying, "This is My beloved Son with whom I am well pleased; hear Him."

(9) When the disciples heard this they fell on their faces and were much afraid, (10) until Jesus came to them and touched them and said, "Arise and be not afraid."

(11) Lifting up their eyes they looked around and saw no one with them except Jesus Himself alone.

(12) As they were coming down from the mountain Jesus commanded the disciples saying, "Tell the vision to no one until the Son of Man has risen from the dead." (13) They seized upon that statement, discussing with one another what rising from the dead might mean.

(14) His disciples asked Jesus, "Why then do the scribes say that Elijah must come first?"

(15) Jesus said, "Elijah does first come and restore everything. Yet how is it written of the Son of Man that He should suffer many things and be treated with contempt? (16) I say to you that Elijah already came, and they did not recognize him, but did to him whatever they wished. So also the Son of Man is going to suffer at their hands."

(17) Then the disciples understood that Jesus had spoken to them about John the Baptist. (18) They kept silent, though, and reported to no one in those days any of the things which they had seen.

Notes: Both Matthew and Mark wrote that it was six days later, but Luke wrote that it was about eight days later. This is not necessarily a discrepancy between the different accounts of the Gospel. Matthew and Mark could have been counting the number of full days between the two events whereas Luke could have been counting also the parts of days, the balance of the day on which the previous event occurred and the part of the day prior to the time on which the current event happened. This could have happened because the written accounts were in Greek whereas the spoken language of the time and place was Aramaic.

By tradition, the site of the transfiguration was Mount Tabor. If that's true, Jesus and the disciples were no longer in the vicinity of Caesarea Philippi but in Galilee. The scriptures say the mountain was a high mountain, but Mount Tabor is not a very high mountain, rising only about 1,748 feet above sea level. By contrast, Mount Hermon is the highest mountain in Israel. It rises about 9,400 feet above sea level and is in the vicinity of Caesarea Philippi.

The face of Jesus shone like the sun, probably because He had been talking to His Father. You may remember that the face of Moses also shone after he had been talking to God. Exodus 34:29-30 reads, "And it came about when Moses was coming down from Mount Sinai (and the two tablets of the testimony were in Moses' hand as he was coming down from the mountain), that Moses did not know that the skin of his face shone because of his speaking to Him. So when Aaron and all the sons of Israel saw Moses, behold the skin of his face shone, and they were afraid to come near him."

A fuller as used in this passage is a cloth dresser or launderer. The dictionary says it is one who fulls cloth, and that to full is to shrink and thicken woolen cloth by moistening, heating, and pressing. You may be familiar with a product called fuller's earth. This is a very fine white powder which is used to clean and purify a product such as in the refining of vegetable oil.

Jesus, Moses, and Elijah were discussing the imminent departure of Jesus. The KN renders this "decease" instead of "departure." The Greek word from which it is translated is "exodus" and means death or parting. As used here, "departure" probably included the crucifixion, death, burial, resurrection, and ascension in its meaning.

Peter's suggestion that they build three tabernacles to honor Jesus, Moses, and Elijah, if carried out, would have meant that the three men would have been on the same level of importance. God made it clear that the Messiah was superior to and succeeded the Law and the Prophets. When God ceased speaking, Moses and Elijah were no longer there, only Jesus remained. The Law and the Prophets had disappeared, but the Messiah was still there-the old law shall be fulfilled and the prophecies have or will come to pass but Jesus is forever.

Malachi 4:5 reads, "Behold, I am going to send you Elijah the prophet before the coming of the great and terrible day of the Lord." Citing this passage, the Jewish scribes or teachers of the law insisted that Elijah must come again before the Messiah came.

That prophecy, as Jesus told the disciples, was referring to John the Baptist and not to an actual rebirth or reappearing of Elijah. Elijah was representative of the restorer of Judaism, but that part of the history of the Jewish people was already past. Elijah could not restore Christianity, because Christianity had not yet been established. It must follow, then, that the figure of Elijah was only figurative and that the fulfillment of the prophecy was through John.

88 Jesus Heals the Demoniac Boy

(Matt. 17:14-21; Mark 9:14-29; Luke 9:37-43a)

(1) The next day Jesus and the three who were with Him came down from the mountain. They saw a large crowd around the other disciples, and scribes were arguing with them. (2) Immediately when the entire crowd saw Jesus, they were amazed and began running up to greet Him.

(3) Jesus asked the disciples, "What are you discussing with them?"

(4) A man separated himself from the multitude and came up to Jesus and, falling down on his knees before Him, said, "Lord, have mercy on my son. I beg You to look at him for he is my only boy. (5) He is possessed by a spirit of epilepsy and when it seizes him it throws him into convulsions and he foams at the mouth and grinds his teeth and stiffens out. (6) He is very ill and he often falls into the fire and often into the water.

(7) I brought him to Your disciples and begged them to cast it out and they could not."

(8) Jesus said, "O unbelieving and perverted generation, how long shall I be with you? How long shall I put up with you? Bring your son here to **Me**."

(9) They brought the boy to Jesus, and when the boy saw Jesus immediately the spirit threw him into a convulsion, and, falling to the ground, he began rolling about and foaming at the mouth.

(10) Jesus asked the father, "How long has this been happening to him?"

The father said, "From childhood, (11) and it has often thrown him both into the fire and into the water to destroy him. But if You can do anything, take pity on us and help us!"

(12) Jesus said, "'If You can!' All things are possible to him who believes."

(13) Immediately the boy's father cried out and began saying, "I do believe; help me in my unbelief."

(14) When Jesus saw that a crowd was rapidly gathering, He rebuked the unclean spirit, saying to it, "You deaf and dumb spirit, I command you, come out of him and do not enter him again."

(15) After crying out and throwing the boy into terrible convulsions the spirit came out, and the boy became so much like a corpse that most of the crowd said, "He is dead!"

(16) But Jesus took the boy by the hand and raised him up and gave him back to his father, and the people were all amazed at the greatness of God.

(17) When Jesus had come into the house, His disciples came and began questioning Him privately, "Why is it that we could not cast it out?"

(18) Jesus said to them, "Because of the smallness of your faith; for truly I say to you, if you have faith as a mustard seed you shall say to this mountain, 'Move from here to there,' and it shall move; and nothing shall be impossible to you. (19) But this kind does not go out by anything but prayer and fasting."

Notes: What reason could Jesus have had in asking the man to tell Him about his son? Jesus could already know exactly the answers to His questions. He had often before demonstrated that He knew the thoughts of men before they spoke. In this case, Jesus probably wanted the multitude of people to hear from the man himself the nature and duration of his son's ailment.

In what manner and how deeply did the man reveal his faith in the power of Jesus? Instead of showing that he believed in the power of Jesus, he showed a lack of faith by what he said, "If You can do anything ..."

Compare this man's faith to that of the centurion at Capernaum. The centurion, a Gentile, had absolute and unquestioning faith in the power of Jesus to heal his servant, but this Jew showed that he didn't have a great deal of faith in Jesus. It seems that the man came to Jesus with a desire and in desperation but with very little hope.

89 Death and Resurrection of Jesus Again Foretold

(Matt. 17:22-23; Mark 9:30-32; Luke 9:43b-45)

(1) While everyone was marveling at all that Jesus was doing, Jesus and His disciples went out from the region of Caesarea Philippi and began to go through Galilee, but Jesus was unwilling for anyone to know about it. (2) As they were gathering together Jesus was teaching His disciples, telling them, "Let these words sink into your ears-the Son of Man is to be betrayed into the hands of men and they will kill Him, and when He has been killed He will rise again three days later."

(3) The disciples were deeply grieved for they did not understand this statement. It was concealed from them so that they might not perceive it, and they were afraid to ask Jesus about it.

Notes: This was the second time Jesus had spoken to the disciples about His death. In section 86 (Matt. 16:21), He had also told them that He was to be killed.

The reason the disciples were grieved and didn't understand what Jesus told them was probably because, even though they did believe that Jesus was the Messiah, they still did not understand the mission of Jesus on earth. If He was the Messiah, how could He die before He returned Israel to its former glory!

90 Jesus Pays Tribute (Matt. 17:24-27)

(1) When Jesus and His disciples had come to Capernaum those who collected the temple tax came to Peter and asked, "Does your teacher not pay the two drachma tax?"

(2) Peter said, "Yes."

When Peter came into the house Jesus spoke to him first, saying, "What do you think, Simon? From whom do the kings of the earth collect customs or poll-tax, from their sons or from strangers?"

(3) Peter answered, "From strangers."

Then Jesus said to him, "Consequently the sons are exempt.

(4) But lest we give them offense, go to the sea and throw in a hook. Take the first fish that comes up and when you open its mouth you will find a shekel. Take that and give it to them for you and Me."

Notes: Under the Law as given to Moses, every male Jew was required to pay a half-shekel annually for the support of the temple. Exodus 30:12-16 reads, "When you take a census of the sons of Israel to number them, then each one of them shall give a ransom for himself to the Lord, when you number them, that there may be no plague among you when you number them. This is what everyone who is numbered shall give: half a shekel according to the shekel of the sanctuary (the shekel is twenty gerahs), half a shekel as a contribution to the Lord. Everyone who is numbered, from twenty years old and over, shall give the contribution to the Lord. The rich shall not pay more, and the poor shall not pay less than the half shekel, when you give the contribution to the Lord to make atonement for your souls. And you shall take the atonement money from the sons of Israel, and shall give it for the service of the tent of meeting, that it may be a memorial for the sons of Israel before the Lord, to make atonement for your souls."

The Jews did not issue their own money but used the money of common trade in whatever region and time in which they resided. According to Josephus, two drachmas were equal in value to the half shekel of the temple tax. Albert Barnes was of the opinion that this temple tax was a voluntary tax and not one that was required by law. However, the wording of the passage from Exodus which was quoted above seems to require the payment of the tax by all males twenty years old and older. In that passage, the words "shall give" appear several times, indicating that at the time the law was given payment of the tax was a definite requirement and not a voluntary contribution. From the original text in Exodus, it's unclear whether this tax was to be a one time tax, a tax to be collected any time the people were numbered or was to be a yearly tax. However, when Jesus lived, this tax may have been changed by tradition to a voluntary contribution.

91 The Greatest in the Kingdom of Heaven

(Matt. 18:1-11, 14; Mark 9:33-50; Luke 9:46-50, 17:1-2)

(1) On the way an argument arose among the disciples as to which of them might be the greatest. (2) When they came to Capemaum they went into the house and Jesus began to question the disciples, "What were you discussing on the way?" But they kept silent.

(3) Sitting down, Jesus called the twelve and said to them, "If any one wants to be first he shall be last of all and servant of all."

(4) They asked, "Who then is greatest in the kingdom of heaven?"

(5) Jesus called a child to Himself and stood him in their midst and, taking the child in His arms, He said to the disciples, (6) "Truly I say to you, unless you are converted and become like children you shall not enter the kingdom of heaven. (7) Whoever then humbles himself as this child, whoever is least among you is the greatest in the kingdom of heaven.

(8) "Whoever receives one such child in My name receives Me, and whoever receives Me is not receiving Me but Him who sent **Me.**"

(9) John said to Jesus, "Master, we saw someone casting out demons in Your name and we tried to hinder him because he was not following with us."

(10) But Jesus said, "Do not hinder him for there is no one who shall perform a miracle in My name and be able soon afterward to speak evil of Me. (11) He who is not against us is for us. (12) Whoever gives you a cup of water to drink because of your name as followers of Christ, truly I say to you, he shall not lose his reward.

(13) "If anyone causes one of these little ones who believe in Me to stumble it would be better for him that a heavy millstone be hung around his neck and that he be cast into the depth of the sea and drowned. (14) Woe to the world because of its stumbling blocks! It is inevitable that stumbling blocks come but woe to that man through whom the stumbling block comes.

(15) "If your hand causes you to stumble cut it off. It is better for you to enter life crippled than having two hands to go into hell, into the unquenchable fire. (16) And if your foot causes you to stumble cut it off. It is better for you to enter life lame than having your two feet to be cast into hell. (17) And if your eye causes you to stumble pluck it out and throw it from you. It is better for you to enter the kingdom of God with one eye than having two eyes to be cast into the hell of fire, (18) where their worm does not die and the fire is not quenched.

(19) "For everyone will be salted with fire. (20) Salt is good, but if the salt becomes unsalty with what will you make it salty again? Have salt in yourselves and be at peace with one another.

(21) "See that you do not despise one of these little ones, for I say to you that their angels in heaven continually behold the face of My Father who is in heaven. (22) Thus it is not the will of your Father who is in heaven that one of these little ones perish."

Notes: At this time, the disciples still didn't know the nature of the kingdom of heaven, continuing to believe it was a kingdom that was to be set up on earth. Believing that, it may have been natural for a person to wonder who, in this new kingdom, would be the chiefs and sub-chiefs and all the other administrators. The disciples were curious to know which of them would have what job, perhaps thinking that it was for this purpose Jesus had chosen them.

"Become as little children!" How did Jesus mean that? Little children have a capacity for belief in things which are nonsense to more mature people. But that's the way people must believe in Jesus, like little children, never doubting. Little children don't care who is to be the greatest-perhaps at some particular moment, they care about who can run the fastest or who's afraid to climb to the top of the tree or who can burp the loudest, but their thoughts are not about future greatness.

So many people in our time believe that God and Jesus are just myths that we Christians use to help us conquer our fear of dying. The Jews do believe in Jesus, but not that He is the Messiah nor that He arose from the dead. They believe that the Messiah is still to come.

What Jesus said in reply to John's statement, that they had seen someone else casting out demons in the name of Jesus, could be used as a text by those who would attempt to prove that people other than those who are strictly obedient to the commandments of Christ are saved. No one can say with certainty that only people who are members of certain congregations of some church will be saved. Jesus is the only judge and no one else has the power to know the answer to that. *But* . . . according to the scriptures, more is required for salvation than a mere belief that Jesus is the Son of God. God... or Jesus... *may* make exceptions but, if so that's entirely up to them and only they have the power to make any exceptions. *But* can a person base his hope of salvation on the *possibility* that he will be granted an exception (or exemption) to the commandments set forth in the Scriptures?

What did Jesus mean when He said it would be better for a person to have a millstone hung around his neck and that he be drowned than to cause a believer to stumble? Did He mean that that person would go to hell? Or did He mean that only a person's mortal life on earth would be affected? Albert Barnes was of the opinion that it would have been better for that person to have died before he committed the sin of seducing a soul away from Christ. Regardless of the language of this passage and its exact meaning, it is a sin to cause others to sin. Therefore, unless that person repents, he would, like any other sinner who did not repent of his sins, be cast into hell.

The words of Jesus regarding the cutting off one's foot or hand or plucking out his eye are for a figurative punishment of the body and should not be taken literally. It is not a foot or a hand or an eye that sins-it is the mind and heart of a person that causes him to sin. What Jesus is actually saying, in plain language, is that if there is any attachment, any person, any job, or any other thing that causes us to sin against God we are to get rid of it.

92 Sin and Forgiveness Between Brethren

(Matt. 18:15-35; Luke 17:3-4)

(1) "If your brother sins against you go and reprove him in private. If he listens to you you have won your brother. (2) But if he does not listen to you take one or two more with you, so that by the mouth of two or three witnesses every fact may be confirmed. (3) If he should refuse to listen to them tell it to the church and if he refuses to listen even to the church let him be to you as a Gentile or a tax-gatherer.

(4) "Truly I say to you, whatever you shall bind on earth shall have been bound in heaven and whatever you loose on earth shall have been loosed in heaven. (5) Again I say to you that if two of you agree on earth about anything that they may ask it shall be done for them by My Father who is in heaven, (6) for where two or three have gathered together in My name there I am in their midst."

(7) Then Peter came and said to Jesus, "Lord, how often shall my brother sin against me and I forgive him? Up to seven times?"

(8) "Jesus said to him, "If he sins against you seven times a day and returns to you seven times saying, 'I repent,' forgive him. (9) But I do not say to you up to seven times but up to seventy times seven.

(10) "For this reason the kingdom of heaven may be compared to a certain king who wished to settle accounts with his slaves. (11) When he had begun to settle there was brought to him one who owed him ten thousand talents, (12) but since he did not have the means to repay, his lord commanded him to be sold, along with his wife and children and all that he had, and repayment to be made. (13) The slave, falling down, prostrated himself before his master and said, 'Have patience with me and I will repay you everything.' (14) The lord of that slave felt compassion and released him and forgave him the debt.

(15) "But that slave went out and found one of his fellow slaves who owed him a hundred denarii and he seized him and began to choke him saying, 'Pay back what you owe.' (16) So his fellow-slave fell down and began to entreat him saying, 'Have patience with me and I will repay you.' (17) He was unwilling, however, but went and threw him in prison until he should pay back what was owed.

(18) "When his fellow-slaves saw what he had done they were deeply grieved and came and reported to their lord all that had happened. (19) Then, summoning him, his lord said to him, 'You wicked slave, I forgave you all that debt because you entreated me. (20) Should you not also have had mercy on your fellow-slave even as I had mercy on you?' (21) His lord, moved with anger, handed him over to the torturers until he should repay all that was owed him.

(22) "So shall My heavenly Father also do to you if each of you does not forgive his brother from his heart."

Notes: In the previous section, Jesus warned His disciples against offending others. Now He is telling them how to react to a person who offends or sins against them.

Is it possible to follow the formula Jesus gave for dealing with a person who has sinned against you? Is it possible to follow that formula if we get angry about the offense and use abusive or foul language or something of that sort? If someone offends you should you forgive him if he doesn't ask you for forgiveness or should you forgive him before he asks?

Some time ago that subject was being discussed in a Bible class in which I was a participant. Several people said that they would forgive a person who offended them without being asked for forgiveness. But should they do that? The person who offends another person may not know that what he did or said was offensive unless the person who was offended goes to him and tells him. Or if he did know he had offended another person, should he be allowed to go through life trampling on the rights of others because the offended person has already forgiven him. If we sin against God, does He forgive us if we refuse to repent or to ask for His forgiveness? Jesus said that if we go to the person who offended us and he listens to us we've gained a brother. Isn't that what our Christian life is about, helping our brothers and sisters in Christ?

The last step in the instructions of Jesus was to tell the offense to the church if the process gets that far. You know, of course, that the church of which Christ is the head had not been established at that time. But a church is not unique to the Christian religion. The word "church" means merely an assembly, but through the years has gradually come to mean a religious assembly. However, since Jesus was preparing the apostles for the coming of His kingdom, which is the church as we know it; perhaps He was referring to the church which was to come-His church.

Back in section 85, Matthew 16:19, Jesus had said to Peter that whatever Peter bound or loosed on earth would be bound or loosed in heaven. Jesus said the same thing here to all the apostles, but in a different context, that is, regarding the treatment of a person who has offended a brother and refused to make it right. Jesus was saying to all the apostles that in the matter of church discipline whatever the church as a whole did in this regard had the approval of heaven. He was saying that all the apostles had the same power in this regard as Peter did.

Seventy times seven was not to be taken as a literal figure for the number of times a brother should be forgiven if he asks for forgiveness. In the Hebrew apocryphal numbers seven was a sacred figure and ten (seven times ten to make seventy) was the number for completeness. The actual number of times a brother should be forgiven if he asks was infinitely-without end.

The parable of the unjust servant was a reference, not about paying our just debts but about the sins we all commit. Our debts of sin against God are so great that there is no hope or possibility of our ever being able to pay it. Each day, the debt would get larger because there's no way we can ever do as much good as to compensate for the sins we commit. Some years ago, there was a popular song entitled "Sixteen Tons." In the words of that song, every day the worker got deeper into debt to the company store. That's the way sin against God works-every day deeper in debt. Without being forgiven, there is no hope of getting rid of that debt. But we can't be forgiven of our sins if we refuse to forgive the debts of sin against us-and the debts of sin of others against us are trifling compared to our debts of sin against God.

93 Sacrifice Is Necessary in Serving Christ

(Matt. 8:19-22; Luke 9:57-62)

(1) As Jesus and His disciples were going along a certain scribe came and said to Jesus, "Teacher, I will follow You wherever You go."

215

(2) Jesus said to the scribe, "The foxes have holes and the birds of the air have nests but the Son of Man has nowhere to lay His head."

(3) Jesus said to another of the disciples, "Follow Me."

But that disciples said, "Lord, permit me first to go and bury my father."

(4) But Jesus said to him, "Follow Me and allow the dead to bury their own dead, but as for you, go and proclaim everywhere the kingdom of God."

(5) And another also said, "I will follow You, Lord, but first permit me to say good-bye to those at home."

(6) But Jesus said to that one, "No one, after putting his hand to the plow and looking back, is fit for the kingdom of God."

Notes: This incident is recorded early in Matthew's Gospel and late in Luke's. The two accounts, very similar in wording, were probably the same incident but may not have been. It's likely that similar conversations took place on different occasions between different people. It's possible, too, that this conversation took place between Jesus and one or more of the twelve when those men (who later became apostles) were weighing their intentions to join themselves to Jesus. Too, the fact that Matthew recorded an incident (or, for that matter, any number of incidents) which he had personally witnessed and Luke recorded things about which he had heard may account for the order in which the time or place of each was recorded.

94 Journey to the Feast of Tabernacles (John 7:2-10)

(1) Now the feast of the Jews, the Feast of Tabernacles (or Booths), was at hand. (2) Jesus' brothers said to Him, "Depart from here and go into Judea so that Your disciples also may behold Your works which You are doing. (3) No one does anything in secret when he himself seeks to be known publicly. If You do these things, show Yourself to the world." (4) For not even His brothers were believing in Jesus.

(5) Jesus said to His brothers, "My time is not yet at hand but your time is always opportune. (6) The world cannot hate you but it hates Me because I testify that its deeds are evil.

(7) "Go up to the feast yourselves. I do not go up to this feast yet because My time has not yet come." (8) Having said these things to His brothers Jesus stayed in Galilee.

(9) But when Jesus' brothers had gone up to the feast then He Himself also went up, not publicly but in secret.

Notes: The Feast of Tabernacles (or Feast of Booths as it was sometimes called) began on the fifteenth day of the seventh month, the Jewish month of Tisri, which was the month of harvest, corresponding to the months of September or October in the Gregorian calendar. (Read Leviticus 23:34ff.) As to time, this was about six months before the crucifixion of Jesus.

The Greek word for brethren or brothers is *adelphos*. It does not necessarily mean literal brothers but neither does it exclude that meaning. However, in this instance, the chances are very remote that it did not mean the literal brothers of Jesus. The scriptures don't tell us how many of the brothers and sisters of Jesus eventually came to believe that Jesus was the Messiah or when those who did believe came to do so. We do know that James and Jude (or Judah or Judas) did accept Jesus as the Messiah but not that any of the others did or did not.

Some versions of the Bible read that Jesus told His brothers He wasn't going to the feast, but that He did go. We must assume that what is written in those versions is incorrect, otherwise what Jesus told His brothers would have been a lie. We know, though, that to lie is sinful and that Jesus had no sin. What would seem to be more accurate is, as stated in other versions of the Bible, that Jesus said He wasn't going up to the feast *yet*.

95 Jesus in the Temple at the Feast of Tabernacles

(John 7:11-30)

(1) The Jews were seeking Jesus at the feast and were asking, "Where is He?"

(2) There was much disagreement among the multitude concerning Jesus. Some were saying, "He is a good man"; others were saying, "No,

on the contrary, He leads the multitude astray." (3) Yet no one was speaking openly of Him for fear of the Jews.

(4) But when it was now the midst of the feast Jesus went up into the temple and began to teach.

(5) The Jews were marveling and saying, "How has this man become learned, having never been educated?"

(6) Jesus, answering them, said, "My teaching is not Mine but His who sent Me. (7) If any man is willing to do God's will he shall know of the teaching, whether it is of God, or whether I speak from Myself. (8) He who speaks from himself seeks his own glory but He who is seeking the glory of the one who sent Him is true and there is no unrighteousness in Him.

(9) "Did not Moses give you the law, and yet none of you carries out the law? Why do you seek to kill Me?"

(10) The multitude answered, "You have a demon! Who seeks to kill You?"

(11) Jesus answered, "I did one deed and you all marvel.

(12) On this account Moses has given you circumcision (not because it is from Moses but from the fathers) and on the Sabbath you circumcise a man. (13) If a man receives circumcision on the Sabbath that the Law of Moses may not be broken, are you angry with Me because I made an entire man well on the Sabbath? (14) Do not judge according to appearance, but judge with righteous judgment."

(15) Some of the people of Jerusalem were saying, "Is this not the man whom they are seeking to kill? (16) Look, He is speaking publicly and they are saying nothing to Him. The rulers do not really know that this is the Christ, do they? (17) We know where this man is from but whenever the Christ may come no one knows where He is from."

(18) Jesus cried out in the temple, teaching and saying, "You both know Me and know where I am from. I have not come of Myself, but He whom you do not know, He who sent Me, is true. (19) I know Him because I am from Him and He sent Me."

(20) Therefore the Jews were seeking to seize Jesus but no man laid hands on Him because His hour had not yet come.

Notes: As it is used in this and many other passages, the word "Jews" denoted those Jews who resisted the teachings of Jesus and who, generally speaking, belonged to the ruling classes, whereas the word "multitude" was used to denote the common people even though all of them, both groups, were in reality Jews.

It's unclear why the Jews were looking for Jesus. Possibly, it was that they were just curious to see whether or not He would show up there in Jerusalem. It seems to have been common knowledge in Jerusalem that the Jews wanted to have Jesus killed, yet when they found Him, they did nothing except marvel that He had so much knowledge even though He had never been formally educated. Themselves being the ones who would have done the teaching, they would have known that Jesus had no formal education, so they couldn't understand where or how He had received His knowledge.

The scripture says that "in the midst of the feast" Jesus began to teach in the temple. The Feast of Booths was a seven day event, so it was about the third or fourth day of the feast when Jesus appeared openly in the temple.

In Malachi 3:1, it is written, "'Behold, I am going to send My messenger, and he will clear the way before Me. And the Lord, whom you seek, will suddenly come to His temple, and the messenger of the covenant, in whom you delight, behold, He is corning,' says the Lord of hosts."

Jesus said, "He who speaks from himself seeks his own glory but He who is seeking the glory of the One who sent Him is true and there is no unrighteousness in Him." The fact that so many people are seeking their own glory is what has caused all the splitting and dividing and doubting and confusion in the so called Christian world. Whether being egotistical or just misguided (or, as in so many cases, unguided) someone will say, *"I* think... " or *"I* believe... " or *"I* feel..." and tell why that person believes that what he or she thinks takes precedent over what the scriptures say and by so doing lead a part of the Lord's church astray. And when that has happened hundreds of times, the church that the Lord Jesus founded has become so fragmented that it can, like humpty-dumpty, never be put back together again.

96 Chief Priests and Pharisees Try to Arrest Jesus

(John 7:31-8:1)

(1) Many of the multitude believed in Jesus and they were saying, "When the Christ shall come will He perform more signs than those which this man has done?"

(2) The Pharisees heard the multitude muttering these things about Jesus and the chief priests and the Pharisees sent officers to seize Him.

(3) Jesus said, "For a little while longer I am with you then I go to Him who sent Me. (4) You shall seek Me and shall not find Me, and where I am you cannot come."

(5) The Jews said to one another, "Where does this man intend to go that we shall not find Him? Is He intending to go to the Dispersion among the Greeks and teach the Greeks? (6) What is this statement that He said, 'You will seek Me and will not find Me and where I am you cannot come'?"

(7) Now on the last day, the great day of the feast Jesus stood and cried out, "If any man is thirsty let him come to Me and drink. (8) He who believes in Me, as the Scripture said, 'From his innermost being shall flow rivers of living water.'"

(9) But in this Jesus spoke of the Spirit whom those who believed in Him were to receive, for the Spirit was not yet given because Jesus was not yet glorified.

(10) When they heard these words some of the multitude were saying, "This certainly is the Prophet." (11) Others were saying, "This is the Christ."

Still others were saying, "Surely the Christ will not come from Galilee, will He? (12) Has not the Scripture said that the Christ comes from the offspring of David and from Bethlehem, the village where David was?"

(13) So there arose a division in the multitude because of Jesus. (14) Some of them wanted to seize Him but no one laid hands on Him.

(15) The officers returned to the chief priests and Pharisees and they were asked, "Why did you not bring Him?"

(16) The officers answered, "Never did a man speak the way this man speaks."

(17) The Pharisees answered them, "Have you also been led astray? (18) Has any one of the rulers or Pharisees believed in Him? (19) But this multitude which does not know the law is accursed."

(20) Nicodemus (he who came to Jesus before, being one of them) said to them, (21) "Does our Law judge a man unless it first hears from him and knows what he is doing?"

(22) They answered and said to him, "Are you also from Galilee? Search and you will see that no prophet arises out of Galilee."

(23) Everyone went to his own home, (24) but Jesus went to the Mount of Olives.

Notes: Those people who believed in Jesus were saying in effect that Jesus was doing the things which they would expect the Messiah to do and asking that if Jesus was not the Messiah what could the Messiah do more than what Jesus had done.

The Jews didn't understand what Jesus was talking about when He said that He would be there a while longer and that they wouldn't be able to find Him or to follow Him. What He was saying was that He would be on earth for a little while longer and then He would return to His Father Who had sent Him. The Jews, having rejected Jesus as the Messiah, would continue to look forward to the coming of the Messiah and, because they had rejected Jesus, they would not be able to go where He was going-they would not be allowed to enter heaven.

Jewish writers, writing at a later date, state that at that time it was the custom of the priests to fill a golden pitcher or vial from the pool of Siloam and, with great solemnity, carry it to the altar and pour it on the sacrifice. That may have been done to commemorate the water Moses caused to flow from the rock, or it may have been done because of improperly interpreting Isaiah 12:3, which reads, "Therefore you will joyously draw water from the springs of salvation." If that was the custom and, regardless of the reason (and probably the passage in Isaiah is the one they used), the words and actions of Jesus would be adequately explained. The text says this incident and discussion took place on the last day of the feast and the ceremonial ritual of taking the water from Siloam to the altar was supposed to have taken place on that day. Notice the similarity of what Jesus said on this occasion with what He said to the Samaritan woman at Jacob's well. Jesus said in John 4:13-14, "Everyone who drinks of this water shall thirst again; but whoever drinks of the water I shall give him shall never thirst; but the water that I shall give him shall become in him a well of water springing up to eternal life." And Zechariah 14:8, "And it will come about in that day that living waters will flow out of Jerusalem, half of them toward the eastern sea and the other half toward the western sea; it will be in summer as well as in winter." The last part of that passage probably meant that the "living water" would be for all people in all nations and would be available at all times, summer and winter.

The passage of scripture (if such it was) which Jesus quoted is not found in the scriptures, at least not in the same words nor in a form recognizable as being the same. Some commentators believe that statement was not meant to be a direct quotation from a particular place in the Old Testament, but that it was meant to refer to an idea or a doctrine which runs throughout the Old Testament.

In speaking of the Spirit which believers were to receive later, Jesus was speaking of the Holy Spirit. The first and second chapters of Acts are probably the best commentary on that subject. We won't go into that now, but it will be a part of the last lesson in this study.

Some of the people present at that time believed that Jesus was the prophet of whom Moses wrote in Deuteronomy 18:15, "The Lord your God will raise up for you a prophet like me from among you, from your countrymen, you shall listen to him." The language used seems to indicate that this was a Messianic prophecy, but it was not generally accepted to be such by the Jews. They believed that this prophet was to come but not that he was the Messiah.

Some of the people didn't believe that Jesus was the Messiah for no other reason than that He made His home in Galilee instead of Bethlehem, not knowing that Jesus had been born in Bethlehem. They didn't know that Jesus had already overcome all of their objections and that He did fulfill all the requirements about which most of the Jewish people were well informed.

The officers which were sent to seize Jesus were probably Levites or temple police. Under Roman law they had no legal standing.

The statement the Jews made, that no prophet had come out of Galilee, was probably incorrect because Jonah is believed to have come out of that region which later, in the time of Jesus, was Galilee. There is no clear evidence concerning some of the other prophets as to whether they did or did not come from the region of Galilee.

The Mount of Olives was to the east of the city of Jerusalem and the Garden of Gethsemane was on its western slope. The town of Bethany, the home of Mary, Martha, and Lazarus, was on the eastern side of the mountain.

97 The Adulteress Brought to Jesus (John 8:2-11)

(1) Early in the morning Jesus came again into the temple. All the people were coming to Him and He sat down and began to teach them. (2) The scribes and the Pharisees brought a woman caught in adultery, and having sat her in their midst, (3) they said to Jesus, "Teacher, this woman has been caught in adultery, in the very act. (4) Now in the Law Moses commanded us to stone such women. What then do You say?"

(5) They said this to test Jesus in order that they might have grounds for accusing Him.

But Jesus stooped down and with His finger wrote on the ground. (6) When they persisted in asking Him, He straightened up and said to them, "If there is one among you who is without sin let him be the first to throw a stone at her."

(7) And again Jesus stooped down and wrote on the ground.

(8) When the scribes and Pharisees heard this they began to go out one by one, beginning with the older ones. And Jesus was left alone with the woman where she had been in the midst of them.

(9) Straightening up, Jesus asked the woman, "Woman, where are your accusers? Did no one condemn you?"

(10) She said, "No one, Lord."

Jesus said, "Neither do I condemn you. Go your way and from now on sin no more."

Notes: In Leviticus 20:10 and again in Deuteronomy 22:22, the Law of Moses stated that it was required that an adulterer or adulteress be put to death. The method of execution was not specified. When this woman was brought to Jesus, the usual method of execution was by stoning (note the death of Stephen). At other times in the history of the Jews, some other method may have been used.

In all probability, the woman was first taken to the council of the Jews. The council saw in this woman a way that might have been used to confound or accuse Jesus. But if the woman had been taken in the "very act" of adultery as her accusers claimed, there must of necessity have been a man caught in the very same act. Where was the man now? According to the Law, the man was as guilty as the woman, and under that Law, the same punishment was required of him as was required of the woman. When the Law was given through Moses, there was equality of the sexes, but since no mention of the man was made in this passage, it seems that such equality no longer existed in the minds of the Jews.

The Law did not specifically address the dilemma to which Jesus was subjected by the scribes and Pharisees who brought the woman to Him. It was not just a matter of wondering what Jesus would say. The dilemma was, would Jesus uphold the Law of Moses and agree with the scribes and Pharisees that the woman should be put to death or would He conform to Roman law which did not allow anyone but a Roman to pass and carry out the death sentence.

Jesus said He did not condemn the woman. In John 3:17, Jesus said, "For God did not send the Son into the world to judge the world, but that the world should be saved through Him." On that day, Jesus saved the life of that woman. Let's hope that eventually, by saving her life that day, Jesus was responsible for saving her soul as well.

98 Attempt to Stone Jesus Because of His Messianic Claims

(John 8:12-59)

(1) Again Jesus spoke to the scribes and the Pharisees, saying, "I am the light of the world. He who follows Me shall not walk in the darkness but will have the light of life."

(2) But the Pharisees said to Jesus, "You are bearing witness of Yourself. Your witness is not true."

(3) Jesus answered, "Even if I bear witness of Myself My witness is true, for I know where I came from and where I am going. You do not know where I come from or where I am going. (4) You people judge according to the flesh but I am not judging any one. (5) Even if I do judge My judgment is true. I am not alone in it-I am with Him who sent Me. (6) Even in your law it has been written that the testimony of two men is true. (7) I am He who bears witness of Myself and the Father who sent Me bears witness of Me."

(8) So they asked Jesus, "Where is Your Father?"

Jesus answered, "You know neither Me nor My Father. If you knew Me you would know My Father also."

(9) These words Jesus spoke in the treasury as He taught in the temple and no one seized Him because His hour had not yet come.

(10) Again Jesus spoke to them, "I go away and you will seek Me and you will die in your sin. Where I am going you cannot come."

(11) Therefore the Jews were saying, "Surely He will not kill Himself since He says, 'Where I am going you cannot come.'"

(12) Jesus said to them, "You are from below; I am from above. You are of this world; I am not of this world. (13) I said to you that you shall die in your sins, for unless you believe that I am He you will die in your sins."

(14) So they asked Jesus, "Who are You?"

Jesus said to them, "What have I been saying to you from the beginning? (15) I have many things to speak and to judge concerning you but He who sent Me is true, and the things which I heard from Him I speak to the world." (16) But they did not realize that He had been speaking to them about the Father.

(17) Jesus said, "When you lift up the Son of Man you will know that I am He. I do nothing on My own initiative but I speak these things as the Father taught Me. (18) He who sent Me is with Me. He has not left Me alone for I always do the things that are pleasing to Him." (19) As Jesus spoke these things many came to believe in Him.

(20) Then Jesus said to those Jews who had believed Him, "If you abide in My word then you are truly disciples of Mine; (21) and you shall know the truth and the truth shall make you free."

(22) They answered Him, "We are Abraham's offspring and have never yet been enslaved to anyone. How is it that You say, 'You shall become free'?"

(23) Jesus answered them, "Truly I say to you, every one who commits sin is the slave of sin. (24) The slave does not remain in the house forever but the son does remain forever. (25) If the Son shall make you free you shall be free indeed.

(26) "I know that you are Abraham's offspring, yet you seek to kill Me because My word has no place in you. (27) I speak the things which I have seen with My Father. You also do the things which you heard from your father."

(28) They answered and said to Him, "Abraham is our father."

Jesus said, "If you are Abraham's children then do the deeds of Abraham. (29) But as it is you are seeking to kill Me, a man who has told you the truth which I heard from God. This Abraham did not do. (30) You are doing the deeds of your father."

They answered, "We were not born of fornication. We have one Father, even God."

(31) Jesus said, "If God were your Father you would love Me, for I proceeded forth and have come from God. I have not even come on My own initiative but He sent Me. (32) Why do you not understand what I am saying? It is because you cannot hear My word. (33) You are of your father the devil and you want to do the desires of your father. He was a murderer from the beginning and does not stand in the truth because there is no truth in him. Whenever he speaks a lie he speaks from his own nature, for he is a liar and the father of lies.

(34) "But because I speak the truth you do not believe Me.

(35) Which of you convicts Me of sin? If I speak the truth why do you not believe Me? (36) He who is of God hears the words of God. For this reason you do not hear them, because you are not of God."

(37) The Jews said, "Do we not say rightly that You are a Samaritan and have a demon?"

(38) Jesus answered, "I do not have a demon. I honor My Father and you dishonor Me. (39) I do not seek My glory. There is one who seeks and judges. (40) I say to you truly, if anyone keeps My word he will never see death."

(41) The Jews said, "Now we know that You have a demon. Abraham died, and the prophets also, but You say, 'If anyone keeps My word he shall never taste of death.' (42) Surely You are not greater than our father Abraham who died? The prophets died, too. Whom do You make Yourself out to be?"

(43) Jesus answered, "If I glorify Myself, My glory is nothing. It is My Father, of whom you say, 'He is our God,' who glorifies Me. (44) You have not come to know Him but I know Him. If I say that I do not know Him I shall be a liar like you, but I do know Him and keep His word. (45) Your father Abraham rejoiced to see My day, and he saw it and was glad."

(46) The Jews said to Jesus, "You are not yet fifty years old and have You seen Abraham?"

(47) Jesus said, "I say to you truly, before Abraham was born I **AM.**"

(48) Therefore they picked up stones to throw at Jesus but He hid Himself and went out of the temple.

Notes: Under the Law, two witnesses were required to establish the truth of any fact. A man can testify only to what he has done or has seen for himself. Jesus and the Father, on the other hand, know everything and can testify to the truth of anything. The prophets testified of Jesus because the word was given to them by God, but the people didn't believe the prophets. Earlier we learned that the people testified that Jesus was not of the city of David and because of that He could not be the Messiah. We know their testimony was not true, though, because they were testifying to something about which they had no knowledge.

The Jews claimed to believe in God, but how deep was their faith? They claimed to believe the prophets, but did they? The wise kings from the Orient knew of Jesus, that He was the promised Messiah. They even told Herod about Jesus. They knew and believed the scriptures but the scribes and Pharisees, who should have known the scriptures much better than foreigners, refused to believe because Jesus didn't fit their preconceived ideas of His mission.

Jesus said, "The truth shall make you free." How does the truth make us free? It frees us from sin! It frees us from the clutches of Satan! In Romans 6:17, Paul wrote, "... Though you were servants of sin... " and on down in verse 19, "... You presented your members as slaves to impurity... " And in Acts 8:23, Peter said to Simon the sorcerer, "For I see that you are in the gall of bitterness and in the bondage of iniquity."

The claim of the Jews that they had never been enslaved to anyone was, as we know and as they surely knew, incorrect. Surely, they had not forgotten that for many years their nation had been held captive in foreign lands. Apparently, they refused to remember that even at that time and for quite a number of years before that they had been in subjection first to Greece and then to Rome. Even now they were not free, being in subjection to the Roman Empire.

When Jesus said, "Before Abraham was born I AM," He was conveying the meaning that His existence was timeless. God the Father used the same words in identifying Himself to Moses at the burning bush. In Exodus 3:14, God said, "I AM who I AM: thus you shall say to the sons of Israel, 'I AM has sent me to you.'" At any time and at all times God IS. But just saying that God exists now, has always existed and always will exist doesn't convey the whole meaning of God. He said to Abram, "I am thy shield," and "I am the almighty God." He said to Isaac, "I am the God of your father Abraham," and "I am with you and bless you." Jesus said on other occasions, "For where two or three have gathered together in My name, there I am in their midst." He said, "I am with you always" and "I am the bread of life" and "I am the light of the world" and "I am the door; if anyone enters through Me, he shall be saved" and "I am the good shepherd." Jesus said, "I am the resurrection and the life; he who believes in Me shall live even if he dies." He said, "I am the way, and the truth, and the life; no one comes to the Father but through Me." He said, "I am the true vine." Jesus is all things to all people who believe in Him and obey His commandments.

99 Contention Because Jesus Gave Sight to a Man Born Blind

(John 9:1-41)

(1) As Jesus passed by He saw a man who was blind from birth. (2) His disciples asked Him, "Rabbi, who sinned, this man or his parents, that he should be born blind?"

(3) Jesus answered, "It was neither that this man sinned nor his parents, it was in order that the works of God might be displayed in Him. (4) We must work the works of Him who sent Me as long as it is day. Night is coming when no man can work. (5) While I am in the world I am the light of the world."

(6) When He had said this Jesus spat on the ground and made a clay of spittle and applied the clay to the blind man's eyes (7) and said to him, "Go, wash in the pool of Siloam" (which is translated, Sent). So the blind man went away and washed and came back seeing.

(8) The man's neighbors and those who previously saw the blind man as a beggar were asking, "Is not this the one who used to sit and beg?"

(9) Others were saying, "This is he."

Still others were saying, "No, but he is like that one." But the man himself kept saying, "I am the one."

(10) Everyone was asking him, "How then were your eyes opened?"

(11) He answered, "The man who is called Jesus made clay and anointed my eyes and said to me, 'Go to Siloam and wash'; so I went away and washed and I received sight."

(12) They asked, "Where is He?" He said, "I do not know."

(13) Then they took him who was formerly blind to the Pharisees. (14) Now the day when Jesus made the clay and opened the man's eyes was a Sabbath.

(15) Then the Pharisees asked the man how he received his sight. He said to them, "He applied clay to my eyes, and I washed, and I see."

(16) Some of the Pharisees were saying, "This man is not from God because He does not keep the Sabbath."

But others were saying, "How can a man who is a sinner perform such signs?" And there was a division among them.

(17) Therefore they said again to the blind man, "What do you say about Him, since He opened your eyes?"

The man said, "He is a prophet."

(18) The Jews did not believe that the man had been blind and had received his sight until they called the parents of the very one who had received his sight, (19) and questioned them, asking, "Is this your son who you say was born blind? Then how does he now see?"

(20) His parents answered them and said, "We know that this is our son and that he was born blind, (21) but how he now sees we do not know, or who opened his eyes we do not know. Ask him. He is of age. He shall speak for himself." (22) His parents said this because they were afraid of the Jews because the Jews had already agreed that if any one should confess Jesus to be Christ he should be put out of the synagogue. (23) For this reason the man's parents said, "He is of age, ask him."

(24) So a second time they called the man who had been blind and said to him, "Give glory to God, we know that this man is a sinner."

(25) He therefore answered, "Whether or not He is a sinner I do not know. One thing I do know, and that is that whereas I was blind now I see."

(26) They said to him, "What did He do to you? How did He open your eyes?"

(27) He answered them, "I told you already and you did not listen. Why do you want to hear it again? Do you want to become His disciples, too?"

(28) They reviled him and said, "You are His disciple but we are disciples of Moses. (29) We know that God has spoken to Moses, but as for this man we do not know where He is from."

(30) The man answered and said to them, "Well, here is an amazing thing-you do not know where He is from and yet He opened my eyes. (31) We know that God does not hear sinners, but if any one is God-fearing and does His will God hears him.

(32) Since the beginning of time it has never been heard that any one opened the eyes of a person born blind. (33) If this man were not from God He could do nothing."

(34) They said to him, "You were born entirely in sins, and are you teaching us?" And they put him out.

(35) Jesus heard that the Pharisees had put the man out and finding him, Jesus asked, "Do you believe in the Son of Man?"

(36) The man answered and said, "Who is He, Lord, that I may believe in Him?"

(37) Jesus said, "You have both seen Him, and He is the one who is talking with you."

(38) The man said, "Lord, I believe." And he worshiped Jesus.

(39) Jesus said, "For judgment I came into this world that those who do not see may see and that those who see may become blind."

(40) Those of the Pharisees who were with Jesus heard these things and said to Him, "Are we blind, too?"

(41) Jesus said to them, "If you were blind you would have no sin, but now you say, 'We see.' Your sin remains."

Notes: There is some disagreement among scholars as to when this incident took place. Some of them are of the opinion that it was at the Feast of Tabernacles in the September or October time frame but others claim it was at the Feast of Dedication in December citing John 20:22 as their authority. Judging from the language of the text, it seems more likely that it took place immediately after the disappearance of Jesus from the temple about which we learned in the previous section.

Biblical scholars say that in those days the Jews believed that deformities, including blindness, were caused by sin, either of the person so afflicted or by the parents of that person. It was also their belief that the soul of a person could leave one body and enter another and that the second body could be afflicted because of the sins of the first body or the parents of that body. In Exodus 20:5 and Numbers 14:18, the statement is made that the sins of the father are visited on his offspring even to the third and fourth generations. It is unclear as to whether they believed that it was the result of sin which was passed on or the guilt of it. We know that it is actually only the result of sin which can be passed on. The health of an unborn infant, for instance, can be affected by its mother smoking or using drugs or otherwise abusing her own body. There have been accounts published of babies having to go through drug withdrawal because the mother was a drug addict.

In this passage, Jesus made another reference to the fact that His life as a mortal man was drawing to a close. As a man, His life would end as the lives of all mortals end. Never truer than now is the statement that man's work is done when night comes. Ecclesiastes 9:11 reads, "Whatsoever thy hand findeth to do, do it with thy might, for there is no work, nor device, nor knowledge, nor wisdom, in the grave, whither thou goest."

There may have been two reasons that Jesus made clay from dirt and His spittle and anointed the eyes of the blind man. It may have been just a device to help the man's faith so that he would do what he was told to do, or it may have been open defiance of the traditions of the Pharisees and Jews who considered what Jesus did to have been a breach of Sabbath law. Spittle was believed to have medicinal value when used to anoint the eyes. If it was done for medicinal purposes on the Sabbath, the Jews considered that to be work although it was all right to do the same thing for pleasure on the Sabbath. If Jesus did this as an act of defiance, perhaps it was also to show how ridiculous some of the traditions of the Jews had become.

We don't read of many people besides Jesus who argued with the Pharisees, scribes, and elders, but this blind man who had received his sight did so, giving back at least as good as he got. And for that, he was put out of the synagogue. Some scholars believe that this man was only put out from the presence of the Pharisees, but the fact that Jesus had to search him out afterwards seems to indicate that their contention is wrong. To have been put out of the synagogue was worse for a Jew than excommunication would be for a Catholic. The Jew would have had no church, no country, and no religious fellowship. He was to be considered and treated as though he was a heathen.

100 Discourse on the Good Shepherd (John 10:1-21)

(1) "Truly I say to you, he who does not enter by the door into the fold of the sheep but climbs up some other way is a thief and a robber. (2) He who enters by the door is the shepherd of the sheep. (3) To him the doorkeeper opens, and the sheep hear his voice, and he calls his own sheep by name, and leads them out. (4) When he puts forth all his own

he goes before them and the sheep follow him because they know his voice. (5) A stranger they simply will not follow, but will flee from him because they do not know the voice of strangers."

(6) This figure of speech Jesus spoke to the Jews but they did not understand those things which He had been saying to them.

(7) Jesus said to them again, "Truly I say to you, I am the door of the sheep. (8) All who come before Me are thieves and robbers, but the sheep did not hear them. (9) I am the door. If anyone enters through Me he shall be saved and shall go in and out and find pasture. (10) The thief comes only to steal and kill and destroy. I came that they might have life and might have it abundantly.

(11) "I am the good shepherd. The good shepherd lays down His life for the sheep. (12) He who is a hireling, and not a shepherd, who is not the owner of the sheep, beholds the wolf coming and leaves the sheep and flees, and the wolf snatches them and scatters them. (13) He flees because he is a hireling and is not concerned about the sheep.

(14) "I am the good shepherd and I know My own and My own know Me, (15) even as the Father knows Me and I know the Father, and I lay down My life for the sheep. (16) I have other sheep which are not of this fold. I must bring them also; and they shall hear My voice, and they shall become one flock with one shepherd.

(17) "The Father loves Me because I lay down My life that I may take it up again. (18) No one takes it away from Me but I lay it down on My own initiative. I have authority to lay it down and I have authority to take it up again. This commandment I received from My Father."

(19) There arose a division again among the Jews because of these words.

(20) Many of them were saying, "He has a demon and is insane. Why do you listen to Him?"

(21) Others were saying, "These are not the sayings of one who is demon-possessed. A demon cannot open the eyes of the blind, can he?"

Notes: The Old Testament contains prophecies of the coming of false shepherds. Ezekiel 34:1-6 says, "Then the word of the Lord came to me saying, 'Son of man, prophesy against the shepherds of Israel. Prophesy and say to those shepherds, "Thus says the Lord God, 'Woe, shepherds of Israel who have been feeding themselves! Should not the shepherds feed the flock? You eat the fat and clothe yourselves with the wool, you slaughter the fat sheep without feeding the flock. Those who are sickly you have not strengthened, the diseased you have not healed, the broken you have not bound up, the scattered you have not brought back, nor have you sought for the lost; but with force and with severity you have dominated them. And they were scattered for lack of a shepherd, and they became food for every beast of the field and were scattered. My flock wandered through all the mountains and on every high hill, and My flock was scattered over all the surface of the earth; and there was no one to search or seek for them.'"" Those words could be an admonition to the leaders of the church who are not doing their work, a warning to those leaders who aren't qualified and don't do the work that their office requires.

There are also prophecies of the true shepherd such as in Psalm 23, 70:20, 80:1-2, 95:7, and Jeremiah 31:10. The Pharisees, scribes, and priests fulfilled the scriptures concerning the false shepherds, and Jesus fulfilled the scriptures which told of the true shepherd. The people who should have been looking out after all the Jews were taking advantage of them instead, valuing their traditions and the Law above the souls of those who were their charges.

Jesus said the good shepherd knows his sheep well enough to call them all by name. That means that Jesus, the Good Shepherd, knows the name of every one of His subjects, and in the book of Revelation, it tells of those whose names are written in the Book of Life. The meaning of what Jesus said was that the elders, the men who are supposed to be leading the flock, should know every one of those people over whom they are overseers by name and the spiritual needs of each of them.

With our knowledge of the Gospels and looking back to what Jesus said about what a good shepherd would do for his sheep, we can understand that Jesus was telling us what He would (and did) do for His followers. We understand that Jesus was telling His hearers that He was going to lay down His life for His followers, not just at that time but down through the ages. It was not just a matter of His willingness to lay down His life for us, but that it was a certainty that He would (and did) do so.

Anyone can lay down his life for any reason, but no one other than Jesus has ever been able to take up his life again after it has once been taken. God gave that power to no one but His own Son.

101 The Lawyer Tests Jesus, and the Parable of the Good Samaritan (Luke 10:25-37)

(1) Then a certain lawyer stood up and put Jesus to the test asking, "Teacher, what shall I do to inherit eternal life?"

(2) Jesus asked the lawyer, "What is written in the Law? How does it read to you?"

(3) The lawyer said, "'You shall love the Lord your God with all your heart and with all your strength and with all your mind, and your neighbor as yourself.'"

(4) Jesus said to him, "You have answered correctly. Do this and you will live."

(5) Wishing to justify himself the lawyer asked, "Who is my neighbor?"

(6) Jesus replied, "A certain man was going down from Jerusalem to Jericho and fell among robbers. They stripped him and beat him and went off leaving him half dead. (7) By chance a certain priest was going down on that road, and when the priest saw the beaten man he passed by on the other side.

(8) And a Levite also, when he came to the place and saw the beaten man, passed by on the other side.

(9) "But a certain Samaritan who was on a journey came upon the beaten man and when he saw his condition felt compassion (10) and came to him and bandaged up his wounds, pouring oil and wine on them. He put the man on his own beast and brought him to an inn and took care of him.

(11) "The next day he took out two denarii and gave them to the innkeeper and said, 'Take care of him, and whatever more you spend, when I return I will repay you.' (12) Which of these three do you think proved to be a neighbor to the man who fell into the robbers' hands?"

(13) The lawyer said, "The one who showed mercy toward him." Jesus said to the lawyer, "Go and do the same."

Notes: One biblical scholar has suggested that the terms "scribe" and "lawyer" mean the same thing and are interchangeable. The Greek word translated "scribe," however, *grammateus* (gram-mat-yooce') means a professional writer, secretary, or clerk. The word translated as "lawyer" is *nomikos* (nom-ik-os') and means an expert in the Mosaic Law or pertaining to the Law. A lawyer, then, would be expected to be of a higher or more respected profession. His opinions and his words would have carried more weight than those of a scribe, and generally, like the scribes, a lawyer would have been sympathetic to the traditions of the Pharisees.

This lawyer probably expected Jesus to give some new instruction or tell of some new way to be saved, but Jesus only asked the lawyer what the Law said about the matter. The lawyer, an expert in the Law, was forced by his own pride and self-esteem to give the answer that he and Jesus knew to be the right one.

The locale of the parable was the road between Jerusalem and Jericho. Since both cities were large ones, there would have been much travel between them. The distance between the two cities was about eighteen miles, and there was a thirty five hundred foot drop in elevation from Jerusalem down to Jericho. The road passed through only one town, Bethany, which was about two miles from Jerusalem, and the rest of the road was through very rough mountainous terrain. The only other building on that road was an inn, the ruins of which can still be seen. That stretch of highway, according to Josephus and Jerome, was made perilous by numerous highwaymen. Even as late as the middle of the nineteenth century, travelers were forced to use an armed escort for safety.

The Bible has many small, almost unnoticeable, things, which, when their meaning is known, testify to the truth of the scriptures. One of those little things is included in the parable that Jesus told. In the parable Jesus said, "... Was going *down* from Jerusalem to Jericho... " The road from Jerusalem to Jericho does go down in elevation a matter of thirty-five hundred feet.

Perhaps Jesus chose as the characters in this parable a priest and a Levite because both of these men would have known the Law and would have known that the Law required them to give assistance to the beaten man, a fellow Jew. And perhaps, Jesus wanted the lawyer to see himself in those two men, someone who knew the Law but didn't obey it when it was inconvenient or distasteful to do so.

102 Jesus Is the Guest of Mary and Martha

(Luke 10:38-42)

(1) Now as they were traveling along Jesus entered a certain village, and a woman named Martha welcomed Him into her home. (2) Martha had a sister called Mary who was listening to the Lord's word seated at His feet.

(3) But Martha was distracted with all her preparations and she came to Jesus and said, "Lord, do you not care that my sister has left me to do all the serving alone? Then tell her to help me."

(4) But the Lord said to her, "Martha, Martha, you are worried and bothered by so many things (5) but only a few things are necessary, really only one, and Mary has chosen the good part which shall not be taken away from her."

Notes: In the Gospels, as well as in time, this is the first mention of Martha and Mary. The name of the town is not mentioned in this passage of scripture, but we know from later scriptures that it was Bethany. The scripture says that Martha welcomed Jesus into her home, leading to an inference that the house belonged to Martha. Also it was Martha who had made herself responsible for preparing the meal they were to eat. It's not clear in this passage whether Mary or Lazarus or both of them lived with Martha, but the general assumption is that they did live there.

In that country and at that time, it was the custom for pupils or disciples to sit at the feet of their teacher while they were being taught. Paul said in Acts 22:3 that he had been brought up at the feet of Gamaliel, meaning, of course, that Gamaliel had been his teacher or tutor.

By saying Martha's name twice, the rebuke of Jesus was milder than it would have been if He had not used her name at all or had said it only once. Jesus also said, in effect, that what Mary was doing was more important than what Martha was doing. I suppose we've all known people who thought it was more important to prepare a good Sunday dinner for guests than it was to attend morning worship services. They were anxious for their dinner to turn out the way they wanted it to. Remember what Jesus said about anxiety in Matthew 6:25-34, that we're not to be anxious about food or clothing.

103 Jesus Teaches and Encourages his Disciples to Pray

(Luke 11:1, 5-8)

(1) It happened that Jesus was praying in a certain place and after He had finished one of His disciples said to Him, "Lord, teach us to pray just as John taught his disciples."
(2) Jesus said to them, "Suppose one of you shall have a friend and shall go to him at midnight and say to him, 'Friend, lend me three loaves. (3) A friend of mine has come to me from a journey and I have nothing to set before him'; (4) and from inside he shall answer and say, 'Do not bother me. The door has already been shut and my children and I are already in bed. I cannot get up and give you anything.' (5) I tell you, even though he will not get up and give you anything because he is your friend, yet because of your persistence he will get up and give you as much as you need."

Notes: You may recall that in His "Sermon on the Mount," Jesus had already told His disciples how to pray. Perhaps the disciple who now asked Jesus to teach them to pray was not one of the twelve or, more than likely, he had forgotten what Jesus had said or wasn't present at that time. Or perhaps, he reasoned that such a short prayer was not sufficient considering the length of time in which Jesus sometimes spent in prayer. It was the custom for rabbis or teachers to give their disciples the forms of prayers to be prayed and maybe that was what John had done for his disciples.

Midnight doesn't seem to be such an unreasonable hour to us, because it's usually ten or eleven o'clock before most of us get to bed anyway. But back, then midnight was just what the word implied-the middle of the night. If there was no radio to listen to or television to watch, no electric lights to read by, most of us would be in bed soon after darkness fell each night too.

In extremely hot countries, it's the custom for people who travel, especially those who must walk, to do so at night to escape the worst of the heat. The custom of the land at that time *required* a host to show hospitality, and the greatest inconvenience or the deepest poverty didn't relieve him of that obligation. The occasion of a guest arriving in the night would call for the setting out of three loaves of bread-one for the guest, one for the host and the other as evidence of the liberality of the host.

In those days, most of the homes were very small, usually having only one or two small rooms. The room that was used for sleeping usually had a raised platform or divan along part of the inside walls. Pallets or thin mattresses were spread on this platform and the family slept on the pallets. The whole family usually slept in one room, so to be stumbling around in the dark to find three loaves of bread and open the door was indeed a lot of trouble. Judging by what Jesus reported the man to have said, it may make one think that the man's children slept with him on his pallet. Such was not the case, however, but the children did sleep on the same platform or divan with him thus the statement that they were in bed with him.

104 Jesus Dines with a Pharisee {Luke 11:37-54)

(1) Now when Jesus had spoken, a Pharisee asked Jesus to have lunch with him, and Jesus went in and reclined at table.

(2) When the Pharisee saw this he was surprised that Jesus had not first ceremonially washed before the meal.

(3) But the Lord said to the Pharisee, "Now you Pharisees clean the outside of the cup and the platter but inside you are full of robbery and wickedness. (4) You foolish ones, did not He who made the outside make the inside also? (5) Give that which is within as charity and then all are clean for you.

(6) "Woe to you, Pharisees! You pay tithe of mint and rue and every kind of garden herb and yet disregard justice and the love of God. These are the things you should have done without neglecting the others. (7) Woe to you, Pharisees! You love the front seats in the synagogue and the respectful greetings in the market places. (8) Woe to you! You are like concealed tombs, and the people who walk over them are unaware of it."

(9) One of the lawyers said to Jesus in reply, "Teacher, when You say this You insult us, too."

(10) Jesus said, "Woe to you lawyers as well! You weigh men down with burdens hard to bear while you yourselves will not even touch the burdens with one of your fingers. (11) Woe to you! You build the tombs of the prophets and it was your fathers who killed them. (12) Consequently you are witnesses and approve the deeds of your fathers because it was they who killed them and you build their tombs. (13) For this reason also the wisdom of God said, 'I will send to them prophets and apostles and some of them they will kill and some they will persecute, (14) in order that the blood of all the prophets shed since the foundation of the world may be charged against this generation, (15) from the blood of Abel to the blood of Zechariah, who perished between the altar and the house of God. Yes, I tell you, it shall be charged against this generation.' (16) Woe to you lawyers! You have taken away the key of knowledge. You did not enter in yourselves and those who were entering in you hindered."

(17) When Jesus left there the scribes and the Pharisees began to be very hostile and to question Him closely on many subjects, (18) plotting against Him to catch Him in something He might say.

Notes: In those days, it was the custom among the Jews (and Greeks and Romans as well) to eat but two principal meals a day. The first would have been lighter and would have been eaten at about ten or eleven o'clock in the morning. It would have consisted mainly of fruit, milk, and cheese. The second meal would have been much heavier, being the main meal of the day. This meal would have been eaten at about three o'clock in the afternoon. It was the earlier meal to which Jesus had been invited by the Pharisee.

We don't know whether or not Jesus washed His hands before He reclined at the table-we do know that He didn't observe the practice of ceremonially washing as had become the tradition observed by the Pharisees. Of course, there was nothing wrong with washing before a meal, and particularly so, because everyone ate with their hands and not with utensils. In the course of a meal everyone would at one time or another dip food from each of the dishes with their hands. What was wrong with the tradition of ceremonially washing before a meal was that the Pharisees had made of it a religious observance. It wouldn't be surprising if Jesus had deliberately refrained from washing His hands in order to draw forth comments from the Pharisee and provide Him an opening for the remarks he made. Rue, the herb Jesus mentioned here together with mint, is a strongly scented woody shrub with red flowers. It has bitter tasting leaves which are used to flavor wines and for medicinal purposes.

In talking about the concealed tombs, Jesus was referring to a section of the Law. Numbers 19:16 reads, "Also, anyone who in the open field touches one who had been slain with a sword or who has died naturally, or a human bone or a grave, shall be unclean for seven days." To be certain that they didn't touch a grave by accident, the Jews made sure that all graves were clearly marked, even going to the extreme of whitewashing them once a year. Jesus drew a parallel by saying that the Pharisees were like unmarked graves over which people walked without knowing about them, implying thereby that the people who did so became unclean without knowing it. He was, in effect, saying that the Pharisees concealed their true nature from others by pretending to be what they were not. In doing so, they were corrupting others and those who were being corrupted didn't know it. It is like what we see so much of today, a person professing knowledge and teaching his personal religious doctrines to people who will not study for themselves and, instead of converting people to Christianity, is converting them only to his own institution.

The term "the wisdom of God" is a puzzling one to many commentators and biblical scholars. Some of them refer back to Proverbs 8 in which it appears that "Wisdom" is doing the talking and they believe that "Wisdom" is a personification of Jesus. BUT...

241

in I Corinthians 1:30 Paul wrote, "But by His doing you are in Christ Jesus, who became to us *wisdom from* God, and righteousness and sanctification, and redemption ... " It appears that Jesus was speaking of Himself in the third person as he so often did at those times when He referred to Himself as the Son of Man. Earlier in this study, we were reminded of all the things Jesus said of Himself that He was the resurrection, the life, the light, the way, the truth, the door, the bread of life, the true vine, the good shepherd, and so on. Also in the first chapter of the book of John, Jesus was called the Word.

The death of Zechariah is recorded in 2 Chronicles 24:21.

Knowledge of the scriptures is the door to salvation. They contain the Word and the words that show the way. Jesus said that He was the word and that no one enters the kingdom except through Him. Although the Gospels and the Epistles had not yet been written, the Old Testament scriptures were available and they told of the coming of the Messiah. Those Old Testament writers were looking forward to the coming of the Messiah and to the salvation He would bring just as we must look to the past for our salvation. The lawyers and scribes and priests had made it difficult for the people to know the scriptures, teaching them instead all the man-made rules and traditions which were only an outward show. They left the inner man completely ignorant of the will and wisdom of God. The lawyers did not teach nor follow the will of God and made it difficult for the common people to do so.

105 Jesus Teaches on the Folly of Covetousness

(Luke 12:13-21)

(1) Someone in the crowd said to Jesus, "Teacher, tell my brother to divide the family inheritance with me."

(2) But Jesus said to him, "Man, who appointed Me a judge or arbiter over you?"

(3) Then Jesus said to the crowd, "Beware and be on your guard against every form of greed, for not even when one has an abundance does his life consist of his possessions."

(4) Then Jesus told them a parable, saying, "The land of a certain rich man was very productive, (5) and he began reasoning to himself, saying, 'What shall I do since I have no place to store my crops?'

(6) "And he said, 'This is what I will do–I will tear down my barns and build larger ones and there I will store all my grain and my goods. (7) Then I will say to my soul, "Soul, you have many goods laid up for many years to come so take your ease; eat, drink and be merry."'

(8) "But God said to him, 'You fool! This very night your soul is required of you, and now who will own what you have prepared?' (9) This is so of the rich man who lays up treasure for himself and is not rich toward God."

Notes: Jesus said that possessions had nothing to do with life, whether it was long, short, blessed, or cursed. A lot of people spend the greater part of their lives in pursuit of wealth or success at the expense of their family life and their spiritual life and sometimes their own health. They will use the excuse that they are working for the welfare of their families, but in most cases, the families would be much happier with less of the world's goods and more of the person's time.

The barns in this parable are not at all like we would picture barns that we're used to seeing. Those barns that were used to store grain were actually holes dug in the ground and covered over. Whether or not this method of storing grain was better than in a barn or silo, as we know them, was not an issue because lumber was not available in quantities large enough for building barns.

In the parable, the rich man used the word, "I" six times and the word "my" five times. No other person is involved or even mentioned. The rich man said nothing about sharing what he had with people who were less fortunate or even anything about giving the Lord His share. There's an old saying with which many people are familiar, "Early to bed and early to rise makes a man healthy, wealthy, and wise." More often than not, wealth is not accompanied by health and not always by wisdom. Some men ruin their health in pursuit of wealth which is not a wise thing to do. Then those same men have to spend their wealth in a vain effort to regain their lost health.

106 About Faithful and Unfaithful Servants

(Luke 12:35-48)

(1) "Be dressed in readiness and keep your lamps lit. (2) Be like men who are waiting for their master when he returns from the wedding feast so that they may immediately open the door to him when he comes and knocks. (3) Blessed are those slaves whom the master finds on the alert when he comes. Truly I say to you that he will gird himself to serve and have them recline at table and will come up and wait on them. (4) Whether he comes in the second watch or even the third and finds them so, blessed are those slaves.

(5) "Be sure of this, if the head of the house had known at what hour the thief was coming he would not have allowed his house to be broken into. (6) You too, be ready, for the Son of Man is coming at an hour that you do not expect."

(7) Peter said, "Lord, are You addressing this parable to us or to everyone else as well?"

(8) The Lord said, "Who then is the faithful and sensible steward whom his master will put in charge of his servants, to give them their rations at the proper time? (9) Blessed is that slave whom his master finds so doing when he comes. (10) Truly I say to you that he will put him in charge of all his possessions. (11) But if that slave says in this heart, 'My master will be a long time in coming,' and begins to beat the slaves, both men and women, and to eat and drink and get drunk, (12) the master of that slave will come on a day when he is not expected and at an hour the slave does not know, and will cut him to pieces and assign him a place with the unbelievers. (13) That slave who knew his master's will and did not get ready or act in accord with his will shall receive many lashes, (14) but the one who did not know it and committed deeds worthy of a flogging will receive but few. From everyone who has been given much shall much be required, and to whom they entrusted much of him they will ask all the more."

Notes: Instead of "be dressed in readiness," the KJV says, "let your loins be girded about." The term "girding the loins" is figurative and means simply being or getting prepared for physical activity. The long garments that were worn would have been very cumbersome for a person engaged in physical activities, so the garment was pulled up and tucked in at the waist in front freeing the legs so that the wearer could move around freely. In India and other Far Eastern locations, some of the men wear what appears to be a long skirt. It is actually a cylinder of cloth gathered at the waist and tucked in there in the same way a person might wrap a towel around himself and tuck it in so that it would stay in place. When they need to engage in more strenuous activity than normal or to wade in water, they reach down between their ankles, grasp the back of their garment at the bottom, pull it up between their legs, and tuck it in the front at the waist. It then becomes like short pants instead of a skirt.

What did Jesus mean in that reference to the master serving the slaves? Had that been done already? No! Would it be done? Yes! When? Jesus would serve the twelve apostles at that last Passover feast by washing their feet and serving them bread and wine.

Almost everyone could recognize this parable for what it is a warning (or promise) that Jesus Himself is coming back and that His coming will be at a time which will be unexpected. In another passage, Jesus said that no one except God Himself knows when that second coming will be, and Jesus could give no signs or hints as to when it would be. A person might wonder how some people can be so egotistical as to believe that this information would be revealed to them even though Jesus, the One who will be coming, didn't know when it would be. A large and prominent religious group was founded by a man who claimed that he had knowledge as to when the world would come to an end. He named the day and on that day, with a number of his followers, he sat down to wait for Jesus to come. When nothing happened, the man said his calculations must have been in error, and he figured out a new date. That new date, and many more like predictions, have now come and gone, and Jesus hasn't come yet. That man is now long dead, but his followers still predict a date for the end of the world then sit and watch it pass like all the other predicted dates have done.

Peter asked Jesus if what He said was only for those disciples there or for everyone. It's obvious that some of the sayings of Jesus were only for the person (or persons) to whom they were spoken, but that others are for the whole world to know and heed. But some of the sayings addressed to but one person contain a principle of conduct or obedience that is beneficial or necessary for all Christians to observe. And it should be fairly easy to determine which is which.

107 Jesus Came not to Bring Peace but Division

(Luke 12:49-56)

(1) "I have come to cast fire upon the earth, and how I wish it were already kindled! (2) But I have a baptism to undergo, and I am much distressed until it is accomplished!

(3) "Do you suppose that I came to grant peace on earth? I tell you no, but rather division. (4) From now on five members in one household will be divided three against two and two against three. (5) They will be divided father against son and son against father, mother against daughter and daughter against mother, mother-in-law against daughter-in-law and daughter-in-law against mother-in-law."

(6) Jesus also said to the multitude, "When you see a cloud rising in the west immediately you say, 'A shower is coming,' and so it turns out. (7) When you see a south wind blowing you say, 'It will be a hot day,' and it turns out that way.

(8) "You hypocrites! You know how to analyze the appearance of the earth and the sky but why do you not analyze this present time?"

Notes: Fire has many uses-to keep us warm, to cook our food, to light our way, to refine products, and to destroy forests and homes. Fire is used as a simile for some things, too-to fire from a job, to fire someone up to do something, and to try someone by fire as a test. In the vast majority of places where "fire" is used in the New Testament, the meaning is the fire of hell. Albert Barnes wrote, "Fire, here, is the emblem of discord and contention, and consequently of calamities. Thus it is used in Psalms 66:12 and Isaiah 43:2." In those two references that probably is the meaning in which "fire" is used. But in some other places, fire is shown to be a refining agent, a trial in which to prove oneself. Although the word "fire" is not actually used, in Job 23:10 and Isaiah 66:10 there is an implication of fire in which fire was used as a means of refining or testing a person. All of you have probably heard the expression, "On fire for the Lord," and it seems that in this passage that may be the meaning which Jesus intended-to stir up the people so that they would turn back to a true worship of the Father or, you might say, to rekindle the flames of zeal for God. Because of His love for the souls of all people, Jesus was not wishing that the fires of hell be lighted and that the souls of some of those people be consigned to them. Jesus did stir up some of the people to return to a true worship of the Father, but He also stirred up the flames of opposition. There were deep divisions among the people because of Him.

The baptism which Jesus would have to undergo was probably a reference to His trial and crucifixion which He knew was in the near future. The distress He was suffering was reflected in the prayers He prayed on the night He was betrayed.

There has probably never been presented in all the history of the world any idea or any contemplated course of action to which there was no opposition. In politics, for instance, even the most popular candidates have a great deal of opposition. In our national elections the difference in the popular vote is usually only a very few percentage points. It would be understandable, then, that Jesus would experience a great deal of opposition to the things He said and taught. He knew that what He said would cause divisions among the people, even within families. Whole families have withdrawn from one of their members who married outside their own religion or denomination. A member of one denomination may marry a member of another denomination and perhaps the couple will experience rejection from both sides of the family. Or this may happen when a member of one religion marries a member of another religion. It may even happen when a Christian marries a non-Christian. Jesus knew this and warned that it would happen.

108 The Necessity of Repentance {Luke 13:1-9)

(1) Now on the same occasion there were some present who reported to Jesus about the Galileans whose blood Pilate had mingled with their sacrifices.

(2) Jesus said to them, "Do you suppose that these Galileans were greater sinners than all other Galileans because they suffered this fate? (3) I tell you no, but unless you repent you will all likewise perish. (4) Or do you suppose that those eighteen on whom the tower in Siloam fell and killed were worse culprits than all the men who live in Jerusalem? (5) I tell you no, but unless you repent you will all likewise perish."

(6) Jesus began telling this parable: "A certain man had a fig tree which had been planted in his vineyard, and when he came looking for fruit on it he did not find any. (7) He said to the vineyard-keeper, 'Look, for three years I have come looking for fruit on this fig tree without finding any. Cut it down! Why does it even use up the ground?' (8) The keeper answered him, 'Let it alone, sir, for this year too, until I dig around it and put in fertilizer. (9) If it bears fruit next year, fine, but if not, cut it down.'"

Notes: Some of the people who were there to hear Jesus told Him of in incident in which Pilate, the Roman governor of Judea, had some Galileans killed as they were offering their sacrifices on the altar. This incident is not recorded in the gospels nor in the annals of Josephus, but Josephus said of Galileans that they were very wicked and disposed to brawls and seditions. Too, there was said to have been enmity between Pilate and Herod Antipas, who at that time was ruling in Galilee. It's recorded in Luke 23:12 that Herod and Pilate had been enemies but that they then became friends. What, if anything, the Galileans had done, the reason Pilate had them killed, is not known, but it may have been because of the enmity between him and Herod although that seems unlikely, people generally being free to travel at will between the two provinces.

Word of mouth was the way news was spread and it was by the passing on of news in this manner that the Jews were able to keep abreast of what was happening in that area. Possibly it was only for this reason that these people, not believing (or not knowing) that Jesus was omniscient, included Him with those to whom they would impart such news. Possibly, also, they told Him in order to see His reaction and possibly to hear Him say something against Pilate or the Romans that they could use in testimony against Him.

It's implied that the bearers of the news about the Galileans believed that such misfortunes were caused by the evil actions of the victims. You may remember that the disciples of Jesus asked Him whether it was the sins of the man who was born blind or the sins of his parents that were the cause of the man having been born blind. It seems to have been the belief of most Jews that when something bad happened to a person it happened because of sin. This was confirmed when Jesus asked the news bearers if they thought those Galileans were worse sinners than others.

Jesus said what He said so that He could teach about repentance. Sins would not be forgiven if the sinners did not repent. In the model prayer which Jesus taught His disciples He said that those who forgave others their trespasses would have their trespasses forgiven. Now we read what Jesus said about repentance-that there would be no forgiveness without the sinner first repenting-if they didn't repent they would perish.

109 Healing a Woman on the Sabbath {Luke 13:10-17)

(1) Jesus was teaching in one of the synagogues on the Sabbath. (2) There also was a woman who for eighteen years had had a sickness caused by a spirit. She was bent double and could not straighten up at all.

(3) When Jesus saw the woman He called her over and said to her, "Woman, you are freed from your sickness." (4) He laid His hands upon her and immediately she was made erect again and began glorifying God.

(5) The synagogue official, indignant because Jesus had healed on the Sabbath, began saying to the multitude in response, "There are six days in which work should be done. Come during them and get healed and not on the Sabbath day."

(6) But the Lord answered him and said, "You hypocrites! Does not each of you on the Sabbath untie his ox or his donkey from the stall and lead him away to water him? (7) This woman, a daughter of Abraham as she is, whom Satan has bound for eighteen long years, should she not have been released from this bond as the Sabbath day?"

(8) As Jesus said this all His opponents were being humiliated and the entire multitude was rejoicing over all the glorious things being done by Jesus.

Notes: The woman in this passage was all bent over because of what Satan had done to her. We don't know whether this was some disease, either common or obscure, or if it was something special which Satan had done.

The woman didn't go to Jesus. She didn't beg Him to heal her as so many people in her position would have done. Apparently she had gone to the synagogue only to worship and, possibly, if she had known in advance that Jesus would be there, to hear Jesus teach. As we are told in so many of the times when Jesus healed someone, apparently He had compassion for the woman and healed her-and for that the synagogue official criticized Jesus.

110 Jesus Attends the Feast of Dedication (John 10:22- 42)

(1) At that time the Feast of Dedication took place at Jerusalem. (2) It was winter and Jesus was walking in the temple in the portico of Solomon. (3) The Jews gathered around Him and asked Him, "How long will You keep us in suspense? If You are the Christ tell us plainly." (4) Jesus answered, "I told you and you do not believe. The works that I do in My Father's name bear witness of Me. (5) But you do not believe because you are not of My sheep. (6) My sheep hear My voice, and I know them, and they follow Me. (7) I give eternal life to them and they shall never perish, and no one shall snatch them out of My hand. (8) My Father who has given them to Me is greater than all, and no one is able to snatch them out of the Father's hand. (9) I and the Father are one."

(10) Again the Jews took up stones to stone Jesus.

(11) Jesus said to them, "I showed you many good works from the Father. For which of them are you stoning Me?"

(12) The Jews answered Him, "For a good work we do not stone You, but for blasphemy; and because You, being a man, make Yourself out to be God."

(13) Jesus answered them, "Has it not been written in your Law, 'I said, you are gods'? (14) If he called gods them to whom the Word of God came (and the Scripture cannot be broken) (15) do you say of Him whom the Father sanctified and sent into the world, 'You are

blaspheming,' because I said, 'I am the Son of God'? (16) If I do not do the works of My Father do not believe Me; (17) but if I do them, though you do not believe Me, believe the works that you may know and understand that the Father is in Me and I in the Father."

(18) Therefore they were again seeking to seize Jesus and He eluded their grasp.

(19) Jesus went away again beyond the Jordan to the place where John was first baptizing and He was staying there. (20) Many came to Him and they were saying, "While John performed no sign yet everything John said about this man was true." (21) And many believed in Jesus there.

Notes: In the year 167 BC, Antiochus Epiphanes, a Seleucid king, conquered Judea. It was reported that he had forty thousand people killed and another forty thousand sold into slavery. He had a sow, a female pig, sacrificed to his god Zeus on the altar of burnt offerings in the temple in Jerusalem. He ordered a broth to be made of the drippings from the sacrificed pig and had this broth sprinkled over the entire temple. This event was prophesied in the book of Daniel and Flavius Josephus referred to that prophecy in his Antiquities of the Jews, book 12, chapter 7, and section 6.

In 164 BC, Judas Maccabaeus reconquered Jerusalem and one of the first orders of business was the purification of the temple. The purification and rededication of the temple are recorded in the apocryphal book of I Maccabees 4:52-59 as follows, "On the twenty-fifth of the ninth month, Chislev, in the year one hundred and forty-eight [that was the one hundred forty-eighth year of the Greek calendar and not one hundred forty-eight BC], they rose at dawn and offered a lawful sacrifice on the new altar of holocausts which they had made. The altar was dedicated, to the sound of zithers, harps and cymbals, at the same time of year and on the same day on which the pagans had originally profaned it. The whole people fell prostrate in adoration, praising to the skies him who had made them so successful. For eight days they celebrated the dedication of the altar, joyfully offering holocausts, communion sacrifices and thanksgiving. They ornamented the front of the Temple with crowns and bosses of gold, repaired the gates and the storerooms and fitted them with doors. There was no end to the rejoicing among the people, and the reproach of the pagans was lifted from them. Judas, with his brothers and the whole assembly of Israel, made it a law that the days of the dedication of the altar should be celebrated yearly at the proper season, for eight days beginning on the twenty-fifth of the month Chislev, with rejoicing and gladness." The Jews call this feast Hanukkah. Josephus recorded the rededication of the temple in his Antiquities in book 12, chapter 7, and section 6. He called it the "feast of lights" because so many candles were burned. According to our calendar, this took place about the fifteenth or twentieth of December and would have been about three or four months before the crucifixion.

Solomon's porch was a covered portico on the eastern side of the temple. It was called "Solomon's porch" because the floor of this section of the temple was the only part of the temple, Herod's temple, that is, which could be identified as being part of the original temple which Solomon had built.

On many occasions previous to this, Jesus had *intimated* that He was the Messiah. He had never said, "I am the Christ," or "I am the Messiah whom you have been expecting." Jesus had performed many, many miracles, all kinds of miracles, and He had spoken of Himself in such a way that the people who were expecting the Messiah to come with pomp and glory and military power... *may* ... have been honestly confused about His true identity. They may have been tom between what the scriptures said about the Messiah and their desires for a king who could lead an army against Rome and free them from Roman rule. And they may have been using this occasion to try to get Jesus to speak words whereby they could accuse Him of blasphemy.

Jesus said that the people who were questioning Him were not His sheep. The fact that they were not His sheep was the evidence, not the cause, of their disbelief. They could have been His sheep by making the choice that many others had made.

The statement Jesus made about no one being able to take His sheep out of the Father's hand is used by some people to support their theory of the impossibility of apostasy. The truth is that although no one else can take us out of the Father's hand, we can leave any time we choose to do so. Paul wrote in Romans 8:38-39, "For I am convinced that neither death, nor life, nor angels, nor principalities, nor things present, nor things to come, nor powers, nor height, nor depth, nor any other created thing, shall be able to separate us from the love of God, which is in Christ Jesus our Lord."

The quotation, "I said, 'You are gods,'" is from Psalms 82:6.

111 The Death and Resurrection of Lazarus

(John 11:1-46)

(1) Lazarus, a man of Bethany the village of Mary and her sister Martha, was sick. (2) Lazarus was the brother of Mary who was to anoint the Lord with ointment and wipe his feet with her hair.

(3) The sisters therefore sent to Jesus a message that said, "Lord, look, he whom You love is sick."

(4) When Jesus heard it He said, "This sickness is not unto death but for the glory of God that the Son of God may be glorified by it."

(5) Now Jesus loved Martha and her sister and Lazarus, (6) but when He heard that Lazarus was sick He stayed two days longer in the place where He was.

(7) After that Jesus said to the disciples, "Let us go to Judea again."

(8) The disciples said to Him, "Rabbi, the Jews were just now seeking to stone You. Are You going there again?"

(9) Jesus answered, "Are there not twelve hours in a day? If anyone walks in the day he does not stumble because he sees the light of this world. (10) But if anyone walks in the night he stumbles because the light is not in him."

(11) After that Jesus said to the disciples, "Our friend Lazarus has fallen asleep. I will go now that I may wake him up."

(12) Then His disciples said, "Lord, if he has fallen asleep he will get well." (13) Now Jesus had spoken of Lazarus' death but they thought that He was speaking of taking rest in sleep.

(14) Then Jesus said to them plainly, "Lazarus is dead, (15) and I am glad for your sake that I was not there so that you may believe. Let us go to him."

(16) Then Thomas, who is called Didymus, said to his fellow disciples, "Let us also go that we may die with Him."

(17) When Jesus arrived He found that Lazarus had already been in the tomb four days.

(18) Now Bethany was near Jerusalem, about two miles away, (19) and many of the Jews had come to Martha and Mary to console them concerning their brother. (20) Then Martha, when she heard that Jesus was coming, went to meet Him, but Mary stayed in the house.

(21) Martha said to Jesus, "Lord, if You had been here my brother would not have died. (22) But even now I know that whatever You ask of God, God will give You."

(23) Jesus said to her, "Your brother will rise again."

(24) Martha said to Jesus, "I know that he will rise again in the resurrection on the last day."

(25) Jesus said to her, "I am the resurrection and the life. He who believes in Me shall live again even if he dies, (26) and everyone who lives and believes in Me shall never die. Do you believe this?"

(27) Martha said to Him, "Yes, Lord, I believe that You are the Christ, the Son of God, He who is to come into the world."

(28) When Martha had said this she went away and called Mary her sister, saying to her secretly, "The Teacher is here and is calling for you."

(29) When Mary heard this she arose quickly and went to meet Jesus. (30) Now Jesus had not yet gone into the village but was still in the place where Martha had met Him.

(31) When the Jews who were with Mary in the house consoling her saw that she rose up quickly and went out they followed her, supposing that she was going to the tomb to weep.

(32) Then when Mary came to where Jesus was and saw Him she fell down at His feet, saying to Him, "Lord, if you had been here my brother would not have died."

(33) When Jesus saw Mary and the Jews who came with her all weeping, He was deeply moved in Spirit and was troubled.

(34) He asked, "Where have you laid him?" They said to Jesus, "Lord, come and see."

(35) Jesus wept.

(36) Then the Jews said, "See how He loved him."

(37) But some of them said, "Could not this Man who opened the eyes of the blind also have kept this man from dying?"

(38) Jesus, groaning again to Himself, came to the tomb. The tomb was a cave and a stone lay against it.

(39) Jesus said, "Remove the stone."

Martha, the sister of him who was dead, said to Jesus, "Lord, by this time there will be a stench for he has been dead four days."

(40) Jesus said to Martha, "Did I not say to you that if you would believe you would see the glory of God?" (41) So they removed the stone.

Jesus raised His eyes and said, "Father, I thank You that You have heard Me. (42) I know that you always hear Me, but because of the people who are standing by I said this, that they may believe that You sent Me."

(43) When Jesus had said these things He cried out in a loud voice, "Lazarus, come forth." (44) And he who had died came out bound hand and foot with graveclothes, and his face was wrapped with a cloth.

Jesus said to them, "Unbind him and let him go."

(45) Then many of the Jews who had come to Mary and had seen the things Jesus did believed in Him. (46) But some of them went away to the Pharisees and told them the things which Jesus had done.

Notes: After Mary and Martha sent for Jesus so that He would heal their brother Lazarus, Jesus waited two more days so that Lazarus would be dead and buried and that the disciples could see Jesus raise him up again. Jesus had been in an area to the east of the Jordan River. Since it took some time to walk from that point to the town of Bethany or from Bethany to there, Lazarus may have already been dead by the time the messengers found Jesus.

It was the custom to bury a body immediately after death. Even though this probably happened in early spring, the weather would have been hot during the day but cool at night and since bodies were not embalmed they could not be preserved at all in warm weather. Acts 5:6 and 10 records that Ananias and Sapphira were both buried immediately after their deaths.

Many people had come to be with Mary and Martha in order to mourn with them and to console them. Four days after the burial of Lazarus, the people were still there because Jewish custom decreed an extended period of mourning. The *Mishna*, which is the first part of the Jewish *Talmud*, prescribed seven days of mourning for close relatives. The standard period of mourning for an important or distinguished person was seven days of public mourning and thirty days of private mourning.

The first words that both Martha and Mary said to Jesus were that if He had been there, Lazarus would not have died. Martha apparently didn't believe that Jesus would (or could) restore Lazarus to life. Whether or not she had heard that Jesus had restored life to others, we don't know, but if she had it was an impersonal type of knowledge and perhaps she didn't believe it had happened. Martha did believe in an eventual resurrection of the dead, as did most of the Jews except for the Sadducees. With her, as with most people, it was probably something to which she gave but little thought, something that would happen sometime in the distant future.

With those people, mourning was done in such a way as to let it be known to all other people that they were mourning. They showed their mourning visibly and audibly. The American Indians mourned openly and loudly too. After the death of one of them, the whole village, especially the women, would wail as a sign of their grief.

It says here that Jesus groaned to Himself. The Greek word translated "groaned" has the additional meaning of indignation. Jesus was upset by the grief of Mary and Martha and the people who were mourning with them. Jesus didn't groan aloud as we probably would have done. The KJV says that Jesus groaned in the Spirit and that He groaned to Himself.

When Jesus wept it wasn't because of the death of Lazarus. It was because of His compassion for the people who were grieving over their loss. When we mourn because of the death of someone dear to us, we're not mourning for the person who has departed so much as we're mourning because of our own loss.

The tombs used in those days were mostly caves in the hills or recesses cut into rocks. They were sealed by rolling a large stone over the opening. That was necessary in order to keep scavenging animals away from the bodies.

Jesus could have used His own miraculous powers to roll the stone away from the entrance to the tomb, but a miracle wasn't needed for that to be done. Jesus never performed a miracle when a miracle wasn't necessary to rectify whatever was wrong, and in this case, there were enough people there with strength enough to roll the stone away.

The prayer of Jesus has been criticized by some people as being "a prayer for show." But this prayer was not to show that He was a prayerful man or to attract attention or admiration to Himself like those Pharisees who prayed aloud on the street corners. It was to show the people that it was through the power of God that Jesus was able to do such things.

There were no incantations, no charms, no hocus-pocus, involved here-just a simple command by the Son of God. Brother Marshall Keeble, an old preacher of the church of Christ, now long dead, once said that Jesus called Lazarus forth by name because, if He hadn't used the name of Lazarus, all the people in that cemetery would have arisen and come forth at the command of Jesus.

This miracle is all the proof we need that some day Jesus will do the same for all the people who are in His kingdom. On that day, Jesus will speak, and all the saved will come forth to be with Him eternally. If Jesus can do it for one person, He can do it for all people.

There was no question in the minds of any of the people who witnessed Jesus restore life to Lazarus that this miracle was, in fact, a miracle. Some of them became disciples of Jesus because of it and others, although they couldn't deny the miracle, remained enemies of Jesus.

112 The Jews Plot Against Jesus and He Goes to Ephraim

(John 11:47-54)

(1) The chief priests and the Pharisees convened a council and asked, "What are we doing? This man is performing many signs. (2) If we let Him go on like this all men will believe in Him, and the Romans will come and take away both our place and our nation."

(3) Then one of them, Caiaphas who was high priest that year, told them, "You know nothing at all, (4) nor do you take into account that it is expedient for you that one man should die for the people rather than that the whole nation should perish."

(5) Now Caiaphas did not say this on his own initiative, but being high priest that year he prophesied that Jesus was going to die for the nation, (6) and not for the nation only, but that He might also gather together into one the children of God who are scattered abroad.

(7) So from that day on they planned together to kill Jesus.

(8) Jesus therefore no longer continued to walk publicly among the Jews, but went away from there to the country near the wilderness into a city called Ephraim, and there He stayed with the disciples.

Notes: The council which was convened by the chief priests and Pharisees was the Sanhedrin, the Jewish ruling body, which had the oversight of both religious and civil affairs for the Jews. From what they said, it seems that they believed in the power of Jesus to perform miracles and, perhaps, that He really was the Messiah. But since Jesus did not display any military prowess, they did not believe in His power to lead the Jews in a revolt against the Romans and mold them into a nation as they had hoped. We don't know why they were afraid the Romans would interfere unless it was because they thought Jesus would try to lead a revolt and fail. We do know, though, that due to the revolt of the Jews in AD 70, the Romans did destroy many of the Jews, did destroy them as a nation, and did destroy the temple which had only recently been completed by Herod the Great.

Caiaphas, the high priest (who, according to Josephus, served in that capacity from AD 18 to AD 36) seems to have prophesied correctly in spite of himself as did Balaam and Saul, the accounts of which are recorded in the Old Testament. The "one" into which Jesus would gather the children of God was His church which would be established shortly after His ascension.

The city here called Ephraim was possibly the city of Ophrah which is listed with other cities in Joshua 18:23 and in other places in the Old Testament. It might also have been the town which was called Ephraim in 2 Chronicles 13:19. Some biblical scholars believe it was the city which is now called et Taiyibeh, which is situated on a hill about sixteen miles northeast of Jerusalem and about five miles east of Bethel, and in that location on some maps purporting to show a representation of Palestine in the time of Christ there is a town named Ephraim. It is doubtful, though, that because of the humor of the Jews at that time Jesus would have remained so close to Jerusalem.

113 Jesus Determined to Go to Jerusalem {Luke 9:51- 56)

(1) When the days were approaching for His ascension Jesus resolutely set His face to go to Jerusalem. (2) He sent messengers on ahead of Him, and the messengers went and entered a village of the Samaritans to make arrangements for Him. (3) But the Samaritans did not receive Him because He was journeying with His face toward Jerusalem.

(4) When Jesus' disciples James and John saw this they asked, "Lord, do You want us to command fire to come down from heaven and consume them?"

(5) But Jesus turned and rebuked them [and said, "You do not know of what kind of spirit you are, (6) for the Son of Man did not come to destroy lives but to save them."] And they went on to another village.

Notes: The Samaritans who refused to receive Jesus into their village were doing what was natural for them to do, that is, they refused hospitality to Jews. The Samaritans and Jews had been natural enemies dating as far back as the splitting of the kingdom after the death of Solomon. You may remember that the woman in Sychar at Jacob's well reminded Jesus that Jews and Samaritans would not have anything to do with each other. These Samaritans, too, probably had no knowledge of that conversation between Jesus and the woman in Sychar in which Jesus told the woman about the living water.

There is some concern about the placement of this passage in this manuscript, but this seems to be the most likely place for it.

Many early manuscripts do not contain the bracketed portion of the text.

114 Jesus Heals the Ten Lepers {Luke 17:11-19)

(1) While Jesus was on His way to Jerusalem He passed along the borders between Samaria and Galilee. (2) As He entered one of the villages ten leprous men who had been standing at a distance met Him. (3) The ten men raised their voices saying, "Jesus, Master, have mercy on us!"

(4) When Jesus saw the men He said to them, "Go and show yourselves to the priests." As they were on their way to do so they were cleansed.

(5) Now one of them, a Samaritan, when he saw that he had been healed, turned back, glorifying God with a loud voice, (6) and he fell on his face at the feet of Jesus, giving thanks to Him.

(7) Jesus asked, "Were there not ten cleansed? The other nine, where are they? (8) Was there no one found who turned back to give glory to God except this foreigner?"

(9) Then Jesus said to the Samaritan, "Rise and go your way. Your faith has made you well."

Notes: Some biblical scholars put forth the theory that Jesus, with His disciples, journeyed from Ephraim up through Samaria to the border between Samaria and Galilee, then traveled down the wadi or gully between the two provinces, and that when Jesus reached the place where the Jordan River ran southward out of the Sea of Galilee, He crossed over into the province of Perea. They theorized that there He met up with a caravan of travelers who were traveling together toward Jericho on their way to Jerusalem to observe the Passover. They also think that Jesus joined Himself to the caravan and traveled along with it. That scenario may very well have happened, but the scholars do not cite any scriptures or other source to support their premise.

Lepers, whether single or in groups, did not frequent places where people who were free of the disease congregated because there were laws forbidding it. This group of ten lepers, then, did not come down to the road where the people traveled, but stood back at some distance from the road but at a place from which they could see the travelers. The law required such a separation because leprosy was a highly contagious disease. In the law, there had been set a minimum distance closer than which lepers could not approach anyone who did not have the disease. Until recent years, there was no cure for leprosy and almost everyone who had leprosy was condemned by the disease to die from it.

In the Law of Moses, there had been included complete instructions concerning how anyone who had leprosy was to be treated. One part of that Law stated that a leper who had been cleansed of the disease could show himself to a priest, and if he was then free of the disease, the priest could declare that he had been cleansed. After the priest had made that declaration, the former leper could then resume his life and intermingle freely with other people.

At least one of the lepers involved in this incident was a Samaritan. The nationality of the other nine was not given, perhaps leading to the belief that they were all Jews. All ten lepers could have been Samaritans or up to nine of them could have been Jews because Jews and Samaritans, who were normally enemies, were made friends, or at the least, companions, by the disease that was common to them-they could have no other friends or companions. It's said that in modern times, Jewish lepers and Mohammedan lepers live together in harmony even though members of their respective religions without the disease are bitter enemies.

One of the ten former lepers, the Samaritan (or perhaps one of the Samaritans), turned back to thank Jesus for making him clean. Can you imagine the happiness, euphoria even, that a person who had been cleansed of leprosy would experience?

How wonderful it would be to be suddenly freed from the sentence of a miserable death under which he had been living? But the other nine men didn't thank Jesus! Were those nine people so different from so many people we meet today? Have you ever opened a door for someone or held it open for someone who completely ignored your courtesy? Perhaps they just walked on through as if the door had opened itself, never looking at you, nor smiling at you, nor thanking you. They act as if such courtesy is *due* them but that they have no obligation to show any courtesy whatsoever in return. Some people pray to God every day, thanking Him for very meager blessings He's given them and other people never even thank Him for bountiful blessings. Whether our blessings are great or small, we owe thanks to our Heavenly Father for them.

115 Jesus Answers the Pharisees about the Kingdom

(Luke 17:20-21)

(1) Jesus had been questioned by the Pharisees as to when the kingdom of God was coming and He said to them, "The kingdom of God is not coming with signs to be observed, (2) nor will people say, 'Look, here it is!' or, 'There it is!' because the kingdom of God is in your midst."

Notes: It seems likely, knowing the Pharisees as we do, that they were not asking for information, but that they were trying to draw attention to the fact that Jesus had been around for some time (we know it to have been about three years) preaching and teaching and trying to prepare the people for the coming of the kingdom of God, and it still hadn't come. They were expecting the kingdom of God to come with pomp and ceremony and military power, in a way that would be visible to everyone because that's the way they wanted it to be.

Luke 19:11 reads, "And while they were listening to these things, He went on to tell a parable, because He was near Jerusalem, and they supposed that the kingdom of God was going to appear immediately." That was in the same time period as our current text and shows that not only the Pharisees, but everyone else was expecting the kingdom of God to come immediately with pomp and power and ceremony. In fact, they tried to hurry things along as reported in John 6:15, "Jesus therefore perceiving that they were intending to come and take Him by force, to make Him king, withdrew again to the mountain by Himself alone." Even after the resurrection, the apostles still didn't understand about the kingdom of God because as Jesus was preparing for His ascension into heaven, they asked Him, "Lord, is it at this time You are restoring the kingdom of Israel?" {Acts 1:6)

Paul wrote in Romans 14:17, "... The kingdom of God is not eating and drinking, but righteousness and peace and joy in the Holy Spirit."

And in John 18:36, Jesus said to Pilate, "My kingdom is not of this world. If My kingdom were of this world, then My servants would be fighting, that I might not be delivered up to the Jews; but as it is, My kingdom is not of this realm."

116 Jesus Teaching in the Villages {Luke 13:22-33)

(1) Jesus was passing through from one city and village to another, teaching and proceeding on His way to Jerusalem.

(2) Someone asked Jesus, "Lord, are there just a few who are being saved?"

(3) Jesus said to them, "Strive to enter by the narrow door, for many, I tell you, will seek to enter and will not be able. (4) When the Head of the house gets up and shuts the door and you come and stand outside and knock on the door, saying, 'Lord, open up to us!' then He will say to you, 'I do not know where you are from.' (5) Then you will say, 'We ate and drank in Your presence and You taught in our streets'; (6) and He will say, 'I tell you, I do not know where you are from. Depart from Me, all you evildoers.'

(7) "There will be weeping and gnashing of teeth there when you see Abraham and Isaac and Jacob and all the prophets in the kingdom of God but yourselves being cast out. (8) They will come from east and west and from north and south and will recline at the table in the kingdom of God. (9) Look, some are last who will be first and some are first who will be last."

(10) Just at that time some Pharisees came up and said to Jesus, "Go away and depart from here for Herod wants to kill you."

(11) Jesus said to them, "Go and tell that fox, 'Behold, I cast out demons and perform cures today and tomorrow, and the third day I reach My goal.' (12) Nevertheless I must journey on today and tomorrow and the next day, for it cannot be that a prophet should perish outside of Jerusalem."

Notes: The person who asked Jesus the question was not identified, but it's likely that it was someone other than one of the twelve apostles. According to Lightfoot, the Jews, knowing that only two of the people who set out from Egypt eventually entered the Promised Land, believed that only a proportionate number of people (only two of millions) would enter heaven and that all of that number would be Jews. You may remember that after the conversion of Cornelius, the Jewish Christians had to be persuaded that Gentiles, too, were acceptable to God. By making reference to the four corners of the earth, Jesus was telling His listeners that, not only Jews, but people from all over the world would be saved.

The Herod spoken of here was probably Antipas, who was ruler over Galilee and Perea at that time. Jesus was probably in Perea on His way to Jerusalem. It's likely that any normally cautious person, being warned by a person who had always been an enemy that someone intended to have Him killed, would be suspicious of that messenger's motive. Jesus, of course, would have been able to divine the motive of the Pharisees in warning Him. Most biblical scholars are of the opinion that under the guise of a pretended friendship, these Pharisees were merely messengers of Herod and that Herod didn't actually want to kill Jesus because he feared what the common people would have done if he had committed such an act, but he did want Jesus out of his territory.

The message which Jesus gave the Pharisees for Herod showed that Jesus had no fear of Herod. In effect, Jesus was telling Herod that He (Jesus) was proceeding on His way at His own pace and that in a short time He would be out of Herod's territory.

117 Jesus Dines With a Pharisee and Heals on the Sabbath

(Luke 14:1-14)

(1) Jesus went into the house of one of the leaders of the Pharisees on the Sabbath to eat bread, and the other people who were there were watching Him closely (2) because there was in front of Jesus a certain man who was suffering from dropsy.

(3) Jesus asked the lawyers and Pharisees, "Is it lawful to heal on the Sabbath or not?"

(4) But they all kept silent. Jesus then took hold of the man with dropsy and healed him and sent him away.

(5) Then Jesus said to them, "Which one of you shall have a son or an ox fall into a well and will not immediately pull him out on a Sabbath day?" (6) And they could make no reply to this.

(7) Then Jesus began speaking a parable to the invited quests when He noticed how they had been picking out the places of honor at the table. He said to them, (8) "When you are invited by someone to a wedding feast do not take the place of honor lest someone more distinguished than you may have been invited by him, (9) and he who invited you both shall come and say to you, 'Give place to this man,' and then in disgrace you proceed to occupy the last place. (10) But when you are invited, go and recline at the last place so that when the one who invited you comes he may say to you, 'Friend, move up higher.' Then you will have honor in the sight of all who are at the table with you. (11) Everyone who exalts himself shall be humbled and he who humbles himself shall be exalted."

(12) Jesus also went on to say to the one who had invited Him, "When you give a luncheon or a dinner do not invite your friends or your brothers or your relatives or your rich neighbor lest they also invite you in return and repayment come to you.

(13) But when you give a banquet invite the poor, the crippled, the lame, the blind, (14) and you will be blessed since they do not have the means to repay you. You will be repaid at the resurrection of the righteous."

Notes: The invitation for Jesus to dine at the home of the Pharisee seems to have been planned with certain arrangements having been made beforehand. The man with dropsy was seated across from Jesus so that He couldn't fail to see the man and note his condition. The Pharisee and his other guests were watching Jesus closely to see what He would do about the man with dropsy, whether out of mere curiosity or to see if Jesus would do or say something that they could use against Him is not clear.

According to the dictionary, "dropsy" is an abnormal accumulation of serous fluid and is a shortened form of the Middle English word "ydropesie" and refers to an edema, which is a watery swelling. The Greek word from which "dropsy" was translated is *hudropikos* (hoo-dro-pik-os') and meant "looking watery."

The lawyers and Pharisees, especially the lawyers, were supposed to be very knowledgeable about the Law of Moses, but they remained silent when Jesus asked them if it was lawful to heal on the Sabbath. Since acts of mercy on the Sabbath were not forbidden by the Law, the lawyers could have made no legal objection to Jesus healing the man with dropsy.

Jesus noticed and commented on the practice of some of the Jews to find and use the choicest seats (or rather, places, since the practice was to recline at the dinner table) at a banquet. The *triclinia* or Grecian table then in use was actually three tables arranged in the form of the letter "U." The diners reclined on the outer perimeter of the three tables leaving the space inside the "U" free for the servants to use when they served the food. It was the opinion of one biblical writer that the center position in each of the three tables were the seats of greatest honor and that the honor declined in proportion to the distance one sat from those seats. Another writer stated that the host sat in the seat of highest honor, the center of the middle table, and proximity to the host indicated the rank or honor of the diners, those closest to the host being the most honorable and those farther away being of lesser honor.

In teaching humility, Jesus was also teaching other lessons which all Christians should know. Politeness and courtesy should be a part of the Christian's character as are humility and love. Paul wrote in 1 Corinthians 13:4-7, "Love is patient, love is kind, and is not jealous; love does not brag and is not arrogant, does not act unbecomingly; it does not seek its own, is not provoked, does not take into account a wrong suffered, does not rejoice in unrighteousness, but rejoices with the truth; bears all things, believes all things, hopes all things, endures all things."

Jesus was also teaching that there are some distinctions in society which should be observed-that some people are due more honor or respect than others because of age, sex, position, character, or whatever. Thus a preacher should be given more honor than a teacher, an elder should be honored above a deacon, and a Christian mother should be honored above her children.

Jesus was not teaching that social gatherings among family and friends were wrong. He was not saying that we shouldn't entertain them by inviting them to eat with us, because we love them and are close to them. What He is saying is that we should not entertain people because of their social position or their wealth or fame if there is an expectation of being repaid in kind. He is saying that spiritually it is more profitable to feed people who are unable to repay us. For that kind of entertaining, repayment is from God.

118 The Parable of the Great Banquet (Luke 14:15-24)

(1) When one of those who were reclining at the table with Jesus heard this he said to Jesus, "Blessed is everyone who shall eat bread in the kingdom of God!"

(2) But Jesus said to him, "A certain man was giving a big dinner and he invited many. (3) At the dinner hour he sent his slave to say to those who had been invited, 'Come, for everything is ready now.' (4) But they all alike began to make excuses. The first one said to him, 'I have bought a piece of land and I need to go out and look at it. Please consider me excused.' (5) Another one said, 'I have bought five yoke of oxen and I am going to try them out. Please consider me excused.' (6) And another one said, 'I have married a wife and for that reason I cannot come.'

(7) "The slave went back and reported this to his master. Then the head of the household became angry and said to his slave, 'Go out at once into the streets and lanes of the city and bring in here the poor and crippled and blind and lame.' (8) The slave said, 'Master, what you commanded has been done and still there is room.' (9) And the master said to the slave, 'Go out into the highways and along the hedges and compel them to come in that my house may be filled, (10) for I tell you, none of the men who were invited shall taste of my dinner.'"

Notes: The person who spoke to Jesus seems to have understood to some extent, but certainly only partially, the meaning behind the parable Jesus had just told (in the previous section). Revelation 19:9 reads, "And he said to me, 'Write, "Blessed are those who are invited to the marriage supper of the lamb.'" And he said to me, 'These are true words of God.'" Like all the other Jews, this man probably had no real understanding of what the kingdom of God would be like and, therefore, was speaking from his wishes and expectations rather than from any knowledge. Jesus, knowing the lack of understanding of that man, told the parable of the great banquet. The meaning of that parable was that since the Jews were rejecting Jesus because He didn't fit their preconceived ideas, they would not be able to enter into the kingdom of God, and the Samaritans and Gentiles whom the Jews considered to be inferior to them, would fill the places that the Jews refused to fill.

119 The Conditions and Cost of Discipleship

(Luke 14:25-35)

(1) Now great multitudes were following along with Jesus, and He turned and said to them, (2) "If anyone comes to Me and does not hate his own father and mother and wife and children and brothers and sisters, yes, and even his own life, he cannot be My disciple. (3) Whoever does not carry his own cross and come after Me cannot be My disciple.

(4) "Which one of you when he wants to build a tower does not first sit down and calculate the cost to see if he has enough to complete it? (5) Otherwise when he has laid a foundation and is not able to finish, all who observe it begin to ridicule him, (6) saying, 'This man began to build and was not able to finish.'

(7) "Or what king when he sets out to meet another king in battle will not first sit down and take counsel whether he is strong enough with ten thousand men to encounter the one coming against him with twenty thousand? (8) Or else while the other is still far away he sends a delegation and asks terms of peace.

(9) "So therefore, no one of you can be My disciple who does not give up all his own possessions. (10) Salt is good but if even salt has become tasteless with what will it be seasoned?

(11) It is useless either for the soil or for the manure pile; it is thrown out. He who has ears to hear let him hear."

Notes: The word here translated "hate" is from the Greek word *miseo* (mis-eh'-o). It has two meanings, the first, to abhor as from hatred, and the other to love less, that is, as used here, by comparison to a person's love of Jesus. He said, then, that Christians must love Him more than they love their spouses, their parents, their brothers and sisters, and so on, or conversely, that they must love their relatives less than they love Him.

The parable Jesus told illustrated the foolishness of entering into some enterprise without first considering all the ramifications and the consequences of failure. If a person should lightly enter into a decision to become a Christian and should then fall away as soon as he encounters some obstacle he had not thought about, he wouldn't have counted the cost.

120 Parables of the Lost Sheep and Lost Coin

(Matt. 18:12-13; Luke 15:1-10)

(1) Now all the tax-gatherers and the sinners were coming near Jesus to listen to Him, (2) and both the Pharisees and the scribes began to grumble, saying, "This man receives sinners and eats with them."

(3) Then Jesus told them this parable, (4) "What do you think? If any man among you has a hundred sheep and one of them strays and becomes lost does he not leave the ninety-nine in the mountain wilderness and go and search for the one that is lost until he finds it? (5) And when he has found it he lays it on his shoulders, rejoicing. (6) When he comes home he calls together his friends and his neighbors saying to them, 'Rejoice with me, for I have found my sheep which was lost!' (7) Truly I say to you, he rejoices over it more than over the ninety-nine which have not gone astray. (8) I tell you that in the same way there will be more joy in heaven over one sinner who repents than over ninety-nine righteous persons who need no repentance.

(9) "Or what woman if she has ten silver coins and loses one coin does not light a lamp and sweep the house and search carefully until she finds it? (10) And when she has found it she calls together her friends and neighbors saying, 'Rejoice with me, for I have found the coin which

I had lost!' (11) In the same way, I tell you, there is joy in the presence of the angels of God over one sinner who repents."

Notes: Here, as in so many other places in the Gospels, we read about the publicans (or tax-gatherers) and sinners lumped together. These were the common people. These people were looked down upon by the Pharisees and the scribes and the lawyers because they were considered to be beneath them in social standing. But what bothered these "elites" most at this time was that Jesus accepted them. Why, He even condescended to eat with them, showing the whole world that He accepted them as being equal to anyone else spiritually.

And the scribes and Pharisees were jealous. It seems to be human nature to want to associate with prominent people like politicians and actors and television personalities, even if we don't particularly like them or don't agree with them. The scribes and Pharisees apparently liked to be around Jesus even if they didn't agree with what He said and did. But Jesus associated with people whom the scribes and Pharisees deemed unworthy. Even though they didn't agree with the things Jesus taught, still they resented it when He didn't prefer to associate with them rather than with those inferior people.

Both of the parables Jesus told concerned something that was lost and the rejoicing when that object was found. We know that what the parables are trying to teach is that some people need rescuing from sin and others don't. Probably the Pharisees and scribes understood the point made in both parables, but considered themselves to have no need to repent. If a person had two children and one of them was rescued from some grave danger, that rescued child would be the center of attention for a while and the other child might feel resentment for being ignored. It could be that way in a spiritual sense with some people. People who like attention, such as the Pharisees, might resent all the attention that a sinner who repented was receiving.

In reading this scripture, it might seem to some people that God is more pleased over the sinners who repented than He was over all those people who didn't need rescuing, those people already in His kingdom. Perhaps, they have forgotten that when they first repented and became Christians, the rejoicing at that time was for them. God's love is for all people, both sinners and the righteous. The ones who don't fall and need to repent are a source of constant joy to God. Those who sin and fall and then repent are at first a source of grief to God which turns to rejoicing when they repent. And when the rejoicing because of their return to the fold is finished, they join with those who are a source of constant joy. Unfortunately, quite often some of those who have repented like the attention they received so much that when the rejoicing over their return is done they lose their enthusiasm for Christ, their faith wanes, and they fall again.

121 The Parable of the Prodigal Son (Luke 15:11-32)

(1) Jesus said, "A certain man had two sons, (2) and the younger of them said to his father, 'Father, give me the share of the estate that falls to me.' So the father divided his wealth between the two sons.

(3) "Not many days later the younger son gathered everything together and went on a journey into a distant country. There he squandered his estate with loose living.

(4) "When he had spent everything a severe famine occurred in that country and he began to be in need. (5) He went and attached himself to one of the citizens of that country who sent him into the fields to feed the swine. (6) He longed to fill his stomach with the pods that the swine were eating for no one gave anything to him.

(7) "But when he came to his senses he said, 'How many of my father's hired men have more than enough bread, but I am dying here with hunger. (8) I will get up and go to my father and say to him, "Father, I have sinned against heaven and in your sight. (9) I am no longer worthy to be called your son. Make me as one of your hired men."' (10) And he got up and went to his father.

"While he was still a long way off his father saw him and felt compassion for him and ran and embraced him and kissed him.

(11) "The son said to him, 'Father, I have sinned against heaven and in your sight. I am no longer worthy to be called your son.'

(12) "But the father said to his slaves, 'Quickly bring out the best robe and put it on him and put a ring on his finger and sandals on his feet. (13) Bring the fattened calf, kill it, and let us eat and be merry, (14)

because this son of mine was dead and has come to life again. He was lost and has been found.' And they began to be merry.

(15) "Now his older brother was in the fields and when he came and approached the house he heard music and dancing.

(16) He summoned one of the servants and began inquiring what these things might be. (17) The servant said to him, 'Your brother has come and your father has killed the fattened calf because he has received him back safe and sound.'

(18) "But the older son became angry and was not willing to go in, so his father came out and began entreating him. (19) but he said to his father, 'Look! For so many years I have been serving you and I have never neglected a command of yours and yet you have never given me a kid that I might make merry with my friends. (20) But when this son of yours came, the one who devoured your wealth with harlots, you killed the fattened calf for him.'

(21) "His father said to him, 'My child, you have always been with me and all that is mine is yours. (22) But we had to be merry and rejoice for this brother of yours was dead and is alive. He was lost and has been found.'"

Notes: This parable has the same theme that Jesus emphasized in His last two parables, that is, something that had been lost and was now found. In this parable it was the father who rejoiced because his youngest son had repented and returned. Anytime a prodigal returns to the fold we should rejoice but, sadly, like the older brother, not everyone is happy that a fallen brother or sister has repented.

In Deuteronomy 21:17, it states that the firstborn or eldest son is to be given a double portion of his father's estate. Therefore if a man had two sons, as did the father in this parable, the eldest would receive two-thirds of the estate, and the younger son would receive one-third. Or if a man had six sons, the eldest would receive two-sevenths of the estate and the others one-seventh each. Too, it was not out of line for a son to ask for and receive his portion of his father's estate while the father was still living.

In Genesis 25:1-6, it says that after the death of Sarah, Abraham married a second time. By his second wife, Keturah, Abraham had six more sons. He gave gifts to these six sons (actually the scripture says that he gave gifts to all his sons by his concubines and whether or not the sons of Keturah were included with the sons of the concubines we don't know) while he still lived, and he gave all that he had to Isaac. Abraham, of course, lived before the Law was given and was not required to divide his estate according to that Law.

In ancient Roman and Syrophoenician societies, it was the custom that when a son reached his majority, he could demand and receive his share of the estate of his father. Can you imagine what this country would be like if that custom was a law here!

In order to show how far the prodigal son had fallen, the parable says that he took a job feeding swine. To a Jew, that was the absolute lowest level to which a person could sink. Some Jews loathed swine so much that they refused to call those animals by name when speaking of them, ref erring to a pig as *dabhar acheer* meaning "the other thing."

It is still the custom among some of the people of the East to always keep a calf, penned and fattened, in readiness to celebrate some great or joyful occasion. They didn't wait for a guest to arrive before they made preparations to welcome him, but always had a calf on hand and ready should the need for it arise.

If the scribes and Pharisees had bothered to analyze this parable, they would have recognized themselves in the person of the elder brother. They resented the attention Jesus gave the publicans and sinners, believing that they, that is, the scribes and Pharisees, should be the ones drawing His attention. They believed that they were the ones who had remained true and faithful to God. From the way they thought about publicans and sinners we may suppose that they would have abandoned these poor souls to the clutches of Satan with no thought of trying to save them.

122 The Parable of the Unrighteous Steward

(Luke 16:1-13)

(1) Jesus also said to the disciples, "There was a certain rich man who had a steward and this steward was reported to be squandering his

master's possessions. (2) The rich man called the steward and said to him, 'What is this I hear about you? Give an account of your stewardship for you can no longer be steward.'

(3) "The steward said to himself, 'What shall I do since my master is taking the stewardship away from me? I am not strong enough to dig and I am ashamed to beg. (4) I know what I shall do so that when I am removed from the stewardship they will receive me into their homes.'

(5) "He summoned each of his master's debtors and he said to the first one, 'How much do you owe my master?'

(6) "The debtor said, 'A hundred measures of oil.'

"The steward said to him, 'Take your bill and sit down quickly and write fifty.'

(7) "Then he asked another, 'How much do you owe?' "He said, 'A hundred measures of wheat.'

"The steward said, 'Take your bill and write eighty.'

(8) "His master praised the unrighteous steward because he had acted shrewdly, for the sons of this age are more shrewd in relation to their own kind than the sons of light. (9) I say to you, make friends for yourselves by means of the riches of unrighteousness so that when it fails they may receive you into the eternal dwellings.

(10) "He who is faithful in a very little thing is faithful also in much, and he who is unrighteous in a very little thing is unrighteous also in much. (11) If therefore you have not been faithful in the use of unrighteous riches who will entrust the true riches to you? (12) If you have not been faithful in the use of that which is another's who will give you that which is your own?

(13) "No servant can serve two masters for either he will hate one and love the other, or else he will hold to one and despise the other. You cannot serve God and money."

Notes: This parable was probably told immediately after Jesus told the last three parables we read. It was most likely aimed chiefly at the publicans in the audience, but, as with so many other teachings, would be profitable for everyone who might have dealings in money or property belonging to others.

The unrighteous steward would not have been a slave as were so many other people in like positions of employment, else he would have been punished rather than being discharged.

Judging by the substances of the debts owed to the steward's master, these debtors might have been tenant farmers or sharecroppers. If not, the debts would most likely have been in money rather than in goods.

People who have dealings with a dishonest master and dishonest tenants must of necessity be dishonest, too, in order to deal properly. Jesus said that the worldly minded are better able to deal with dishonest people than the people who are not worldly minded-a thief thinks all people are thieves, and an honest man considers all people to be honest.

The application of this parable to Christians is rather difficult. It seems that Jesus is saying to Christians that they must be as shrewd in their stewardship of God's property as a dishonest person would be in trying to get personal gain at the expense of his master. All we own is God's, and we are only God's stewards when we are using it. If we do the best we can with everything over which we are stewards, we will probably still be misusing "our" property. Perhaps Jesus is saying, too, that a way we can succeed in gaining our reward in heaven even though we may fail miserably as stewards is in wisely making friends by the proper use of the "riches of unrighteousness."

What we gain by helping those people who are less fortunate and who are unable to help themselves is not by merit but by grace. How can we gain by merit when what we have is the property of another person-in this instance, God's? We can be selfish and use all of it for our own benefit or we can be unselfish and use part of it to help others. The lesson we are to learn from this parable is that we are to use the property over which we have control on earth to secure comfort and happiness in the world to come. The unrighteous steward used what belonged to his master to secure a future for himself after he would no longer have the means to support himself. In the same way, we are to use the property of God in such a way as to help us attain our place in heaven. Be sure to notice that Jesus did not say that we are to use what we have in the same way the steward did because what the steward did was wrong. But we are to work to secure the results the steward was able to achieve.

We are not judged by the size or prominence of our actions but by the principles that inspired those actions. If we refuse to compromise with our faith when something great is at stake, we aren't likely to compromise when less is at stake. If we forget our principles because what we want to do isn't a very big sin, how can we resist greater temptation? Or we might ask, "How much is your honor worth?" Do we sell it for the price of a pencil taken from our employer or take one of his postage stamps for our own use?

123 The Pharisees Scoff at Jesus and Are Reproved

(Luke 16:14-17)

(1) Now the Pharisees, who were lovers of money, listened to all these things and they scoffed at Jesus. (2) Jesus said to them, "You are those who justify yourselves in the sight of men but God knows your hearts. That which is highly esteemed among men is detestable in the sight of God.

(3) "The Law and the Prophets were proclaimed until John. Since then the gospel of the kingdom of God is preached and everyone is forcing his way into it. (4) But it is easier for heaven and earth to pass away than for one stroke of a letter of the Law to fail."

Notes: This is the first place where we read that the Pharisees were openly derisive of Jesus. Until now they hadn't been openly hostile to Jesus because they were afraid of the reaction of the common people. Matthew 21:45-46 says, "And when the chief priests and the Pharisees heard His parables, they understood that He was speaking about them. And when they sought to seize Him, they feared the multitudes, because they held Him to be a prophet."

In the parable about the unrighteous steward that Jesus had told and His subsequent remarks the Pharisees could recognize themselves because they were comparatively wealthy and also demonstrably religious. They were trying to serve two masters, God and money, and not doing a very good job of serving God. It's possible that some of them thought that because Jesus had no earthly wealth; He was envious and because of that He had said the things He said about money. It is more probable that because most of them recognized themselves in the characters in the parable, they were trying to draw attention away from their own faults by making fun of Jesus.

The priests and Pharisees had perverted the Law in a variety of ways, including subverting it to their traditions, but Jesus said that in spite of their efforts the Law would remain until it was completely fulfilled.

124 The Rich Man and Lazarus (Luke 16:19-31)

(1) "Now there was a certain rich man and he habitually dressed in purple and fine linen, gaily living in splendor every day, (2) and a certain poor man named Lazarus who was covered with sores was laid at his gate. (3) Lazarus was longing to be fed with the crumbs which fell from the rich man's table and even the dogs came and licked his sores.

(4) "Now it happened that the poor man died and was carried away by the angels to Abraham's bosom and the rich man also died and was buried.

(5) "In Hades the rich man lifted up his eyes, being in torment, and saw Abraham far away with Lazarus in his bosom. (6) He cried out and said, 'Father Abraham, have mercy on me and send Lazarus to dip the tip of his finger in water and cool off my tongue for I am in agony in this flame.'

(7) "Abraham said, 'Child, remember that during your life you received your good things and Lazarus received bad things so now he is being comforted here and you are in agony. (8) Besides all this, between us and you there is a great chasm fixed so that those who wish to come over from here to you are not able, and that none may cross over from there to us.'

(9) "The rich man said, 'Then I beg you, Father, that you send him to my father's house, (10) to my five brothers, that he may warn them lest they also come to this place of torment.'

(11) "But Abraham said, 'They have Moses and the Prophets. Let your brothers hear them.'

(12) "But he said, 'No, Father Abraham, but if someone goes to them from the dead they will repent.'

(13) "Abraham said to him, 'If they do not listen to Moses and the Prophets neither will they be persuaded if someone rises from the dead.'"

Notes: It may be observed that the story of the unjust steward dealt with the proper (or improper) use of money and the story of Lazarus and the rich man dealt with the consequences of improper use of money.

Some biblical scholars, writers, and commentators have assigned to the rich man the name of "Dives" simply for the sake of convenience. That was not his name, however, but a word which means "rich man" or "wealthy."

The rich man was very wealthy. That is known because the scripture says that he wore purple and fine linen. Along the coast of the Mediterranean Sea, in the vicinity of Tyre, there lives a very rare shellfish from which with great expense, a purple dye is obtained. Cloth colored by this dye was worn by kings and nobles or people of great wealth. In the book of Acts, there is recorded the account of a woman named Lydia who was a seller of purple. Also, in chapters 17 and 18 of Revelation, we can read about people arrayed in purple and fine linen as a sign of their wealth.

The "fine linen" was probably made from flax grown along the Nile River in Egypt. Such linen would have been very white, and it was said to have been worth twice its weight in gold.

To further illustrate the great wealth of the rich man, the scripture states that he fared sumptuously every day.

The beggar in this story was named Lazarus. That was also the name of the brother of Mary and Martha, the man whose life Jesus restored after he had been dead for several days. This man (and Abraham, of course) is the only character in any of the stories or parables of Jesus to have a name. Because this character had a name, some biblical writers believe this story is the telling of something which actually did happen. Other writers disagree, believing it to be a parable only and that the descriptions of the places of eternal abode were made to fit the beliefs of the Jews of that time in that the souls that were lost went to one place and the souls of the saved to another place and that there was a deep impassable gorge between the two places. It may have been that Jesus chose that name because He had already raised up Lazarus from the dead and certainly some of the people there knew about it. It can't matter a great deal whether this is a true story or a parable-the lesson learned from it would be the same either way.

The scripture doesn't say what either the rich man or Lazarus did to deserve going to the destination to which he was consigned. In Matthew 19:23-24, it is recorded that Jesus said, "Truly I say to you, it is hard for a rich man to enter the kingdom of heaven. Again I say to you, it is easier for a camel to go through the eye of a needle, than for a rich man to enter the kingdom of God."

Abraham is reported to have said that if people wouldn't obey Moses and the Prophets, they wouldn't believe even if someone should rise from the dead. At least some of the people knew this to be true, because they knew that Jesus had raised up Lazarus, the poor man's namesake, and that he still lived in Bethany. Too, perhaps some of them knew about Jairus's daughter. In John 12:10-11, it says, "But the chief priests took counsel that they might put Lazarus to death also; because on account of him many of the Jews were going away, and were believing in Jesus."

We know, too, that even after Jesus Himself arose from the dead and after that fact was known to the people, many of them refused to become His followers because it would have meant that they would have had to change their way of life or that they'd be expelled from the synagogue. They chose to have their reward on earth rather than to receive a greater reward in heaven. Isn't that true of people today? Some of them are ashamed to confess that they believe in a supreme being. Some of them confess to believing in God but are too concerned with their lives to be bothered with religion. And many of them don't believe there's such a thing as a God of heaven.

125 Jesus Teaches His Disciples (Luke 17:5-10)

(1) The apostles said to the Lord, "Increase our faith!"

(2) The Lord said, "If you had faith like a mustard seed you would say to this mulberry tree, 'Be uprooted and be planted in the sea,' and it would obey you. (3) Which of you having a slave plowing or tending sheep will say to him when he has come in from the field, 'Come immediately and sit down to eat'? (4) Will he not rather say to the slave, 'Prepare something for me to eat and properly clothe yourself and serve me until I have eaten and drunk and afterwards you will eat and drink'?

(5) "He does not thank the slave because he did the things which were commanded, does he? (6) So you too, when you do all the things which are commanded you, say, 'We are unworthy slaves. We have done only that which we ought to have done.'"

Notes: It appears from this passage that the teachings of Jesus had convinced the apostles that they did not have enough faith to do the things Jesus taught them to do. Perhaps they felt that they didn't love as they should or that they couldn't forgive others for offenses as they should, or that they didn't have the faith to perform cures as they wanted to.

Jesus told the apostles that the most faithful and most diligent of people could do no more than it was their duty to do and that, therefore, we can not earn nor merit salvation. Salvation is by grace and grace is a gift from God for all the people who are faithful and who obey His commandments and do His will.

126 Parable on Prayer or the Importunate Widow

(Luke 18:1-8)

(1) Jesus told the disciples a parable to show that they ought to pray at all times and not to lose heart. (2) He said, "In a certain city there was a judge who did not fear God and did not respect man. (3) There was also a widow in that city and she kept coming to the judge saying, 'Give me legal protection from my opponent.'

(4) "For a while the judge was unwilling, but afterwards he said to himself, 'Even though I do not fear God nor respect man (5) yet because

this widow bothers me I will give her legal protection lest by continually coming she wear me out.'"

(6) The Lord said, "Hear what the unrighteous judge said.

(7) Now shall not God bring about justice for His elect who cry to Him day and night, and will He delay long over them?

(8) "I tell you that He will bring about justice for them speedily. However, when the Son of Man comes will He find faith on the earth?"

Notes: The stated purpose of this parable was to urge the followers of Jesus to always maintain a prayerful attitude and to continue to pray for the things we need or want even when previous prayers have long gone unfulfilled. We are not to become tired of praying because our prayers haven't been answered to our satisfaction or to quit praying.

In this parable, God is represented by the judge, saved people by the widow, and the petitions of God's people by the cries of the widow. This parable is similar to the parable about the man who went to borrow bread from a friend when unexpected guests came. Jesus is not urging people to continue to pray for their wants and desires above their needs but that we should continue to pray for things like our health or the health and welfare of friends or family members.

Perhaps, one reason God doesn't answer some of our prayers to our satisfaction is that to do so would be harmful or contrary to our real needs or to the needs of others. How could He answer the prayers of two sports teams when members of both are praying for victory? How could He answer the prayers of millions of people who are all praying to win the same lottery? And perhaps, somewhere there is a sinner to whom God is giving one more opportunity to become a Christian when answering someone else's prayer might prevent it.

Some people may think that Paul stopped praying too soon for the removal of his "thorn in the flesh," but in 2 Corinthians 12:7-9 Paul reported that his prayer was answered by God when God said to him, "My grace is sufficient for you, for power is perfected in weakness." Perhaps, it's unfortunate that we don't receive a spoken answer from God to each of our prayers, for then we could continue to pray for some things and stop praying for others. Some people may think that God answers every prayer with a "yes" or a "no" or that He doesn't answer them at all, but He could be saying, "Wait just a little while longer."

127 Parable on Prayer: The Pharisee and the Publican

(Luke 18:9-14)

(1) Jesus also told this parable to certain people who trusted in themselves, that they were righteous, and viewed others with contempt. (2) "Two men went up into the temple to pray. One of them was a Pharisee and the other was a tax-gatherer. (3) The Pharisee stood and prayed to himself thusly, 'God, I thank You that I am not like other people: swindlers, unjust, adulterers, or even like this tax-gatherer. (4) I fast twice a week and I pay tithes of all that I get.'

(5) "But the tax-gatherer, standing some distance away, was even unwilling to lift up his eyes to heaven but was beating his breast saying, 'God, be merciful to me the sinner!'

(6) "I tell you, the tax-gatherer went down to his house justified rather than the Pharisee, for everyone who exalts himself shall be humbled but he who humbles himself shall be exalted."

Notes: This parable was told specifically for the benefit of those people who could never bring themselves to admit that they may have been wrong about anything and were contemptuous of people whom they observed sinning. In Proverbs 30:12-13, that subject is addressed like this, "There is a king who is pure in his own eyes, yet is not washed from the filthiness. There is a king-oh how lofty are his eyes! And his eyelids are raised in arrogance."

In 2 Corinthians 13:1-3, Paul addressed that subject in these words, "If I speak with the tongues of men and of angels, but do not have love, I have become a noisy gong or a clanging cymbal. And if I have the gift of prophecy, and know all mysteries and all knowledge; and I have all faith, so as to remove mountains, but do not have love, I am nothing. And if I give all my possessions to feed the poor, and if I deliver my body to be burned, but do not have love, it profits me nothing." The Pharisee in this parable was apparently a man of outstanding character, because it isn't recorded that he lied about himself. But he was boastful and filled with pride, and he looked down on others because he thought they weren't as good as he was. He didn't confess his sins (he probably thought he didn't have any sins to confess), but he did confess all his virtues. He stood up as he prayed so that other people could see that he prayed. The scripture says that he prayed to himself, so he firmly believed that what he said in his prayer was true.

But the tax gatherer confessed that he was a sinner and he showed great remorse. He was so ashamed of his sins that he stood in a remote part of the temple (we can assume that it was a remote part of the temple because he was far away from the Pharisee and the Pharisee would have been in the most prominent part of the temple) and considered himself to be so unworthy that he wouldn't even look toward heaven. He offered no justification for what he had done and he made no excuses. As in the parable of the prodigal son, it seems that an unrighteous person who is penitent is more acceptable to God than a man who considers himself to be righteous but will not confess his sins. The apostle John wrote in 1 John 1:8-9, "If we say that we have no sin, we are deceiving ourselves, and the truth is not in us. If we confess our sins, He is faithful and righteous to forgive us our sins and to cleanse us from all unrighteousness."

The Pharisee exalted himself and the tax gatherer humbled himself but, according to Jesus, the Pharisee would be humbled and the tax gatherer would be exalted at some later time.

128 Jesus Answers the Pharisees about Divorce

(Matt. 19:1-12; Mark 10:1-12)

(1) When Jesus had finished these words He rose up and departed from Galilee and went into the region of Judea beyond the Jordan. (2) Great crowds gathered around Him again and He healed them there, and, according to His custom, He once more began to teach them.

(3) Some Pharisees came up to Jesus to test Him and asked, "Is it lawful for a man to divorce his wife for any cause at all?"

(4) Jesus answered, "Have you not read that from the beginning of creation God made them male and female (5) and said, 'For this reason a man shall leave his father and mother and shall cleave to his wife and the two shall become one flesh'? (6) Consequently they are no longer two people but one. Then what God has joined together let no man separate.

(7) "But what did Moses command you?"

(8) They answered, "Moses permitted a man to write a certificate of divorce and send his wife away. Why did he do this then?"

(9) Jesus answered, "Because of your hardness of heart Moses permitted you to divorce your wives but in the beginning it was not this way.

(10) "I say to you, whoever divorces his wife except for immorality and marries another woman commits adultery against her, and if the woman divorces her husband and married another man she is committing adultery."

(11) In the house the disciples began questioning Jesus about this matter again and they said to Him, "If the relationship of the man and his wife is like this it is better not to marry."

(12) Jesus said, "Not all men can accept this statement but only those to whom it has been given. (13) There are eunuchs who were born that way from the womb of their mother, and there are eunuchs who were made eunuchs by men, and there are also eunuchs who made themselves eunuchs for the sake of the kingdom of heaven. He who is able to accept this, let him accept it."

Notes: After the last trip of Jesus to Galilee before His crucifixion, He returned to Judea by way of Perea which was a province to the east of the Jordan River. As usual in those days, a crowd followed Jesus, some to hear His teachings and others to be healed by Him.

While they all were on the way, some Pharisees came to Jesus and asked Him about divorce, whether or not it was right or legal for a man to divorce his wife for whatever reason he wanted to. This was another of the Pharisees' attempts to entrap Jesus. Perhaps they wanted to see if He would say something different from what He had said in His Sermon on the Mount. He had said in Matthew 5:31-32, "And it was said, 'Whoever sends his wife away, let him give her a certificate of divorce'; but I say to you that everyone who divorces his wife, except for the cause of unchastity, makes her commit adultery; and whoever marries a divorced woman commits adultery." The Law concerning divorce was recorded in Deuteronomy 14:1-3. If Jesus confirmed what He had said on the mountain, it would appear that He was disputing the authority of the Law of Moses, but if He agreed with the Law it would mean that He was being inconsistent. The Pharisees thought they had Jesus backed into a comer either way He answered and that at last they had penetrated His armor, so to speak.

In the modem world, there are a lot of different views about divorce and remarriage. People who aren't religious give no thought to whether it's right or wrong and go about marrying and divorcing, observing only the civil laws in doing so. Many people, who do consider themselves religious, ignore all biblical teaching on the subject and do just the same as those people who have no religion. The Catholic Church has rules of it's own concerning marriage and divorce, and those rules don't agree with what Jesus said. For instance, a Catholic who marries a non-Catholic can get the marriage annulled and, to them, it was like there had been no marriage at all. That action does not, however, affect the civil union which must be dissolved by a civil divorce. They seem to forget, though, that if there was no marriage, there was the sin of fornication. Even in some so-called fundamentalist churches, there is a lot of liberality about the sin involved, and it is too often ignored. Also, some people go to the other extreme, making their own rules concerning remarriage based on their own assumptions and their own interpretation of this scripture. It would be difficult to know for sure all the rights and wrongs of marriage, divorce, and remarriage but we do know it is a sin, and that it is sin because Jesus said so.

129 Jesus Blesses the Children

(Matt. 19:13-15; Mark 10:13-16; Luke 18:15-17)

(1) People were bringing children, and even their babies, to Jesus so that He might lay His hands on them and pray, but when the disciples saw what was happening they rebuked those people.

(2) When Jesus saw this He was indignant and said to the disciples, "Permit the children to come to Me and do not hinder them for the kingdom of God belongs to such as these. (3) Truly I say to you, whoever does not receive the kingdom of God like a child shall not enter in at all."

(4) Jesus took the children into His arms and began blessing them and laying His hands on them. Afterwards He departed from there.

Notes: It isn't heard much anymore, but there used to be a lot of joking about politicians kissing babies in order to influence the parents to vote for them. Why those parents wanted their children kissed by politicians is a mystery, but in this passage, the parents wanted their children blessed by this great man. Some of them probably believed that Jesus was the Messiah, but others undoubtedly did not. Whether or not they believed Jesus was the Messiah or only a prophet, it would have been their desire to have their children blessed by Him.

When the disciples objected that the people were bothering Jesus with the children, Jesus told them that the kingdom of heaven was made up of such people as were like children. Some people try to use this passage to prove that babies can be members of the church. But there's nothing to show that's true. Jesus only blessed them. What Jesus *did* say was not that babies made up the kingdom of heaven but that people who did make up the kingdom of heaven must be childlike in their faith. They must accept the truth of the Gospel with the same kind of faith that a child accepts what its parents tell it. And like children learn as they grow, Christians must learn as they grow in spirituality and in faith.

130 The Rich Young Ruler

(Matt. 19:16-26; Mark 10:17-27; Luke 18:18-27)

(1) As Jesus was setting out on a journey a certain ruler ran up to Him and knelt before Him and asked Him, "Good Teacher, what shall I do to inherit eternal life?"

(2) Jesus said to him, "Why do you call Me good? No one is good except God alone. But if you wish to enter into life keep the commandments."

(3) The young man asked Jesus, "Which ones?"

Jesus answered, "You shall not commit murder; you shall not commit adultery; you shall not steal; you shall not bear false witness; (4) honor your father and mother; and you shall love your neighbor as yourself."

(5) The young man said to Jesus, "Teacher, I have kept all these things from my youth up. What am I still lacking?"

(6) Looking at the young man Jesus felt a love for him and said to him, "One thing you still lack. Go and sell all that you possess and distribute it to the poor and you shall have treasure in heaven. Then come follow me."

(7) When the young man heard this statement his face fell and he went away grieved for he was one who owned much property and was extremely rich.

(8) Jesus looked around at His disciples and said to them, "How hard it will be for those who are wealthy to enter the kingdom of God!"

(9) The disciples were amazed at these words of Jesus. Again Jesus said to them, "Children, how hard it is to enter the kingdom of God! (10) It is easier for a camel to go through the eye of a needle than for a rich man to enter the kingdom of God."

(11) The disciples were even more astonished and asked Jesus, "Then who can be saved?"

(12) Looking upon them Jesus said to them, "With men it is impossible but not with God, for all things are possible with God."

Notes: The story of this rich young ruler who came to Jesus seeking eternal life is a very familiar one. The young man knew that he had kept the Law all his life but he knew, too, that there was still something he lacked.

Perhaps, this young man had made the mistake of believing that he could do enough good works to earn his way into heaven, but he feared that he had not done quite enough. A prominent religious organization made that same mistake when they came up with what they call the doctrine of supererogation. That is a belief that a person can earn extra credit in heaven by doing more good works than are required of a Christian. We know this doctrine is not taught in the scriptures and is, therefore, erroneous and that there is no way a person can merit or earn salvation.

The instructions Jesus gave to this young man were not meant to be applied as a general rule by which Christians are to live but was a specific answer to the specific question of this one man. It would, however, apply to anyone else who had the same problem that the young man had. This man had great wealth, but it wasn't his wealth that would keep him out of heaven. It was his love for his wealth which put the wealth ahead of his desire for salvation. Jesus didn't mean that every person who had wealth had to get rid of it. What he did mean was that every person must get rid of anything and everything that stands between him and salvation. A very poor person could put a desire for wealth ahead of his spiritual well-being and be just as lost as a wealthy person. None of the twelve apostles was wealthy (with the possible exception of Matthew), but what they did have they gave it all up to follow Jesus-and all to them was as much as all to this young ruler.

This is a further illustration and confirmation of the truth of the statement which Jesus had previously made about people who are wealthy, that is, that a person cannot serve two masters, particularly if one of those masters is money.

131 The Disciples' Reward

(Matt. 19:27-30; Mark 10:28-31; Luke 18:28-30)

(1) Then Peter said to Jesus, "Look, we have left everything and followed You. What then will there be for us?"

(2) Jesus said to the disciples, "Truly I say to you that you who have followed Me, in the regeneration when the Son of Man will sit on His glorious throne, you also shall sit upon twelve thrones judging the twelve tribes of Israel. (3) Everyone who has left houses or brothers or sisters or father or mother or children or farms for My name's sake and for the sake of the gospel and the kingdom of God (4) shall receive a hundred times as much now in the present age, houses and brothers and

sisters and mothers and children and farms, along with persecutions; and in the age to come, eternal life. (5) But many who are first will be last and the last first."

Notes: After Jesus had told the rich young ruler, he must sell all his possessions and give everything to the poor, the young man refused to do that. Then Peter said, in effect, "We, the apostles *have* left everything we owned and followed You. If that young man would have inherited eternal life by doing the same, what will we get for doing it?"

The term "twelve tribes of Israel" as used here and in Luke 22:30, may or may not have meant only the literal twelve tribes of Israel, or it could have meant all the saved in all generations. Whatever the meaning Jesus put upon that phrase it is evident that He meant that the apostles would be accorded great honor, but probably not nearly as great in earthly life as in the heavenly hereafter.

There will be a slight digression from the main subject here to offer an explanation of an apparent anomaly in the scriptures. The eleven men who were left as apostles after Judas Iscariot hanged himself were later referred to as the "twelve" in some places. In Acts 6:2, it reads, "And the twelve summoned the congregation of the disciples and said, 'It is not desirable for us to neglect the Word of God in order to serve tables.'" You will remember, though, that the eleven remaining apostles had voted to add Matthias to their number. Matthias is almost universally accepted as being the replacement for Judas, and he may very well have been worthy of that honor, but if you will study the passage in which Matthias was chosen, you will find that he does not fulfill all the requirements for being an apostle-he was not chosen by Jesus. In 1 Corinthians 14:3- 5 Paul wrote, "For I delivered to you as of first importance what I also received, that Christ died for our sins according to the Scriptures, and that He was buried, and that He was raised on the third day according to the Scriptures, and that He appeared to Cephas, and then to the twelve." At the time of which Paul wrote, there were only the eleven-Judas was already dead, and Matthias had not been added to their number, yet he used the term "the twelve" to refer to the remaining apostles. On the other hand, Paul did fulfill all the requirements for being an apostle and, it is my contention, that he was the twelfth apostle, the person replacing Judas.

Now back to the original subject!

A hundred times, the number of fathers or mothers or sisters or brothers which the Christians had left behind in order to follow Jesus most likely referred to the spiritual relatives who would be in their spiritual family. Christians consider all other Christians to be their brothers and sisters-our spiritual family. About the houses or the farms we leave to follow Jesus-that is unclear. We would never have a need for a hundred houses or a hundred farms. But the persecutions! Many of the early Christians did have that experience. Down through the ages, beginning shortly after the establishment of the church, other Christians have been persecuted in many places and in many ways. Even today, there are places on earth where Christians may be persecuted because of their religion.

Concerning the last verse above, one biblical writer has suggested that the meaning of that phrase is that it is a warning against pride in sacrificial accomplishments; the pride such as Peter had shown when he asked Jesus what they, the apostles, would get.

132 The Parable of Laborers in the Vineyard

(Matt. 20:1-16)

(1) "The kingdom of heaven is like a landowner who went out early in the morning to hire laborers for his vineyard. (2) When he had agreed with the laborers for a denarius for the day he sent them into his vineyard.

(3) "He went out again about the third hour and saw others standing idle in the market place. (4) To those he said, 'You too go into the vineyards and what is right I will give you.' So they went.

(5) "Again he went out about the sixth and the ninth hour and he did the same thing. (6) About the eleventh hour he went out and found others standing and he said to them, 'Why have you been standing here idle all day long?' (7) They said to him, 'Because no one hired us.' He said to them, 'You too go into the vineyard.'

(8) "When evening had come the owner of the vineyard said to his foreman, 'Call the laborers and pay them their wages beginning with the last group to the first.' (9) When those hired about the eleventh hour came each one received a denarius.

(10) And when those hired first came they thought that they would receive more, but each one of them also received a denarius.

(11) "When they received it they grumbled at the landowner, (12) saying, 'These last men have worked only one hour and you have made them equal to us who have borne the burden and the scorching heat of the day.'

(13) But the landowner answered and said to one of them, 'Friend, I am doing you no wrong. Did you not agree with me for a denarius? (14) Take what is yours and go your way but I wish to give to this last man the same as to you. (15) Is it not lawful for me to do what I wish with what is my own? Or is your eye envious because I am generous?'

(16) "Thus the last shall be first and the first last."

Notes: At that time, in that society, each day was divided into twelve hours beginning at the average hour of sunrise and ending with the average hour of sunset. The beginning time would be roughly equal to six o'clock in the morning our time and the ending time would be about six o'clock in the evening. The first hour of the day would have been from six to seven, the second from seven to eight, and so on. The eleventh hour would have begun at about five o'clock.

This parable is meant to teach that everyone who enters the kingdom of heaven receives the same reward as everyone else. To some of the people who spend their entire adult lives as members of the church, it may seem that they've been cheated when people who become members only in their twilight years receive the same reward as they receive. But anyone who felt that way would not have a true Christlike attitude. Every Christian should be joyful over the saving of another soul because of his love for Christ and his love for the souls of others.

Some of the Jews who accepted Jesus as the Messiah and became Christians resented the fact that Gentiles were allowed into the church, believing that because they were God's chosen people, they should have been the only ones to have been allowed into His kingdom. Acts 11:1-3 says, "Now the apostles and the brethren who were throughout Judea heard that the Gentiles also had received the Word of God. And when Peter came up to Jerusalem, those who were circumcised took issue with him, saying, 'You entered the house of uncircumcised men and ate with them.'"

Some years ago, a well-known preacher during the airing of his regular Sunday sermon stated that of course there would be different degrees of reward in heaven. He didn't say why he believed that, but this parable clearly teaches that everyone who enters the kingdom of God will receive the same reward as everyone else there. How can perfection be improved upon?

This is the second time we've encountered that cryptic phrase, "The last shall be first and the first last." What it means is that those who enter the kingdom of God last shall have the same reward as those who have entered His kingdom first-" the last shall be the same as the first and the first shall be the same as the last." Everyone who would become a Christian is told what he may expect to receive when the gates of heaven are opened to him. And every one of them is told that same thing-what God has promised in His scriptures to give to the faithful. Only in the length of their time to enjoy, the benefits of Christianity on earth do those who enter the kingdom early in life receive more than those who enter it late in life.

133 Jesus Foretells His Death and Resurrection

(Matt. 20:17-19; Mark 10:32-34; Luke 18:31-34)

(1) Jesus and the disciples were on the road going up to Jerusalem and Jesus was walking ahead of the disciples. The disciples were amazed and those who followed were fearful. On the way Jesus took the twelve disciples aside by themselves and began to tell them what was going to happen to Him.

(2) Jesus said, "Look, we are going up to Jerusalem and all things which are written through the prophets about the Son of Man will be accomplished. (3) He will be delivered to the chief priests and the scribes and they will condemn Him to death and will deliver Him to the

Gentiles. (4) And the Gentiles will mock Him and spit upon Him and scourge Him and crucify Him and on the third day He will rise again."

Notes: It may be remembered that the last time Jesus was in Judea, the priests plotted to have Him killed. What amazed the disciples was that Jesus was ignoring that threat, and they were fearful for their own lives because they were His followers. Then Jesus took the twelve disciples aside so that they were by themselves, and He told them plainly what was going to happen to Him in Jerusalem. Back in Matthew 16:21, it says, "From that time Jesus began to show His disciples that He must go to Jerusalem, and suffer many things from the elders and chief priests and scribes, and be killed, and be raised up on the third day."

Many things about the birth, life, and death of the Messiah had been foretold by God's prophets. Most of the Jews, especially the elders, chief priests and scribes, would have been familiar with the Messianic prophecies. Most of them refused to believe the correct interpretation of what the prophets said, preferring instead to put their own interpretation on those prophecies. Things haven't changed so much in the past two thousand years because people still prefer to put their own interpretation on the Bible commandments than to accept the plain truth of what they say.

And perhaps the twelve disciples, too, believed with the majority of the Jews the popular interpretation of what the Messiah would be and do when He came. Remember that even on the day Jesus ascended back to heaven, they asked, "Is it at this time You are restoring the kingdom to Israel?"

134 Salome Asks Preference for Her Sons

(Matt. 20:20-28; Mark 10:35-45)

(1) Then James and John, the two sons of Zebedee, together with their mother came up to Jesus bowing down and making a request of Him. (2) They said to Jesus, "Teacher, we want You to do for us whatever we ask of You."

(3) Jesus said to them, "What do you want Me to do for you?"

(4) The mother of James and John said, "Command that in Your kingdom these two sons of mine may sit one on Your right and one on Your left."

(5) James and John said, "Grant that we may sit in Your glory one on Your right and one on Your left."

(6) But Jesus said to them, "You do not know what you are asking for. Are you able to drink the cup I am about to drink or to be baptized with the baptism with which I am baptized?"

They said to Him, "We are able."

(7) Jesus said to them, "The cup that I drink you shall drink and you shall be baptized with the baptism with which I am baptized, but to sit on My right or on My left, this is not Mine to give but it is for those for whom it has been prepared by My Father."

(8) When the other ten disciples heard this they became indignant with James and John.

(9) Jesus called the disciples to Himself and said to them, "You know that those who are recognized as rulers of the Gentiles lord it over them and their great men exercise authority over them. (10) It is not so among you. Whoever wishes to become great among you shall be your servant (11) and whoever wishes to be first among you shall be servant of all. (12) For even the Son of Man did not come to be served but to serve and to give His life a ransom for many."

Notes: Some biblical scholars believe that the mother of James and John, the sons of Zebedee, was named Salome, and it is by that name she is identified by some writers. That name appears in only two places in the scriptures, Mark 15:40 and Mark 16:1. In neither place is Salome identified as the mother of James and John. The only other person we know of who was named Salome was the daughter of Herodias, who requested the head of John the Baptist. Josephus recorded that Herodias had a daughter named Salome who was the stepdaughter of Herod who had John killed.

Matthew wrote that it was the mother of James and John who asked Jesus for the places of honor in His kingdom, but Mark wrote that it was James and John themselves who asked. Since Matthew was a witness to this affair and Mark only wrote what he was told, it may be best to accept Matthew's account as the more accurate.

Like many mothers, Salome had ambitions for the betterment of her children, but she, like her sons, probably had an inaccurate picture of what the kingdom of Jesus would be.

In earthly kingdoms, to be seated next to the ruler was a great honor, and these men were requesting those places of honor in advance of any requests that might be made by their fellow apostles. And like children, they probably thought that the first to ask would be the ones who received the honor.

James and John said that they were able to suffer what Jesus was about to suffer, but they had no idea about what was to come. James, as we know, was slain by Herod not long after the kingdom was established, and John, although he had a long life, was exiled on the Isle of Patmos for years because of his religious beliefs and activity.

The word here translated "servant" in the NASV and "minister" in the *KN* are both from the Greek word *diakonos* and is translated in other places in the scriptures as "deacon." And the word translated "slave" in the NASV and "servant" in the KJV is from the same Greek word *diakonos* and is also translated "deacon" in other places. *Diakonos* is the noun form and *diakoneo* is the verb form. These words are translated as either "minister," "servant" or "deacon." The original meaning was a servant or waiter who served others and performed menial tasks. The word translated "ransom" meant "a redemption price," "atonement" or "ransom."

135 Bartimaeus and His Friend Receive Sight

(Matt. 20:29-34; Mark 10:46-52; Luke 18:35-43)

(1) Jesus came to Jericho, and as He was going out from Jericho with His disciples and a great multitude, two blind beggars, one of whom was Bartimaeus the son of Timaeus were sitting by the road begging. (2) Hearing a multitude going by Bartimaeus inquired what this might be and he was told that Jesus was passing by.

(3) When Bartimaeus heard that it was Jesus the Nazarene he began to cry out and say, "Jesus, Son of David, have mercy on us!"

(4) Many of those who led the way sternly told him to be quiet but he kept crying out all the more, "Lord, have mercy on us, Son of David!"

(5) Jesus stopped and said, "Call them here."

And they called the blind men, saying to them, "Take courage and arise. He is calling for you."

(6) Casting aside his cloak Bartimaeus jumped up and he and his friend came to Jesus.

(7) Jesus questioned them, asking, "What do you want Me to do for you?"

(8) Bartimaeus said to Jesus, "Lord, we want to regain our sight."

(9) Moved by compassion Jesus touched their eyes and said, "Receive your sight. Your faith has made you well."

(10) Immediately they regained their sight and began following Jesus on the road, glorifying God. And when all the people saw it they gave praise to God.

Notes: Matthew alone records that there were two blind men, while Mark and Luke say there was one. And only Mark records the name of this one blind man. It may be that the man Bartimaeus was the only one who spoke, and for that reason, Mark and Luke didn't mention the other man. Or perhaps their sources of information failed to inform them of the second blind man.

The prefix "bar" before a name means "son of." As "Simon Barjonah" meant "Simon Son of Jonah," "Bartimaeus" meant "Son of Timaeus."

Jericho was located about five miles west of the Jordan River near the northern end of the Dead Sea, and about fourteen or fifteen miles from Jerusalem. Jericho was the first city taken by Joshua when the Israelites came back to the Promised Land. The fall of the city is recorded in the sixth chapter of the book of Joshua. After the city was destroyed, Joshua placed a curse on the man who would rebuild the city. Joshua 6:26 reads, "Then Joshua made them take an oath at that time, saying, 'Cursed before the Lord is the man who rises up and builds this city Jericho; with the loss of his first-born he shall lay its foundation, and with the loss of his youngest son he shall set up its gates.'" That curse was fulfilled in the days of King Ahab, nearly five hundred years later. 1 Kings 16:34 says, "In his days Hiel the Bethelite built Jericho; he laid its foundation with the loss of Ahiram his first-born, and set up its gates with the loss of his youngest son Segub, according to the word of the Lord, which He spoke by Joshua the son of Nun."

Albert Barnes reports in his commentary that Herod the Great died in Jericho of a "wretched and most foul disease." Flavius Josephus, when reporting the death of Herod, didn't say where he died, but that he lived to an old age and was in great pain when he died.

136 Zacchaeus Entertains Jesus (Luke 19:1-10)

(1) Jesus entered and was passing through Jericho. (2) In Jericho there was a man called by the name of Zacchaeus. Zacchaeus was a chief tax-gatherer and was rich. (3) He was trying to see who Jesus was and he was unable to do so because of the crowd for he was small in stature. (4) So he ran on ahead and climbed up into a sycamore tree in order to see Jesus who was about to pass through that way.

(5) When Jesus came to that place He looked up to Zacchaeus and said to him, "Zacchaeus, hurry and come down for today I must stay at your house."

(6) Zacchaeus hurried and came down and received Jesus gladly.

(7) But when the crowd saw this they all began to grumble, saying, "He has gone to be the guest of a man who is a sinner."

(8) Zacchaeus stopped and said to the Lord, "Look, Lord, half of my possessions I will give to the poor and if I have defrauded anyone of anything, I will give back four times as much."

(9) Jesus said to him, "Today salvation has come to this house because he, too, is a son of Abraham. (10) For the Son of Man has come to seek and to save that which was lost."

Notes: Most of the people of Jericho probably had heard about Jesus and word of His passing through the town had preceded His arrival there. Jesus, with a multitude of people following along with Him, was on His way to Jerusalem to observe the Passover. This was only a few days before the crucifixion.

Anyone traveling from the province of Perea to Jerusalem in the province of Judea would have passed through Jericho as that was the first town they would have come to in Judea.

Traders would have been required to pay import duty on their goods as they entered Judea, and it was probably the gathering of those taxes which had made Zacchaeus so rich. Zacchaeus was a *chief* tax gatherer. Whether that meant he had other tax collectors under him or that the particular location in which he served or the amount of taxes he collected was the reason he was called a chief tax gatherer, we don't know.

Curiosity is an odd thing. It makes reasonably sane people do things that they wouldn't do for any other reason. If the president of the United States or some famous movie actor was passing through town, a lot of people would go to almost any lengths just to see that person. That's what Zacchaeus did. Isn't it strange-and wonderful-that God can use a person's curiosity to save his soul!

Being short in stature, Zacchaeus climbed up a sycamore tree so he would be up high enough to see over the people who would otherwise be blocking his view of Jesus. Most of you may be familiar with sycamore trees and what they look like. The sycamore trees about which we know grow to be quite large. They have large multipointed leaves and smooth bark which is shed in patches so that it appears to be green with white patches in it. The sycamore tree which Zacchaeus climbed was not that kind of tree. That tree was a member of the fig family and grows only in very warm climates.

Going to the home of Zacchaeus to eat with him was the only incident of which we know that Jesus invited Himself to be someone's guest. But in the same way that Jesus knew Zacchaeus's name, He knew that He would be welcome there.

As we have already learned, a tax collector set his own rates for collecting. He could collect as much as the traffic would bear and keep the difference between what he collected and what he was required to turn over to the Romans. Zacchaeus was rich, so he had collected quite a bit of money over what he was required to pay.

Zacchaeus was so pleased with the honor of having Jesus as his guest and of gaining eternal salvation through that association that he pledged to give half of his wealth to the poor and to restore fourfold any money he had wrongfully taken. That means that Zacchaeus could not have accumulated more than one eighth of his wealth by unjust means or else he could not have fulfilled his pledge to Jesus. Jesus did not require Zacchaeus to make that pledge or to restore what he had wrongfully taken. To become Christians, people are not required to undo the sins they've committed. They aren't required to return what they've stolen, be it money or a life or a person's good name or even a pencil taken from one's employer. When they've gone through all the steps to salvation and been baptized, all their sins are forgiven and they are as clean as if they've never sinned. That doesn't mean, of course, that they should not compensate for what they've done, whether it's to restore what was taken or to serve time in prison under civil laws for crimes committed.

In a previous section, we learned that Jesus said it was harder for a rich man to enter the kingdom of heaven than for a camel to pass through the eye of a needle. Yet Jesus said that day salvation had come to the house of this rich man-this Zacchaeus.

Zacchaeus was a Jew, as was Matthew, and, like Matthew, Zacchaeus was a Jewish name. Jesus said in Matthew 15:24, "I was sent only to the lost sheep of the house of Israel," and Jesus said that Zacchaeus was a "son of Abraham." Also when Jesus sent out the twelve, He told them to go only to "the lost sheep of the house of Israel." We know, though, that Jesus made exceptions to that restriction, notably the servant of the Roman centurion and the Syrophoenician woman's daughter, although the Roman centurion's servant may have been a Jew even though the centurion wasn't.

137 The Parable about Money Usage (Luke 19:11-27)

(1) While they were listening to these things Jesus went on to tell a certain parable because He was near Jerusalem and His disciples supposed that the kingdom of God was going to appear immediately.

(2) Jesus said, "A certain nobleman went to a distant country to receive a kingdom for himself, after which he would return.

(3) He called ten of his slaves and gave them ten minas and said to them, 'Do business with this until I come back.'

(4) "But his citizens hated him and sent a delegation after him to say, 'We do not want this man to reign over us.'

(5) "When the nobleman returned home after receiving the kingdom he ordered that these slaves to whom he had given the money be called to him so that he might learn what business they had done.

(6) "The first slave came and said, 'Master, your mina has made ten more minas.'

(7) "The master said, 'Well done, good slave. Because you have been faithful in a very little thing be in authority over ten cities.'

(8) "The second came and said, 'Your mina, master, has made five minas.'

(9) "The master said to him also, 'And you are to be over five cities.'

(10) "Another slave came saying, 'Master, behold your mina which I put away in a handkerchief, (11) for I was afraid of you because you are an exacting man-you take up what you did not lay down and reap what you did not sow.'

(12) "The master said to him, 'By your own words I will judge you, you worthless slave. You knew I am an exacting man taking up what I did not lay down and reaping what I did not sow. (13) Then why did you not put the money in the bank and then when I came I would have collected with interest?'

(14) "The master said to the bystanders, 'Take the mina away from him and give it to the one who has ten minas.'

(15) "And they said to him, 'Master, he has ten minas already.'

(16) "'I tell you that to everyone who has shall more be given but from the one who does not have even what he does have shall be taken away.

(17) "'But these enemies of mine who did not want me to reign over them, bring them here and slay them in my presence.'"

Notes: While still in or near Jericho, Jesus told another parable. It says that the reason He told this particular parable was that they were near Jerusalem and the disciples thought that the kingdom of God was going to appear immediately.

This parable, which is similar (if not the same) as the one recorded in Matthew 25:14-30 and known as the parable of the talents, was intended to show that the people must wait some time longer for the kingdom of God to come. The people were expecting Jesus to set up His kingdom when He reached Jerusalem, but through this parable, He was telling them that He was going to a far country to receive a kingdom and that someday He would return. Many of the early Christians thought Jesus would be returning immediately, but of course, they had misunderstood him. Jesus did set up His kingdom on earth on that first day of Pentecost after His ascension, but it was not the kind of kingdom the Jews expected the Messiah to set up or the kind that they would accept.

In the parable, the citizens of the country who hated the new king represent the Jews who rejected Jesus as the Messiah. The people of the new kingdom said they didn't want the nobleman to reign over them, and the Jews later told Pilate that they had no king but Caesar and that Jesus was not the king of the Jews. However, the fact was that because of His ancestry and lineage, Jesus was the heir apparent (or pretender) to the throne of David. The Jews were more than willing to accept Jesus as their king but only if He was to be the kind of king they wanted.

When Jesus does return, He will reward each of His servants who have put into a proper use their money or talents or time or whatever resources they had with which to work. The people who have not used their resources properly, and those who didn't want Jesus as their king, will have no place in His kingdom.

138 Mary Anoints Jesus

(Matt. 26:6-13; Mark 14:3-9; John 12:1-11)

(1) Six days before the Passover Jesus came to Bethany, the town which was the home of Lazarus whom Jesus had raised from the dead. (2) They made a supper there for Jesus at the home of Simon the Leper and Martha was serving, but Lazarus was one of those reclining at the table with Jesus. (3) Meanwhile Mary took a pound of very costly perfume of pure nard and poured it on the head of Jesus and anointed His feet and wiped

His feet with her hair, and the house was filled with the fragrance of the perfume.

(4) But Jesus' disciples became indignant when they saw this and began to scold Mary.

Judas Iscariot, who was intending to betray Jesus, said, (5) "Why this waste? Why was this perfume not sold for the high price of three hundred denarii and the money given to poor people?" (6) Now he said this, not because he was concerned about the poor, but because he was a thief. He had the money box and he used to pilfer what was put in it.

(7) But Jesus, aware of this, said to them, "Let her alone. Why do you bother her? She has done a good deed to Me. (8) The poor you always have with you and whenever you wish you can do them good, but you do not always have Me. She has done what she could. She has kept this for the day of My burial and (9) when she poured the perfume upon My body she has anointed My body beforehand to prepare Me for burial.

(10)   Truly I say to you, wherever the gospel is preached in the whole world what this woman has done shall also be spoken of in memory of her."

(11) A great multitude of the Jews learned that Jesus was there in Bethany and they came, not for Jesus' sake only, but that they might see Lazarus whom Jesus had raised from the dead. (12) The chief priests took counsel so that they might put Lazarus to death also (13) because on account of him many of the Jews were going away and were believing in Jesus.

Notes: The accounts of this incident written by Matthew and Mark are different from the one written by John. If one reads only the account written by John, one could assume that this happened at the home of Lazarus, but it doesn't say just that. What it *does* say is that Bethany was where Lazarus lived. Both Matthew and Mark state that this took place at the home of Simon the Leper. Neither Matthew nor Mark give the woman's name nor do they say that Lazarus was present.

It is quite possible that Simon the Leper and the family of Mary, Martha, and Lazarus were either related or were close friends. This is borne out by the fact that Martha helped with serving the meal and that Lazarus was one of the guests who were reclining at the table.

At that time in His life, Jesus could find very little time to Himself, because there were people constantly crowding around Him either to see a miracle, to be healed, or to listen to Him talk. This time it was even worse, if that's possible, because the people came not only to see Jesus but to see Lazarus, whom they knew Jesus had restored to life after he had died, and it was for this reason that the chief priests wanted to have Lazarus killed too.

There is the remote possibility that this incident was the same as the one which was reported in section 56 from Luke 7:36-50. It's doubtful, though, because none of the conditions or circumstances other than that the woman anointed the feet of Jesus and wiped them with her hair are the same. In that incident, the woman was known to have been a sinner and that doesn't fit the character of Mary as we know it.

Pure nard, or spikenard as it's called in some versions of the scriptures, was a very expensive perfume, the value of a pound of which would be about three to four hundred dollars today. It was imported from Arabia, India, and the Far East. In those days, people used perfume instead of deodorants (which were unknown and consequently unavailable), and this was possibly the most expensive of the perfumes which were available.

139 Jesus Enters Jerusalem

(Matt. 21:1-11; Mark 11:1-11; Luke 19:28-44; John 12:12-19)

(1) The next day Jesus was going on ahead, ascending to Jerusalem. (2) As they approached Jerusalem, at Bethphage and Bethany near the Mount of Olives, Jesus sent out two of His disciples.

(3) He told them, "Go into the village opposite you and immediately you will find a donkey tied there and a colt on which no one yet has ever sat. Untie the colt and bring it here,

(4) and if anyone says to you, 'Why are you doing this?' you say, 'The Lord has need of it,' and immediately he will send it back here."

(5) Now this took place that what was spoken through the prophet might be fulfilled, saying, (6) "Say to the daughter of Zion, 'Fear not. Behold, your King is coming to you, gentle, and mounted on a donkey, even on a colt, the foal of a beast of burden.'"

(7) The two disciples went away and found a colt tied at the door outside in the street and untied it. (8) As they were untying the colt its owner said to them, "Why are you untying the colt?"

(9) The disciples said, "The Lord has need of it," and the owner gave them permission to take it.

(10) They brought the colt to Jesus and threw their garments upon it and then put Jesus on it. (11) Much of the multitude spread their garments in the road and others were cutting branches from palm trees and spreading them in the road.

(12) As Jesus was approaching, near the descent of the Mount of Olives, the whole multitude of the disciples began to praise God joyfully with a loud voice for all the miracles which they had seen.

(13) "Hosanna! Blessed is He who comes in the name of the Lord, even the King of Israel! Blessed is the coming of our father David! Hosanna in the highest!"

(14) When Jesus had entered Jerusalem all the city was stirred, asking, "Who is this?"

(15) The multitudes answered them saying, "This is the prophet Jesus from Nazareth in Galilee."

(16) Then some of the Pharisees in the multitude said to Jesus, "Teacher, rebuke Your disciples."

(17) But Jesus said, "I tell you, if these people become silent even the stones will cry out."

(18) When Jesus approached Jerusalem He had seen the city and wept over it, (19) saying, "If even you had known in this day the things which make for peace! But now they have been hidden from your eyes. (20) For the days shall come upon you when your enemies will throw up a bank before you and surround you and hem you in on every side (21) and will level you to the ground and your children within you, and they will not leave in you one stone upon another because you did not recognize the time of your visitation."

(22) These things Jesus' disciples did not understand at the first but when Jesus was glorified then they remembered that these things were written of Him and that they had done these things to Him.

(23) The multitude that was with Jesus when He called Lazarus out of the tomb and raised him from the dead was bearing Him witness. (24) For this cause also the multitude went and met Jesus because they heard that He had performed this sign.

(25) Because of this the Pharisees said to one another, "You see that you are not doing any good. Look, the world has gone after Him."

(26) Jesus entered Jerusalem and went into the temple. After looking all around He departed for Bethany with the twelve since it was already late.

Notes: Zechariah 9:9 reads, "Rejoice greatly, 0 daughter of Zion! Shout in triumph, 0 daughter of Jerusalem! Behold, your King is coming to you; He is just and endowed with salvation, humble, and mounted on a donkey, even on a colt, the foal of a donkey." This prophesy was written about five hundred years before the birth of Jesus.

The prophecy Jesus made concerning the destruction of Jerusalem was fulfilled in AD 70, when the Romans under the general Titus did build an embankment against the city. This embankment was a mound of dirt piled up to def end the Romans from the citizens of Jerusalem. It stretched completely around the city, and its purpose was to keep any Jew from leaving Jerusalem and to keep any supplies from entering the city thereby starving the people of Jerusalem into submission. Jerusalem was razed, and the only part of Herod's magnificent temple which was identifiable afterwards was part of the foundation and is what is now called "the wailing wall."

140 The Barren Fig Tree Is Cursed and Withers

(Matt. 21:18-22; Mark 11:12-14, 19-26)

(1) In the morning of the next day, when Jesus left Bethany to return to the city, He became hungry. (2) Seeing in the distance by the road a lone fig tree in leaf, He went to see if perhaps He would find anything

on it. But when He came to it He found nothing but leaves because it was not the season for figs.

(3) Then Jesus said to the fig tree, "May no one ever eat fruit from you again, for no longer shall there ever be any fruit from you." And His disciples were listening.

(4) Whenever evening came they would go out of the city,

(5) and as they were passing the next morning they saw the fig tree withered from the roots up for it had withered at once.

(6) Seeing this the disciples marveled, and being reminded Peter said to Jesus, "Rabbi, look, the fig tree which You cursed has withered. How did it wither so quickly?"

(7) Jesus answered, saying to them, "Have faith in God! Truly I say to you, if you have faith and do not doubt you shall not only do what was done to the fig tree but even if you say to this mountain, 'Be taken up and cast into the sea,' it shall be granted you. (8) Therefore I say to you, all things for which you pray and ask, believe that you have received them and they shall be granted you. (9) And whenever you stand praying, forgive if you have anything against anyone so that your Father who is in heaven also may forgive you your transgressions.

(10) But if you do not forgive neither will your Father who is in heaven forgive your transgressions."

Notes: The text states that it was not the season for figs. Albert Barnes in his commentary wrote that it was not too early in the season for figs and that there should have been figs on the tree. He wrote that what is meant is that it was the time for figs to be ripe but that the end of the time for harvesting them had not yet come. This may have been an attempt by Barnes to explain something which he did not understand, that is, why Jesus would have cursed a perfectly healthy fig tree for not bearing fruit when it was not the season for it to do so. The scripture clearly stated that it was not the season for figs. The time would have been about the first part of April and, unless the growing season for figs in Israel is considerably earlier than it is here, a fig tree *could* perhaps have had figs on it but certainly none of them would have been big enough or ripe enough to eat.

In my humble opinion, Jesus knew from the beginning that it was not the season for figs to be ripe and that the fig tree would have no figs on it. This incident may have been an occasion for Jesus to teach His disciples another lesson. There is no season when our efforts cannot bear fruit for the kingdom of God. Paul wrote in 2 Timothy 4:2, "... Be ready in season and out of season... " This phrase is more familiar to us in the language of the KJV which reads, ". . . Be instant in season, out of season..."

141 The Temple Cleansed

(Matt. 21:12-17; Mark 11:15-18; Luke 19:45-48)

(1) Jesus and the disciples came to Jerusalem and Jesus entered the temple and began to cast out those who were buying and selling there. He overturned the tables of the moneychangers and the seats of those who were selling doves,

(2) and He would not permit anyone to carry goods through the temple.

(3) Then Jesus began to teach and He said to the people, "It is written, 'My house shall be called a house of prayer for all the nations,' but you have made it a robbers' den."

(4) Jesus was teaching daily in the temple and the blind and the lame came to Him and were healed. (5) But when the chief priests and the scribes saw the wonderful things He had done and heard the children crying out in the temple and saying, "Hosanna to the Son of David!" they became indignant (6) and said to Jesus, "Do You hear what these are saying?"

Jesus said to them, "Yes. Have you never read, 'Out of the mouths of infants and nursing babes You have prepared praise for Yourself'?"

(7) When the chief priests and the scribes and the leading men among the people heard this they began seeking a way to try to destroy Jesus, for they were afraid of Him because all the multitude was astonished at His teaching. But they could not find anything that they might do, for all the people were hanging upon His words.

(8) And Jesus left them and went out of the city to Bethany and lodged there.

Notes: This is the second time Jesus cleansed the temple of the merchants and the moneychangers. He did this at the beginning of His ministry, and He did it again here at the end of His ministry. Knowing the animosity of the Pharisees and the chief priests and the scribes, we don't have to wonder why that first cleansing didn't take.

The moneychangers weren't just people who sat behind their tables and exchanged coins for dollar bills or some such activity-they were the bankers of their day. They borrowed and loaned money at interest. In the parable of the talents or pounds, the unprofitable servant was criticized by his master because he didn't lend the money to the moneychangers instead of hiding it in the ground.

The quotation, "My house shall be called a house of prayer for all nations," is from Jeremiah 7:11; and, "Out of the mouths of infants and nursing babes You have prepared praise for Yourself," is from Psalms 8:2.

142 Greeks Seek Jesus; He Foretells His Death (John 12:20-50)

(1) Certain Greeks were going up to worship at the feast, (2) and they came to Philip, who was from Bethsaida of Galilee, and said to him, "Sir, we wish to see Jesus."

(3) Philip came and told Andrew and together they came and told Jesus.

(4) Jesus said to them, "The hour has come for the Son of Man to be glorified. (5) Truly, I say to you, unless a grain of wheat falls into the earth and dies it remains by itself alone, but if it dies it bears much fruit. (6) He who loves his life loses it and he who hates his life in the world shall keep it to life eternal. (7) If anyone serves Me let him follow Me and where I am there shall My servant also be. If anyone serves Me the Father will honor him.

(8) "Now My soul has become troubled. What shall I say, 'Father, save Me from this hour'? But for this purpose I came to this hour. (9) Father, glorify Thy name."

Then there came a voice out of heaven: "I have both glorified it and will glorify it again."

(10) The multitude, who stood by and heard it, were saying that it had thundered. Others were saying, "An angel has spoken to Him."

(11) But Jesus said, "This voice has not come for My sake but for your sakes. (12) Judgment is upon this world. Now the ruler of this world shall be cast out. (13) And I, if I be lifted up from the earth, will draw all men to Myself."

(14) Jesus was saying this to indicate the kind of death by which He was to die.

(15) The multitude answered Jesus, "We have heard out of the Law that the Christ is to remain forever. How can You say, 'The Son of Man must be lifted up'? Who is this Son of Man?"

(16) Jesus said to them, "For a little while longer the light is among you. Walk while you have the light that darkness may not overtake you. He who walks in the darkness does not know where he goes. (17) While you have the light believe in the light in order that you may become sons of light." Jesus spoke these things and then departed and hid Himself from them.

(18) Though Jesus had performed so many signs before them still they were not believing in Him (19) so that the word that Isaiah the prophet spoke might be fulfilled, "Lord, who has believed our report? And to whom has the arm of the Lord been revealed?"

(20) For this reason they could not believe, for Isaiah said again, (21) "He has blinded their eyes and He hardened their hearts lest they see with their eyes and perceive with their hearts and be converted and I heal them." (22) These things Isaiah said because he saw the glory of Jesus and he spoke of Him.

(23) Nevertheless many even of the rulers believed in Jesus but because of the Pharisees they were not confessing Him lest they should be put out of the synagogue, (24) for they loved the approval of men rather than the approval of God.

(25) Jesus cried out and said, "He who believes in Me does not believe in Me but in Him who sent Me, (26) and he who beholds Me beholds the One who sent Me.

(27) "I have come as light into the world that everyone who believes in Me may not remain in darkness.

(28) "If anyone hears My sayings and does not keep them I do not judge him, for I did not come to judge the world but to save the world. (29) He who rejects Me and does not receive My sayings has one who judges him. The word I spoke is what will judge him at the last day. (30) I did not speak on My own initiative but the Father Himself who sent Me has given Me commandment what to say and what to speak. (31) I know that His commandment is eternal life therefore the things I speak I speak just as the Father has told Me."

Notes: The reason the Greeks who asked to speak to Jesus had come to Jerusalem is unclear. There are three possible reasons for their coming: they could have been Jews who lived in Greece and had come to celebrate the Passover; they could have been Greek proselytes to the Jewish religion and had come for the same reason; or they could have been Greeks who had heard about Jesus and just wanted to talk to Him because, as it was recorded in Acts 17:21, "Now all the Athenians and the strangers visiting there used to spend their time in nothing other than telling or hearing something new." It is probable that the reason was either of the first two which are listed above. Living in Greece, these people may have heard about Jesus and all the signs He performed and, for that reason mainly, they wanted to look at him, perhaps hoping also to see one of His signs. It seems that the first discourse of Jesus in this section was delivered mainly to those Greeks.

The second discourse of Jesus was for the purpose of informing His listeners of what was going to happen to Him and the reason it was going to happen. It had been ordained that Jesus would die for the sins of mankind and that without His death those sins could not be erased. Because His death without His subsequent resurrection would stifle all hope, He had to be raised up so that hope could live in the hearts of all people. If Jesus had not been raised up after His death, the people who had hope through Him (including the apostles) probably would have thought that Jesus was just another in the long line of pretenders to the throne of David (and of God). With the resurrection an accomplished fact, all people would know that faith could save them through obedience and the grace of God.

143 The Jews Question Jesus's Authority

(Matt. 21:23-27; Mark 11:27-33; Luke 20:1-8)

(1) Jesus and the disciples came again to Jerusalem. As Jesus was walking in the temple and teaching the people and preaching the gospel, the chief priests and scribes and elders came and confronted Him.

(2) They asked Jesus, "By what authority are You doing these things and who gave You this authority?"

(3) Jesus said to them, "I will ask you one question also and if you answer Me then I will tell you by what authority I do these things. (4) Was the baptism of John from heaven or from men? Answer Me."

(5) They began reasoning among themselves, saying, "If we say, 'From heaven,' He will say, 'Then why did you not believe him?', (6) but if we say, 'From men,' all the people will stone us to death for they are convinced that John was a prophet."

(7) Answering Jesus they said, "We do not know."

Jesus said to them, "Neither will I tell you by what authority I do these things."

Notes: In those last few days before the crucifixion, Jesus had made it His custom to spend the days in the temple teaching and preaching and to spend the nights in Bethany or on the Mount of Olives. This was in early April and the nights were warm enough at that time of year so that a person who stayed outside overnight wouldn't suffer from cold.

The scriptures don't say anything that would indicate that the chief priests and scribes and elders were trying to trap Jesus into saying something for which they could accuse Him when they asked by what authority He was doing the things He was doing, probably meaning by that the cleansing of the temple as well as teaching and preaching. But the authority to regulate and direct the affairs of the temple belonged to the priests, the Levites, and Jesus was neither a priest in the sense that the Levites were, nor a Levite. They wanted to know, then, why

Jesus had taken it upon Himself to change the traditions that they had allowed to develop and which they had maintained. Probably, in this instance, these men were themselves usurping the authority of the priests.

It could have been that these men were aware that Jesus was the rightful heir to the throne of David, in addition to claiming to be the Messiah, and that they resented Him because He wasn't doing what they thought the Messiah should be doing, because He hadn't been sent down to earth to set up an earthly kingdom rather than a heavenly one.

144 The Parable of the Two Sons (Matt. 21:28-32)

(1) "What do you think? A man had two sons and he went to the first and said, 'Son, today go work in the vineyard.' (2) The son answered and said, 'I will, sir'; but he did not go.

(3) "The man went to the second son and said the same thing. This son answered and said, 'I will not,' yet afterwards he regretted it and went. (4) Which of the two did the will of his father?"

They said, "The latter."

Jesus said, "Truly I say to you that the tax-gatherers and harlots will get into the kingdom of God before you. (5) John came to you in the way of righteousness and you did not believe him but tax-gatherers and harlots did believe him. You, seeing this, did not even feel remorse afterward so as to believe him."

Notes: In the parable, the first son who pretended to be obedient, but wasn't, represented the Jewish religious leaders who had perverted their religion by their traditions to the point that most people didn't even know how to worship God as He intended they do. They pretended to be zealous for God but made no effort to uplift the people or to help them in any way. Instead of trying to bring sinners back into the fold, they shunned them. They listened to the preaching of John the Baptist and ignored his message.

The second son, the one who said he would not go work in the vineyard but did, represented the people who through the ages had made no special claims to religious fervor or faithfulness. But those were the people who had heard the preaching of John and had repented.

The vineyard represented the fertile fields where sinners are gathered, ready to receive the message of anyone trying to lead them into the kingdom of God.

This parable was told as part of the answer to the question asked of Jesus concerning His authority. Those people hadn't accepted as authoritative what John the Baptist had said about Jesus, but the common people had believed John and had believed that he was a prophet. The religious leaders hadn't believed John and hadn't repented nor been baptized as the common people had done. If they refused to accept John as a prophet, how could they accept Jesus as the one about whom John prophesied?

145 The Parable of the Wicked Husbandmen

(Matt. 21:33-46; Mark 12:1-12; Luke 20:9-19)

(1) Jesus said, "Listen to another parable. There was a landowner who planted a vineyard and put a wall around it and dug a vat under the wine press and built a tower. He rented it out to vine-growers then went on a journey for a long time.

(2) "At the harvest time he sent a slave to the vine-growers in order to receive some of the produce of the vineyard from the vine-growers. (3) They took the slave and beat him and sent him away empty-handed. (4) The owner sent another slave to them and they wounded this one in the head and treated him shamefully. (5) He sent another and that one they killed, and so it was with many others, beating some and killing others.

(6) "The owner of the vineyard said, 'What shall I do?' He had one more person to send, a beloved son, 'I know,' he said, 'I will send my beloved son. Perhaps they will respect him.'

(7) "But when the vine-growers saw the son they reasoned among themselves and said, 'This is the heir. Come, let us kill him and seize his inheritance and it will be ours.' (8) So they took the son and killed him and threw him out of the vineyard.

(9) "When the owner of the vineyard comes what will he do to those vine-growers? (10) He will bring those wretches to a wretched end and will rent out the vineyard to other vine growers who will pay him the proceeds at the proper season."

(11) When they heard this they said, "May it never be!"

(12) But Jesus looked at them and said, "Have you not even read this scripture: 'The stone which the builders rejected became the chief corner stone. This came about from the Lord, and it is marvelous in our eyes'?

(13) "Then I say to you, the kingdom of God will be taken away from you and will be given to a nation producing the fruit of it. (14) He who falls on this stone will be broken to pieces but on whomever it falls it will scatter like dust."

(14) When the chief priests and scribes and Pharisees heard the parables of Jesus they understood that He was speaking about them. They tried to seize Him but they feared the people because the people held Him to be a prophet.

Notes: This parable is recognizable as a short history of the relationship between God and the Jewish people. The landowner is God; the vine-growers are the Jewish people; the servants sent to collect from the vine-growers were the prophets who were mistreated or killed; the son was Jesus; and the other vine-growers are the rest of the people in the world.

This parable also reminds us of the long-suffering and forgiving nature of God in His dealings with His chosen people.

Read Isaiah 5:5-7, "So now let Me tell you what I am going to do to My vineyards: I will remove its hedge and it will be consumed; I will break down its walls and it will become trampled ground. And I will lay it waste; it will not be pruned or hoed, but briars and thorns will come up. I will also charge the clouds to rain no rain upon it. For the vineyard of the Lord of hosts is the house of Israel, and the men of Judah His delightful plant. Thus He looked for justice, but behold, bloodshed; for righteousness, but behold, a cry of distress."

The scripture which Jesus quoted is from Psalms 118:22-23.

146 Parable of the King's Son's Marriage Feast

(Matt. 22:1-14)

(1) Jesus spoke to them again in a parable, saying, (2) "The kingdom of heaven may be compared to a king who gave a wedding feast for his son. (3) He sent out his slaves to call those who had been invited to the wedding feast, but they were unwilling to come. (4) Again he sent out other slaves saying, 'Tell those who have been invited, "Look, I have prepared my dinner, my oxen and my fattened livestock are all butchered and everything is ready. Come to the wedding feast."' (5) But they paid no attention and went their way, one to his own farm, another to his business, (6) and the rest seized his slaves and mistreated them and killed them.

(7) "The king was enraged and sent his armies which destroyed those murderers and set their city on fire.

(8) "Then he said to his slaves, 'The wedding is ready but those who were invited were not worthy. (9) Go then to the main highway and as many as you find there invite to the wedding feast.'

(10) "The slaves went out into the streets and gathered together all they found, both evil and good, and the wedding hall was filled with dinner guests. (11) But when the king came in to look over the dinner guests he saw there a man not dressed in wedding clothes (12) and said to him, 'Friend, how did you come in here without wedding clothes?' And the man was speechless.

(13) "Then the king said to the servants, 'Bind him hand and foot and cast him into outer darkness. In that place there shall be weeping and gnashing of teeth.' (14) Many are called but few are chosen."

Notes: This parable is very similar to the parable of Jesus which was written up in section 117 and which was taken from Luke 14:15-24. The theme of this parable is the same as the last one about the wicked husbandmen. It was changed somewhat from the way it was told in Luke to suit the different circumstances. The first invitees were, of course, the Jews and the others who were brought in later were the Gentiles.

Something which was in this parable and which was not in the other one in Luke is the incident of the wedding guest who wasn't dressed properly. The fact that all the other guests were dressed in wedding garments and that the one who was not dressed properly and had nothing to say in his defense indicates that it was well known that wedding garments were required and that they were readily available. The king here represents the Lord at the final judgment and the inappropriately dressed man represents those people who don't have the proper spiritual attire-their attire is not that of Christians but of interlopers. They may think they have the proper spirit and attitude or they may think that what they lack will be overlooked on that final day, but without the proper furnishings they will be denied access to a home in heaven. Matthew 7:21-23: "Not everyone who says to Me, 'Lord, Lord,' will enter the kingdom of heaven; but he who does the will of My Father who is in heaven. Many will say to Me on that day, 'Lord, Lord, did we not prophesy in Your name, and in Your name cast out demons, and in Your name perform many miracles?' And then I will declare to them, 'I never knew you, *depart from me, you who practice lawlessness.*'"

147 Paying Tribute to Caesar (Matt. 22:15-22; Mark 12:13-17; Luke 20:20-26)

(1) Then the Pharisees went and counseled together how they might trap Jesus in what He said. (2) They watched Hirn and sent spies of their disciples and Herodians who pretended to be righteous in order that they might catch Him in some statement so as to deliver Him up to the rule and the authority of the governor.

(3) These came and said to Jesus, "Teacher, we know that You speak and teach correctly and that You are truthful and defer to no one and You are not partial to any but teach the way of God in truth. (4) Tell us then what You think-is it lawful to pay a poll-tax to Caesar or not? Shall we pay or shall we not pay?"

(5) But Jesus detected their trickery and malice and, knowing their hypocrisy, said to them, "Why are you testing Me, you hypocrites? Bring Me a denarius so I can look at the coin used for the poll-tax."

(6) They brought Jesus a denarius and He asked them, "Whose likeness and inscription does it have?"

(7) They said to Jesus, "Caesar's."

Then Jesus said to them, "Then render to Caesar the things that are Caesar's and to God the things that are God's."

(8) They were unable to catch Jesus in a saying in the presence of the people and, marveling at His manner, they became silent and went away.

Notes: The Roman government required a very large annual payment of tribute by the Jews because of and as an acknowledgment of the subjection of the Jews to Rome. About twenty years prior to this time, a man called Judas of Galilee had stirred up the people against Rome because of that tribute, the Jewish people in general being bitterly opposed to it.

By this time, the Pharisees, the priests, and the scribes had learned that they themselves could not succeed when they tried to entangle Jesus in their traps and had almost stopped trying. But they hadn't given up entirely. They had made an alliance of sorts with the Herodians, a political party of sorts which was pro-Roman, and for some undisclosed reason, anti-Jesus. The Herodians and some of the disciples of the Pharisees were sent to Jesus with a question which they thought could not be answered without alienating someone. If He said that the tribute should be paid He would turn the Jewish people against

Him, because they were so bitterly opposed to the tax. But if He said that the tribute should not be paid He would have alienated the Roman governor-and it is certain that if He had said the tax should not have been paid the Roman officials would have learned of it very quickly.

The money which was in use in Judea was Roman money, and that in itself showed that Judea was under Roman rule-a conquered nation uses the money of the conqueror. The answer that Jesus gave also confirmed the fact that it was not contrary to the law of God to be in subjection to and to pay tribute to another nation. In some of his writings, Paul stated clearly that Christians should be in subjection to their rulers, whether elected by themselves or forced upon them by a conqueror.

The people who had posed the question to Jesus were amazed-amazed, that is, to learn that there was an answer which would alienate neither the Jewish people nor the Roman governors and that Jesus had the wisdom to know and to give that answer.

148 Sadducees Question the Resurrection

(Matt. 22:23-33; Mark 12:18-27; Luke 20:27-40)

(1) On that day some of the Sadducees (who say there is no resurrection) came to Jesus and questioned Him, saying, (2) "Teacher, Moses wrote for us that if a man dies leaving no child but leaves a wife his brother should take the wife and raise up an offspring to his brother. (3) Now there were seven brothers with us and the first one married and died and, having no offspring, left his wife to his brother. (4) The second one took her and died leaving behind no offspring, and the third likewise, (5) and on down until all seven had died leaving no children. (6) Finally the woman died also. (7) In the resurrection, when they rise again, which one's wife will she be? All seven had her as wife."

(8) Jesus said to them, "Is this not the reason you are mistaken, that you do not understand the scriptures nor the power of God? (9) The sons of this age marry and are given in marriage, (10) but those who are considered worthy to attain to that age and the resurrection from the dead neither marry nor are given in marriage. (11) Neither can they die anymore for they are like angels and are sons of God being sons of the resurrection. (12) But regarding the fact that the dead rise again have you not read in the book of Moses, in the passage about the burning bush, how God spoke to him saying, 'I am the God of Abraham and the God of Isaac and the God of Jacob'? (13) He is not the God of the dead but of the living. You are greatly mistaken."

(14) When the multitude heard this they were astonished at the teaching of Jesus and some of the scribes said to Him, "Teacher, You have spoken well." And they did not have courage to question Him longer about anything.

Notes: Most people who are familiar with the Bible have some knowledge of the two more prominent Jewish religious sects during the time Jesus was on earth-the Pharisees and the Sadducees. Neither sect is even mentioned in the Old Testament.

Josephus, the Jewish historian, wrote that these two religious sects began about the same time. That happened during the reign of a man named Jonathan who was high priest from 159 BC to 144 BC. Though the sects were not formalized until then, the sentiments which led to the formation of the two sects had been in the minds of the people for years going back to the release of the Jews from the Babylonian captivity.

The word "Pharisee" means "to separate" or "the separate." The Pharisees believed that they should maintain strict separation between themselves, that is, the Jews and all other people. They held to four major beliefs: (1) that there was a resurrection of the dead; (2) that there was a future state or life with rewards and punishment; (3) that there were angels and spirits; and (4) that there was a special providence of God carried out by angels and spirits. Originally, the Pharisees were true patriots and reformers but eventually they became mere formalists. During the time of Christ, there was supposed to have been more than six thousand members of the sect. They were the chief proponents of patriotism. The "Zealots" were also Pharisees and were the extremists of the sect. The Pharisees had gained a great deal of influence over the common people by a great show of their supposed virtues. We know from the accounts of their confrontations with John the Baptist and with Jesus that most of them were selfish, self righteous, and self-centered and that they tried to cover these traits with religious formality and feigned piety.

The Sadducees were much more liberal in their dealings with people outside Judaism, and they resented any attempts at restraints in that respect. They accepted no restraints outside the scriptures themselves, and they interpreted the scriptures as liberally and as laxly as possible. The father of the sect of Sadducees was a man named Zadok whose followers were originally called Zadokites. In time, the name was corrupted until it became "Sadducees." Although Zadok was the father of the sect, he was not the founder. Zadok lived about 260 BC, long before the sect was formalized. Zadok was a pupil of a man named

Antigonus Sochaeus, who taught that God should be served without hope of reward or fear of punishment. That doctrine was the basis for the beliefs of Zadok and, later, of the sect of the Sadducees. The Sadducees denied all four of the major beliefs of the Pharisees, believing instead that God's promises were for this life only. They didn't believe in trying to relieve the distress of the poor people-they believed that the poor were consigned to live in poverty as punishment for past wrongs. To them, then, poverty and disease and distress of all kinds were the evidence of their own wrongdoing and were God's curse on them for that wrongdoing. Generally, the Sadducees were the aristocrats of the Jews. They were the party of the high priests, they were mostly wealthy, and they were consenting to the rule of the Romans. These three factors made them respected and powerful although they were far fewer in number than the Pharisees.

It may be noted here that although Jesus often said things such as, "Woe to you, scribes and Pharisees, hypocrites... " He didn't say the same things to or about the Sadducees.

There does not appear to have been an ulterior motive of the Sadducees in asking their question as was so often the case in the questioning by the Pharisees. The chief priests, however, were often involved in the conspiracy against Jesus and many of them were Sadducees. The writing in the Law of Moses to which the Sadducees referred is in Deuteronomy 25:5-6. That Law, however, didn't originate with Moses. Back in Genesis 38:6-11, we read that Er, the first-born son of Judah, was married and died before he had children. Then at Judah's request, his daughter-in-law married Judah's second son, Onan, so that she could have a child to Er, her first husband.

None of the Pharisees seem to have been wise enough or, at least, able to prove to the Sadducees the error of their beliefs. The Pharisees couldn't be persuaded that the Sadducees were right, but they weren't able to prove they were wrong either. The Sadducees didn't deny the existence of God, in fact, they believed in Him. But according to the beliefs of the Sadducees, the power of God was much less to them than it was to the Pharisees because of their belief that there was neither reward nor punishment beyond the grave.

149 The Great Commandment

(Matt. 22:34-40; Mark 12:28-34)

(1) When the scribes and Pharisees heard that Jesus had put the Sadducees to silence they gathered themselves together. (2) One of them, a lawyer, recognizing that Jesus had answered the Sadducees well and testing Him, asked a question, (3) "Teacher, which is the great commandment in the Law, the foremost of all?"

(4) Jesus answered, "'Hear, 0 Israel! The Lord our God is one Lord, (5) and you shall love the Lord your God with all your heart and with all your soul and with all your mind and with all your strength.' (6) This is the great and foremost commandment. (7) The second is like it, 'You shall love your neighbor as yourself.' (8) On these two commandments depend the whole Law and the Prophets. There is none greater than these."

(9) A scribe said to Jesus, "Right, Teacher. You have truly stated that He is One and there is no one else besides Him, (10) and to love Him with all the heart and with all the understanding and with all the strength and to love one's neighbor as himself is much more than all burnt offerings and sacrifices."

(11) When Jesus saw that he had answered intelligently He said, "You are not far from the kingdom of God."

(12) After that no one would venture to ask Jesus any more questions.

Notes: According to Jewish writers, for ages, there had been disagreements among the Jewish rabbis and religious leaders as to which of God's Laws was greatest. Since, according to them, there were more than six hundred commandments of Moses, there was a great deal of room for disagreement. But this question was not asked in an effort to settle that age-old argument-it was used as another occasion to test Jesus.

Paul wrote in Romans 13:8-10, "Owe nothing to anyone except to love one another; for he who loves his neighbor has fulfilled the law. For this, 'You shall not commit adultery, you shall not murder, you shall not steal, you shall not covet,' and if there is any other commandment, it is summed up in this saying, 'You shall love your neighbor as yourself.' Love does no wrong to a neighbor; love therefore is the fulfillment of the law." In Leviticus 19:18, the Law read, "You shall not take vengeance, nor bear any grudge against the sons of your people, but you shall love your neighbor as yourself; I am the Lord." Jesus had previously quoted that Law in Matthew 19:19 and He quoted it again here in Matthew 22:39.

150 Whose Son Is the Christ?

(Matt. 22:41-46; Mark 12:35-37; Luke 20:41-44)

(1) As Jesus taught in the temple, while the Pharisees were gathered together there, He asked them a question, (2) saying, "What do you think about the Christ? Whose son is He?"

They said to Him, "The Son of David!"

(3) Jesus asked, "How is it that the scribes say that the Christ is the son of David? David himself in the Holy Spirit said in the book of Psalms, (4) 'The Lord said to my Lord, "Sit at My right hand until I make thine enemies a footstool for Thy feet."' (5) David calls Him 'Lord,' and how is He his son?"

(6) The great crowd enjoyed listening to Jesus, but no one was able to answer Him a word, nor did anyone dare from that day on to ask Him another question.

Notes: Jesus probably asked the question for several reasons. First, He probably wanted to show the Pharisees that their knowledge of the Messiah was incomplete and that they didn't know as much as they thought they knew. And perhaps, He also wanted to show the general public that the Pharisees were ignorant on that subject. A third reason would have been that Jesus sincerely wanted all the people who heard Him speak to know the true answer to His question. Jesus pointed out that although the Messiah was physically a descendant of David, He was alive when David wrote his Psalms and was acknowledged by David as his Lord. The word "Lord" does not refer only to divinity but it can also mean authority. The scripture that Jesus quoted is from Psalms 110:1.

151 The Last Public Discourse of Jesus: He Denounces the Scribes and the Pharisees

(Matt. 23:1-36; Mark 12:38-40; Luke 20:45-47)

(1) While all the people were listening Jesus spoke to them and to His disciples saying, (2) "The scribes and the Pharisees have seated themselves in the chair of Moses, (3) so do and observe all that they tell you but do not do according to their deeds for they say things and do not do them. (4) They tie up heavy loads and lay them on men's shoulders but they themselves are unwilling to move them with so much as a finger.

(5) "They do all their deeds to be noticed by men for they broaden their phylacteries and lengthen the tassels of their garments. (6) They like to walk around in long robes. They love the place of honor at banquets and the chief seats in the synagogues (7) and respectful greetings in the market places and being called 'Rabbi' by men.

(8) "Do not be called 'Rabbi' for One is your Teacher, and you are all brothers. (9) Do not call anyone on earth your father for only One is your Father-He who is in heaven. (10) Do not be called leaders for only One is your Leader and that one is Christ.

(11) "The greatest among you shall be your servant. (12) Whoever exalts himself shall be humbled and whoever humbles himself shall be exalted.

(13) "Woe to you, scribes and Pharisees, hypocrites, because you shut off the kingdom of heaven from men. You do not enter in yourselves nor do you allow those who would enter to go in.

(15) "Woe to you, scribes and Pharisees, hypocrites, because you devour widows' houses even while for the sake of appearance you make long prayers. For that reason you shall receive even greater condemnation.

(16) "Woe to you, scribes and Pharisees, hypocrites, because you travel about on sea and land to make one proselyte and when he becomes one you make him twice as much a son of hell as you yourselves.

(17) "Woe to you, blind guides, who say, 'To swear by the temple is nothing, but whoever swears by the gold of the temple is obligated.'

(17) You fools and blind men, which is more important, the gold or the temple that sanctified the gold? (18) "You say, 'To swear by the altar is nothing, but whoever swears by the offering that is on it is obligated.' (19) You blind men, which is more important, the offering or the altar that sanctifies the offering? (20) He who swears by the altar swears by it and by everything on it. (21) He who swears by the temple swears by the temple and by Him who dwells within it. (22) And he who swears by heaven swears by the throne of God and by Him who sits upon it.

(23) "Woe to you, scribes and Pharisees, hypocrites, for you tithe mint and dill and cummin and have neglected the weightier provisions of the law-justice and mercy and faithfulness. These are the things you should have done without neglecting the others. (24) You blind guides, who strain at a gnat and swallow a camel.

(25) "Woe to you, scribes and Pharisees, hypocrites, for you clean the outside of the cup and the dish but inside they are full of robbery and self-indulgence. (26) You blind Pharisees, first clean the inside of the cup and the dish so that the outside of it may become clean also.

(27) "Woe to you, scribes and Pharisees, hypocrites, for you are like white-washed tombs which on the outside appear beautiful but inside are full of dead men's bones and all uncleanness. (28) Outwardly you too appear righteous to men but inwardly you are full of hypocrisy and lawlessness.

(29) "Woe to you, scribes and Pharisees, hypocrites, for you build the tombs of the prophets and adorn the monuments of the righteous (30) and say, 'If we had been living in the days of our fathers we would not have been partners with them in shedding the blood of the prophets.' (31) Therefore you are witnesses against yourselves that you are descendants of those who murdered the prophets. (32) Fill up then the measure of the guilt of your fathers.

(33) "You serpents, you brood of vipers, how shall you escape the sentence of hell? (34) Look, I am sending you prophets and wise men and scribes. Some of them you will kill and crucify and some of them you will scourge in your synagogues and persecute from city to city (35) so that upon you may fall the guilt of all the righteous blood shed on earth from the blood of righteous Abel to the blood of Zechariah,

the son of Berechiah, whom you murdered between the sanctuary and the altar. (36) Truly I say to you, all these things shall come upon this generation."

Notes: Jesus said the scribes and Pharisees had seated themselves in the chair of Moses, because they were the ones who taught the Law to the people. Since the Laws of God were given through Moses to teach them to the people would have been like a teacher taking the place of Moses.

Phylacteries (or frontlets) were first mentioned in Exodus 13:16, "So it shall serve as a sign on your hand, and as phylacteries on your foreheads, for with a powerful hand the Lord brought us out of Egypt." It seems that this statement was meant to have been taken figuratively, but the Pharisees especially had taken it literally. Compare this to what is written in Proverbs 6:20-21, "My son, keep your father's commandment, and forsake not the law of your mother; bind them continually upon your heart, and tie them about your neck."

Phylacteries contained four bits of scripture which were written on thin strips of parchment, put into a small leather case, and bound either on the forehead or on the left arm. The four scriptures were Exodus 12:2-10, Exodus 13:11-21, Deuteronomy 6:4-9, and Deuteronomy 11:18-21.

The Pharisees made their phylacteries as conspicuous as possible and wore them all the time whereas most of the people wore them only at prayer.

Concerning the tassels, Numbers 15:38-40 reads, "Speak to the sons of Israel, and tell them that they shall make for themselves tassels on the corners of their garments throughout their generations, and that they shall put on the tassel of each corner a cord of blue. And it shall be a tassel for you to look at and remember all the commandments of the Lord, so as to do them and not follow after your own heart and your own eyes, after which you played the harlot, in order that you may remember to do all My commandments, and be holy to your God." The Pharisees made their tassels longer than was customary so that they could be looked upon as having a greater respect for the Law.

Peter said in his address to the council at Jerusalem as recorded in Acts 15:10, "Now therefore why do you put God to the test by placing upon the neck of the disciples a yoke which neither our fathers nor we have been able to bear?" The Pharisees had added immeasurably to the burdens of the people by binding on them traditions in addition to the burdens already imposed upon them by the Law.

The Jewish religion had its "rabbbis," and the Catholics have their "fathers," and the Protestants have their "reverends." It's "the Reverend this" and "the Reverend that" wherever you read or hear about a Protestant preacher. With the Catholics, it's "Father this" and "Father that." Jesus said plainly that they were not to be called "rabbi" and that they were to call no man "Father," but like so many things in the Bible, this, too, is being ignored. The word "reverend" appears only once in the entire Bible and that one time it is in reference to God. Psalms 111:9 reads, "He sent redemption unto His people; He had commanded His covenant forever; holy and reverend is His name."

We aren't told how the Pharisees "devoured the houses of widows" or if this was a simile rather than an actual deed. It would seem, though, that the Pharisees were taking advantage of widows and in some way causing them to lose their homes rather than helping them. James wrote in 1:27, "Pure religion and undefiled before God and the Father is this, to visit the fatherless and widows in their affliction, and to keep himself unspotted from the world."

The proselytes whom the Pharisees and scribes were so diligently seeking weren't just people whom they were trying to convert from paganism to Judaism, but they were also Jews whom they were trying to persuade to become Pharisees. They weren't being converted to the *religion* of the Pharisees but to the sect of the Pharisees and therefore to the *greed and deceit* of the Pharisees, such proselytes becoming worse than those who converted them. Albert Barnes wrote that some of the proselytes were from paganism and that the Pharisees took advantage of them to as great an extent as possible then abandoned them. They had lost their old gods and been abandoned (so they thought) by their new one, so they became godless persons worse than they had been before.

The oaths taken or required by the Pharisees meant more or less according to the object on which they were sworn. This points out dramatically what the Pharisees considered to be of more importance, the gold in the temple, donations to the temple, and the physical matter on the altar as opposed to the holiness of the temple and the altar.

Concerning the cleaning of the outside of the cup, this meant that the scribes and Pharisees were more concerned with appearances than with character. As long as they could appear to the people to be pious and to be obeying all the Laws of Moses, it didn't matter to them what their spiritual lives were like. Whether they stole or cheated or committed adultery or whatever, they didn't care as long as it wasn't generally known to the people.

When speaking of the tombs here, Jesus was teaching a lesson which was different from the lesson He taught about the tombs in Luke 11:44. In Luke 11, the graves were said to be so disguised or hidden that people didn't know when they walked on or over them or touched them. Here, Jesus is comparing the scribes and Pharisees to whitewashed tombs which were so beautiful on the outside that people didn't think too much about the fact that they were so filthy and rotten inside.

It isn't clear as to the identity of the Zechariah about whom Jesus spoke here. The prophet Zechariah from the book of Zechariah was said to be the son of Berechiah, but there is no mention in that book of how or where or under what circumstances he died. There is another Zechariah in the scriptures about whom it was written in 2 Chronicles 24:20-21 that he was killed "in the court of the house of the Lord." The death of this Zechariah fits the manner of death of the Zechariah about whom Jesus spoke but his father's name was Jehoiada. Albert Barnes attempted to reconcile this apparent inconsistency by stating that men quite often were called by two different names such as Matthew was also Levi and Peter was Simon or Cephas and therefore Jehoiada may also have been called Berechiah. Also, the father-in-law of Moses was called by two different names-Reuel and Jethro. There are many men written of in the scriptures who were named Zechariah, and the fathers of several of them were named, but the only one whose father was said to have been named Berechiah was the prophet of the biblical book of Zechariah. Because of what Jesus said, we may assume either that the men named Berechiah and Jehoiada were the same person or that they were two different men and that the sons of both of them were slain in the same manner.

Of course, it is well known what befell the Jews about forty years later in AD 70 when the Roman Emperor Titus captured and razed Jerusalem.

152 Jesus Laments Over Jerusalem

(Matt. 23:37-39; Luke 13:34-35)

(1) "O Jerusalem, Jerusalem, the city that kills the prophets and stones those sent to her! How often I wanted to gather your children together just as a hen gathers her brood under her wings but you would not have it so! (2) Look, your house is being left to you desolate (3) and I say to you, you shall not see Me from now on until the time comes when you say, 'Blessed is He who comes in the name of the Lord!'"

Notes: In His lament for the people of Jerusalem, Jesus was acknowledging what they had done in the past and predicting what was going to happen to them in the near future. But He was also leaving the door open for the return of the Jews to God's kingdom when they recognize Jesus as the Messiah and accept Him as their Savior. On this subject, read what Paul wrote in Romans 11:25-32, "For I do not want you, brethren, to be uninformed of this mystery, lest you be wise in your own estimation, that a partial hardening has happened to Israel until the fullness of the Gentiles has come in; and thus all Israel will be saved; just as it is written, 'The Deliverer will come from Zion, He will remove ungodliness from Jacob. And this is My covenant with them, when I take away their sins.' From the standpoint of the gospel, they are enemies for your sake but from the standpoint of God's choice they are beloved for the sake of the fathers; for the gifts and the calling of God are irrevocable. For just as you once were disobedient to God, but now have been shown mercy because of their disobedience, so these also now have been disobedient, in order that because of the mercy shown to you they also may now be shown mercy. For God has shut up all in disobedience that He might show mercy to all."

153 The Widow's Mites (Mark 12:41-44; Luke 21:1-4)

(1) Jesus sat down opposite the treasury and began observing how the multitude were putting money into the treasury. Many rich people were putting in large sums, (2) and Jesus saw that a certain poor widow came and put in two small copper coins, which amount to a cent.

(3) Calling His disciples to Him Jesus said to them, "Truly I say to you that this poor widow put in more than all the contributors to the treasury, for all the others put into the offering out of their surplus but she, out of her poverty, put in all she owned, all she had to live on."

Notes: In the outer court of the temple, the Court of Women, there were thirteen chests. Each chest had a trumpet-shaped opening and was labeled with the particular use to which the money which was deposited therein was to be used.

The NASV says that the widow put into the treasury "two small copper coins which amount to a cent." The *KN* says, "two mites which make a farthing." The original Greek says the coins were "lepta" and made up a "quadrans." Whatever the coins were called, whether lepta or small copper coins or mites, they were made of brass and were the smallest coins in use at that time.

154 Jesus Foretells the Destruction of Jerusalem

(Matt. 10:17-23, 24:1-35; Mark 13:1-31;
Luke 12:11-12, 17:23-25, 37, 21:5-33)

(1) Jesus came out of the temple and was going away when one of His disciples came up to point out the temple buildings to Him, (2) that they were adorned with beautiful stones and votive gifts, and said, "Teacher, look what wonderful stones and what wonderful buildings!"

(3) Jesus answered, saying, "These great buildings that you are looking at, truly I say to you, the days will come in which there will not be left one stone upon another which will not be torn down."

(4) Later as Jesus was sitting on the Mount of Olives opposite the temple His disciples, Pater and James and John and Andrew, came to

Him privately and questioned Him, asking, "Tell us, when will these things be? What will be the sign when these things are about to take place, and what will be the sign of Your coming and the end of the age?"

(5) Jesus said to them, "See to it that no one misleads you,

(6) for many will come in My name saying, 'I am the Christ,' and, 'The time is at hand,' and will mislead many, but do not go after them.

(7) "You will hear of wars and rumors of wars and disturbances but do not be frightened. These things must take place but that is not yet the end."

(8) Then Jesus continued, "Nation shall rise against nation and kingdom against kingdom. (9) There will be great earthquakes and in various places plagues and famines and there will be terrors and great signs from heaven. (10) But these things are merely the beginning of birth pangs.

(11) "Be on your guard, for before all these things they will deliver you up to retribution. They will lay hands on you and will persecute you and they will deliver you to the courts and the synagogues and prisons. (12) You will be flogged in the synagogues and you will be sent to stand before governors and kings for My name's sake as a testimony to them. (13) But all these things will lead to opportunities for your testimony of Me.

(14) "When they arrest you and bring you before the synagogues and the rulers and authorities and deliver you up, do not be anxious. Make up your minds not to prepare beforehand to defend yourselves and do not become anxious about how or what you shall apeak in your defense or what you should say for I will give you utterance of what you are to say,

(15) and wisdom which none of your opponents will be able to resist or refute. (16) Say whatever is given to you in that hour for the Holy Spirit will teach you what you ought to say, for it is not you who speak, but the Holy Spirit.

(17) "At that time many will fall away and will deliver up one another and hate one another. (18) Brother will deliver brother to death and father his child, and even children will rise up against parents and have them put to death. (19) Some of you will be delivered up even by parents and brothers and relatives and friends and they will put some

of you to death. You will be hated by all on account of My name (20) yet not a hair of your head will perish.

(21) "Many false prophets will arise and will mislead many. Because lawlessness will be increased most people's love will grow cold. (22) By your endurance you will gain your lives, for the ones who endure to the end shall be saved.

(23) "This gospel of the kingdom shall be preached in the whole world for a witness to all the nations, and then the end shall come.

(24) "When you see Jerusalem surrounded by armies recognize that her 'Abomination of Desolation,' which was spoken of through Daniel the prophet, is standing in the holy place where it should not be" (let the reader understand) (25) "then let those who are in Judea flee to the mountains. (26) Let him who is on the housetop not go down or enter in to get anything out that is in the house. (27) Let him who is in the field not turn back to get his cloak and let those who are in the midst of the city depart and let not them who are in the country enter the city, (28) because these are days of vengeance in order that all things which are written may be fulfilled.

(29) "Woe to those who are with child and to those who nurse babes in those days for there will be great distress upon the land and wrath to the people. (30) They will fall by the edge of the sword and will be led captive into all the nations, and Jerusalem will be trampled under foot by the Gentiles until the times of the Gentiles be fulfilled.

(31) "Pray that your flight may not be in the winter or on a Sabbath. (32) Those days will be a time of great tribulation such as has not occurred since the beginning of the creation which God made until now, and never shall. (33) Unless those days had been cut short by the Lord no life would have been saved, but for the sake of the elect whom He chose He cut short those days.

(34) "Then people will say to you, 'See, here is the Christ,' or, 'Look, there He is.' If they do, do not believe them and do not go away nor run after them. (35) False Christs and false prophets will arise and will show great signs and wonders in order to, if possible, lead even the elect astray. (36) But take heed! I have told you everything in advance.

(37) "Then if anyone says to you, 'Look, He is in the wilderness,' do not go forth; or, 'Look, He is in the inner rooms,' do not believe

them. (38) Just as the lightning flashes out of one part of the sky from the east and shines even to the other part of the sky in the west so will the coming of the Son of Man be in His day. But first He must suffer many things and be rejected by this generation."

The disciples asked Jesus, "Where, Lord?"

(39) Jesus said to them, "Wherever the corpse is, there will the vultures be gathered.

(40) "But immediately after the tribulation of those days there will be signs-the *sun will be darkened and the moon will not give its light and the stars will fall* from the sky. (41) Upon the earth there will be dismay among the nations, perplexity at the roaring of the sea and the waves, (42) men fainting from fear and the expectation of the things which are coming upon the world, and the powers of the heavens will be shaken. (43) Then the sign of the Son of Man will appear in the sky and all the tribes of the earth will mourn. They will see the *son of man coming on the clouds of the sky* with great power and glory. (44) He will send forth His angels with *a great trumpet* and *they will gather together* His elect from the four winds, from the farthest end of the earth to the farthest end of heaven. (45) But when these things begin to take place, straighten up and lift up your heads because your redemption is drawing near."

(46) Then Jesus told them a parable: "Now learn the parable from the fig tree and all the trees. When its branch has already become tender and it puts forth its leaves you see it and know for yourselves that summer is now near. (47) Even so, you too, when you see all these things happening, recognize that the kingdom of God is near, right at the door.

(48) "Truly I say to you, this generation will not pass away until all these things take place. (49) Heaven and earth will pass away but My words shall not pass away."

Notes: Many people try to use this passage as a means of forecasting the coming of the end of the world. But notice! The question the disciples asked Jesus is a two-part question, and the answer Jesus gave is a two-part answer. There have always been wars between nations, and there will continue to be wars until Jesus returns. There have always been earthquakes and plagues and famines, and there will continue to be earthquakes and plagues and famines. These things are not signs of the end of the world or of the second coming of Jesus. They are signs that things are normal in the world. Notice again what Jesus said,"... Many will come in My name saying,'... The time is at hand... ' and will mislead many, but do not go after them." As you are probably aware these false prophecies of the end of time have been made several times in the past, at least once in our time, and those who predicted them have, of course, always been wrong. It may be that God will always make sure that such predictions are wrong as proof that no man can ever know the mind of God.

The prediction of Jesus concerning the destruction of the temple was fulfilled in AD 70. The Romans almost completely destroyed the city of Jerusalem, and no stone of the temple remained atop another. The only part of Herod's magnificent temple that is identifiable today is a part of the foundation which the Jews call the "wailing wall." It's called that because that is where many pious Jews gather to bemoan the destruction of Jerusalem and the temple.

There have been times in the history of Christianity when family members delivered other family members for persecution and death, and they probably thought they were doing the right thing just as Paul thought he was doing God's will when he persecuted Christians. The repression of Christianity has occurred down through the ages and even into modern times. And some parts of Christianity have persecuted or repressed other parts because of a difference in doctrines.

There have been false prophets in the past and, if we are to consider preachers as prophets, the world is full of them now. Consider the many different churches which call themselves Christian churches but teach so many different doctrines. And they all believe that their doctrines are acceptable to God and therefore are all right to teach. These people don't accept God's Word, the Bible, to be authoritative, partly because they don't know His word and don't study to learn it-or else they think God doesn't mean what He said.

Jesus said, "Because lawlessness will be increased most people's love will grow cold." Most people aren't old enough to know how things used to be before the end of the Second World War. Back then, it seemed that more people attended worship services on Sunday than didn't. Now there's probably no more that one person in about twenty who attends services on Sunday morning on a regular basis and considerably less than half that many who attend on Sunday or Wednesday evenings.

Those things about which Jesus warned were things that have already come to pass, and they are not signs of the end of the world. We will know that anyone pretending to be the Christ at the second coming will be a liar and pretender because when Jesus does come again, there will be no warning whatsoever and everyone from the east to the west will know about it at the same time. Jesus did give information as to some signs that would accompany His return. What He did not do was give any information about when that would be. Flavius Josephus wrote that many men arose about that time claiming to be the Messiah and drawing men away after them.

There have been many times when a person left a burning building and then returned to try to rescue some cherished personal belongings and died because of it. Jesus warned His disciples that when the fall of Jerusalem was imminent that they were not to return to their homes for any reason whatsoever because their time to flee the coming ruin would be very short. It has been stated that no Christians were left in Jerusalem when the Romans took it.

155 Jesus Tells of His Second Coming

(Matt. 24:36-51; Mark 13:32-37; Luke 17:22, 26-36, 21:34-38)

(1) Jesus said to the disciples, "The days shall come when you will long to see one of the days of the Son of Man but you will not see it. (2) But of that day and hour no one knows, not even the angels in heaven, nor the Son, but the Father alone.

(3) For the days of the coming of the Son of Man will be like what happened in the days of Noah. (4) As in those days which were before the flood people were eating and drinking, they were marrying and giving and being given in marriage, until the day that Noah entered the ark, (5) and they did not understand until the flood came and took them all away and destroyed them. So shall it be at the coming of the Son of Man.

(6) "It was the same as happened in the days of Lot. They were eating and drinking, they were buying and selling, they were planting, they were building, (7) but on the day that Lot went out from Sodom it rained fire and brimstone from heaven and destroyed them all.

(8) "It will be the same on the day that the Son of Man is revealed. (9) On that day let not the one who is on the housetop and whose goods are in the house go down to take them away, and likewise let not the one who is in the field turn back. (10) Remember Lot's wife. (11) Whoever seeks to keep his life shall lose it and whoever loses his life shall preserve it.

(12) "At that time there will be two men in the fields; one will be taken, and one will be left. (13) There will be two women grinding at the mill; one will be taken and one will be left. (14) I tell you, that night there will be two people in one bed; one will be taken and the other will be left.

(15) "Therefore take heed and be ready, for you do not know which is the appointed day when your Lord is coming.

(16) But be sure of this, that if the head of the house had known at what time of the night the thief was coming, he would have been on guard and would not have allowed his house to be broken into. (17) For this reason you be ready, too; for the Son of Man is coming at an hour when you do not think He will.

(18) "It is like a man who went away on a journey and who upon leaving his house put his slaves in charge, assigning to each one his task. He also commanded the doorkeeper to stay on the alert. (19) Therefore, lest the master of the house come suddenly and find you asleep, be on the alert for you do not know when he is coming, whether in the evening, at midnight, or cockcrowing, or in the morning.

(20) "Be as the faithful and sensible slave whom his master put in charge of the members of his household to give them their food at the proper time. (21) Truly I say to you that he will put him in charge of all his possessions. (23) But an evil slave will say in his heart, 'My master is not coming for a long time,' (24) and he will begin to beat his fellow slaves and eat and drink with drunkards. (25) Then the master of that slave will come on a day and at an hour when the slave does not expect

him, (26) and shall cut the slave into pieces and assign him a place with the hypocrites. Weeping shall be there and the gnashing of teeth.

(27) "Be on guard, that your hearts may not be weighted down with dissipation and drunkenness and the worries of life nor that day come on you suddenly like a trap; (28) for it will come upon all those who dwell on the face of all the earth. (29) But stay on guard at all times, praying that you may have strength to escape all those things that are about to take place and that you will stand before the Son of Man.

(30) "And what I say to you I say to all, 'Be on the alert!'"

(31) Now during the day Jesus was teaching in the temple but at evening He would go out and spend the night on the mount that is called Olivet. (32) And all the people would get up early in the morning to come to Him in the temple to listen to Him.

Notes: As you can see, throughout this entire section, Jesus was telling about His second coming in several different ways. He warned the disciples that when He came again, it would be suddenly and without any warning and that everyone should make certain to be ready when that time came.

156 The Parable of the Ten Virgins (Matt. 25:1-13)

(1) "The kingdom of heaven will be comparable to ten virgins who took their lamps and went out to await the bridegroom. (2) Five of them were foolish and five were prudent, (3) for the foolish ones took their lamps but took no oil for them, (4) but the prudent ones took oil in flasks along with their lamps.

(5) "Now while the bridegroom was delaying all the virgins got drowsy and went to sleep. (6) Then at midnight there was a shout, 'Look, the bridegroom! Come out to meet him.'

(7) "Then all the virgins arose and trimmed their lamps. (8) The foolish ones said to the prudent ones, 'Give us some of your oil-our lamps are going out.'

(9) "But the prudent ones answered, 'No, there will not be enough for you and us too. Instead you go to the dealers and buy some oil for yourselves.'

(10) "While the foolish ones were away purchasing oil, the bridegroom came and those who were ready went in with him to the wedding feast and the door was shut.

(11) "Later the other virgins returned saying, 'Lord, lord, open up for us.' (12) But he answered, 'Truly I say to you, I do not know you.'

(13) "Be on the alert then, for you do not know the day nor the hour."

Notes: This is another parable with the lesson which shows how foolish it is not to be prepared at all times to meet Jesus when He comes again. It might be noted here that regardless of the actual day and year when Jesus comes again, for each of us as individuals that day is the day we die and that day is as uncertain as the time Jesus will come again.

157 The Parable of the Talents (Matt. 25:14-30)

(1) "It is like a man who was going on a journey. He called his slaves and entrusted his possessions to them. (2) To one slave he gave five talents, to another he gave two talents, and to another one talent, each according to his ability. Then the man left on his journey.

(3) "Immediately the slave who had received five talents traded with them and received five more talents. (4) In the same manner the one who received two talents gained two more. (5) But he who received one talent went away and dug in the ground and hid his master's money.

(6) "Now after a long time the master of those slaves returned and settled accounts with them. (7) The one who had received five talents came up and brought five more talents and said, 'Master, you entrusted five talents to me. Look, I have gained five more talents.'

(8) "His master said to him, 'Well done, good and faithful slave. You have been faithful with a few things so I will put you in charge of many things. Enter into the joy of your master.'

(9) "The slave who had received two talents came and said, 'Master, you entrusted to me two talents. Look, I have gained two more talents.'

(10) "His master said to him, 'Well done, good and faithful slave. You have been faithful with a few things so I will put you in charge of many things. Enter into the joy of your master.'

(11) "Then the one who had received one talent came and said, 'Master, I knew you were a hard man who reaped where you did not sow and gathered where you scattered no seed.

(12) I was afraid and I went away and hid your talent in the ground. Look, I give you back what is yours.'

(13) "But the master said to him, 'You wicked, lazy slave! You knew that I reap where I did not sow and gather where I scattered no seed, (14) so you ought to have put the money in a bank and when I returned I would have received it back with interest. (15) Therefore take the talent away from him and give it to the one who has ten talents.'

(16) "For to everyone who has more will be given and he will have an abundance, but from the one who does not have even what he does have will be taken away. (17) That worthless slave will be cast into the outer darkness and in that place will be weeping and gnashing of teeth."

Notes: This parable is very similar to the parable of the ten pounds which was recorded in a previous section. The message in this parable is that everyone who has a talent should use it for the glory of God and His kingdom. Anyone who can preach should preach. Anyone who can teach should teach. Anyone who can do personal work should do personal work. Anyone who has a talent that can be profitable in the Lord's work and doesn't use it is like that unprofitable servant who hid his talent in such a way that it was useless to anyone.

Jesus said,"... To everyone who has more will be given... " That "more" about which He spoke is the reward that Christians will receive upon His second coming. And "... The one who does not have even what he does have will be taken away... " possibly refers to the final destination of the people who do not accept Jesus as savior or who do not obey the commandments Jesus gave that anyone who becomes a Christian must have obeyed. Jesus said in Revelation 3:5, "He who overcomes shall thus be clothed in white garments; and I will not erase his name from the book of life, and I will confess his name before My Father, and before His angels." And Revelation 20:12 and 15, "And I saw the dead, the great and the small, standing before the throne, and books were opened; and another book was opened, which is the book of life; and the dead were judged from the things which were written in the books, according to their deeds... And if anyone's name was not found written in the book of life, he was thrown in the lake of fire."

158 Judgment of the Nations (Matt. 25:31-46)

(1) "When the Son of Man comes in His glory with all the angels then He will sit on His glorious throne. (2) All the nations will be gathered before Him and He will separate them from one another as the shepherd separates the sheep from the goats. (3) He will put the sheep on His right and the goats on His left.

(4) "Then the King will say to those on His right, 'Come, you who are blessed of My Father. Inherit the kingdom prepared for you from the foundation of the world. (5) I was hungry and you gave Me food to eat. I was thirsty and you gave Me drink. I was a stranger and you invited Me in, (6) naked and you clothed Me. I was sick and you visited Me. I was in prison and you came to Me.'

(7) "Then the righteous will answer Him, 'Lord, when did we see You hungry and feed you or thirsty and give You drink? (8) When did we see You a stranger and invite You in or naked and clothe You? (9) When did we see You sick or in prison and come to You?'

(10) "The King will answer them, 'Truly I say to you that to the extent that you did it to one of these brothers of Mine, even the least of them, you did it to Me.'

(11) "Then He will say to those on His left, 'Depart from Me, accursed ones, into the eternal fire that has been prepared for the devil and his angels. (12) I was hungry and you gave Me no food to eat. I was thirsty and you gave Me nothing to drink. (13) I was a stranger and you did not invite Me in, naked and you did not clothe Me, sick and in prison and you did not visit Me.'

(14) "Then they too will answer and say, 'Lord, when did we see You hungry or thirsty or a stranger or naked or sick or in prison and did not take care of You?'

(15) "Then He will say to them, 'Truly I say to you, to the extent that you did not do it to one of the least of these you did not do it to Me.'

(16) "And these will go away into eternal punishment but the righteous will enter into eternal life."

Notes: The glorious throne of Christ will be evident to everyone on that day and not just to the people who have believed in Him and obeyed His commandments. What will happen on that day is not just that the believers will be separated from the unbelievers (the unbelievers will know then, though they never believed it before, that there is a heaven and a hell and that they are lost). What will happen is that the true believers, the people who have been obedient to the will of God, will be separated from the people who have fooled themselves or tried to fool the world into believing that they are true Christians. These last are the people who have followed after other men or chosen their own way of worship, people who haven't bothered to find out what God required of them. These are the people who thought that just because they believed that Jesus lived or that there is a savior and that there is a God that they should and would be saved the same as the people who were obedient to the will of God. The atheists and agnostics and the willfully disobedient believers will know of a certainty that they aren't saved, and they won't need to be convinced of that fact by Jesus.

159 Jesus Is Sought in Jerusalem

(Matt. 26:1-5; Mark 14:1-2; Luke 22:1-2; John 11:55-57)

(1) When Jesus had finished all these words He said to His disciples, (2) "You know that after two days the Passover is coming and the Son of Man is to be delivered up for crucifixion."

(3) Now the Feast of Unleavened Bread, which is called the Passover of the Jews, was approaching, but before the Passover many people went up out of the country to purify themselves.

(4) Then the chief priests and the scribes and the elders of the people were gathered together in the court of the high priest who was named Caiaphas, and they plotted together seeking how they could seize Jesus by stealth and kill Him. (5) But they were saying, "Not during the festival lest a riot occur among the people." For they were afraid of the people.

(6) In Jeursalem the people were seeking for Jesus and as they stood in the temple they were asking one another, "What do you think? Will He come to the feast at all?"

(7) They were curious because the chief priests and the Pharisees had given orders that if anyone knew where Jesus was that person should report it so that they might seize Him.

Notes: Upon what day of the week this occurred is in doubt. We know it was two days before the Passover, but the day of the week the Passover was on is not clear either. In counting back from the first day of the week, the day upon which Jesus arose, it would seem that the day on which Jesus was presently speaking would be the second day of the week, or Monday, as we count the days. The Passover meal would have been eaten the night of the fourth day which would have preceded the day of the fourth day. Jesus would have been crucified on the fourth day of the week, have spent three days and three nights in the grave, and would have arisen on the first day of the next week. Conventional thinking is that the crucifixion was on Friday because the day after the crucifixion was a Sabbath day. However, Jesus said specifically that He would be in the grave three days and three nights which would have made the crucifixion to have been on Wednesday. Further, the Passover was followed by the Feast of Unleavened Bread which covered seven days, the first and seventh of which were also Sabbaths. For further information on this subject see Leviticus 23:5-8 (see appendix).

160 Judas Agrees to Betray Jesus

(Matt. 26:14-16; Mark 14:10-11; Luke 22:3-6)

(1) Then Satan entered into Judas Iscariot, who was one of the twelve, (2) and Judas went away and discussed with the chief priests and officers how he might betray Jesus to them.

(3) Judas asked them, "What are you willing to give me to deliver Jesus up to you?"

(4) The Jews were glad when they heard this and consented to give Judas money, and they weighed out to him thirty pieces of silver.

(5) Judas agreed to do it for that amount and from then on he began seeking a good opportunity to betray Jesus to the Jews at some place apart from the multitude.

Notes: It isn't known why Judas decided to betray Jesus to the chief priests. It may have been that he was offended because his advice about selling the ointment wasn't taken. Some people are offended because of such minor things as that. Too, we know he was the treasurer for the twelve apostles and that he was stealing some of the money for his own use. Perhaps, he thought the money from selling the ointment would have been put into the treasury and that he could then steal part of it. Perhaps, he was one of those people who choose to serve money rather than to serve Jesus. It could have been for any one of a number of other reasons, too. And it could have been that Judas was chosen to be one of the twelve, because Jesus knew his character was such that he would choose to betray Jesus but it would not have been just of God to *make* Judas be what he was just so that he would betray Jesus. God is a just God.

One biblical writer speculated that Judas may have become impatient waiting for Jesus to establish His kingdom and decided that betraying Him to the chief priests would accomplish that. How that would have forced or brought about the immediate establishment of the kingdom the writer didn't explain. The scriptures bear out the fact that Judas was a thief with a thief's mentality and a desire for things he couldn't have without stealing, and that his desires for the present were greater than his hopes for the future.

It might be pointed out, too, that Judas, knowing the desires of the chief priests and the elders, went to them seeking a reward by betraying Jesus rather than waiting in hopes of them approaching him for that purpose, which would have been a rather forlorn hope.

161 Preparing for the Passover

(Matt. 26:17-19; Mark 14:12-16; Luke 22:7-13)

(1) On the first day of Unleavened Bread when the Passover lamb was to be sacrificed (2) Jesus said to Peter and John, "Go and prepare the Passover for us, that we may eat it."

(3) They asked Him, "Where do You want us to prepare it?"

(4) Jesus said to them, "Go into the city and when you have entered the city you will meet a man carrying a pitcher of water. Follow him into the house he enters, (5) and you shall say to the owner of the house, 'The Teacher says to you, "My time is at hand. Where is the guest room in which I may eat the Passover with My disciples?"' (6) Then he will show you a large upper room furnished and ready. Prepare it there."

(7) Peter and John departed and did as Jesus had directed them and found everything just as He had told them, and they prepared the Passover.

Notes: The Law regarding the observance of the Passover and the Feast of Unleavened Bread is recorded in Leviticus 23:4-8.

Josephus, the Jewish historian, reported it in different places as being seven days and also eight days and as beginning on the fourteenth and again on the fifteenth of the month. The Law was clear, though, that the Passover was on the fourteenth day of the first month and that the Feast of Unleavened Bread began on the fifteenth of that month and lasted seven days.

Leaven had come to be regarded as a symbol of corruption because it caused bread to become stale much quicker than if the leaven had been left out of the bread. Jesus Himself referred to leaven in a disparaging way. The Jews remove all leaven from their homes on the night between the thirteenth and fourteenth of the month of Nisan, and there is no leaven in Jewish households during the days of the feast.

The method Jesus used to locate a place in which He and the apostles could eat the Passover meal could have been dictated by the fact that Jesus didn't want Judas to know in advance the location of the place where they were to eat. If Judas had known, that would have been a perfect time for him to betray Jesus because only Jesus and His disciples would have been there and none of the people would have known about Jesus being taken until later, perhaps not until after He had been killed.

Because so many Jews who lived in other places, even in foreign lands, went to Jerusalem to observe the Passover and the Feast of Unleavened Bread, it had become a custom for the residents of Jerusalem to open up their homes to guests at that time. It has been suggested that the man in whose home Jesus and the disciples ate the Passover was personally acquainted with Jesus and was possibly a close friend of Jesus. That may have been true but there is nothing in the scriptures to confirm it to be either true or false.

The reason Jesus wanted particularly to eat this, His last Passover meal, with the disciples may have been that the original of this event began with the sacrifice of a lamb and because of that sacrifice the angel of death passed over those who made the sacrifice. That first sacrifice was symbolic of the upcoming sacrifice of the Lamb of God, Jesus the Son of God, so that all people who take advantage of that sacrifice could be freed from their sins and saved from death. Too, this was to be the last opportunity before His crucifixion that Jesus would have to institute what has become known as the Lord's Supper or the Last Supper (see appendix).

162 Jesus Washes the Feet of the Disciples (John 13:3- 20)

(1) Knowing that the Father had put all things into His hands and that He had come from God and was going back to God,

(2) Jesus rose from the supper and laid aside His garments. He took a towel and girded Himself with it. (3) Then He poured water into a basin and began to wash the disciples' feet and to wipe them with the towel with which He had girded Himself.

(4) When Jesus came to Simon Peter, Peter said to Him, "Lord, are You going to wash my feet?"

(5) Jesus said to Peter, "You do not realize now what I do but you will understand later.'

(6) But Peter said to Jesus, "You shall never wash my feet!"

Jesus answered, "If I do not wash you, you have no part with Me."

(7) Simon Peter said, "Lord, not my feet only but also my hands and my head."

(8) Jesus said to Peter, "He who has bathed needs only to wash his feet but is completely clean. You are clean, but not all of you." (9) Jesus knew the one who was to betray Him and for this reason He had said, "Not all of you are clean."

(10) After Jesus had washed the disciples' feet and taken His garments and reclined again at the table He asked them, "Do you know what I have done to you?

(11) "You call Me Teacher and Lord, and you are right for so I am. (12) Then if I, the Lord and Teacher, washed your feet you ought also to wash one another's feet. (13) I gave you this example that you also should do as I did to you. (14) I tell you this truth, a slave is not greater than his master and neither is one who is sent greater than the one who sent him. (15) If you know these things you will be blessed if you do them.

(16) "I do not speak of all of you. I know the ones I have chosen, but I said it so that this scripture may be fulfilled: 'He who eats My bread has lifted up his heel against Me.'

(17) "From this time on I will tell you something before it comes about so that when if does happen you may believe that I am He. (18) In truth I say to you that he who receives whomever I send receives Me and he who receives Me receives Him who sent Me."

Notes: In those days, in that place, people didn't wear shoes and socks or stockings as we do, but they wore sandals over bare feet. There were very few paved roads and streets, and it wasn't possible for anyone to walk any distance on the dirt roads and streets without getting his feet dirty from the dust or mud. Ordinarily, there would have been a servant whose duty it was to wash the feet of all the men, but on this night, Jesus had chosen to be alone with the twelve men who were His particular disciples.

This was not just a person performing a menial task that no one else wanted to do, but it was a chance for Jesus to teach a valuable lesson to the men who would carry on His work when He was no longer there with them. They had been chosen to serve rather than to be served.

Some people have elected to treat this incident as a commandment, a necessary religious ritual, using as proof the fact that Jesus said, "I gave you this example that you also should do as I did to you." But the example was not the washing of the disciples' feet-it was showing them that no service was below the dignity of a Christian when that person did something, anything that needed doing. The washing of feet was not a rite of servitude or humility, but just a task that needed to be done.

163 Jesus Foretells His Betrayal and Judas Leaves

(Matt. 26:20-25; Mark 14:17-21; Luke 22:21-23; John 13:1-2, 21-30)

(1) Before the Feast of the Passover Jesus knew that the time had come that He should leave this world and return to the Father, and having loved His own who were in the world He loved them to the end.

(2) When it was evening Jesus was with the twelve, (3) and as they were reclining at the table and eating Jesus became troubled in spirit and said, "I say to you truly that one of you will betray Me-one who is eating with Me. (4) Indeed the Son of Man is to go, just as it has been determined and is written of Him, but woe to that man by whom the Son of Man is betrayed! It would have been better for that man if he had not been born."

(5) The disciples began looking at one another, at a loss to know of which one Jesus was speaking, (6) and they began to discuss among themselves which one of them it might be who was going to do this thing.

(7) Being deeply grieved they each one began to say to Jesus, "Surely not I, Lord."

(8) Jesus answered, "It is one of the twelve. He who dipped his hand with Me in the bowl is the one who will betray Me,

(9) and his hand is with Me on the table."

(10) Judas, who was betraying Jesus, said, "Surely it is not I, Rabbi?" Jesus said to Judas, "You have said it yourself."

(11) There was reclining close to Jesus one of His disciples, the one whom Jesus loved. (12) Simon Peter gestured and said to that disciple, "Tell us who it is of whom He is speaking."

(13) He, leaning back to Jesus, said to Him, "Lord, who is it?"

(14) Jesus answered, "That is the one for whom I shall dip the morsel and give it to him."

So when Jesus had dipped the morsel, He took it and gave it to Judas, the son of Simon Iscariot. (15) After the morsel Satan entered into Judas, having already put into his heart to betray Jesus.

Jesus said to Judas, "What you are going to do, do quickly."

(16) No one of the others reclining at the table knew why Jesus had said this to Judas. (17) Some were supposing, because Judas had the money box, that Jesus was saying to him, "Buy the things we have need of for the feast;" or else that he should give something to the poor. (18) After receiving the morsel Judas went out immediately, and it was then night.

Notes: Like many of the things in the life of Jesus, His betrayal by Judas was foretold in the Old Testament. Psalms 41:9 says, "Even my close friend, in whom I trusted, who ate my bread, has lifted up his heel against me." The companionship of Jesus and Judas over a period of three years would ordinarily have made them close friends; else, it would seem that Judas would have left the discipleship long before this. Jesus, of course, had known from the beginning that Judas would betray Him when the time came. But before that happened, Jesus told the other disciples that He would be betrayed so that later when they remembered that He had told them about it before the actual event, they would have more proof to offer confirming the fact that Jesus is the Messiah.

Even though Jesus knew from the beginning that Judas would betray Him, it appears that it still hurt Jesus when it happened. And it is very possible that Judas himself didn't know he would betray Jesus until only a short time before this. All the other disciples seem to have thought so highly of each other that each of them would as soon believe it was he who would betray his Lord as to believe that another of the twelve would do so. The form of the question in the original Greek indicates that each of them, when he asked if it was he, expected the answer to be "no."

Jesus was following the path that had been preordained for Him from the beginning and which had been revealed a little at a time by the prophets down through the ages. Although the betrayal had been predetermined, Judas was free to make the decision for himself. He was chosen to be one of the twelve because of his character. Jesus knew

Judas would do what he did, but the decision belonged to Judas alone. At any time, he could have changed his mind and repented. If Judas had been forced to do this against his will, and had then been punished by eternal damnation for doing so, that would not have been the act of a just God, and God is a just God. No! Judas, like all of us, was free to do as he wished, and he wished to do what he did.

164 Contention for Preference among the Twelve

(Luke 22:24-30)

(1) There arose a dispute among the twelve as to which one of them was regarded as the greatest.
(2) Jesus said to them, "The kings of the Gentiles lord it over them, and those who have authority over them are called 'Benefactors.' (3) But not so with you, but let him who is greatest among you become as the youngest, and the leader as the servant. (4) Who is greater, the one who reclines at the table or the one who serves? Is it not the one who reclines at the table? But I am among you as the One who serves, (5) and you are those who have stood by Me in My trials. (6) Just as My Father has granted Me a kingdom I grant you (7) that you may eat and drink at My table in My kingdom and you will sit on thrones judging the twelve tribes of Israel."

Notes: When Jesus said, "My time has come," the disciples must have thought He was ready to set up the earthly kingdom they expected, and here at the Passover meal they got into another argument as to which of them would be greatest in that kingdom. But they still had the wrong idea about greatness in the Lord's kingdom. This was the same argument that all of them had engaged in about six months previously. And the mother of James and John had gone with her sons to request the highest honors in the new kingdom. None of them had as yet any idea of what the new kingdom would be like.

165 The New Commandment (John 13:31-35)

(1) After Judas had gone out Jesus said, "Now the Son of Man has been glorified and God has been glorified in Him. (2) If God is glorified in Him, God will also glorify Him in Himself and will glorify Him immediately.

(3) "Little children, I am with you for a little while longer. You shall seek Me, and as I said to the Jews, I now say to you also, 'Where I am going, you cannot come.'

(4) "I give you a new commandment, that is, that you love one another. Even as I have loved you, you also shall love one another. (5) By this all men will know that you are My disciples, if you have love for one another."

Notes: When Judas left the upper room, he probably went directly to the priests who had given him the thirty pieces of silver. He knew where Jesus had been spending the nights, and he probably reasoned that Jesus would go to the same place this night too.

In calling the eleven "little children" Jesus was showing the tenderness of His love for them. After being with them for three years as mentor, teacher, example, and father figure He was going to leave them as orphans. They now would have to assume the roles for which He had been preparing them. They would have to look after themselves, make their own decisions, instead of Jesus being there to guide and direct them.

John, in his Epistles, called his readers "little children." Whether this was because he was emulating Jesus or not, we don't know. If it was for that reason, John could have had no better example.

Back in John 7:36 (section 96), we read about a conversation Jesus had with the Jews. At that time Jesus told the Jews that they couldn't go where He was going. It's that conversation and that statement to which Jesus is referring here.

In Leviticus 19:18 the Law stated,"... You shall love your neighbor as yourself ...," but this new commandment Jesus gave called for greater love than that. They (and we) should love others as Jesus loved His disciples. That love was not as brother for brother, or father for son, or mother for daughter, and not even as husband for wife, but as Jesus loved those disciples. How great was that love? Listen to what Jesus said in John 15:13: "Greater love has no man than this, that one lay down his life for his friends."

166 The Lord's Supper

(Matt. 26:26-29; Mark 14:22-25; Luke 22:14-20)

(1) When the hour to eat the Passover had come Jesus reclined at the table with the apostles. (2) Jesus said to them, "I have earnestly desired to eat this Passover with you before I suffer."

(3) While they were eating Jesus took some bread and, after a blessing, He broke it and gave it to the disciples and said, "Take it and eat. This is My body. Do this in remembrance of **Me.**"

(4) In the same way Jesus took the cup and gave thanks and gave it to them, saying, "Drink from it, all of you. (5) This is My blood of the covenant which is poured out for you and the many for forgiveness of sons. (6) Truly I say to you, I will never again drink of this fruit of the vine until the day when I drink it new with you in My Father's kingdom."

And they all drank from the cup.

Notes: This is the account of the institution of what we call "the Lord's supper" or "communion." Of the four accounts of the Gospel, John's is the only one that doesn't include a record of that event. That seems rather strange because the eating of the Lord's Supper is one of the very few rituals we have in the Christian church. If Matthew hadn't recorded this, the account by Paul in 1 Corinthians may have been the only account we would have of the beginning of this ritual and the details of how it began.

Part of the dogma of the Catholic Church is a doctrine which Catholics call "transubstantiation." That means that they believe the bread and the wine are literally changed into the body and the blood of Jesus when it has been blessed by a priest. The only argument that can be presented in support of that doctrine are the words of Jesus when He said, "This is My body," and, "This is My blood." However, that is also one of the principal arguments against the doctrine because at the first "Lord's Supper" the bread and the wine were not literally the body and blood of Jesus even when He said, "This is My body," and, "This is My blood." His body had not yet been sacrificed nor His blood shed.

In those days, in Eastern countries and among Eastern people, it was the custom to seal agreements with blood. This was true of God's people too. For the forgiveness of sin, a blood sacrifice was required. Jesus said His blood was poured out for many. Paul wrote that Jesus died for *all-for* our sins that was the blood sacrifice. That was the blood that seals the pact between God and all others who become a part of the agreement.

Jesus didn't say when or how often we should observe communion. He did say that when we did observe it we were to do it in remembrance of Him. Paul reported in 1 Corinthians 11:25 that Jesus said, "This cup is the new covenant in My blood; do this, as often as you drink it, in remembrance of Me." We do have an example cited in Acts 20:7 which reads, "And on the first day of the week, when we were gathered together to break bread... " In one other place there is an implication that the saints met on every first day of the week and the assumption is that this meeting was for the purpose of observing the Lord's supper. 1 Corinthians 16:2 reads, "On the first day of every week let each one of you put aside and save, as he may prosper, that no collection be made when I come."

In the absence of a direct command to partake of the Lord's Supper every first day of the week many denominations hold to the opinion that they may observe it only once a month or once a quarter or even once a year. Whether or not they are technically correct, it certainly would not be out of line to partake of it weekly. The important thing must be how we partake and not how often we partake. It would be better to partake only once a year in reverence, humility, and, above all, remembrance, than to partake weekly with no thought for the meaning of what we do.

167 Peter's Denial Foretold (Matt. 26:31-35;

Mark 14:27-31; Luke 22:31-34; John 13:36-38)

(1) Simon Peter said to Jesus, "Lord, where are You going?" Jesus answered, "Where I am going you cannot follow Me now, but you shall follow Me later."

(2) Peter said, "Lord, why can I not follow You right now? I will lay down my life for You."

(3) Jesus answered, "Will you lay down your life for Me?

(4) Simon, Simon! Listen, Satan has demanded permission to sift you like wheat (5) but I have prayed for you, that your faith may not fail. When once you have turned again strengthen your brothers."

(6) Then Jesus said to the disciples, "You will all fall away because of Me this night for it is written, 'I will strike down the shepherd and the sheep of the flock shall be scattered.' (7) But after I have been raised I will go before you to Galilee."

(8) Peter said to Jesus, "Even though all may fall away because of You, I will never fall away."

(9) Jesus said to him, "The truth is that you yourself this very night before a cock crows shall deny three times that you know Me."

(10) But Peter kept insisting, "Lord, with You I am ready to go both to prison and to death! Even if I have to die with You I will not deny You!"

And all the other disciples were saying the same thing.

Notes: The prophecy Jesus quoted is from Zechariah 13:7.

The words of Jesus indicate that He knew what Satan could do and that He knew Satan wanted to put the faith of Peter and the other disciples on trial like he had tried the faith of Job. We don't know what kinds of trials Satan would have used nor how the apostles, *at this time,* would have handled them. We know that later in their lives the faith of these same apostles was tried in a lot of ways and in a lot of places, some of them about which we know being imprisonment or death because of their faith. Jesus knew what trials Peter and the others would face and that afterwards Peter would need to repent or, as one version puts it, be converted.

Too, the language Jesus used seems to suggest that after Peter overcomes his trials he will have become stronger and that his strength will be needed to help the others through their trials.

Mark's Gospel says that Peter would deny Jesus three times before the cock would crow twice, but all three of the other accounts of this incident say nothing about the cock crowing more than once. The commentators ignore this apparent discrepancy, and it is certainly not an important difference.

168 Disciples Told to Have Purse, Bag, and Sword

(Luke 22:35-38)

(1) Jesus asked the disciples, "When I sent you out without purse and bag and sandals did you lack for anything?"

They answered, "No, nothing."

(2) Jesus said, "But now let those who have a purse and a bag take them along, and let him who has no sword sell his outer garment and buy one. (3) I tell you that this which is written must be fulfilled in Me, 'And He was numbered with transgressors,' for that which refers to Me has its fulfillment."

(4) They said, "Lord, look, here are two swords." Jesus said to them, "It is enough."

Notes: You will recall that much earlier in His ministry Jesus sent out the twelve men whom He had chosen to be apostles. They went out two by two to preach, to heal, and to do the work of the Lord. Jesus told them not to take with them money nor extra clothing nor extra sandals, that whatever they needed would be furnished by the people to whom they preached and served. Now Jesus is telling them that things will be different after He is gone-that they are to take extra clothing and money and provisions and a weapon with which to defend themselves. With the exception of Peter's use of a sword to cut off the ear of Malchus, it isn't recorded that any of them ever used a weapon for self-defense or for any other reason, even though they were told by Jesus to take a sword.

The prophecy Jesus quoted is from Isaiah 53:12. It tells what people in general would think of Jesus and, because they thought of Him in that way, they would think of the apostles in that same way.

Jesus was not telling the apostles that carrying a sword would keep them safe, rather He may have been warning them that they would face many perils after He was gone, and certainly some of them did die a violent death. Or perhaps, Jesus was saying that we are allowed to use weapons in defense of our own lives and the lives of our loved ones-such defensive actions have not been forbidden.

Many Bible students have taken the position that the scriptures say that a person may not kill another person for any reason, even in defense of their own lives. A few have even gone so far as to take the position that a person could not kill any living thing. Such thinking is in error. At the time Moses received this (and the other) commandment(s), the Israelites were actively engaged (or would soon be) in the annihilation of the people in the land they were to occupy. Too, the popular translation of that particular commandment should have been rendered as "thou shalt not commit murder" rather than "thou shalt not kill."

169 The Farewell Discourse of Jesus (John 14:1-16:33)

(1) "Let not your heart be troubled. Believe in God, believe also in Me.

(2) "In My Father's house are many dwelling places. If it were not so I would have told you, for I go to prepare a place for you. (3) And if I go and prepare a place for you I will come again and receive you to myself, so that where I am you may be also. (4) And you know the way where I am going."

(5) Thomas said to Jesus, "Lord, we do not know where You are going. How do we know the way?"

(6) Jesus said to him, "I am the way and the truth and the life. No one comes to the Father but through Me. (7) If you had known Me you would have known My Father also. From now on you know Him and have seen Him."

(8) Philip said to Jesus, "Lord, show us the Father and it is enough for us."

(9) Jesus said to him, "Have I been so long with you and yet you have not come to know Me, Philip? He who has seen Me has seen the Father. How do you say, 'Show us the Father'?

(10) "Do you not believe that I am in the Father and the Father is in Me? I do not speak the words that I say to you on My own initiative, but the Father abiding in Me does His works. (11) Believe Me that I am in the Father and the Father in Me. Otherwise believe on account of the works themselves.

(12) "Truly, truly, I say to you, he who believes in Me shall also do the works that I do. Greater works than these shall he do because I go to the Father. (13) And whatever you ask in My name I will do so that the Father may be glorified in the Son. (14) If you ask Me anything in My name I will do it. (15) If you love Me you will keep My commandments.

(16) "I will ask the Father and He will give you another Helper so that He may be with you forever. He is the Spirit of truth whom the world cannot receive because it does not behold Him or know Him. You know Him because He abides with you and will be in you. (18) I will not leave you as orphans; I will come to you.

(19) "After a little while the world will behold Me no more, but you will behold Me. Because I live you shall live also. (20) In that day you shall know that I am in My Father, and you in Me and I in you.

(21) "He who has My commandments and keeps them is he who loves Me, and he who loves Me shall be loved by My Father, and I will love him and will disclose Myself to him."

(22) Judas (not Iscariot) said to Jesus, "Lord, what then has happened that You are going to disclose Yourself to us and not to the world?"

(23) Jesus answered him, "If anyone loves Me he will keep My word, and My Father will love him. We will come to him and make Our abode with him, (24) He who does not love Me does not keep My words. The word which you hear is not Mine but the Father's who sent Me.

(25) "These things I have spoken to you while abiding with you. (26) But the Helper, the Holy Spirit whom the Father will send in My name, will teach you all things and bring to your remembrance all that I said to you.

(27) "Peace I leave with you. My peace I give to you, not as the world gives do I give to you. Let not your heart be troubled nor let it be fearful.

(28) "You heard that I said to you, 'I go away and I will come to you.' If you loved Me you would have rejoiced because I go to the Father, for the Father is greater than I.

(29) "Now I have told you before it comes to pass so that when it comes to pass you may believe. (30) I will not speak much more with you for the ruler of the world is coming, and he has nothing in Me. (31) But that the world may know that I love the Father, and as the Father gave Me commandment even so I do.

"Arise, let us go from here.

(32) "I am the true vine and My Father is the vine-dresser. (33) Every branch in Me that does not bear fruit He takes away, and every branch that bears fruit He prunes that it may bear more fruit.

(34) "You are already clean because of the word which I have spoken to you. (35) Abide in Me and I in you. As the branch cannot bear fruit of itself unless it abides in the vine, so neither can you unless you abide in Me. (36) I am the vine, you are the branches. He who abides in Me, and I in him, bears much fruit, for apart from Me you can do nothing. (37) Anyone who does not abide in Me is thrown away as a branch and dries up. The dried branches are gathered and cast into the fire and burned. (38) If you abide in Me and My words abide in you, ask whatever you wish and it shall be done for you. (39) By this is My Father glorified, that you bear much fruit and so prove to be My disciples.

(40) "Just as the Father has loved Me I have also loved you. Abide in My love. (41) If you keep My commandments you will abide in My love, just as I have kept My Father's commandments and abide in His love. (42) These things I have spoken to you that My joy may be in you and that your joy may be made full.

(43) "This is My commandment, that you love one another just as I have loved you. (44) Greater love has no one than this, that one lay down his life for his friends. (45) You are My friends if you do what I command you. (46) No longer do I call you slaves for the slave does not know what his master is doing. I have called you My friends for all things that I have heard from My Father I have made known to you.

(47) "You did not choose Me but I chose you and appointed you that you should go and bear fruit and that your fruit should remain so that whatever you ask of the Father in My name He may give to you. (48) This I command you, that you love one another.

(49) "If the world hates you you know that it has hated Me before it hated you. (50) If you were of the world the world would love its own.

Because you are not of the world, but I chose you out of the world, the world hates you.

(51) "Remember the word that I said to you, 'A slave is not greater than his master.' If they persecuted Me they will also persecute you. If they kept My word they will keep yours also.

(52) "All these things they will do to you for My name's sake because they do not know the One who sent Me. (53) If I had not come and spoken to them they would not be with sin but now they have no excuse for their sin. (54) He who hates Me hates My Father also.

(55) "If I had not done among them the works which no one else did they would not have sin, but now they have both seen and hated Me and My Father as well. (56) They have done this in order that the word that is written in their Law may be fulfilled, 'They hated Me without a cause.'

(57) "When the Helper comes, whom I will send to you from the Father, that is the Spirit of truth who proceeds from the Father, He will bear witness of Me, (58) and you will bear witness also because you have been with Me from the beginning.

(59) "I have spoken these things to you that you may be kept from stumbling. (60) They will make you outcasts from the synagogue, but an hour is coming for everyone who kills you to think that he is offering service to God. (61) They will do these things because they have not known the Father or Me.

(62) These things I have spoken to you, when their hour comes, you may remember that I told you of them. I did not say these things to you at the beginning because I was with you.

(63) "Now I am going to Him who sent Me and none of you asks Me, 'Where are You going?' (64) Because I have said these things to you sorrow has filled your heart.

(65) "I tell you the truth, it is to your advantage that I go away because if I do not go away the Helper shall not come to you. If I go I will send Him to you. (66) And He, when He comes, will convict the world concerning sin and righteousness and judgment; (67) concerning sin because they do not believe in Me, (68) concerning righteousness because I go to the Father and you no longer behold Me, (69) and concerning judgment because the ruler of this world has been judged.

(70) "I have many more things to say to you but you cannot bear them now. (71) But when He, the Spirit of truth, comes He will guide you into all the truth, for He will not speak on His own initiative but whatever He hears He will speak, and He will disclose to you what is to come. (72) He shall glorify Me for He shall take of Mine and shall disclose it to you. (73) All things that the Father has are Mine, therefore I said that He takes of Mine and will disclose it to you.

(74) "A little while and you will no longer behold Me, and again a little while and you will see Me."

(75) Some of Jesus' disciples said to one another, "What is this thing He is telling us, 'A little while and you will not behold Me, and again a little while and you will see Me,' and, 'because I go to the Father'?"

(76) And they were saying, "What is this that He says, 'A little while'? We do not know what He is talking about."

(77) Jesus knew that they wished to question Him and He said to them, "Are you deliberating together about this that I said, 'A little while and you will not behold Me, and again a little while and you will see Me'? (78) Truly, truly, I say to you that you will weep and lament but the world will rejoice. You will be sorrowful but your sorrow will be turned to joy. (79) Whenever a woman is in travail she has sorrow because her hour has come but when she gives birth to the child she remembers the anguish no more because of the joy that a child has been born into the world. (80) You now have sorrow but I will see you again and your heart will rejoice, and no one will take your joy away from you.

(81) "In that day you will ask Me no questions. Truly, truly, I say to you, if you shall ask the Father for anything He will give it to you in My name. (82) Until now you have asked for nothing in My name. Ask and you will receive that your joy may be made full.

(83) "These things I have spoken to you in figurative language. An hour is coming when I will speak no more to you in figurative language, but will tell you plainly of the Father.

(84) In that day you will ask in My name, and I do not say to you that I will request the Father on your behalf (85) for the Father Himself loves you because you have loved Me and have believed that I came forth from the Father. (86) I came forth from the Father and have come into the world. I am leaving the world again and going to the Father."

(87) Jesus' disciples said, "Lo, now You are speaking plainly and are not using figures of speech. (88) Now we know that You know all things and have no need for anyone to question You. By this we believe that You came from God."

(89) Jesus answered them, "Do you now believe?

(90) "Behold, an hour is coming, and has already come, for you to be scattered each to his own home and to leave Me alone. Yet I am not alone because the Father is with Me.

(91) "These things I have spoken to you that in Me you may have peace. In the world you have tribulation, but take courage, I have overcome the world."

Notes: This last discourse of Jesus to the apostles took place the night before the crucifixion. At least parts of it are familiar to all of us. Some of it is used in many funeral services. Probably every part of it has been the basis of numerous sermons. And all of it teaches lessons we need to know. What Jesus said here, this last discourse, was only partly for the apostles-it was also partly a lesson for all the world to know.

The Old Testament scripture that Jesus quoted, "They hated Me without a cause," is from Psalms 35:19 and Psalms 69:4.

170 Jesus's Prayer for His People (John 17:1-26)

(1) Jesus spoke these things and, lifting up His eyes to heaven, He said, "Father, the hour has come. Glorify Your Son that the Son may glorify You, (2) even as You gave Him authority over all mankind, that to all those You have given Him, He may give eternal life. (3) This is eternal life, that they may know you, the only true God, and Jesus Christ whom You sent.

(4) "I glorified You on the earth, having accomplished the work which You gave Me to do. (5) Now glorify Me together with Yourself, Father, with the glory that I had with You before the world was.

(6) "I manifested Your name to the men whom You gave Me out of the world. They were Yours and You gave them to Me, and they have kept Your word. (7) Now they have come to know that everything You have given Me is from You, (8) for I have given to them the words which

You gave Me. They have received Your words and truly understood that I came forth from You, and they believed that You did send Me.

(9) "I ask on their behalf (I do not ask on behalf of the world but of those You have given Me) for they are Yours. (10) All things that are Mine are Yours and Yours are Mine, and I have been glorified in them.

(11) "I am no more in the world and yet they themselves are in the world, and I come to You. Holy Father, keep them in your name, the name which You have given Me, that they may be one even as We are. (12) While I was with them I was keeping them in Your name which You have given Me. I guarded them and not one of them perished but the son of perdition, that the scripture might be fulfilled.

(13) "Now I come to You, and these things I speak in the world that they may have My joy made full in themselves. (14) I have given them Your word and the world has hated them because they are not of the world even as I am not of the world.

(15) I do not ask You to take them out of the world but to keep them from the evil one. (16) They are not of the world even as I am not of the world. (17) Sanctify them in the truth-Your word is truth.

(18) "As You did send Me into the world I also have sent them into the world. (19) For their sakes I sanctify Myself that they themselves also may be sanctified in truth.

(20) "I do not ask in behalf of these alone but for those also who believe in Me through their word, (21) that they may all be one even as You, Father, are in Me and I in You and that they also may be in Us, so that the world may believe that You did send Me. (22) The glory which You have given Me I have given to them so that they may be one just as We are one, (23) I in them and You in Me, and that they may be perfected in unity. This is so that the world may know that You did send Me and did love them even as You did love Me.

(24) "Father, I also desire that these whom You have given Me may be with Me where I am in order that they may behold My glory, the glory which You have given Me, for You did love Me before the foundation of the world.

(25) "O righteous Father, although the world has not known You, yet I have known You, and these have known that You did send Me.

(26) I have made Your name known to them and will make it known so that the love wherewith You did love Me may be in them and I in them."

Notes: In this prayer, Jesus is speaking to His Father as though God had no knowledge of those things about which He was speaking. In praying to His Father, only on a very few occasions were the prayers of Jesus recorded as having been spoken aloud. We don't know whether all the prayers of Jesus to God were spoken aloud or if some of them were spoken silently. This one was spoken aloud, and it was spoken for the benefit of the apostles who heard it rather than to inform God to whom it was prayed. When a public prayer is offered for the benefit of one of us who is present at the time, for some reason that person seems to feel more humble and closer to God than at other times. Perhaps that's the reason Jesus prayed aloud on this occasion.

171 Jesus and His Disciples Go to the Garden of Gethsemane on the Mount of Olives

(Matt. 26:30; Mark 14:26; Luke 22:39; John 18:1)

(1) When Jesus had spoken these words He and the disciples sang a hymn and afterwards they went forth, as was the custom of Jesus, over the ravine of the Kidron to the Mount of Olives.
(2) There was a garden there into which He Himself entered with his disciples.

Notes: The scriptures don't tell us for sure, but probably until now, Jesus and the eleven were still in the upper room where they had eaten the Passover meal together.

The Kidron brook and ravine ran along the eastern wall of the city of Jerusalem between the temple and the Mount of Olives.

172 The Agony in the Garden

(Matt. 26:36-46; Mark 14:32-42; Luke 22:40-46)

(1) Jesus came with the disciples to a place called Gethsemane and said to them, "Sit here while I go over there and pray."

(2) Jesus took with Him Peter and the sons of Zebedee, James and John, and began to be grieved and distressed. (3) Then He said to them. "My soul is deeply grieved to the point of death. Remain here and keep watch with Me."

(4) Then Jesus went a little beyond them, about a stone's throw, and fell to the ground on His face and began to pray that if it were possible the hour might pass Him by. (5) He prayed, "My Father, all things are possible for You, remove this cup from Me. Yet not what I will but what You will."

(6) Now an angel from heaven appeared to Jesus, strengthening Him, (7) and being in agony He was praying very fervently, and His sweat became like drops of blood falling down upon the ground.

(8) When Jesus rose from prayer He came to the disciples and found them sleeping. He said to Peter, "Simon, are you asleep? Could you men not keep watch with Me for one hour?

(9) Keep watching and praying that you may not enter into temptation. The spirit is willing but the flesh is weak."

(10) Jesus went away a second time and prayed, "My Father, if this cannot pass away unless I drink it Your will be done."

(11) Again Jesus came and found the disciples sleeping, for their eyes were very heavy, and they did not know what to answer Him.

(13) Jesus left them again and went away and prayed a third time saying the same thing once more. (13) Then He came back to the disciples and said to them, "Are you still sleeping and taking your rest? It is enough. The hour is at hand and the Son of Man is being betrayed into the hands of sinners. (14) Arise, let us be going. The one who betrays Me is at hand!"

Notes: Why did Jesus pray to His Father that the things that were going to happen right away wouldn't happen? That has to be a rhetorical question, because we can't know the answer. The reason Jesus had to die was the reason He had come into the world-to die as a sacrifice for the sins of all the people who would accept Him as their savior. He had known from the beginning not only that He had to die but what manner of death it was to be. Long before this, in His ministry, Jesus had made many references to "the cross," "being lifted up," "people bearing their own crosses," etc.

All animals have instinctive fears. Dumb animals fear death without understanding the meaning of death. They fear other animals, they fear man, and their fears are born with them. Human babies are said to be born with an instinctive fear of falling. As they grow in knowledge and understanding, they come to fear other things that can harm them, too, like fire and water. And they come to fear death too. Most people have a fear of death during at least some parts of their lives. In most cases, though, the fear is not of death but of the uncertainty of what follows death. With Jesus, though, He had no fear of death itself, because He knew it couldn't hold him, but as a man He could feel pain just like any other person, and He knew the intense physical agony that He would have to suffer in crucifixion, and like any other sane person, he dreaded that. There are various opinions among biblical scholars as to the reason for the intense sorrow Jesus had, but since the scriptures don't reveal the answer, it would be useless to speculate further. There are two things concerning the coming crucifixion that Jesus must have felt; that, as a man, He dreaded the pain, the agony, the humiliation, and the death which were before Him; and that as God, He feared that whatever He did, it wouldn't be enough to convince and to save all people.

The writer Doddridge wrote, "Aristotle and Diodorus Siculus both mention bloody sweats as attending some extraordinary agony of mind; and I find Loti [Pierre, pseudonym of Louis-Marie-Julien Viaud], in his Life of Pope Sextus V., and Sir John Chardin in his History of Persia, mentioning a like phenomena, to which Dr. Jackson [Jesse Louis] adds another from Thuanus." Also, Voltaire [pseudonym of Francois-Marie Arouet] in his *Universal History* wrote of Charles IX of France, "He died in his thirty fifth year. His disorder was of a very remarkable kind; the blood oozed out of all his pores. This malady, of which there have been other instances, was owing either to excessive fear, or violent agitation, or to a feverish and melancholy temperament." We can see from these writings that when Jesus sweated blood, it was not unique in the annals of mankind.

At the last Jesus was not telling those three disciples that they could continue their sleep, but that they had had enough sleep already. Now it was time to arise and go to meet His betrayer and the people who would have Him killed. Those people were on their way to take Him and they were drawing near.

173 Betrayal and Arrest of Jesus

(Matt. 26:47-56; Mark 14:43-52; Luke 22:47-53; John 18:2-11)

(1) While Jesus was still speaking a multitude came with officers from the chief priests, Pharisees, scribes and elders of the people bearing lanterns and torches and with swords and clubs. Judas, who was betraying Jesus, was preceding the multitude. (2) Now Judas knew the place also for Jesus had often met there with His disciples.

(3) Jesus, knowing all the things that were to come upon Him, went forward and said to the multitude, "Whom do you seek?"

(4) They answered Him, "Jesus the Nazarene."

Jesus answered, "I am He." Judas, who was betraying Jesus was standing with them.

(5) When Jesus said to them, "I am He," they drew back and fell to the ground.

(6) Again Jesus asked them, "Whom do you seek?" They said, "Jesus the Nazarene."

(7) Jesus answered, "I told you that I am He. If you seek Me let these go their way." (8) He said this that the word which He spoke might be fulfilled, "Of those whom You have given Me I lost not one."

(9) Then Jesus said to the chief priests and officers of the temple and elders who had come against Him, "Have you come out with swords and clubs to arrest Me as though I am a robber? Every day I used to sit with you in the temple teaching and you did not lay hands on Me. (10) But all this has taken place that the Scriptures of the prophets may be fulfilled, but this hour and the power of darkness are yours."

(11) Now Judas had given them a sign. He said, "Whomever I shall kiss, He is the one. Seize Him and lead Him away under guard." (12) Judas, having received the Roman cohort, approached Jesus to kiss Him.

(13) Then Jesus said to Judas, "Friend, do what you have come for."
(14) Immediately Judas went to Jesus and said, "Hail, Rabbi!" and kissed Him.

(15) Jesus said to Judas, "Judas, are you betraying the Son of Man with a kiss?" (16) Then they came and seized Jesus.

(17) When those who were around Jesus saw what was going to happen they said, "Lord, shall we strike with the sword?" (18) Then Simon Peter, having a sword, drew it and struck the high priest's slave and cut off his right ear (the slave's name was Malchus).

(19) But Jesus said, "Stop! No more of this. Let them do as they will." And He touched the ear of Malchus and healed him.

(20) Then Jesus said to Peter, "Put your sword back into its sheath. All those who take up the sword shall perish by the sword. (21) Do you think that I cannot appeal to My Father and He will at once put at My disposal more than twelve legions of angels? (22) Shall I not drink the cup which the Father has given Me? (23) How then shall the Scriptures be fulfilled, that it must happen this way?" (24) Then all the disciples left Him and fled.

(25) A certain young man was following Jesus and he was wearing nothing but a linen sheet over his naked body, and the multitude seized him, (26) but he left the linen sheet behind and escaped naked.

Notes: Even though the moon was supposed to be full at that time, the lanterns and torches were necessary because the Garden of Gethsemane was located in the Kidron Valley between the Mount of Olives and the hills upon which Jerusalem was built. The moon would have been low in the west below the horizon as seen from the valley so it would have been quite dark in the garden.

When Jesus identified Himself to the people who comprised the mob, they all stepped backward and some of them fell to the ground. Probably there were some people in the mob who had seen Jesus perform miracles. Some of them had seen Him in the temple and heard Him teaching. Perhaps there were some there who had tried to entrap Him with their questions. Perhaps some of them, having seen the miracles Jesus performed, had fears that He could and would harm them because of what they were doing. Certainly it would have been difficult for any of those people not to have admiration for Jesus, even though they were determined to have Him killed. Perhaps some of them even believed what the chief priest had said about it being expedient for one person to die for the many.

We might wonder a little bit about the lack of proficiency of Peter with his sword. He was a simple fisherman and probably had never used a sword either to defend himself or to attack anyone else. If he had been proficient with the weapon, he might have severely wounded or killed Malchus. But for Jesus, to restore a life would have been as simple as restoring an ear.

Jesus said, "Of those whom You have given Me I lost not one," so that the scriptures might be fulfilled. Such a passage cannot be found in the Old Testament. However, in His recent prayer for the people that is included in section 169, Jesus did say in that prayer, "While I was with them, I was keeping them in Your name which You have given Me; and I guarded them, and not one of them perished but the son of perdition, that the scripture might be fulfilled."

The young man who came with only a linen cloth wrapped around him is unidentified. Perhaps he was someone who had heard the noise of the mob and got up out of bed to see what was happening, wrapping himself with the handiest thing he could find at the moment. He was not one of the eleven, and he was not one of the mob. Albert Barnes speculated that perhaps he was the owner of the garden and a friend of Jesus who came to see what was going on and to see if there was anything he could do to help.

174 Jesus Examined by Annas (John 18:12-14, 19-23)

(1) The Roman cohort and the commander and the officers of the Jews arrested Jesus and bound Him (2) and led Him to Annas first, for he was father-in-law of Caiaphas who was high priest that year. (3) Now Caiaphas was the one who had advised the Jews that it was expedient for one man to die on behalf of the people.

(4) The high priest questioned Jesus about His disciples and about His teaching.

(5) Jesus answered, "I have spoken openly to the world. I always taught in the synagogues and in the temple where all the Jews come together and I spoke nothing in secret. (6) Why do you question Me? Question those who have heard what I spoke to them. Look, they know what I said."

(7) When Jesus had said this one of the officers standing by gave Him a blow and asked, "Is that the way you answer the high priest?"

(8) Jesus asked him, "If I have spoken wrongly bear witness of the wrong, but if I spoke rightly why do you strike **Me?**"

Notes: Annas was the father-in-law of Caiaphas the high priest. Caiaphas served as high priest from AD 18 to AD 36. A parenthetical phrase here states that it was Caiaphas who had told the Jews that it was expedient that one man should die for the people. That was reported in chapter eleven of John, section 112, when the Jews were plotting and trying to decide what they could do about Jesus.

Jesus was probably taken to Annas instead of Caiaphas, because the Jews considered Annas to be the real or true high priest. According to Jewish tradition, a high priest served in that office for life. The Romans, however, had removed Annas from office and replaced him with several others and eventually with Caiaphas. Flavius Josephus reported the succession of high priests as follows:

This man [Valerius Gratus] deprived Annus [sic] of the high priesthood, and appointed Ismael, the son of Phabi, to be high priest. He also deprived him in a little time, and ordained Eleazar, the son of Ananus, who had been high priest before, to be high priest; which office, when he had held for a year, Gratus deprived him of it, and gave the high priesthood to Simon, the son of Camithus; and when he had possessed that dignity no longer than a year, Joseph Caiaphas was made his successor.

Even though Annas had been removed from office by the Romans, the Jews still honored him as their high priest and considered him to be above Caiaphas. It is said that Annas made five of his sons and sons-in-law high priests.

175 Jesus Examined by Caiaphas and Condemned by the Sanhedrin

(Matt. 26:57, 59-68; Mark 14:53, 55-65;
Luke 22:54a, 63-71; John 18:24)

(1) Annas had Jesus bound and those who had seized Him led Him away to Caiaphas the high priest, where the chief priests and the scribes and the elders were gathered together.

(2) When it was day the Council of elders of the people assembled, both chief priests and scribes, and they led Jesus away to the council chamber.

(3) Now the chief priests and the whole Council kept trying to obtain false testimony against Jesus in order that they might put Him to death, but they did not find any. (4) Even though many false witnesses came forward and gave false testimony against Jesus their testimony was not consistent.

(5) But later on two men came forward and stood up and began to give false testimony against Jesus. They said, (6) "We heard Him say, 'I will destroy this temple of God made with hands and in three days I will build another not made with hands.'" (7) Not even in this was their testimony consistent.

(8) Then the high priest stood up and came forward and questioned Jesus, "Do you make no answer?" he asked. "What is it that these men are testifying against You?"

(9) But Jesus kept silent and made no answer. Again the high priest questioned Him, "I command You by the living God that You tell me whether You are the Christ, the Son of God."

(10) Jesus said to him, "You have said it yourself. If I tell you, you will not believe, and if I ask a question you will not answer. (11) Nevertheless I tell you that hereafter you shall see the Son of Man sitting at the right hand of the power of God and coming on the clouds of heaven."

(12) They all asked, "Are You the Son of God then?" Jesus said to them, "Yes, I am."

(13) Then the high priest tore his robes and said, "He has blasphemed! What further need do we have of witnesses? You also have now heard the blasphemy. (14) What do you think?"

(15) They answered, "He is deserving of death!"

(16) The men who were holding Jesus in custody were mocking Him and beating Him. (17) Some began to spit at Him and they blindfolded Him and beat Him with their fists and said to Him, "Prophecy to us, You Christ. Who is the one who hit You?" And the officers received Him with slaps to the face.

(18) And they were saying many other things against Jesus, blaspheming Him.

Notes: The text reads, "Even though many false witnesses came forward and gave false testimony against Him their testimony was not consistent." In Deuteronomy 17:6, the Law reads, "On the evidence of two witnesses or three witnesses, he who is to die shall be put to death; he shall not be put to death on the evidence of one witness." Because the testimony of the false witnesses was inconsistent, that is, no two witnesses testified to the same thing, their testimony couldn't be used to convict Jesus.

Eventually, two men came forward with testimony against Jesus, testimony which seemed to be consistent to some degree. Even though their testimony didn't agree, it was close enough so that it was acceptable to the council. The actual words of Jesus as recorded in John 2:19 were, "Destroy this temple, and in three days I will raise it up." The chief priests and Pharisees might have pretended not to understand what Jesus meant, but they stated to Pilate in Matthew 27:63, "Sir, we remember that when He was still alive that deceiver said, 'After three days I am to rise again.'" That was proof that they did understand what Jesus meant.

That Jesus would not defend Himself against the charges brought against Him was prophesied in Isaiah 53:7 as follows: "He was oppressed and He was afflicted, yet He did not open His mouth; like a lamb that is led to slaughter, and like a sheep that is silent before its shearers, so He did not open His mouth."

The question Jesus was asked, whether He was the Christ, the son of God, was, to the Jews, a two-part question, because to them the

Christ was not necessarily the Son of God. In the days of the prophets, the Messiah was believed to be the Son of God, but these Jews no longer believed that. Their Messiah was a physical deliverer in the same way that the judges were physical deliverers, and the Messiah was supposed to deliver them from the oppression and rule of the Romans. For Jesus to answer both parts of the question in the affirmative would, in the eyes of His questioners, brand Him a braggart and a blasphemer.

176 Peter Denies Jesus

(Matt. 26:58, 69-75; Mark 14:54, 66-72;
Luke 22:54b-62; John 18:15-18, 25-27)

(1) Simon Peter was following Jesus at a distance and so was another disciple. Now that other disciple was known to the high priest and he entered with Jesus into the courtyard of the high priest. (2) Peter, though, was standing at the door outside. So the other disciple, the one who was known to the high priest, went out and spoke to the doorkeeper and brought in Peter.

(3) The slaves and officers had kindled a charcoal fire in the middle of the courtyard for it was cold and they were standing there warming themselves. Peter was there with them standing and warming himself at the fire, waiting to see the outcome.

(4) As Peter was below in the courtyard the slave girl of the high priest who kept the door came (5) and, seeing Peter as he sat in the firelight, she looked intently at him and said, "You are also one of this man's disciples, are you not? You were with Jesus the Galilean."

(6) But Peter denied it saying, "Woman, I am not. I do not know Him. I neither know nor understand what you are talking about." And he went out to the gateway.

(7) At the gateway another servant girl saw Peter and said to those who were there, "This man was with Jesus the Nazarene."

They said to Peter, "Surely you are one of His disciples for you are a Galilean, too. The way you talk gives you away."

(8) Again Peter denied it with an oath, "I do not know the man you are talking about."

(9) After about an hour had passed one of the slaves of the high priest, a relative of the man whose ear Peter had cut off, said, "Did I not see you in the garden with Him?"

(10) Peter began to curse and swear, "I do not know the man!" Immediately, while he was still speaking, a cock crowed.

(11) The Lord turned and looked at Peter. Then Peter remembered the word which Jesus had said, "Before the cock crows today you will deny Me three times," (12) and Peter went out and wept bitterly.

Notes: Peter knew that to deny Jesus was wrong, and he thought he would never do such a thing. We, too, know that to deny Jesus as our Lord after we have professed to be Christians is wrong. But one thing must be said in Peter's favor-he was there! Both Peter and John were there, but where were the others?

The identity of that "other disciple" is assumed to have been John. Only John recorded that another disciple was there, and in writing of himself, John never used his own name, most often referring to himself as "the disciple whom Jesus loved."

John was known to the high priest, presumably Caiaphas, because it was to Caiaphas that Jesus had now been taken. We don't know to what extent John was known to Caiaphas or whether the relationship was of a social, business, or religious nature. At any rate, John seems to have been known by the gatekeeper, a slave girl, and known well enough so that he would be allowed to enter without being questioned and that he could bring guests.

The average houses of that day were built in a rectangular shape with one or two stories. There was usually only one door which opened onto a porch which in turn opened onto a courtyard in the center of the building. There was a stairway on the porch which led to the second floor or to the roof. The roof was flat and was often used as a sitting area. It was surrounded by a parapet for safety and privacy. The courtyard was surrounded by rooms all of which opened onto the courtyard. It was into such a courtyard in the house of Caiaphas that John brought Peter. John himself probably went into the room where Jesus was being questioned.

Some biblical writers are of the opinion that the place where Jesus was taken, first to Annas and then to Caiaphas, were in the same building, a very large house or perhaps a palace of some sort. That may have been true because the courtyard was large enough to hold a large number of people. Whether or not Annas and Caiaphas were in the same building, the building to which they took Jesus to be questioned by Caiaphas was a large one because the scriptures say they took Jesus to where the elders, the chief priests, the scribes, and the whole Sanhedrin were assembled.

As in many other countries, our own country for instance, the part of the country from which a person comes can often be determined by his manner of speech or accent. There are linguists in America who claim they can tell by his speech within a hundred miles what part of this country a person is from. Before television became common, the differences in speech were much more pronounced than they are now.

John seems to have had no fear or shame in having it known that he was a disciple of Jesus. He went boldly into the house of Caiaphas. It makes one wonder if perhaps Peter would have been treated in the same way if he had answered, "Yes," when asked if he was a disciple of Jesus. Though his faith may have been shaken by what was happening, Peter's love for Jesus was strong enough to take him into what he would have considered a hostile environment so that he could see for himself what was happening to Jesus. We might wonder if Peter cursed and swore from exasperation at being questioned or if he did it deliberately so that by doing so he would be disassociated from the person of Jesus, a person known to be very religious.

Peter's denial of Jesus shows that no matter how strong in the faith we might consider ourselves to be, if the circumstances are right for it, we are in danger of falling. This is a lesson that all Christians should keep in mind-that if Peter could fall so could any of us.

177 Remorse and Suicide of Judas (Matt. 27:3-10)

(1) When Judas, who had betrayed Jesus, saw that He had been condemned he felt remorse and returned the thirty pieces of silver to the chief priests and elders, (2) saying, "I have sinned by betraying innocent blood."

But they said, "What is that to us? See to that yourself!"

(3) Then Judas threw the pieces of silver into the sanctuary and departed, and he went away and hanged himself.

(4) The chief priests took the pieces of silver and said, "It is not lawful to put them into the temple treasury since it is the price of blood."

(5) They counseled together and with the money bought the potter's field as a burial place for strangers. (6) For this reason that field has been called the Field of Blood to this day. (7) Then that which was spoken through Jeremiah the prophet was fulfilled, saying, "And they took the thirty pieces of silver, the price of the One whose price had been set by the sons of Israel;

(8) and they gave them for the potter's field as the Lord directed me."

Notes: The word that's translated "repented" in the *KN* (in the NASV the word is translated as "felt remorse") is from the Greek word *metamellomai* (met-am-el'-lom-ahee) and means "to care afterwards, regret, repent." Judas had no reason to fear anyone (unless it was God) because of what he had done, so fear of what some person might do to him had nothing to do with his repentance. Neither is there anything in the scriptures to indicate that it was because of any affection for Jesus. Rather, it appears that his conscience was bothering him because what he had done was sinful.

The chief priests and elders knew the money they had given Judas was blood money, and Judas said it was the price of "innocent blood." It should be recognized, then, that the chief priests and elders knew that the purpose for which they had paid Judas the money was not a righteous purpose.

Actually, there was nothing in the Law that prohibited putting the money into the treasury, but it was a part of the tradition of the Jews which forbade them to return the money to the treasury. Apparently, the elders and chief priests saw nothing wrong with paying money out of the treasury for such a purpose, but they thought it was wrong to return it to the treasury. It seems that just the opposite should have been true-wrong to take money from the treasury to pay out as blood money but not wrong to put it into the treasury.

The reason for the purchase of a separate piece of land in which to bury Gentiles who died in Jerusalem is that the Jews didn't believe in having Gentiles buried in Jewish cemeteries. A potter's field was a field of clay from which the potter took the clay which he used to make his merchandise, and after the clay had been removed, the field was almost worthless for any other use and could be bought for a very low price.

The scripture states that the quotation is from Jeremiah but it's really in Zechariah 11:12-13. This apparent discrepancy was probably caused by a transcribing error. In the original Greek the names are very similar.

178 The First Trial of Jesus by Pilate

(Matt. 27:1-2, 11-14; Mark 15:1-5;
Luke 23:1-7; John 18:28-38)

(1) Early in the morning the chief priests with the elders and scribes and the whole Council held a consultation against Jesus to put Him to death. (2) Binding Jesus, the whole body of them arose and led Him away and delivered Him up to Pilate the governor.

(3) From Caiaphas they led Jesus into the Praetorium, but they themselves did not enter the Praetorium so that they might not be defiled but might eat the Passover.

(4) So Pilate went out to them and asked, "What accusation do you bring against this Man?"

(5) They answered, "If this Man were not an evildoer we would not have delivered Him up to you."

(6) Then they began to accuse Jesus, saying, "We found this Man misleading our nation and forbidding to pay taxes to Caesar and saying that He Himself is Christ the King."

(7) Pilate again entered the Praetorium and summoned Jesus and asked Him, "Are You the King of the Jews?" Jesus answered, "It is as you say."

(8) Then Jesus asked, "Are you saying this on your own initiative or did others tell you about Me?"

(9) Pilate answered, "I am not a Jew. Your own nation and the chief priests delivered You up to me. What have You done?"

(10) Jesus answered, "My kingdom is not of this world. If My kingdom were of this world my servants would be fighting so that I might not be delivered up to the Jews, but as it is, My kingdom is not of this realm."

(12) Pilate said to Jesus, "So You are a king?"

Jesus answered, "You say correctly that I am a king. For this I have been born and for this I have come into the world, to bear witness to the truth. Everyone who is of the truth hears My voice."

(13) Pilate asked Him, "What is the truth?" And when he had said this he went out again to the Jews and said to them, "I find no guilt in Him. (13) Take Him yourselves and judge Him according to your law."

The Jews said, "We are not permitted to put anyone to death," (14) that the word Jesus spoke might be fulfilled, signifying what kind of death he was about to die.

(15) But the chief priest accused Jesus harshly, (16) and Pilate questioned Jesus again, "Do You make no answer? See how many charges they bring against You!"

(17) But Jesus did not answer Pilate with regard to even a single charge so that the governor was quite amazed.

(18) The Jews kept on insisting and they said, "He stirs up the people, teaching all over Judea, starting from Galilee, even as far as this place."

(19) When Pilate heard this he asked whether Jesus was a Galilean, (20) and when he learned that He belonged to Herod's jurisdiction, he sent Jesus to Herod who was in Jerusalem at that time.

Notes: It was very early on Wednesday morning. Even though the Jews had tried Jesus and sentenced Him to death, they couldn't carry out the death sentence themselves, because it was illegal under Roman law for anyone to be executed without permission or concurrence of the Roman governors.

This scripture says that the Jews couldn't enter the Praetorium because if they did so, they would be unclean and couldn't eat the Passover. The Passover festival included not only the *day* of the Passover feast but also the following seven days which were known as the Feast of Unleavened Bread. Probably all pious Jews had eaten the Passover meal (or Seder) at about the same time Jesus had done so, but they had to remain ceremonially clean in order to continue to observe the feast days which followed.

You will probably note that the things for which the Jews had condemned Jesus were not the same things they told Pilate that Jesus had done. The Jews refused to enter the Praetorium for fear of being made unclean, but they could lie so as to have an innocent man killed without any qualms of guilt.

Pilate was probably a fairly intelligent man and he would have known that if the things the Jews were saying about Jesus were true then the Jews would have been the very last people to have wanted Him killed. They chafed under Roman rule and any man who urged them to withhold tribute from Caesar and who called himself a king in defiance of Rome would have been a hero to the Jews. They would have been more likely to have hidden him and protected him than to have turned him over to the Romans.

When Pilate said that he found no fault in Jesus, he was in essence saying that as the Roman governor, he believed Jesus to be innocent of any crime worthy of death and that he didn't believe the charges brought against Jesus by the Jews.

The reason Jesus remained silent and refused to answer the charges against Him was probably because He could have successfully defended Himself to Pilate and have been released from custody. But to have done so would have thwarted the express purpose for which Jesus had come to earth, to die for sinners. That would only have delayed the inevitable. Jesus had to die and the Jews would have found another way, either legally or illegally, to have killed Him.

The Herod written about in this scripture was Herod Antipas who ruled as Tetrarch of an area that included Galilee. He had absolutely no authority in Judea because Judea was ruled directly by the Romans, specifically by Pilate as governor. Herod was in Jerusalem for the Passover, and Pilate sent Jesus to him only as a matter of courtesy because Jesus was from Galilee.

179 Herod Antipas Questions Jesus (Luke 23:8-12)

(1) Now Herod was very glad when he saw Jesus. He had wanted to see Jesus for a long time because he had been hearing about Him and was hoping to see some sign performed by Him. (2) Herod questioned Jesus at some length, but Jesus answered him not at all. (3) The chief priests and scribes were standing there accusing Jesus vehemently (4) and Herod and his soldiers treated Jesus with contempt and mocked Him. Afterwards they dressed Him in a gorgeous robe and sent Him back to Pilate.

(5) Herod and Pilate became friends with one another that very day. Before that they had been at enmity with each other.

Notes: Luke 9:7-9 (section 71) reads, "Now Herod the tetrarch heard of all that was happening and he was greatly perplexed, because it was said by some that John had risen from the dead, and by some that Elijah had appeared, and by others, that one of the prophets of old had risen again. And Herod said, 'I myself had John beheaded; but who is this man about whom I hear such things?' And he kept trying to see Him." Herod was the only person about whom the scriptures tell us Jesus expressed contempt. Luke 13:31-32 says, "Just at that time some Pharisees came up, saying to Him, 'Go away and depart from here, for Herod wants to kill You.' And He said to them, 'Go tell that fox, "Behold, I cast out demons and perform cures today and tomorrow, and the third day I reach My goal."'"

Herod, having no authority in Judea, probably questioned Jesus about things having nothing to do with His guilt or innocence. His questions were more apt to have been about things aimed at satisfying the curiosity he had expressed about Jesus.

180 The Second Trial by Pilate

(Matt. 27:15-26; Mark 15:6-15; Luke 23:13-25; John 18:39-40, 19:4-16)

(1) Now at the feast the governor was accustomed to release for the multitude any one prisoner whom they wanted released.

(2) A man named Barabbas had been imprisoned for insurrection in the city and had committed murder in the insurrection. (3) So the multitude went up and asked the governor to do as he had been accustomed to do for them.

(4) So Pilate summoned the chief priests and the rulers and the people and when they were gathered together he said to them, (5) "You brought this Man to me as one who incites the people to rebellion but I have examined Him in front of you and have found no guilt in this Man regarding the charges that you make against Him. (6) No, nor has Herod, for Herod sent Him back to us, and look, nothing deserving of death has been done by Him. (7) I will, therefore, punish Him and release Him.

(8) "But you have a custom, that I should release someone for you at the Passover. Do you wish then that I release for you Jesus who is called Christ the King of the Jews?" (9) For he was aware that the chief priests had delivered Jesus up because of envy.

(10) But they cried out all together, saying, "Away with this Man and release to us Barabbas!"

(11) Now the chief priests and the elders had stirred up the multitude and persuaded them to ask the governor to release Barabbas for them and to put Jesus to death.

(12) Pilate, wanting to release Jesus, addressed them again and said, "Which of the two do you want me to release for you?"

They said, "Barabbas!"

(13) Pilate asked them, "Then what shall I do with Jesus who is called Christ the King of the Jews?"

They all shouted back, "Let Him be crucified!" and, "Crucify Him, crucify Him!"

(14) Pilate said to them the third time, "Why? What evil has this Man done? I have found in Him no guilt demanding death. I will therefore punish Him and release Him."

But they were insistent and kept shouting all the more, "Let Him be crucified!"

(15) Pilate came out again and said to the multitude, "Look, I am bringing Jesus out to you that you may know that I find no guilt in Him."

(16) Then Jesus came out and Pilate said to them, "Behold the Man!"

(17) When the chief priests and officers saw Jesus they cried out, saying, "Crucify, crucify!"

Pilate said to them, "Take Him yourselves and crucify Him for I find no guilt in Him."

(18) The Jews answered, "We have a law and by that law He ought to die because He made Himself out to be the Son of God."

(19) When Pilate heard this statement he was more afraid, and he entered the Praetorium again and said to Jesus, "Where are You from?" But Jesus gave him no answer.

(20) Pilate said, "Do You not speak to me? Do You not know that I have authority to release You and I have authority to crucify You?"

(21) Jesus answered, "You would have no authority over Me if it had not been given to you from above. For that reason he who delivered Me up to you has the greater sin."

(22) As a result of this Pilate made further efforts to release Jesus but the Jews cried out saying, "If you release this Man you are no friend of Caesar. Everyone who makes himself out to be a king opposes Caesar."

(23) When Pilate heard these words He brought Jesus out and sat down on the judgment seat at a place called the Pavement (but in Hebrew Gabbatha). (24) While Pilate was sitting on the judgment seat his wife sent to him saying, "Have nothing to do with that righteous Man, for last night I suffered greatly in a dream because of Him."

(25) Now it was the day of preparation for the Passover at about the sixth hour. Pilate said to the Jews, "Behold your King!"

(26) But they cried out, "Away with Him, away with Him, crucify Him!"

Pilate asked them, "Shall I crucify your King?"

The chief priests answered, "We have no king but Caesar."

(27) When Pilate saw that he was accomplishing nothing but rather that a riot was beginning he took water and washed his hands in front of the multitude and said, "I am innocent of this Man's blood. See to that yourselves."

(28) All the people answered and said, "His blood be on us and on our children!"

(29) Seeing that there was nothing more he could do and wishing to satisfy the multitude Pilate pronounced sentence that their demand should be granted. (30) Then he released Barabbas for them, and he had Jesus scourged and delivered Him to be crucified.

Notes: There is no record in the scriptures of how or when the custom arose concerning the release of a prisoner at the Feast of the Passover.

Josephus recorded that at about that time there was an insurrection of the Jews because Pilate's government took money from the temple treasury to build an aqueduct. Many people were killed in that insurrection and that may have been the insurrection in which Barabbas was involved and for which he was imprisoned.

Pilate could have released Jesus in spite of the wishes of the Jews. He had the power to do so, and he was convinced that Jesus was innocent of any crime. Whether from a lack of courage to oppose the Jews or a wish not to offend them, Pilate didn't release Jesus. It is ironic that the Jews delivered up Jesus on a false charge of insurrection against Rome and asked for the release of a man known to have been guilty of insurrection.

The scriptures say that Pilate's wife in a dream had seen bad things happening because of Jesus. The Romans attached great significance to dreams, and historians tell us that both Julius and Augustus Caesar thought dreams were of great importance. Scourging was a particularly vicious method of punishment.

A scourge had multiple leather thongs to which were attached bits of metal and bone which cut into the flesh when applied. Because it was easily possible for a person to die while being scourged, the law set a limit on the number of lashes that were allowed to have been given a prisoner.

Roman soldiers were noted for being hard, callous men. They were made to be that way because of the training and treatment to which they were subjected. They had no personal reason to hate or revile Jesus, but they took this occasion to mock the Jews by mistreating their king.

When the Israelites had demanded a king like the nations around them had, Samuel warned them how they would be treated by a king. Now these Jews were rejecting their rightful king and pledging allegiance to a foreign power, because this king wasn't going to lead them in a revolt against that foreign power to which they were pledging their allegiance. Jesus had already foretold what was going to happen to Jerusalem and its inhabitants in Luke 19:41-44 and Luke 23:27-31, and of course, about forty years later, that prediction was fulfilled by the same Roman nation.

Pilate is condemned in history because, as a judge, he didn't do his duty but allowed himself to be influenced by outside pressure. The symbolic washing of his hands changed nothing. Because he didn't do what he knew was the right thing to do, he might as well have personally executed Jesus. By allowing Jesus to be crucified, he may as well have ordered it to be done. It was within his power as the highest official in Judea to have ruled either way (see appendix).

181 The Soldiers Mock Jesus

(Matt. 27:27-31; Mark 15:16-20; John 19:1-3)

(1) Then Pilate took Jesus and scourged Him. (2) Then the soldiers of the governor took Jesus away into the palace (that is, the Praetorium), and they called together the whole Roman cohort around Him. (3) Then they stripped Jesus and put a purple robe on Him.

(4) After weaving a crown of thorns the soldiers put it on Jesus' head and put a reed in His right hand. They kneeled down before Him and mocked Him and began to acclaim Him, saying, "Hail, King of the Jews!" (5) The soldiers kept beating Jesus' head with the reed and spitting on Him and striking Him in the face and kneeling and bowing before Him.

(6) When the soldiers had finished mocking Jesus they took the purple robe off Him and put His own garments on Him. Then they led Him away to crucify Him.

Notes: As stated in the previous section, the Roman soldiers had no personal reason for the way they treated Jesus. To some people, cruelty to others gives them pleasure. And it was only for their personal pleasure that they treated Jesus as they did. The crown of thorns must have been very painful and to be continually hit on the head by a reed would certainly have produced a headache at the very least.

A reed was not only a very slender form of grass with a jointed stem, but could also have been a much larger plant such as bamboo, which can be as much as five inches in diameter. They can also be the plants similar to bamboo which is often called "fishing poles" which usually grow to about an inch or more in diameter. Such grasses were often used as whips in schoolrooms a century or more ago. The use of such reeds for that purpose was called "caning."

182 The Crucifixion (Matt. 27:32-44;

Mark 15:21-32; Luke 21:26-38; John 19:17-24)

(1) They took Jesus out, and He was bearing His own cross.

(2) As they were coming out they pressed into service a passer by coming from the country, Simon the Cyrene (the father of Alexander and Rufus), to bear the cross behind Jesus. (3) Following Jesus there were a multitude of the people and many women who were mourning and lamenting Him.

(4) Jesus, turning to the women, said, "Daughters of Jerusalem, stop weeping for Me but weep for yourselves and for your children. (5) The days are coming when they will say, 'Blessed are the barren and the wombs that never bore and the breasts that never nursed.' (6) Then they will begin to say to the mountains, 'Fall on us,' and to the hills, 'Cover us.' (7) For if they do these things in the green tree what will happen in the dry?"

(8) Two others who were criminals were also being led away to be put to death with Jesus. (9) When they came to the place called in Hebrew Golgotha, which is translated "Place of a Skull," there they crucified Jesus and the two criminals, one on the right side of Him and the other on the left. (10) [And the Scripture was fulfilled which says, "And He was numbered with transgressors."] (11) They gave Jesus wine mingled with gall and myrrh to drink, but after tasting it Jesus was unwilling to drink.

(12) And Jesus said, "Father, forgive them for they do not know what they are doing."

(13) The people who were passing by were hurling abuse at Jesus, wagging their heads (14) and saying, "Ha! You who are going to destroy the temple and rebuild it in three days, save Yourself! If You are the Son of God come down from the cross." (15) And some of the people stood by looking on.

(16) The rulers, the chief priests along with the scribes and elders, were also mocking Jesus and saying, (17) "He saved others, now let Him save Himself. If He is the Christ of God, His Chosen One, and the King of Israel let Him now come down from the cross and we shall believe in Him. (18) He trusts in God, let God deliver Him now if He takes pleasure in Him, for He said, 'I am the Son of God.'"

(19) The robbers who had been crucified with Jesus were also casting the same insult at Him.

(20) The soldiers, when they had crucified Jesus, took His outer garments and made four parts, a part to every soldier, and also the tunic. Now the tunic was seamless, woven in one piece. (21) They said to one another, "Let us not tear it but let us cast lots for it to decide whose it shall be." They said this so that the Scripture might be fulfilled, "They divided My outer garments among them and for My clothing they cast lots."

(22) The soldiers also mocked Jesus, coming up to Him and offering Him sour wine (23) and saying, "If You are the King of the Jews save yourself!" (24) Then, sitting down, they began to keep watch over Him there.

(25) Pilate wrote the charge against Jesus in an inscription and put it on the cross. The inscription was written, "JESUS THE NAZARENE, THE KING OF THE JEWS," and it was written in Hebrew, Latin, and in Greek. (26) Therefore many of the Jews read this inscription for the place where Jesus was crucified was near the city.

(27) The chief priests of the Jews said to Pilate, "Do not write, 'The King of the Jews,' but that He said, 'I am King of the Jews.'"

(28) Pilate answered, "What I have written I have written."

(29) And it was the third hour when they crucified Jesus.

Notes: In the twenty-four hours preceding the crucifixion, Jesus had had no sleep. He had been mocked and spat upon and scourged. He had been beaten with hands and reeds, humiliated, lied about, and now He had been burdened with a heavy wooden cross. As a man, His physical strength had been exhausted. Even the Romans saw that He was not physically capable of carrying the cross and pressed another man into service to carry it.

There are nine men named Simon about which something is written in the New Testament. The man whom the Romans forced to carry the cross of Jesus was the seventh in order in the scriptures. This Simon was a Jew from the city of Cyrene which is located in what is now Libya in North Africa. Mark further identified him as the Father of Alexander and Rufus as though they were known to the readers of his account of the Gospel. There is a man named Rufus mentioned by Paul in Romans 16:13, but there's nothing to indicate that he was the son of the Simon about whom Mark wrote. Five men named Alexander are mentioned in the New Testament. There's nothing to indicate whether or not this Alexander was the same as any one of the other four. Because of what Mark wrote in his Gospel and of Paul's mention of Rufus in Romans, there is an opinion, widespread among some scholars, that Simon and his family later became Christians.

The account of Simon being pressed into service to carry the cross of Jesus is told in the Gospels of Matthew, Mark, and Luke. John wrote that Jesus carried His own cross to the place called "the Place of the Skull." It seems that John would be the more reliable witness since he alone of the eleven apostles (and Mark and Luke who were not apostles) was the only one about which we know who was actually present at the crucifixion. However, in the days following the crucifixion, there arose a rumor to the effect that Simon was substituted for Jesus, not only to carry His cross, but in the crucifixion as well. It may have been to counter that rumor that John wrote of the journey to the cross as he did. Another possibility is that Simon carried only one end of the cross and that Jesus carried the other end. In that case, Jesus would still have been carrying the cross.

Jesus expressed sympathy for the women who were following Him and mourning for Him, and at the same time, He was warning them of much worse things that would happen to them later and which did happen in AD 70. In those times, mothers would carry a double burden-the physical suffering to which they themselves would be subjected and the mental suffering for the physical suffering of their children. Wishing for the mountains to fall on them or the hills to hide them was something the people would do when they were suffering at the hands of the Romans. Josephus recorded that as many as two thousand people tried to hide in the subterranean caverns under Jerusalem and were killed when the city was razed by the Romans.

It's possible that the mind of man has thought of no more cruel or more painful or worse manner of punishment than that of death on a cross as practiced by the Romans. There is a written essay extant explaining all of what happens during death by crucifixion.

It was between eight and nine o'clock in the morning modern time, or during the third hour of the day ancient time, when Jesus began the trip from the Praetorium to Golgotha.

The mixture of wine or vinegar and gall or myrrh which they offered Jesus to drink was a mixture designed to be given to people being crucified or on whom great pain was to be inflicted. Its purpose was to stupefy or make the victim insensible or to diminish the intensity of the pain. The reason Jesus refused to drink this mixture is not given. A reason that has been put forward by some scholars is that since Jesus "must drink the cup," He wanted to experience the full intensity of it, that is, He wanted to suffer all that had to be endured without having it made easier for Him. Another possibility is that the dulling of the pain would, of course, have made the experience more endurable, but it would also have prolonged the length of time for the suffering, and by suffering the full intensity of the pain, life would have ended more quickly.

The prophecy, "He was numbered with transgressors," is from Isaiah 53:12, and the prophecy, "They divide My garments among them, and for My clothing they cast lots," is from Psalms 22:18. The garment for which the soldiers cast lots was the tunic of Jesus. This was a very unusual garment in that it was woven in one piece instead of being in two parts as were most such garments. The two-piece tunics were joined at the shoulder by clasps and reached to the knees of the wearer. According to Josephus, the tunic of the high priest was an exception to the general rule, it being woven in one piece as was that of Jesus. The author of the book of Hebrews wrote extensively about the high priesthood of Jesus, so it would have been fitting and appropriate that His tunic be of the one piece design denoting that He, too, was a high priest but of a different order since He was not of the tribe of Levi.

The sign which Pilate had made and put above Jesus on the cross was written in Hebrew, Latin, and Greek so that everyone would be able to read it. The sign read, "THIS IS JESUS THE NAZARENE, THE KING OF THE JEWS." Even though the Jews wanted Pilate to change the sign to read that Jesus *said* He was king of the Jews, the charge that Jesus was the king of the Jews was probably Pilate's only legal reason to have had Jesus crucified. In any case, Pilate was probably not too concerned either way. About six years after the crucifixion of Jesus, in AD 36, Pilate was removed from his post as governor for excessive oppression of the people.

183 The Penitent Thief {Luke 23:39-43)

(1) One of the criminals who were hanged there was also shouting abuse at Jesus, saying, "Are You not the Christ? Save Yourself and us!"

(2) But the other thief rebuked him and said, "Do you not even fear God? You are under the same sentence of condemnation. (3) We are indeed here justly for we are receiving what we deserve for our deeds, but this Man has done nothing wrong."

(4) He turned and said to Jesus, "Jesus, remember me when You come into Your kingdom!"

(5) Jesus said to him, "I say to you truly that today you shall be with Me in Paradise."

Notes: Some people have used this passage of scripture as an example of all that's required to be saved. Who among us, when telling someone the requirements for salvation, has not been asked the question, "What about the thief on the cross?" They believe it is a legitimate model of death-bed repentance and salvation. But we know that isn't true for several reasons. First, the thief lived and died under the Law of

Moses-he never obeyed that form of doctrine which is necessary for a person to become a Christian, and he never had to do so. Before Jesus died, He had the unique power to save anyone in any way He chose and for any reason that was satisfactory to Him. And after the kingdom of Christ was established on the day of Pentecost when Peter preached that first gospel sermon, the criteria for a person to be saved was established and has never changed. The truth is that for the same results to be produced for other people as it was for the thief, the same circumstances leading up to the thief's salvation would have to be reproduced. We know, though, that such a thing is impossible. We can read in Romans 6:10, Hebrews 7:26-27, 10:10, and 1 Peter 3:18 that Jesus died once and that one time was for all time and for all people.

Matthew wrote that both the thieves were jeering at Jesus, but Luke says (and Luke was the only one of the Gospel writers to record it) that one of the thieves repented, confessed his faith in Jesus as the savior, and that he was saved. Of all the people who knew Jesus or who knew of Him, this robber was one of the very few who still believed in the divinity of Jesus at that time. In fact, he may have been the only one.

Due to the way the scriptures have been translated from the original Greek, there is some confusion about heaven and hell. For instance, the word "heaven" could have meant: the sky in which there are clouds and from which rain comes; the firmament in which are located the sun, the moon, and the stars; and the home or abode of God. Also, four different words have all been translated "hell": Hades (hah'-dace); Gehenna or ge-Hinnom (gheh-eh-nah) for "the valley of the Hinnon," a valley just south of Jerusalem; and Tartarus (tar-tar-o'-o). To confuse things even more, some people think paradise is synonymous with heaven and others think it is synonymous with Eden, the garden.

Some theologians believe that departed souls go to either one of the two places to await the final judgment. Those souls destined for eternal punishment go to Hades to wait and the souls destined to be eternally with God go to paradise. They believe that the beggar Lazarus who was with Abraham was in paradise and the rich man was in Hades. After the judgment, the souls in Hades will go to Gehenna or Tartarus, the lake of fire, and the souls in paradise will go to the heaven of God. In confirmation of this last, Jesus said that He and the thief would be together in paradise. We know this wasn't the heaven of God, because in John 20:17, Jesus said that He had not yet ascended to His Father.

If all that isn't confusing enough, the word "paradise" is used only three times in the New Testament: in our current text Luke 23:43, in 2 Corinthians 12:4 in which Paul is writing of the man caught up into paradise, and in Revelation 2:7 which says, "To him who overcomes, I will grant to eat of the tree of life, which is in the Paradise of God." All three times the word is translated from the same Greek word *par-ad'-i-sos* and the definition of that word is: a park, or a place of future happiness. Smith's Bible Dictionary defines "paradise" as:

> This is a word of Persian origin, and is used in the Septuagint as the translation of Eden. It meant "an orchard of pleasure and fruits," a "garden" or "pleasure ground," something like an English park. It is applied figuratively to the celestial dwelling of the righteous, in allusion to the Garden of Eden (2 Cor. 12:4; Rev. 2:7). It has thus come into familiar use to denote both the garden and the heaven of the just.

184 The Death of Jesus (Matt. 27:45-56;

Mark 15:33-41; Luke 23:44-49; John 19:25-30)

(1) All the acquaintances of Jesus and the women who used to follow Him about in Galilee and minister to Him there had followed Him to Jerusalem and were standing at a distance looking on.

(2) Among the women there were standing by the cross of Jesus His mother; His mother's

sister Salome, the mother of the sons of Zebedee; Mary the wife of Clopas, the mother of James the Less and Joseph; and Mary Magdalene.

(3) When Jesus saw His mother and the disciple whom He loved

standing nearby He said to His mother, "Woman, behold! This is your son!"

(4) Then He said to the disciple, "This is your mother!" And from that time on the disciple took Mary into his own household.

(5) It was now about the sixth hour and darkness fell over the whole land until the ninth hour, the sun being obscured.

(6) At about the ninth hour Jesus cried out with a loud voice, "Eloi, Eloi, lama sabachthani?" which is translated, "My God, My God, why have You forsaken Me?"

(7) When some of the bystanders heard this they said, "Listen, He is calling for Elijah." (8) The people said, "Let us see whether Elijah comes to save Him."

(9) After this Jesus, knowing that all things had already been accomplished and so that the Scripture might be fulfilled, said, "I am thirsty."

(10) A jar full of sour wine was standing there and immediately one of the bystanders ran and, taking a sponge, he filled it with sour wine and put it on a branch of hyssop. He brought the sponge to the mouth of Jesus and gave Him a drink. (11) When Jesus had received the sour wine He said, "It is finished."

(12) Then Jesus, crying out with a loud voice, said, "Father, into Your hands I commit My spirit." Having said this He bowed His head and yielded up His spirit. (13) Then the veil of the temple was torn in two from top to bottom and the earth shook and the rocks were split (14) and the tombs were opened. Many bodies of the saints who had fallen asleep were raised, (15) and coming out of the tombs after Jesus' resurrection they entered the holy city and appeared to many.

(16) Now when the centurion and those who were with him keeping guard over Jesus saw the earthquake and the things that were happening they became very frightened. (17) When the centurion, who was standing right in front of Jesus, saw the way He breathed His last he also began praising God and said, "Certainly this man was innocent. Surely He was the Son of God!"

(18) When all the multitudes who had come together for this spectacle observed what happened they began to return beating their breasts.

Notes: We don't know the reason Jesus sent His mother to live with John. At that time, she had at least two living children besides Jesus–James and Jude (or Judas). We don't have any information at all about

Joseph. Because of the language used, we surmise that he was still living during at least a part of the ministry of Jesus, but after Jesus reached the age of twelve, we do not read anything else about Joseph. It would be interesting to know whether or not Joseph rejected Jesus as the Messiah, and about his later years, but that information wasn't recorded for us.

Psalms 69:21 reads, "They also gave me gall for my food, and for my thirst they gave me vinegar to drink." The act of the bystander in giving Jesus vinegar to drink (or sour wine according to some versions) was not another cruel act designed to add to the discomfort of Jesus as He hung on the cross, but vinegar or sour wine was the common drink of Roman soldiers, so instead of being more torture for Jesus, giving Him the vinegar was an act of kindness.

The rending of the veil of the temple from top to bottom is assumed to have shown that people no longer had to go through the priests as intermediaries between man and God. Jesus was the supreme sacrifice and no other sacrifice would be necessary. Previous to this, only the high priest could look beyond the veil into the Holy of Holies in the temple and then only once each year. The priests who were burning incense in the Holy Place could now see what was on the other side of the curtain.

185 The Burial of Jesus

(Matt. 27:57-61; Mark 15:42-16:1; Luke 23:50-56; John 19:31-42)

(1) It was the preparation day, the day before the Sabbath, and the Sabbath was about to begin. (2) So that the bodies should not remain on the cross on the Sabbath (for that Sabbath was a high day), the Jews asked Pilate that the legs of the three who had been crucified might be broken and that the bodies might be taken away.

(3) Therefore the soldiers came and broke the legs of the first man and of the other man who was crucified with Jesus.

(4) But coming to Jesus they saw that He was already dead and they did not break His legs, (5) but one of the soldiers pierced His side with a spear and immediately there came out blood and water. (6) He who has seen has borne witness and this witness is true. He knows that he is telling the truth so that you also may believe. (7) These things came

to pass that the Scripture might be fulfilled, "Not a bone of Him shall be broken." (8) And another Scripture says, "They shall look on Him whom they pierced."

(9) A rich man named Joseph from Arimathea, a city of the Jews, came when it was evening. Joseph was a good and righteous man who himself had also become a disciple of Jesus but a secret one for fear of the Jews. (10) Joseph was a prominent member of the Council (he had not consented to their plan and action) who himself was waiting for the kingdom of God. He gathered up courage and went in before Pilate and asked for the body of Jesus.

(11) Pilate wondered if Jesus was dead by this time and, summoning the centurion, Pilate questioned him as to whether Jesus was already dead. (12) Ascertaining from the centurion that He was, Pilate granted the body to Joseph and Joseph took it away.

(13) Nicodemus, who had first come to Jesus by night, came also and brought a mixture of about a hundred pounds weight of myrrh and spices. (14) He and Joseph took down the body of Jesus and bound it in clean linen, wrapping it with the spices as is the burial custom of the Jews.

(15) Now in the place where Jesus was crucified there was a garden and in the garden was a new tomb belonging to Joseph which he had hewn into the rock and in which no one had yet been laid. (16) Because the tomb was nearby they laid Jesus there. Then they rolled a large stone against the entrance of the tomb and went away.

(17) Two of the women who had come with Jesus out of Galilee, Mary Magdalene and Mary the mother of Joses, followed after and were there sitting opposite the grave and looking on to see where the body of Jesus was laid.

(18) When the Sabbath was over Mary Magdalene, Mary the mother of James and Salome bought spices that they might go and anoint the body of Jesus. (19) They went away and prepared the spices and perfumes and then rested on the Sabbath according to the commandment.

Notes: The Romans often left the bodies of criminals hanging on the cross until birds or animals devoured them or putrefaction took care of them. The Jews, however, had a law which forbade them to leave the body of a man who had been hanged to remain on the tree overnight. Deuteronomy 21:22-23 says, "And if a man has committed a sin worthy of death, and he is put to death, and you hang him on a tree, his corpse shall not hang all night on the tree, for you shall surely bury him on the same day (for he who is hanged is accursed of God), so that you do not defile your land which the Lord your God gives you as an inheritance."

It may have been that the Jews had become somewhat lax in observing that law because the scripture states that it was because the next day was a Sabbath that they wanted the legs of the three men broken. The next day was a Sabbath, the first day of the Feast of Unleavened Bread, and the Jews didn't want the bodies hanging on the crosses in plain sight of all those Jews who had come from far away to celebrate. To have broken the legs of the men instead of killing them outright was probably so that the suffering could continue until death even though the coming of death was brought on considerably sooner by doing so. Jesus was already dead, and the Romans knew He was dead, so there was really no need for them to pierce Him with a spear.

Evidently, the flow of blood mingled with water from the side of Jesus was sufficiently outside the normal to have caused John to make particular mention of it, so much so, in fact, that John felt compelled to assert the truth of his statement. With the coming of death and the stopping of the action of the heart the blood in a body tends to settle in the part of the body that is lowest, in the case of Jesus the legs and feet.

Two, a wound on a dead body doesn't bleed nearly as freely as on a live one, and soon after death, it won't bleed at all. There may have been something symbolic in this in that both elements, blood and water, are required to cleanse us from sin-the blood that Jesus shed for the sins of all mankind and the water of baptism for each of us individually. In 1 John 5:6-8, John wrote, "For this is the one who came by water and blood, Jesus Christ; not with water only, but with the water and with the blood. For there are three that bear witness, the Spirit and the water and the blood, and the three are in agreement."

The prophecy concerning the fact that none of the bones of Jesus would be broken is from Psalms 34:20. And the prophecy which states that the body of Jesus would be pierced is from Zechariah 12:10.

The exact site of the city of Arimathea is not known today, but scholars believe it to have been located about twenty miles northwest of Jerusalem. The fact that a rich man would bury Jesus was prophesied in Isaiah 53:9. It seems ironic that most of the people who were closest to Jesus were afraid to be with Him at His death, but that people who were afraid to be with Him while He was alive were not afraid to go to Pilate to request the body of Jesus so that they could bury it.

It was the custom of the Jews either to embalm the bodies of the dead or to wrap them up with quantities of spices. The length of time before the bodies of Jesus and the thieves would have to have been buried wasn't enough to allow them to be embalmed even if that had been the wish of those who buried them. Nicodemus brought about a hundred pounds of myrrh and spices to use in preparing the body of Jesus for burial. Myrrh was a resin. It was very bitter to the taste and had a narcotic effect if taken internally.

The linen cloth which Joseph brought is believed to have been a sindon, a garment so expensive that it could be worn only by wealthy people. That was also supposed to have been the type of garment which was worn by the young man who was in the garden when Jesus was taken by the Jews and whose wrap was left in the hands of someone in the mob when the young man ran away.

The death of Jesus was at about three o'clock in the afternoon. That certainly wouldn't have left much time to do all that had to be done before the beginning of the Sabbath because the Sabbath began at about six o'clock. Joseph had to go to Pilate for permission to take the body of Jesus down from the cross, physically remove the body from the cross, prepare it for burial, bury it, and seal the tomb. And there were indications that the preparation of the body was incomplete when it was put into the tomb because of the fact that the women who watched as Joseph and Nicodemus buried Jesus intended to buy more spices with which to anoint Jesus after the Sabbath was over (see appendix).

186 A Guard Set over the Tomb (Matt. 27:62-66)

(1) Now on the next day, which was the day after the preparation, the chief priests and the Pharisees met with Pilate

(2) and said, "Sir, we recall that when He was still alive that deceiver said, 'After three days I will rise again.' (3) Therefore give orders for the grave to be made secure until the third day lest His disciples come and steal Him away and say to the people, 'He has risen from the dead,' and the last deception will be worse than the first."

(4) Pilate said to them, "You have a guard. Go and make it as secure as you know how."

(5) Then they went and made the grave secure, and along with the guard they put a seal on the stone.

Notes: There is some disagreement among biblical scholars, but it appears that this took place on the Sabbath, probably shortly after the beginning of the Sabbath which would have been at about six o'clock in the evening. Certainly, it isn't likely that the Jews would have allowed very much time to have passed, certainly not a whole night, before they thought of having a guard put over the tomb. It also seems evident that they knew what Jesus meant when He spoke about the temple being destroyed and raised up on the third day and about "the sign of Jonah."

A person who is honest thinks that all people are honest, and a person who's dishonest considers all people to be dishonest. A person who drives slowly is more apt to pull out in front of oncoming traffic than a speeder because he thinks that all people drive as slowly as he does. If the Jewish leaders had known more about the people they thought would steal the body of Jesus, they would have seen that a guard over the tomb was unnecessary. But they thought the disciples would have done what they would have done, that is, steal the body of Jesus to make it seem that He had risen. But those eleven men were honorable men. They were despondent and dejected.

They thought the death of Jesus ended the hope which they had had of His setting up a kingdom on earth. Without Jesus to lead them, what good would it have done to steal His body and claim He had been raised from the dead? (see appendix)

187 The Empty Tomb

(Matt. 28:1-10, Mark 16:2-11, Luke 24:1-12, John 20:1-18)

(1) Jesus rose early on the first day of the week and He appeared first to Mary Magdalene, from whom He had cast out seven demons. (2) Now after the Sabbath Mary came to the tomb early, while it was still dark, and saw that the stone had been taken away from the tomb. (3) So Mary ran, and went to Simon Peter and the other disciple, the one whom Jesus loved, and said to them, "They have taken the Lord out of the tomb, and we do not know where they have laid Him."

(4) Peter then came out with the other disciple, and they went toward the tomb. (5) They both ran, but the other disciple outran Peter and reached the tomb first; (6) and stooping to look in, he saw the linen cloths lying there, but he did not go in.

(7) Then Simon Peter came, following him. He stooped and looked in then he went into the tomb. (8) He saw the linen cloths lying by themselves, (9) and the napkin, which had been on His head, not lying with the linen cloths but rolled up in a place by itself. (10) Then the other disciple, who reached the tomb first, also went in, and he saw and believed, (11) for as yet they did not know the scripture, that Jesus must rise from the dead.

(12) Then the disciples went back to their homes, and Peter was wondering at what had happened.

(13) And Mary was weeping outside the tomb, and as she wept she stooped to look into the tomb; (14) and she saw two angels in white, sitting where the body of Jesus had lain, one at the head and one at the feet.

(15) The angels said to Mary, "Woman, why are you weeping?"

She said to them, "Because they have taken away my Lord, and I do not know where they have laid Him." (16) Saying this, she turned around and saw Jesus standing, but she did not know it was Jesus.

(17) Jesus said to her, "Woman, why are you weeping? Whom do you seek?"

Supposing Jesus to be the gardener, Mary said to Him, "Sir, if you have carried Him away tell me where you have laid Him, and I will take Him away."

(18) Jesus said to her, "Mary."

Mary turned and said to Jesus in Hebrew, "Rabboni!" (which means teacher).

(19) Jesus said to her, "Do not hold me, for I have not yet ascended to the Father; but go to My brethren and say to them, 'I am ascending to My Father and your Father, to My God and your God.'"

(20) Mary Magdalene then went to the other disciples, those who had been with Jesus, as they mourned and wept, and said to them, (21) "I have seen the Lord"; and she told them that Jesus had said those things to her. (22) But when they heard that Jesus was alive and had been seen by Mary, they would not believe it.

(23) Now after the Sabbath, toward the dawn of the first day of the week when the sun had risen, (24) Mary, the mother of James and Salome also went to see the tomb, taking the spices which they had prepared. (25) And they were saying to one another, "Who will roll away the stone for us from the door of the tomb?" (26) And looking up, they saw that the stone was rolled back; for it was very large.

(27) Behold! There was a great earthquake; for an angel of the Lord descended from heaven and came and rolled back the stone, and sat upon it. (28) His appearance was like lightning, and his raiment white as snow. (29) And for fear of him the guards trembled and became like dead men.

(30) Upon entering the tomb the women did not find the body; (31) but they saw a young man sitting on the right side, dressed in a white robe, and they were amazed.

(32) But the angel said to the women, "Do not be afraid or amazed; I know that you seek Jesus of Nazareth, who was crucified. (33) He is not here; for He has risen, as He said. Come, see the place where they laid Him. (34) Then go quickly, and tell His disciples and Peter that He has risen from the dead, (35) and behold, He is going before you to Galilee; there you will see Him, as He said. Lo, I have told you."

(36) While they were perplexed about this, behold, two men stood by them in dazzling apparel; (37) and as they were frightened and bowed their faces to the ground, the men said to them, "Why do you seek the living among the dead? (38) Remember how He told you, while He was still in Galilee, (39) that the Son of Man must be delivered into the

hands of sinful men, and be crucified and on the third day rise." (40) And they remembered His words.

(41) The women departed quickly and fled from the tomb with fear and great joy, for trembling and astonishment had come upon them; (42) and they said nothing to anyone and ran to tell His disciples.

(43) And behold, Jesus met them and said, "Hail!" And they came and took hold of His feet and worshipped Him.

(44) Then Jesus said to them, "Do not be afraid; go and tell My brethren to go to Galilee, and there they will see Me."

(45) Returning from the tomb the women told all this to the eleven and to all the rest. (46) Now it was Mary Magdalene and Joanna and Mary the mother of James and the other women with them who told this to the apostles; (47) but these words seemed to them an idle tale, and the apostles did not believe them.

Notes: The scripture says that the guards, the Roman soldiers, shook with fear and were like dead men. It sounds as though they fainted dead away, doesn't it? If any of us had been there in their position, we might have fainted too-seeing those angels shining so brightly and a heavy stone being rolled away.

There are some differences between the different accounts in the four Gospels concerning the order of the things which happened on that Sunday morning and who was involved in those happenings. The differences aren't important, and the order in which they are recorded doesn't affect the truth of what did happen.

We don't know why Mary didn't recognize Jesus. We do know that she didn't expect to see Him there. Possibly His appearance was changed somewhat from what it had been before His death, or maybe, it was too dark there in the garden for Mary to see well through her tears. It will be evident later that it was not sight alone that caused the others to believe that the risen Jesus was really their Lord.

Biblical writers and scholars are in disagreement concerning the request of Jesus that Mary not cling to Him because He had not yet ascended to His Father. It seems probable that to get His correct meaning His words could be paraphrased as follows: "You don't have to hold on to Me. I'm not going to ascend to heaven immediately. I'll be here long enough so that you and the others will see Me at other times before I do ascend to heaven."

It's possible that because Jesus didn't say "our Father" and "our God" that He was making a distinction between the relationship that He had with God and the relationship of the disciples to God. Jesus is the offspring of God, the Son of God and One with God, and Christians (the disciples at that time) are the adopted children of God.

An observation: It would seem likely that the fact that the disciples were so reluctant to believe that Jesus had risen from the dead, their unwillingness to believe something so contrary to their knowledge of the natural order of things, that it would make their report of the facts of the resurrection more believable.

188 The Guard Reports to the Jews (Matt. 28:11-15)

(1) While the disciples were on their way some of the guard came into the city and reported to the chief priests all that had happened.

(2) When the chief priests had assembled with the elders and counseled together they gave a large sum of money to the soldiers (3) and said, "You are to say, 'His disciples came by night and stole Him away while we were asleep,' (4) and if this should come to the governor's ears we will win him over and keep you out of trouble."

(5) So the guard took the money and did as they had been instructed; and this story was widely spread among the Jews and is to this day.

Notes: The scripture says that "some of the guard" reported to the chief priests what had happened. Only a third of the total number of soldiers would have been on duty at the time of the happenings which they reported to the chief priests. It's the opinion of some biblical writers that these soldiers had seen Jesus leave the tomb after the angels had rolled away the stone. Other writers take the view that Jesus was gone before the stone was rolled away, that Jesus didn't need doors through which to pass. Later events bear out this last. But the disciples and the women did need the stone to have been rolled away so they could enter the tomb to see that Jesus was no longer there. This latter view is borne out by such passages as Acts 10:40-41 in which Peter is reported as having said, "God raised Him up on the third day, and granted that He should become visible, not to all people, but to witnesses who were chosen beforehand by God, that is, to us, who ate and drank with Him after He arose from the dead." Whether the guard were "like dead men" from having seen the angels or from having seen the risen Christ, we don't know. Either would probably have had the same effect on the soldiers.

This passage graphically points out the character of the Jews. Not only did they close their eyes and their minds to the things Jesus did while He was here on earth, but they refused to accept the testimony of impartial witnesses (witnesses who would have been more apt to have been hostile to Jesus than to favor Him), bribing those witnesses to lie about what they had seen and heard so that the common people would remain ignorant of the facts concerning the Messiah. Their desire for prominence and power and influence on earth was so great that they were willing to damn themselves to hell in order to satisfy that desire.

It was a capital offense for a Roman soldier to sleep on duty. It must have taken a great deal of money and a lot of persuasion to get them to lie about sleeping on duty. And they must have had a great deal of faith in the power of the Jews to persuade the Roman officers not to deal out the punishment such an offense called for. Also, considering the character of the people with whom they were dealing, they must have had firm and believable assurances that the Jews would indeed keep them from being punished. Of course, they may have been assured that no one but Jews would every hear their story. The wording of the passage seems to indicate that there was more than a casual telling of the soldiers' lies from mouth to mouth and friend to neighbor in and around Jerusalem. Rather it seems to have been a widespread effort on the part of the Jews to disseminate the lie in order to counteract the truth about Jesus and His resurrection. About AD 70, Justin Martyr in collaboration with Trypho wrote a dialogue in which he stated that the Jews sent special messengers to every country so that the lies they wanted the people to believe about Jesus could be spread as far and as wide as possible.

189 Jesus Appears to Two Disciples on the Way to Emmaus

(Mark 16:12-13; Luke 24:13-35)

(1) After that Jesus appeared in a different form to two of His disciples who that very day were walking on their way to the country to a village named Emmaus which was about seven miles from Jerusalem. (2) They were conversing with each other about all the things which had taken place (3) and while they were conversing and discussing Jesus Himself approached and began traveling with them, (4) but their eyes were prevented from recognizing Him.

(5) Jesus said to them, "What are these words that you are exchanging with one another as you are walking?" And they stood still looking sad.

(6) One of them, named Cleopas, said to Jesus, "Are You the only one visiting Jerusalem and unaware of the things which have happened here in these days?"

(7) Jesus asked, "What things?"

They answered Him, "The things about Jesus the Nazarene who was a prophet mighty in deed and word in the sight of God and all the people, (8) and how the chief priests and our rulers delivered Him up to the sentence of death and crucified Him.

(9) "We were hoping that it was He who was going to redeem Israel. Indeed, besides all this, it is the third day since these things happened.

(10) "Also some women among us amazed us. When they were at the tomb early in the morning, (11) and did not find His body they came saying that they had also seen a vision of angels who said that He was alive.

(12) "Some of those who were with us went to the tomb and found it just exactly as the women had said, but Him they did not see."

(13) Jesus said to them, "O foolish men and slow of heart to believe in all that the prophets have spoken! (14) Was it not necessary for the Christ to suffer these things and to enter into His glory?" (15) Then beginning with Moses and all the prophets He explained to them the things concerning Himself in all the Scriptures.

(16) As they approached the village where they were going Jesus acted as though He would go further. (17) But they would constrain

Him, saying, "Stay with us for it is getting toward evening and the day is now nearly over." And Jesus went in to stay with them.

(18) When Jesus had reclined at table with them He took the bread and blessed it and broke it and began to give it to them.

(19) Then their eyes were opened and they recognized Him, and He vanished from their sight.

(20) They said to one another, "Were not our hearts burning within us while He was speaking to us on the road, while He was explaining the Scriptures to us?"

(21) Then they arose that very hour and returned to Jerusalem and found gathered together the eleven and those who were with them (22) and reported to them, saying, "The Lord has really risen and has appeared to Simon."

(23) They told of their experiences on the road and how Jesus was recognized by them in the breaking of the bread; but these did not believe them either.

Notes: The site of the town of Emmaus has not been located. Biblical scholars believe it to be the ruins now known as el Kubeibeh which is located less than eight miles northwest of Jerusalem.

Neither of the two disciples Jesus met on the road to Emmaus was any of the eleven apostles. One of them was named Cleopas, but this is the only place in which that name appears in the scriptures. Nothing else in known about him *unless* he is the same person who was listed as being Cleophas *(KN)* or Clopas (NASV), whose wife Mary was listed as being with the other women in John 19:25. His companion was not identified, unless he is the Simon to whom Cleopas is referring as the person to whom Jesus appeared. However, that Simon may possibly have been Peter because in 1 Corinthians 15:5, Paul wrote,"... And that He appeared to Cephas, then to the twelve." We don't have an account of Jesus appearing to Peter prior to this time unless (completing the circle) it was Peter who was with Cleopas on the road to Emmaus. *But* if it had been Peter, it's almost certain that he would have been identified. Further, some biblical scholars without giving a reason believe the companion of Cleopas to have been Luke.

The reason Jesus kept the two disciples from recognizing Him is not given, but it might have been so that He could teach them (or have them recall) the prophecies about the Messiah. They would then be able to determine from their own knowledge the things by which the Messiah could be known and by which He could be identified.

190 Jesus Appears to the Apostles

(Luke 24:36-43; John 20:19-25)

(1) When it was evening on that day, the first day of the week, and when the doors where the disciples were had been shut for fear of the Jews, Jesus came and stood in their midst and said to them, "Peace be with you."

(2) The disciples were startled and frightened and thought they were seeing a spirit.

(3) Jesus asked them, "Why are you troubled and why do doubts arise in your hearts? (4) See My hands and My feet, that it is I Myself. Touch Me and see. A spirit does not have flesh and bones as you see that I have."

(5) When Jesus had said this He showed them His hands and His side. The disciples rejoiced when they saw that it was the Lord. (6) While they still could not believe it for joy and marveling Jesus asked them, "Have you anything to eat?" (7) They gave Him a piece of broiled fish, and He took it and ate it before them.

(8) Jesus said again, "Peace be with you. As the Father has sent Me, I also send you."

(9) When He had said this He breathed on them and said to them, "Receive the Holy Spirit. (10) If you forgive the sins of any their sins have been forgiven them; if you retain the sins of any they have been retained."

(11) But Thomas, one of the twelve also called Didymus, was not with them when Jesus came. (12) The other disciples said to him, "We have seen the Lord!"

But Thomas said, "Unless I shall see in His hands the imprint of the nails and put my finger into the place of the nails and put my hand into His side I will not believe."

Notes: For someone to believe something there must be a will to believe it-belief is from the heart as well as from the mind. The Jewish leaders didn't want to believe that Jesus was the Messiah, and even after seeing what should have been incontrovertible proof, they still refused to believe. And it seems that the apostles weren't much better off in that respect. They had the testimony of at least six eye witnesses to the bodily resurrection of Jesus and still they refused to believe it.

Thomas has the name of being a doubter. People who are subject to many doubts are often called "Doubting Thomases." But Thomas believed as readily as the others. They wouldn't believe until they saw Jesus with their own eyes, and it was the same with Thomas. When they saw Jesus, they believed and when Thomas saw Jesus he believed.

The names "Thomas" and "Didymus" mean the same thing. "Thomas" is Aramaic and "Didymus" is Greek. The meaning of both names is "twin." There is nothing in the scriptures to tell us that Thomas was one of a pair of twins (other than his name, of course) so we don't know anything about his twin, whether it was a brother or a sister or whether it was alive or dead.

It is usually assumed that the Holy Spirit came upon the apostles on the day of Pentecost when Peter preached the first gospel sermon. This passage, however, may give some people the impression that Jesus *may* have bestowed the Holy Spirit on the ten apostles at this time. There is no record of Jesus bestowing the Holy Spirit on Thomas after he believed. That fact would cast some doubt on the Holy Spirit being given to the others at this time, but it certainly doesn't preclude Jesus from having done so and of bestowing it on Thomas at a later though unrecorded time. Taking this one step further, the language of Acts 2 certainly conveys the impression that the Holy Spirit first came upon the apostles at that time. And the words of Jesus in Acts 1 just before His ascension confirm that impression when He said that the apostles *would be* baptized with the Holy Spirit not many days after that and that it would come with power.

191 Jesus Appears to All Eleven Apostles

(Mark 16:14; John 20:26-29)

(1) After eight days again Jesus' disciples were inside reclining at the table and Thomas was with them. Jesus came, the doors having been shut, and stood in their midst and said, "Peace be with you."

(2) Then Jesus reproached Thomas for his unbelief and hardness of heart and said to him, "Reach here your finger and see My hands and reach here your hand and put it into My side, and be not unbelieving but believing."

(3) Thomas said to Jesus, "My Lord and my God!"

(4) Jesus said to him, "Because you have seen Me you have believed. Blessed are they who did not see Me and yet believed."

Notes: When Jesus invited Thomas to feel the nail holes in His hands and the spear wound in His side, it showed that even though He hadn't heard Thomas say what he said about believing that Jesus had arisen, He knew exactly what Thomas had said. Some biblical scholars have assumed that Thomas *did* feel the hands and side of Jesus but the scriptures don't say that he did.

Whatever it was that satisfied the doubts of Thomas, his confession was stronger than any of the others. If Thomas' doubts were greater, his confession was fuller. His words show that he not only believed that Jesus was the Messiah but that he believed Him to be God also.

192 Jesus Appears at the Sea of Tiberias (John 21:1-24)

(1) After these things Jesus made Himself visible again to the disciples at the Sea of Tiberias. He did it in this way:

(2) There together were Simon Peter, Thomas called Didymus, Nathaniel of Cana of Galilee, the sons of Zebedee and two other disciples. (3) Simon Peter said to them, "I am going fishing."

They said to him, "We will come with you."

They went out and got into the boat but that night they caught nothing. (4) When the day was breaking Jesus stood on the beach but the disciples did not know that it was Jesus.

(5) Jesus said to them, "Children, do you have any fish?" They answered Him, "No."

(6) Jesus said, "Cast the net on the right hand side of the boat and you will find a catch."

They cast the net on the right side and then they were not able to haul it in because of the great number of fish.

(7) That disciple whom Jesus loved said to Peter, "It is the Lord." So when Simon Peter heard that it was the Lord he put on his outer garment (for he was stripped for work) and threw himself into the sea. (8) But the other disciples came in the little boat for they were not far from the land, only about one hundred yards away, dragging the net full of fish.

(9) When they got out upon the land they saw a charcoal fire already laid with fish placed on it, and bread.

(10) Jesus said to them, "Bring some of the fish which you have just now caught."

(11) Simon Peter went up and drew to land the net filled with a hundred fifty-three large fish, and although there were so many the net was not torn.

(12) Jesus said to them, "Come and have breakfast." None of the disciples ventured to question Him, "Who are You?" knowing that it was the Lord. (13) Jesus gave them the bread and the fish also. (14) This was now the third time Jesus was manifested to the disciples after He was raised from the dead.

(15) When they had finished breakfast Jesus said to Simon Peter, "Simon, son of John, do you love Me more than these?"

Simon answered, "Yes, Lord, You know that I love You." Jesus said, "Tend My lambs."

(16) Jesus said the second time, "Simon, son of John, do you love Me?"

Simon answered, "Yes, Lord, You know that I love You." Jesus said, "Shepherd My sheep.:

(17) Jesus said to Peter the third time, "Simon, son of John, do you love Me?"

Peter was grieved because Jesus said to him the third time, "Do you love Me?" and he said to Jesus, "Lord, You know all things; You know that I love You."

Jesus said to him, "Tend My sheep.

(18) "I say to you this in truth, when you were younger you used to gird yourself and walk wherever you wished but when you grow old you will stretch out your hands and someone else will gird you and bring you where you do not wish to go." (19) Jesus said this telling by what kind of death Peter would glorify God. When He had said this Jesus said to Peter, "Follow Me!"

(20) Peter, turning around, saw the disciple whom Jesus loved following them, the one who had leaned back on Jesus' breast at the supper, and said, "Lord, who is the one who betrays You?" (21) Peter, indicating him, said to Jesus, "Lord, and what about this man?"

(22) Jesus said to him, "If I want him to remain until I come what is that to you? Follow **Me!**" (23) This saying of Jesus went out among the brethren that that disciple would not die, yet Jesus did not say to Peter that John would not die but only, "If I want him to remain until I come what is that to you?"

(24) This is the disciple who bears witness of these things and wrote these things, and we know that his witness is true.

Notes: It is the opinion of some biblical writers that by going fishing at this time the apostles, the seven listed here, were returning to their previous vocation and were planning to make it their livelihood. Other writers disagree, believing that they had returned to Galilee because Jesus had instructed them to do so and that they were fishing just to pass the time until Jesus came to them in Galilee. In Matthew 28:10, Jesus told the women, "... Go and take word to My brethren to leave for Galilee, and there they shall see Me." This should make it clear that the apostles *had* gone to Galilee to meet with Jesus. The other four were probably in Galilee too, but just not with this seven. Not all the apostles, you will remember, were fishermen before Jesus called them.

There are about six Greek words used in the Gospels which are all translated "children." The particular word Jesus used in this passage is *paidion* (pa-hee-dee' -on) which means roughly "immature children" and, as Jesus used it, would be the equivalent of men being called "boys."

It is reported that a person standing on the shore of the sea of Galilee can see fish in the water. That may have been the reason the disciples immediately did as the stranger (to them at that time) suggested.

This was actually the seventh appearance of Jesus but only the third to a group of the apostles-to the ten, to the eleven and now to the seven.

Peter had repeatedly said by word and by deed that he loved Jesus more than any of the others. In Matthew 26:33 he had said, "Even though all may fall away because of You, I will never fall away." And in John 13:37 he said, "Lord, why can I not follow You right now? I will lay down my life for You." He drew a sword and would have fought for Jesus in the garden-but... he denied Jesus three times.

There are three Greek words which are translated in English as "love." Two of them are used in this passage. The first two times Jesus asked Peter if Peter loved Him He used the stronger of the *words-agapao* (ag-ap-ah'-o). Both of those times, Peter answered with the weaker *word-phileo* (fil-eh'- o). The third time Jesus asked Peter if he loved Him, He used the word *phileo,* and Peter answered using *phileo* again. One can't help but wonder if the reason Peter answered as he did was because, if he used the stronger word *agapao,* he was afraid he would fail Jesus again. He had been so positive on other occasions and failed. Perhaps, this time he wouldn't be so positive and he wouldn't fail Jesus.

John reported that Jesus told Peter that Peter would suffer martyrdom, and tradition has it that Peter was indeed martyred. That tradition says that Peter was crucified upside down about thirty-four years later in Rome. When faced with being crucified, Peter stated that there was no greater honor for him than to be killed as his Lord had been killed. So that he wouldn't be killed in the same way Jesus was killed, the Romans are said to have crucified Peter upside down so that he wouldn't have died the same way Jesus did. There is no evidence available to confirm or to refute that tradition.

The site of John's grave in Ephesus, where he is supposed to have spent his last years, was said to have been well known to the early Christians there.

193 The Great Commission

(Matt. 28:16-20, Mark 16:15-18)

(1) The eleven disciples proceeded to Galilee to the mountain which Jesus had designated. (2) When they saw Jesus they worshiped Him, but some of them were doubtful.

(3) Jesus came up and said to them, "All authority has been given to Me in heaven and on earth. (4) Go into all the world and preach the gospel to all creation and make disciples of all the nations, baptizing them in the name of the Father and the Son and the Holy Spirit, (5) teaching them to observe all that I commanded you, and lo, I am with you always, even to the end of the age.

(6) "He who has believed and has been baptized shall be saved but he who has disbelieved shall be condemned. (7) These signs will accompany those who have believed: in My name they will cast out demons; they will speak with new tongues; (8) they will pick up serpents; and if they drink any deadly poison it shall not hurt them; they will lay hands on the sick and they will recover."

Notes: The eighth appearance of the risen Jesus was on a mountain in Galilee. Matthew wrote that the eleven were present. In 1 Corinthians 15:6, however, the statement is made that Jesus appeared to more than five hundred people at one time. Matthew doesn't say that only the eleven were present, so many biblical scholars believe it was on this occasion that the five hundred people were present.

The wording of the original Greek text makes it clear that it is the disciples they make and not the nations who are to be baptized. It is also clear to anyone studying the passage with an open mind that baptism is part of making disciples and without it there is no salvation.

All those things that Jesus said could happen or could be done to or by the apostles were done to one or another of them as reported in

Acts, except the drinking of poison. If any of them was poisoned, either inadvertently or by an enemy, that fact wasn't recorded. If one of them was poisoned, perhaps that person didn't even know it.

The most encouraging words the apostles heard must have been the promise of Jesus that He would be with them always. Even though those words weren't spoken to us, they would apply to us, and they should be as encouraging to us as they were to the apostles, but we can't receive the rewards of that promise just by sitting in a church pew.

194 Other Appearances and Commands of Jesus

(Luke 24:44-49; John 20:30-31, 21:25; Acts 1:2-3)

(1) Jesus said to the disciples, "These are My words which I spoke to you while I was still with you, that all things which are written about Me in the Law of Moses and the Prophets and the Psalms must be fulfilled."

(2) Then He opened their minds to understand the Scriptures (3) and said to them, "It is written that the Christ should suffer and rise again from the dead the third day (4) and that repentance for forgiveness of sins should be proclaimed in His name to all the nations beginning from Jerusalem. (5) You are witnesses of these things. (6) Listen, I am sending forth the promise of My Father upon you but you are to stay in the city until you are clothed with power from on high."

(7) Jesus was taken up after He had by the Holy Spirit given orders to the apostles whom He had chosen. (8) To these He also presented Himself alive after His suffering by many convincing proofs, appearing to them over a period of forty days and speaking of the things concerning the kingdom of God.

(9) Jesus performed many other signs and did many other things in the presence of the disciples which are not recorded in this book. (10) If they were written in detail I suppose that even the world itself would not contain the books which would have been written, (11) but these things have been written so that you may believe that Jesus is the Christ, the Son of God, and that in believing you may have life in His name.

Notes: The last recorded appearances of Jesus prior to the ascension were to James, the son of Zebedee (see 1 Cor. 15:7) and then to the eleven. Perhaps the appearance of Jesus to James alone was because Jesus knew that James would be the first of the apostles to be killed because of Him.

The opening of the minds of the apostles was probably through the teachings of Jesus, not only in those last appearances but throughout the time He had spent with them. It was not a miraculous infusion of knowledge into their minds, but their memories could have been somewhat miraculously stimulated. At any rate, you may remember that the two disciples whom Jesus had met on the road to Emmaus understood all about Him because of His teachings and not because of any miraculous transmission of knowledge. It was probably that same way with the apostles.

195 The Ascension (Mark 16:19-20;

Luke 24:50-53; Acts 1:4-11)

(1) Gathering the disciples together Jesus led them as far as Bethany. Then He lifted up His hands and blessed them and commanded them not to leave Jerusalem but to wait for what the Father had promised, "Which," He said, "you heard from Me. (2) John baptized with water but you shall be baptized with the Holy Spirit not many days from now."

(3) When the disciples had come together they had asked Jesus, "Lord, is it at this time You are restoring the kingdom to Israel?"

(4) Jesus said to them, "It is not for you to know times or seasons which the Father has fixed by His own authority. (5) But you shall receive power when the Holy Spirit has come upon you, and you shall be My witnesses in Jerusalem and in all Judea and Samaria, and even to the remotest part of the earth."

(6) After Jesus had said these things He was lifted up even while the disciples were looking on, and a cloud received Him into heaven out of their sight, and He sat down at the right hand of God.

(7) As they were gazing intently into the sky while Jesus was departing, suddenly two men in white clothing stood beside them (8) and said, "Men of Galilee, why do you stand looking into the sky? This

Jesus who has been taken up from you into heaven will return in just the same way as you have watched Him go into heaven." (9) The disciples returned to Jerusalem with great joy (10) and were continually in the temple praising God. (11) They went out and preached everywhere while the Lord worked with them and confirmed the word by the signs that followed.

Notes: Can anyone possibly imagine how the apostles must have felt as they stood there watching Jesus ascend into heaven and knowing that He was returning to the place from which He came! Have you ever been so filled with happiness that a little bit of it spilled out through your eyes? If so, you probably know about how the apostles must have felt on that occasion. Beginning when the servants of the high priest took hold of Jesus in the garden, these men had been under quite a lot of stress: the Man to whom all of them looked to establish His kingdom had been crucified; their faith had almost failed them; and they learned that Jesus had risen from the dead. Their faith was restored even deeper than before. Now they *knew* that Jesus lived again and they understood... well, almost understood, about His kingdom.

* * *

That is the end of our study, but hopefully, not the end of our learning. It is a truism that *no one learns as much as he who teaches.* Perhaps, hopefully again, you who have read this entire work have learned much that is useful, informative, and even entertaining in your journey toward salvation.

This study, of course, has been only about the life of Jesus on earth. To learn, as Paul Harvey would say, the "rest of the story," study the rest of the New Testament. In it, you will learn what the Holy Spirit gave the writers to pass on to you so that you could know how to become a Christian, how to live as a Christian, and how to make Christians of others.

Peace to All, and God Bless You All.

APPENDIX

The references to the Feast of Unleavened Bread and its relationship in time to the Passover in Section 159:3 and 161:1 (Matt. 36:17, Mark 14:1 & 12, and Luke 22:1 & 7) do not agree with the Law concerning these festivals as described in Leviticus 23:4-8 which reads: "These are the feasts of the Lord, holy convocations which you shall proclaim at their appointed times. On the fourteenth day of the first month at twilight is the Lord's Passover. And on the fifteenth day of the same month is the Feast of Unleavened Bread to the Lord; seven days you must eat unleavened bread. On the first day you shall have a holy convocation; you shall do no customary work on it. But you shall offer an offering made by fire to the Lord for seven days. The seventh day shall be a holy convocation; you shall do no customary work on it." **(NKJV)**

In his book *Being Jewish*, Ari L. Goldman wrote concerning the Passover: "The holiday begins on the fifteenth day of Nisan and lasts for seven days in Israel and eight in the Diaspora. (Reform Jews keep seven days in the Diaspora.) The first and last days are holy days during which work is prohibited." As you can see, the observance of these days in modern times does not agree with the ancient Law as given to Moses. And apparently that difference existed during the days when Jesus walked the earth. The discrepancy is not explained in the scriptures.

We are, however, familiar with the fact that the leading men of the Jewish nation, the chief priests, scribes, lawyers and Pharisees, held that the traditions which had grown up in their culture during the centuries since the Law was given on Sinai carried more weight with them than the Law itself. What Jesus thought and said about those beliefs and practices regarding traditions is recorded in Section 78:2-11 (Matthew 15:1-6 and Mark 7:1-13).

Evidently the writers of the Gospels were themselves confused about the how, when and why of these two festivals and their juxtaposition as relating to each other, and the truth concerning the observance of those two festivals may have been lost at the time of their writings. The possibility also exists that the translations of the original scriptures were inaccurate and caused the current confusion. However, the fact that the Law stated that the festival of the Passover was to be the *fourteenth* of the first month (Nisan at that time) and the modern date of the festival is on the *fi eenth* of Nisan seems to preclude that possibility. Also the Law stated that the Feast of Unleavened Bread was to begin on the fifteenth day of Nisan and the modern Passover begins on that date.

The celebration of the Passover is still in the month of Nisan but the order of the months in the Jewish calendar has been changed since the Law was given to Moses. The months remain in the same order but the month of Tishrei, formerly the seventh month in order, is now deemed to be the first month in order and the first day of Tishrei is New Years day instead of the first day of Nisan.

The Law stated that the day of the Passover was to begin at twilight. In *Being Jewish,* Mr. Goldman wrote: "As with virtually all Jewish observances, each festival starts the night before the calendar day. This is true of the weekly Sabbath, which begins Friday night at sundown, and so with all the festivals...." Originally the Jews considered *all* days to begin at twilight (or sundown), but now they observe the days generally as the rest of the world, except as noted for the festivals and the Sabbaths.

Regarding the references to the "preparation day" in Sections 180:25, 185:1 and 186:1 (Matthew 27:62, Mark 15:42, Luke 23:54 and John 19:14, 31 & 42), they refer to the day in which the Jews prepared for the beginning of the Feast of Unleavened Bread. In the day or days before the beginning of that feast, in addition to celebrating the Passover, the Jews were required to remove every trace of all the leavening agents from their homes.

Jesus was crucified on the day of the Passover. That day began at the nominal time of sundown (around six o'clock as we count time) and ended at the same time the following day. Jesus ate the Passover meal with his disciples on the evening of the Passover at which time He instituted what we know as The Lord's Supper. He was taken that same night, was tried, crucified and died before the day ended at the next twilight, which marked the end of the day of the Passover. The first day of the Feast of Unleavened Bread began at twilight when the day of the Passover ended and that new day was a Sabbath, the Sabbath before which the executed men were supposed to have been buried.